P9-BJL-848

110
111
29
183

Donated To
CAMROSE LUTHERAN COLLEGE LIBRARY

By _Macmillan Bloedel Research Ltd._

→ Everett Thykeson →

447 KARP CT.

COQUITLAM BC

Personal and Organizational Change

through Group Methods

CONTRIBUTORS

ROBERT R. BLAKE
Scientific Methods, Inc., Austin, Texas

J. F. T. BUGENTAL
Psychological Service Associates, Los Angeles, California

DOUGLAS R. BUNKER
Harvard University

P. G. HANSON
Houston Veterans Hospital and Baylor University College of Medicine

ROGER HARRISON
Yale University

D. L. JOHNSON
Houston Veterans Hospital and Baylor University College of Medicine

DONALD C. KLEIN
Boston University

F. A. LYLE
Houston Veterans Hospital and Baylor University College of Medicine

MATTHEW B. MILES
Columbia University

ROBERT B. MORTON
Formerly Chief, Psychological Service, Director Patient Training Laboratory, Houston Veterans Hospital, Houston, Texas
Harless and Kirkpatrick Associates, Inc., Atlanta, Georgia

JANE SRYGLEY MOUTON
University of Texas

R. MOYER
Houston Veterans Hospital and Baylor University College of Medicine

BARRY OSHRY
Boston University

P. ROTHAUS
Houston Veterans Hospital and Baylor University College of Medicine

ROBERT TANNENBAUM
University of California, Los Angeles

PERSONAL AND ORGANIZATIONAL CHANGE THROUGH GROUP METHODS:

The Laboratory Approach

Edgar H. Schein and Warren G. Bennis

Sloan School of Management
Massachusetts Institute of Technology

John Wiley & Sons, Inc., New York · London · Sydney

← Everett Thykeson →

447 KARP CT.

COQUITLAM BC

BF
637
C653 | 23,774

THIRD PRINTING, APRIL, 1967

Copyright © 1965 by John Wiley & Sons, Inc.

All Rights Reserved
This book or any part thereof
must not be reproduced in any form
without the written permission of the publisher.

Library of Congress Catalog Card Number: 65-19476
Printed in the United States of America

CAMROSE LUTHERAN COLLEGE
LIBRARY

TO THE MEMORY OF DOUGLAS McGREGOR

PREFACE

For a number of years now, we have been engaged in a form of educational enterprise which has come to be called Laboratory Training. For both of us our involvement with this enterprise started as practical action. We worked as staff members of various laboratories, helped organizations to design laboratory training programs, served in an advisory capacity to the National Training Laboratories that, in a real sense, originated and developed laboratory training, and, most important, developed considerable enthusiasm about further developments in laboratory training.

Working as a member of a training staff or as a consultant to an organization which is considering laboratory training is personally exciting and gratifying, but not completely so. The world of action makes us acutely aware of the need for conceptualization and a systematic frame of reference, because the world of action is so diverse, complex, and chaotic. Both of us have for some time felt this need for a conceptual scheme—a coherent explanation of what laboratory training is and what assumptions underlie it. The present book represents our attempt to fulfill our own need for such conceptualization. Hopefully, it will also contribute usefully to the growing literature on this important educational innovation.

The ideas presented in this book are our own best efforts, at this stage, to communicate what we think laboratory training is all about. But it would be presumptuous to ignore the great influence which the ideas of many others have had upon us. Every time a laboratory is run, the staff encounter each other intellectually and emotionally, leading to useful cross-fertilization and personal growth. This indeed is what makes the running of laboratories such an exciting enterprise.

It means also that we are in a real sense indebted to all those other fellow trainers and delegates with whom we have worked and whose ideas have helped us to shape our own.

Particular thanks go to Leland Bradford and Kenneth Benne whose efforts over the years to nurse the delicate child of laboratory training have now produced a robust viable adult. Their encouragement, support, and stimulation, their willingness and desire to help others grow intellectually and emotionally, and their enthusiastic commitment to laboratory training as an educational philosophy have inspired and helped us beyond measure.

From time to time, we have exposed bits and pieces of our emerging manuscript to our colleagues for comment and criticism. Their reactions have always been encouraging and helpful. We would like to thank particularly Chris Argyris, Robert Kahn, Douglas McGregor, and Matthew Miles for their help on this score.

The great job of drafting and redrafting, typing and retyping was ably handled by Mrs. Marian Pruslin and Miss Amy Ventresca. The index was prepared by Mrs. I. Srivastva. Finally, we wish to thank Clurie Bennis and Mary Schein for their stimulation, encouragement, and support during the sometimes difficult hours of meshing our ideas and putting them down on paper.

Cambridge, Massachusetts
March 1965

EDGAR H. SCHEIN
WARREN G. BENNIS

CONTENTS

Part I

WHAT IS LABORATORY TRAINING?

This part of the book is primarily designed to introduce the reader to laboratory training. In Chapter 1 we introduce the concept and discuss some of our considerations in writing this book. Chapter 2 attempts to give the reader "a feel" for laboratory training by describing and commenting on a typical two-week residential laboratory. In Chapter 3 we provide an overview of the issues in laboratory training—the assumptions and values which underlie it, the kinds of learning theory which have been proposed to explain its workings, and the forces in the laboratory setting which work toward learning. The three chapters taken together should give the reader with only a casual interest in laboratory training an adequate overview, on the basis of which he should be able to determine whether or not to read on.

1

Introduction

We wrote this book so that a wide audience could come to understand and evaluate a new and powerful educational medium which we call laboratory training. We believe that this educational approach is an innovation which holds important *practical potentials* for the conduct of human affairs. We are even more certain that it can provide some important *theoretical understanding* of human and social processes of learning and change.

As for the practical side, laboratory training can be employed to influence *personal learning* and *organizational change*. We shall attempt to show later on, how these two "target systems"—the individual and the organization—are affected by laboratory training. On the theoretical side, we became interested in the learning conditions and processes of laboratory training because of their evident impact on the learner. We wished to know just why and how it works. What are the mechanisms of learning and change which underlie its processes?

So this book was written to describe and conceptualize an educational strategy which purports to influence the development of learning in individuals and to induce change in organizations. The readership we have in mind is a very general one: *The book is written for all those individuals who are interested in the complicated social and psychological processes of human learning and change and for all those individuals interested in controlling the outcomes of these change processes.* We wish to communicate to the practical planner of learning and change processes what laboratory training has to offer him. At the other extreme, we wish to communicate to our academic and scientific colleagues a theory of human learning and change which has great promise.

So far we have not said anything about what laboratory training is.[1] In fact, we hope to say a good deal about what laboratory training is in Chapters 2 and 3, where its processes and outcomes are described in detail. For the moment we can say that laboratory training is an educational strategy which is based primarily on the experiences generated in various social encounters *by the learners themselves,* and which aims to influence attitudes and develop competencies toward learning about human interactions. So, essentially, laboratory training attempts to induce changes with regard to the learning process itself and to communicate a particular method of learning and inquiry. It has to do with "learning how to learn." This will become clearer as we go along, though we must recognize at the outset that there are some very real problems in communicating the idea of laboratory training. What we mean by laboratory training unfortunately cannot. be expressed with the clarity and precision we have ordinarily come to expect from scientific undertakings. There are some good reasons for this difficulty in communication, quite apart from the usual pitfalls of social science jargon, and it might be useful to review some of these before continuing with the rest of the chapter.[2]

Some Problems in Communicating the Idea of Laboratory Training

First of all, *laboratory training does not fit into the conventional categories of education or therapy.* It contains elements of both processes but maintains its uniqueness. The domain of laboratory training extends across the social geography of the behavioral sciences and the so-called "helping" professions, and its borders with other disciplines are very fuzzy.

Second, *laboratory training is new.* It started as recently as 1947 in Bethel, Maine. Since then, like most intellectual movements, it has moved along in an erratic rhythm, incorporating and ejecting idéas in a topsy-turvy way.[3] Laboratory training is not, and should not be construed as a monolithic entity. Instead, it is a rapidly growing and ever-changing enterprise, composed of ideas and procedures, practiced

---

[1] The interested reader is advised to read the recent book edited by L. P. Bradford, J. R. Gibb, and K. D. Benne (1964) for an excellent account of the origins, status, and theoretical development of laboratory training.

[2] See Argyris (1962 and 1964) for two clear accounts of laboratory training.

[3] See Bradford et al. (Chapter 4, 1964) for an excellent account of the history of laboratory training.

by social scientists and professionals who share certain beliefs and values, but who, on occasion, disagree on major issues. Because of its newness and novelty, laboratory training has not truly "settled" or codified its concepts and practices, nor should it.

Third, *laboratory training is experience-based learning which besets us with the problem of matching symbols with experience.* An abstract symbol is not identical with the experience it symbolizes. And so it is always difficult to convey our own varied observations and experiences with laboratory training to others who have had other experiences. In this respect, it is tempting to side with Freud's position regarding psychoanalysis and assert that no one is in a position to judge laboratory training unless he has been through a laboratory. We will reject this position, tempting as it is and truthful as it may be, in favor of a more difficult and perhaps tenuous position, based on our desire to develop meaningful reference points for the reader.

Finally, *laboratory training is far from being fully understood, either in terms of processes or outcomes.* As trainers, we are always concerned with the *multitude* of data generated rather than the lack of it; with the many *levels* and wide range of behavior, skills, emotions, and intellect engaged in laboratory training rather than the narrowness of the experience; and with the simultaneity and immediacy of these compounding and interacting factors. The total experience is direct, immediate, dense, occasionally surprising, and engages many levels and many facets of people-in-groups simultaneously.

Thus, the problem of exposition is a difficult one for us because the linear logic of the printed sentence and English syntax cannot adequately capture the rhetoric of laboratory training. Perhaps an "action painting" is more appropriate for this task for it conveys in a glance the power and complexity of human experience more aptly than words.

Laboratory training's failure to fit into conventional categories, its newness and crazy-quilt development, its reliance on concrete experiential referents rather than abstractions, and its complexity, these four factors in combination complicate the task of exposition.

Despite these communication problems, laboratory training has "caught on" and is actively sought and employed by many individuals and by more and more organizations. It would be hard to figure out exactly how many individuals have been exposed to it, but we would venture that 50,000 or so would be a reasonable estimate. We mention this figure, not as a testimonial, but as a fact to reckon with. For if laboratory training is so complicated, so hard to understand, so new, so risky and expensive to apply (as we shall see in Chapter 10), then how is its popularity to be explained? To answer this question, we must turn to an examination of some aspects of contemporary society.

Crises in Contemporary Society

We believe that the growth and success of laboratory training—and, probably, its increasing popularity over the next decade or so—are based on its singular appropriateness for dealing with some of the core crises facing contemporary society. These crises emerge generally from the acceleration of certain forces often summarized under the word, modernization; that is to say, forces which tend toward (1) increased reliance on science and technology for the solution of man's problems, (2) increased urbanization, bureaucratization, and mechanization, particularly of communication systems, and (3) higher rates and frequency of mobility, increased population, and so forth.

This tendency toward modernization makes life problematical for the *individual*. There is already mounting evidence that he is alienated, lonely, anxious, and desperately seeking purpose and identity. It is very difficult to know how far or deep these personal conditions go and what can or should be done to ameliorate them. To make matters worse, the individual is being called on to perform more and more complicated roles in his world of work. It is no longer enough to be a competent specialist or technician or expert or "entrepreneur." Nowadays, the individual is called on to understand the "human side of enterprise," to develop interpersonal competence, to examine the social and political forces within which his work is embedded and has to be transacted. His success and self-esteem may depend on these human skills.

From the point of view of *organizations* within our society, the problems are even more massive. Given the increased complexity and growth of human organizations, given their susceptibility to growth, decay, and rapid change, given the scientific basis for their productive processes and the inevitable diversity of specialists working on these processes and products, the viability and successes of these organizations are precarious. It is becoming increasingly clear that organizations have to develop mechanisms for two overarching tasks: (1) better means for human *communication* and *collaboration*, particularly between levels of hierarchy and between divergent specialists, and (2) better mechanisms for coping with externally induced stress and changes, *adaptability*.

Given the stresses of contemporary society, individuals and organizations must probably learn new ways of adaptation. We think that laboratory training has come along at just that point in time when these twin needs of interpersonal competence of the individual and development of organizational effectiveness are at their peak. Not that laboratory training is itself capable of solving these problems; but it is one tangible and vital method which can be applied to *examining* and *diagnosing* them. At the most, it can provide a basis for improved mechanisms of choice and processes for solving the problems. At the least, it may help in alerting organizations and developing sensitivity in the individual to the foreseeable problems. To what extent and how well laboratory training accomplishes these aims is far from obvious; conclusive evidence is a long way off. What we are attempting to stress at this point, however, is the cultural basis for the emergence of laboratory training. And as far as we can surmise, it is based on laboratory training's perceived ability to solve, or at least to tackle, some of the crises facing us in the contemporary world.

Our Own Values

Any educational mechanism contains a value system and normative structure; i.e., a system of "oughts," and "don'ts," and "ideals" which guide action and toward which commitment of its followers is imperative. Laboratory training is no exception, although unfortunately its most committed advocates often seem to betray an annoying naiveté regarding these values. We tend to be cautious about our own value structure concerning laboratory training. By this we mean that our basic value, the one we think laboratory training depends on, is that of inquiry, examination, diagnosis, and experimentation as opposed to action, procedure, strategy, operation and deed. When we go *beyond* this value, the "spirit of inquiry," we hope that we have not misled ourselves or the reader by evading or obscuring the value implications.

Why do we point this out now? Because laboratory training has activated various controversies since its inception due to the failure of its critics or advocates to articulate exactly the value system underlying their assertions. We have attempted to be as open as we are capable regarding our own biases, predispositions, and value system. We encourage the reader to scrutinize them and, in the process, possibly articulate his own.

This leads us to say something else regarding our value position. To a large extent, laboratory training was pioneered and developed by the National Training Laboratories.[4] In no sense do we want to détract from its essential contribution in developing laboratory training into

---

[4] The recent book edited by Bradford et al. which we cited earlier describes the development of National Training Laboratories and its contribution to laboratory training.

a viable educational medium. In fact, over the years, we have been intimately associated with National Training Laboratories (NTL) in one capacity or another; both of us have served as Directors on the NTL Board. At the same time, laboratory training is not NTL—it is much broader. Therefore we insist on and NTL encourages our separateness from its organization and its activities. We are neither High Priests nor True Believers and we hope that our position of commitment, yet detachment, is evident in this book. We care about making up our own minds in important matters and we want to uphold this value for our readers.

The Plan of This Book

This book is divided into four parts. Part I aims to provide a broad and very general *introduction to laboratory training*. It attempts to give an orientation and perspective to laboratory training which amounts to a basic understanding of its outcomes and processes. In Chapter 2 we present a bird's-eye view from a delegate's standpoint. We imagine a typical delegate going through a typical two-week laboratory and try to capture what he experiences, feels, thinks, and wonders about. Chapter 3 articulates and organizes these experiences in a more systematic way.

Part II is devoted to the *uses of laboratory training*: how it is employed and practiced, how laboratory designs are developed and implemented, under what conditions it is appropriate to use, who the chief users of laboratory training are, and so forth. Chapter 4 is written to provide a panoramic view of the uses and varieties of laboratory training. Chapters 5 through 9 are samples of some of the most effective uses and sophisticated designs for the implementations of laboratory training. Chapter 10 is our attempt to conceptualize the basic principles and strategies in its use.

Part III focuses on *research*. In Chapter 11 we outline a paradigm for locating different types of research strategies. In Chapters 12 and 13 we have invited two distinguished researchers to submit some recent examples of their "evaluation" research and theory on the processes and outcomes of laboratory training.

Part IV represents our conceptualization of the *basic learning processes and mechanisms which govern the processes and outcomes of laboratory training*. This is our attempt to bring laboratory training into the basic field of social psychology by providing a new model for viewing personal learning and organizational change. Chapter 14 gives an overview of our learning theory. In Chapter 15 we examine why organizations do not produce the kind of attitude change which laboratory training can produce, and, in the process, elaborate our model of attitude change. Chapter 16 examines the forces in the lab which underlie and make possible the kind of learning which individuals experience. In Chapter 17 we state some hypotheses about laboratories pertaining to the amount and type of learning which they make possible. Finally, in Chapter 18 we attempt to verbalize some of our own questions and anxieties about laboratory training. "If you want to run a laboratory" yourself, then Appendix 1 offers some help and warnings. In Appendix 2 we have listed and categorized some readings for the reader who wants to delve more deeply into the nature of laboratory training.

In summary, we can say that we wrote this book because we wanted to communicate to a widely growing audience the potentialities and limitations of an important, new educational strategy. We believe that this strategy is capable of releasing some important forces which can enhance man's ability to control more effectively and creatively his human environment. At the same time, we think that the understanding of these change processes will help in reducing the darkness around, and in building a viable theory of, human change.

2

What Is Laboratory Training:

Description of a Typical Residential Laboratory

Many attempts have been made to characterize the nature of laboratory training, but most of them have not been successful for several reasons: (1) laboratories *vary tremendously* in goals, training design, delegate population, length, and setting, making it difficult to describe this experience in general; (2) laboratories attempt to provide a *total* and *integrated* learning experience for the participants, making it difficult to communicate in written words the interdependence of the many separate aspects of the laboratory training design; (3) laboratories intend to provide a learning experience which is, in part, *emotional*, and to provide the opportunity for the participants to explore the interdependence of emotional and intellectual learning. It is difficult without observing the process first-hand to describe and understand the nature of this emotional learning and its meaning to the learner.

In spite of these difficulties, it is important to attempt to communicate some of the flavor of the typical laboratory training experience. By giving a bird's-eye view of laboratory training, we hope to highlight and exemplify the differences in assumptions and methods between the laboratory approach and more traditional educational activities. For our case, we will use a typical *two-week residential* laboratory for a group such as middle level managers in industry. By residential, we mean that all the participants live at the conference center and spend their entire time in training activities. As we will show in Chapter 4, there are many other types of laboratories. We have chosen the two-week residential one as our example because it represents the most typical kind of laboratory. The primary focus of the laboratory is the *personal* learning of the individual delegate.

In the description to be presented below, we will use primarily a chronological approach. However, to highlight the integrative quality of the laboratory and its emotional impact, it will be necessary, from time to time, to insert such comments as an observer might make who is studying the laboratory. In Chapter 3 we shall provide an overview of the different kinds of issues which laboratory training involves.

Orientation to the Laboratory. Participants in a laboratory such as the one we will describe, come from various business and industrial organizations. They are likely to be middle managers in either line or staff jobs. Some have volunteered for the experience while others have been sent by their superiors or at the recommendation of the training department. For most participants, hereafter called "delegates," the total learning experience begins long before the actual laboratory. They have read written brochures and articles about laboratory training, have talked with others who have attended, and have been oriented by supervisors or members of the training department staff in the organization in which they work. These contacts build up expectations of what the laboratory will be like, which in turn influence how the delegate approaches and reacts to the actual laboratory activities.

The brochure for a typical two-week laboratory will advertize the goals of the laboratory as follows:

Human relations training focuses on the individual, the small group, and the organization. A *major training goal* is increased interpersonal competence in the many roles each participant plays—on the job, in the community, even in the family. The objectives include both the individual satisfactions derived from full use of one's capacities and the organizational strength achieved through good working relations. The training activities of the laboratory combine to make it possible to experiment with more effective ways of learning and new ways of behaving.[1]

How the person later responds to laboratory training experiences will depend on (1) whether goals such as these are meaningful to him in terms of the interpersonal and group problems he experiences, and (2) whether or not he genuinely volunteers for the experience. If he feels pressure from his boss or organization to attend the laboratory, it may be unclear to him what kinds of problems others perceive him to have. If he is unclear about the perceptions of others and does not perceive particular problems in himself, he cannot be clear about what to learn at the laboratory.

Because of great differences in initial orientation, we find delegates arriving at laboratories with a whole gamut of initial feelings—at one

---

[1] From the brochure "This is NTL" (1963).

extreme, eager anticipation based on genuine volunteering; at the other, great apprehension and a feeling of having been punished because of "having been sent" without fully understanding why. Most delegates are also puzzled at the outset by the vague and unsatisfactory answers to the question of what the laboratory will be about that they have obained from acquaintances who have attended laboratories. Some will respond to this vagueness by being intrigued; others will be frightened; all will share a certain amount of uncertainty as they arrive at the conference center.

The great variety of initial feelings and universally felt uncertainty can be directly related to the fact that laboratory training has no cultural counterpart. It is not exactly like school; it is clearly different from psychotherapy; and it shares little with other kinds of training activities. The delegate thus has to form stereotypes on minimum information and is vulnerable to whatever anxieties tend to be aroused by any situation alleged to be interpersonally potent.

Arrival at the "Cultural Island." Most laboratories are held somewhere away from the pressures of day-to-day urban living, generally in an isolated comfortable hotel or conference center. The preliminary information sent to the delegate makes it clear that the atmosphere of the laboratory is informal and that the delegate will be expected to live in, in the sense of having minimal contacts with job or family during the course of the laboratory.

When he arrives at the conference center, the delegate is assigned to a room with one or more other delegates—a situation which may be of considerable emotional significance if he has been used to staying alone when traveling or attending conventions. He is given a notebook which contains general information, schedules, and group assignments. He is also given a name tag which has only his name on it, making it clear at the outset that he is at the laboratory as a *person*, not as a representative of the organization.

Initial conversations among the delegates, perhaps while unpacking, often involve attempts to discover what the laboratory is all about and how expert others are about it. The range of responses is likely to be from complete ignorance and confusion among some, to tales of "emotional bloodbaths" among others who have undergone experiences that they believe to have been similar or who have·read about T-groups in popularized articles. The uncertainty about what lies ahead is preoccupying and provokes tension.

This newness, the uncertainty, and the apprehension all work toward a situation in which the delegate arrives at his first orientation session unable to comprehend what is being said. He is too busy trying to get acclimatized and to get control of his own feelings of tension and uncertainty. Some delegates have read portions of their notebook, but these are not informative either, at this stage of the game.

First Session. The orientation session for the entire group of from 50 to 75 delegates is generally held in the early afternoon of the first day. It deals with matters of housekeeping (dining room hours, recreation facilities, how to get laundry done, and so forth), provides an opportunity to introduce the staff of the laboratory, and states in brief form the goals of the laboratory and the kinds of learning activities which hopefully will enable the delegates to achieve these goals.

For example, in a typical introduction, the "dean" of the laboratory or some other staff member points out that the *goals* of the laboratory are to create opportunities for the delegates *to learn* about the following kinds of things:

1. *Self.* The delegates' own behavior in groups and the impact which their behavior has on other members.
2. *Others.* The behavior of others in a group and the impact which their behavior has on them.
3. *Groups.* How groups work; what makes them function.
4. *Larger systems.* How organizations and larger social systems work.
5. *The learning process.* How to learn from their own experience ("learning how to learn").

These are deceptively simple goals and are in general only vaguely understood when first outlined. In discussing the *method* by which we learn in a laboratory setting, the speaker indicates that the basic difference between the laboratory and the traditional learning experience is that in the former we attempt to learn *from an analysis of our own experiences in groups* rather than from what some expert tells us. Thus, the term laboratory implies that the delegate has an opportunity to become a researcher and a student of his own and others' group behavior; he becomes both the subject and the experimenter-observer. The speaker points out that it is easier to explain this method after the delegates have had some experience in the laboratory. He then turns to an explanation of the daily schedule (see Table 2-1), after which he sends the delegates to their groups for the first training group (T-group) session.

From the delegate's point of view, the initial orientation session may be more meaningful as an emotional introduction to the staff and laboratory than it is in its actual content. Whether or not he is aware of it, the delegate is more likely to be paying attention to how the speaker looks and sounds than to what he says. The kinds of feelings which the speaker arouses in him—tension, anticipation, reassurance, hostility, confusion, or whatever—will make it hard for him to listen attentively and to comprehend. Recognition of this fact has led most laboratory staffs to plan introductory sessions which are as short as possible, reserving further explanation for sessions which follow the initial meetings of the training group. If the laboratory staff requires individual information about delegates, either for purposes of an evaluation research project or for the design of certain training activities, questionnaires or tests may be administered as part of the initial general session.

The schedule which is given to the delegate will indicate the major training activities of the laboratory:

1. *T-groups.*[2] These are basic learning groups which continue to meet throughout the course of the laboratory. They usually contain 10 to 15 members with one or two staff members or "trainers." T-groups are generally "unstructured," in the sense that the staff provides a minimum of agenda and formal leadership.

Table 2–1   Typical Schedule for the Week

	Sun.	Mon.	Tues.	Wed.	Thurs.	Fri.
9:00–11:00		T-group	T-group	T-group	T-group	T-group
11:00–11:30		Coffee break	Coffee break	Coffee break	Coffee break	Coffee break
11:30–12:30		General session	General session	General session	General session	General session
12:30–1:30		Lunch	Lunch	Lunch	Lunch	Lunch
1:30–3:30		T-group	T-group	Exercise	Exercise	Exercise
3:30–6:00	Opening session	Free time	Free time	Free time	Free time	Free time
6:00–7:30		Dinner	Dinner	Dinner	Dinner	Dinner
7:30–9:30	T-group	T-group	Tape listening exercise	Free	Exercise or training film	Free

2. *Information or theory sessions.* These are general sessions during which a staff member lectures and/or gives a demonstration to impart some concepts or ideas or research findings about an area relevant to the laboratory goals.

---

[2] The T in T-group stands for training. Such groups have also been called D-groups (development) and study groups.

3. *Focused exercises.* These are activities which may involve small or large groups. They are usually introduced by a staff member who describes the learning goals and the specific activities, such as role-playing or group observation, which are to be engaged in by the delegates.

4. *Other activities.* Most laboratories involve seminars, two-man interview groups (dyads), informal bull sessions, and other activities which may be introduced during its course. Some of these will be described below in our chronicle. They are usually not included on the delegate's regular schedule because of their informal or optional status.

Scheduled activities generally take place from 9 to 12 in the morning, 1 to 3 in the afternoon, and 8 to 10 in the evening. What the schedule can only half-successfully impart, but which is crucial is the degree to which the training design is an attempt to integrate the scheduled activities, and the degree to which informal unscheduled activities form an integral part of the total training. Furthermore, the schedule itself overstates the rigidity of the laboratory. Actually, the staff communicates to delegates that they, as well as the staff, have the power to change the schedule if training needs dictate such changes.

The T-Group

The T-group is, for most delegates, the major emotional focus of their laboratory experience. From their notebooks, they discover which group they are in. Also in the notebook is a roster of all delegates including their job title and organization. Finding out who the other members of their group are, including the staff member, becomes one of the first anchors around which the delegates organize their experience. This anchor takes on additional importance as the delegate discovers the unstructured nature of the T-group.

The group meets in a room around a large table. Each person is given a name card which is placed in front of him. There is usually a tape-recorder on or near the table. When the group has settled down, the staff member gives a short introduction, usually lasting less than five minutes, in which he restates some of the learning goals. He points out that the T-group's primary task is to create learning opportunities for its members, and that it has no formal leader, preset agenda, or rules by which it must operate. It is up to the whole group, including the staff member, to decide what to do and how best to learn from its experience.

Whether he emphasizes it in the introduction or later, the trainer makes it clear that it is legitimate and likely to be profitable for the group to try to learn from its *own* experienced behavior—the "here-and-now" situation—rather than to discuss problems outside the group, from the world they left, the "there-and-then" world. The tape-recorder, which will be running at all times unless the group decides to turn it off, is available as a learning aid to enable the group to recapitulate and study some of its earlier experiences. The tapes are the property of the group and are erased at the end of the laboratory. If the staff member comments on his own role at all, he is likely to state that he does not perceive himself to be the chairman or leader of the group, but rather a person who will help the learning process in whatever way he can.[3]

When the trainer finishes his introduction, the group is suddenly left to its own resources. It is difficult to describe the full emotional impact of the beginning minutes of a T-group because the members are struggling with so many emotional issues at once. They are confronted with a violation of many expectations they have taken for granted in educational settings, most of all that the trainer will define an agenda, some ground rules and some goals which are meaningful for the group. Instead, each member confronts some major problems—"what do we do and what are our goals"; "who am I to be in this unstructured situation and what kind of role should I play"; "how can I keep sufficient control over the group to prevent it from doing things which will make me too uncomfortable?"

In coping with these problems, different members use different strategies. Some ask further questions of the trainer; some try to get him to be more of a leader or guide; some lapse into an anxious watchful silence; some get angry; and some attempt to organize the group with various tasks like "introducing ourselves." As the members fill the vacuum with their behavior, they begin to generate the raw data from which they will have the opportunity to learn about themselves, their impact on others, others' reactions to them, and how groups work.

How the T-group goes about its business of creating learning opportunities during the first and subsequent sessions is hard to characterize because each group has its own unique history. It has its own particular

---

[3] We have had to qualify so often this description of what the staff member does because of the huge variation among trainers in how they open the T-group and the kind of role they make for themselves. For a more complete discussion of the role of the trainer, the reader is referred to Chapter 16 and to the volume on training by Bradford, Gibb, and Benne (1964).

combination of people; its own particular trainer with his own theory of learning and style of intervention; its unforeseen incidents, dilemmas, and crises. It creates, for each member, a unique set of emotional and intellectual experiences.

T-groups do have in common the kinds of issues or dilemmas which have to be resolved in the process of building a group and learning from this procedure—what to do, how to spend the time, how to distribute power, control and influence, how to develop group standards and a climate which permits maximum learning, how to develop group goals and a sense of group progress, how to keep the group process within bounds. It is the particular solutions to such dilemmas which make each group unique.

A Digression: The Learning Process in the T-Group. What does the delegate begin to learn from the unstructured group experience? In what manner does he first discover for himself the meaning of the laboratory method of learning? For some delegates, learning begins immediately with the opportunity to study their own reactions to this novel experience, and to compare their reactions with those of others. For other delegates, the learning process does not begin until they become involved in some incident in the life of the T-group in which they are confronted with unexpected feelings on the part of others, either in reaction to their own behavior or to the behavior of others. Both kinds of delegates gain an *increased awareness of their own feelings and the feelings of others.* What is this increased awareness about?

For many delegates, the learning process first focuses around the problem of *communication.* While most delegates admit at the outset that they are not as good listeners as it might be hoped, rarely do they realize how little listening they or anyone else in the group does during the early sessions. The discovery that they missed many things altogether and that various group members heard the same speaker say entirely different things is shocking and thought provoking. *They become more aware of the complexity of the communication process.*

For some delegates, the problem of communication is not as salient as the problem of structure and organization in the group. Those who wish to get the group organized often find themselves confronted by others who are comfortable in an unstructured setting and vice versa. An important first learning step for this group is the *awareness and acceptance of genuine differences in member needs, goals, and ways of approaching problems.*

Another kind of learning which occurs results from a group member getting reactions from others in areas about which he is relatively blind. The person who leaps into the early power vacuum of the group with the sincere motive of getting the group moving may discover that a number of other members perceived him as attempting to dominate and control the group. The silent member may discover that he communicates more of his feelings through his silence than he realizes, and that for many members his behavior is a subtle but powerful way of controlling the group. The person who tries to help by giving reactions to others whenever the impulse moves him may discover that others do not find his "feedback" helpful, either because it is too evaluative, too ill-timed, or too hostile in undertone. The person who hides his own feelings by being constantly analytical about what the group is doing may discover that several members view his behavior as a real barrier to group progress instead of an aid. For all of these delegates, the crucial learning process is *increased awareness of their own impact on others* which enables them to check the assumptions they have made about themselves.

Some delegates focus their learning effort on the level of group processes. They discover that group decisions are tricky things to observe and to manage intelligently. Sometimes a minority pushes the group into action because each of the silent members erroneously assumes that the silence of the others means consent. Sometimes the group votes and then acts on majority rule only to discover that the minority is effectively able to block the action. The group may elect or appoint a chairman only to discover that he is unable to control the vicissitudes of the meeting because the same members who were willing to have him be chairman discover that they are unwilling to have him exercise any kind of control. Sometimes the group sets up an agenda only to discover that the agenda tyrannizes the group and prevents it from doing what it really wants to do. Yet, no one knows how to undo the group decision, particularly if it was hard won in the first place. *Increased awareness of how groups function and the consequences of certain kinds of group action* are the learning result.

Usually these discoveries result from an emotionally taxing reconstruction of some of the earlier events in the group's life. In the process of making such a reconstruction, members learn how to be better observers of group action, learn what sorts of observation other members have made, and learn what sorts of reaction have been aroused by various incidents in the group's history. Almost in spite of themselves group members become more observant, more analytical, and more cautious in making assumptions about group behavior. They are, in this sense, *learning how to learn* from their own experience.

Out of increased awareness in all these areas comes the possibility of changed attitudes. The delegate develops new attitudes toward the learning process, toward himself, toward others, and toward groups. Out of such attitude changes will come new behavior and greater competence in dealing with others. The major learning outcomes, therefore, will be *increased awareness, changed attitudes*, and *greater interpersonal competence*.[4]

Theory Sessions

It is a basic assumption of laboratory training that experience must precede the introduction of a theoretical concept. Equally important is the assumption that raw experience without some degree of intellectual understanding is insufficient to produce learning which is useful and can be generalized. The delegate must be able to fit his experience into a framework of concepts and ideas which will allow him to relate to situations and persons other than in the laboratory.

In order to optimize learning, delegates attend daily information or theory sessions. The content of these sessions is designed to help them understand the experiences they are having in the T-group by focusing on topics such as the following: what to observe in a group, emotional problems of becoming a member of a new group, decision making and problem solving in groups, the communication process, styles of emotional expression and presentation of self to others.

For example, after the first T-group session, the entire delegate group usually goes to a general session during which the speaker discusses in greater detail the set of assumptions which underlie the laboratory method, in particular why the T-group is so unstructured. He points out that the removal of structure, agenda, and ground rules facilitates a *maximum exposure* of the reactions of the group members to the group situation. There is no place to hide, no agenda or set of rules behind which to obscure feelings. He also points out that merely creating a situation in which members expose some of their typical reactions does not, by itself, lead to learning. In addition, there must develop a *frank sharing of reactions and feelings* and a *climate of support and encouragement* which facilitates further exposure; there must develop a *willingness to engage in genuine mutual exploration* of group phenomena and a group atmosphere in which *experimentation* and *exploration* are viewed as positive sources of learning; there must develop a set of ground rules and a climate

---

[4] A more detailed discussion of these outcomes will be found in Chapter 3 and Part IV.

which permits *behavior to be viewed objectively* as data for analysis, rather than as something to be evaluated, rewarded, or punished. Finally, for the learning experience to be fully useful to the person, there must develop some degree of *intellectual understanding* of what is happening at the emotional level.

The speaker generally attempts to draw his illustrations from his own T-group experience and to show that the seemingly unique events in the groups do fit some theoretical framework and can be generalized, to some extent, to other groups in other settings. When such lectures are well done, the delegates have a genuine sense of integration with the realization that *neither the T-group nor the lectures would make complete sense without the other.* Together, they can make a potent learning experience.

In designing the content of theory sessions, the staff draws on its general knowledge of what issues the T-groups are likely to be facing at any given time and how these relate to other laboratory and back-home realities. In many instances, however, they will introduce new topics on short notice if it appears that several groups are facing some new issue which was not going to be dealt with. This requires close coordination among staff members and a sharing of what they perceive to be happening in their T-groups from day to day.

During the second week, the emphasis in theory sessions usually shifts somewhat from T-group issues to issues which arise in social systems, organizations, and communities. More attention is given to the occupational role which the delegate plays, to problems of authority and delegation, theories of management and organization, the consequences of collaboration or competition, and the like. As we will see below, an attempt is made to integrate this material with experiences generated in focused exercises.

Focused Exercises

The purpose of focused exercises is to generate some specific behavior so that a particular area can be studied (e.g., the communication process), or to practice some skill which is important for further learning (e.g., how to observe group action). An example of the former is an experiment highlighting the differences between one- and two-way communication. A delegate is asked to give some complex instructions to a group under two kinds of conditions: *one-way communication,* defined by the ground rule that the group is not allowed to ask any questions during the instructions, and *two-way communication,* defined by the ground rule that the group may say anything during the instructions. The one-way and two-way conditions can then be compared in terms of accuracy of communication, length of time taken, feelings of the sender and the receivers, and so forth.

An example of the latter, practicing a skill, is an exercise on skills of observation. One half of the T-group is asked to engage in a short role-playing sequence while the other half of the group observes the interaction in terms of categories decided on prior to the exercise. If observation is the sole focus, the different observers then take time to compare their observation and discuss the possible sources of difference in them. If, in addition, the exercise is designed to practice the skill of giving feedback to make the participant group more effective, a period is set aside for the observers to report on their findings to the participants. The participants are then interviewed to obtain their reactions to the feedback, or are allowed to engage in further interaction to determine what difference, if any, the feedback has made. A final portion of the exercise is a joint discussion or a reversal of roles among the groups between that of actor and that of observer.

An exercise such as any of these involves practice in several kinds of activities: actually observing others while remaining silent, analyzing observations and reconciling differences between observers, deciding what observations to report back to the group in order to be helpful, and the actual process of giving the feedback in such a way as to maximize learning opportunities. The behavior to be watched may be left entirely to the observers or may be structured into the exercise through instructions and observational forms. Such forms deal with communication patterns, the kinds of membership roles which different people play, patterns of influence and leadership, methods of group decision, style of expressing emotions, and so forth.

Toward the end of the first week or beginning of the second week, a more complicated and extensive exercise may be introduced. One frequently used exercise is on intergroup competition. Two or three T-groups are each given instructions to produce some product—a one or two page paper on some relevant topic—which is evaluated by a panel of judges consisting of members drawn from the competing groups. For example, the instructions may be to produce a 200-word statement outlining a plan for the conversion of a highly autocratic organization into one which practices participative management techniques, or a plan for the movement of a plant from one city to another with minimum negative consequences. One product is judged the winner. The purpose of the exercise is to give the groups a chance to work on some concrete task and to explore the dynamics of intergroup competition. By the time this exercise is introduced, the groups are usually more ready to begin a concrete task and to test themselves against other groups, a situation which produces high levels of motivation for the exercise.

The group first selects one or two of its members to join the judging panel, after which it works on its product for two hours or so. In the meantime, the judges meet to develop criteria by which the product will be judged. When each group has finished, the paper is turned over to the laboratory secretary for duplication and distribution to the competing groups. In the free time after the work period, one typically sees the groups clustered in separate parts of the conference center reviewing how they worked, expressing confidence in their own product, and generally derogating (though in a joking manner) the other groups. Questionnaire data on how the groups perceive their own effectiveness and that of the other groups are gathered by the staff before the groups begin working on the product and again after they have finished.

The following morning, the groups meet to look at their own product and that of the other groups. They are told that a general session is scheduled at which time they will have a chance to argue for their product through a spokesman who will engage in a debate with spokesmen from the other competing groups. The groups spend some time electing this spokesman and developing a strategy for him to follow in the debate. During the general session, each group sits behind its spokesman and is allowed to pass notes to him but not to communicate with him in any other way. At various points during the morning, data are gathered on each group's opinion of which is the best product, and whether it feels the judges will be influenced primarily by the merit of the product or by loyalty to their group.

After the debate, the judges deliberate in front of all the groups and reach a decision. At this point, feelings run very high, particularly in the losing group or groups. Each group is sent back to its own room for 30 minutes or so to consider how it feels about the decision. In the meantime, the data gathered at various points are being tabulated in preparation for a total feedback and analysis session. After the half hour of separate group meetings, the groups are brought back into general session to be interviewed by a staff member—do they feel the decision was fair, do they feel the judges were swayed by loyalty, and so forth?

In line with the general assumption that for maximum learning the experiences which the groups have had must be analyzed and put into a framework, the final portion of the exercise is devoted to an hour or more of systematic recapitulation supported by the results of the questionnaires which had been administered at various points during the total exercise.[5] One effective way to conduct the general session is to have a staff member make some predictions about group reactions to (1) having a concrete task to perform under time pressure, (2) being in a competitive situation, and (3) actually winning or losing. He may also point out some of the strains of being a judge or being a group spokesman. The delegates are then invited to comment on the predictions—did they observe the phenomenon predicted or not, and if not, why do they feel it did not occur in their group. Finally, the questionnaire data, which also bear on the predictions, are presented. These usually support the predictions in a clear fashion and create a dramatic finale to the exercise.

In this type of exercise, an attempt is made to simulate the realities of organizations and social systems. The exercise highlights for delegates the positive and negative consequences of intergroup competition, what it feels like to be a winner or a loser, a judge or a group representative. The exercise also begins to refocus the delegate on his back-home situation. Where the T-group is oriented to the here-and-now, the intergroup exercise begins to bridge the gap to the job situation with all of its intergroup conflict problems. Delegates usually have little difficulty generalizing some of their observations to labor-management negotiations, staff-line conflicts, interdepartmental rivalries, and majority-minority conflicts in committee meetings and other instances of intergroup discord.[6]

One important learning outcome of the exercise is the discovery by most delegates that the losing group rarely changes its mind about which product was the best; rather, it rationalizes in a variety of ways reasons for its loss. Once a group becomes committed to its product, it has difficulty seeing the merit in another group's product. Even if the delegate already knows that this phenomenon tends to occur, his knowledge takes on a new and more significant meaning when he relates it to his own intense and often irrational feelings of loyalty to his T-group, and when he studies the nature of his own feelings and shares them with other members who have similar feelings.

---

[5] This particular intergroup competition exercise was adapted from a previously employed and systematically conducted experiment, thus permitting some predictions to be made about the outcome. The exercise was developed by Blake and Shepard and is based on experiments conducted by Muzapher Sherif (1961). See Blake et al. (1961, 1964).

[6] For an important recent variation of this exercise, see Chapter 5.

The Second Week

The main task of the first week is entry into the laboratory culture. Re-entry into the back-home world is the primary task of the second week. During this week, the increasing attention on back-home problems is manifested in a variety of ways. Sometimes groups are brought together with the task of discussing how they might apply some of their new knowledge to the back-home situation. Or, meetings of groups are held at which members take turns discussing some particular back-home problem they have, while the other members attempt, through interviewing and careful diagnosis, to give help to each other on the problem. The real benefit of this kind of activity is to give the helpers practice in the art of giving help. If the problem presenter gains new insight into his back-home situation, this is a secondary gain. In some laboratory designs, a new set of groups is started with the purpose of giving every member the experience of making a transition from one group to another. The problems of re-entry into the back-home groups can then be assessed in the light of the transitional experience within the laboratory.

To support the theoretical material on problems of organizations and change, additional exercises are sometimes used. For example, to deepen understanding of the forces which make for or restrain change, the T-groups may be asked to diagnose the forces which have led to greater openness of communication in the group and those forces which have tended to prevent it. To obtain increased insight into organizational phenomena, groups may be given the task of simulating a company to market an actual product, while observers study the procedures used by the groups to establish their organization and to handle the kinds of problems that develop.

Informal Contacts

One other type of activity which takes on increasing importance as the laboratory proceeds is the informal contact made with the staff in individual or seminar sessions. Sometimes seminars are scheduled around topics which are of particular interest to staff members. In some laboratories, the delegates survey their own needs and ask that certain seminar topics be covered by any staff member (or other delegate) who is willing to act as seminar leader. Topics, such as the role of values in business, reconciliation of problems of family and career, the place of religion in modern life, the possibility of a similarity between laboratory training and brainwashing, may be proposed. Even if no one is found to be an expert resource person in the area, the group is encouraged to meet and discuss the issue.

In addition to seminars, a variety of informal contacts with staff develop in which either small groups or individuals get together with a staff member, often the trainer of their own T-group, to discuss anything ranging from the possible applications of the laboratory method to back-home problems to more general issues like the nature of organization theory. The staff member may be asked to elaborate on a lecture he gave or discuss what is new in a given area of research. Or, he may be sought out for guidance relating to a delegate's personal problem. If the staff member feels that the pursuit of such an area would create a problem (because of the special relationship which this would imply between himself and a single member of the T-group or because he might not feel qualified to enter such a counseling relationship), he can suggest that the delegate take the problem to a particular staff member, usually a psychiatrist hired for this purpose, who holds himself more available for individual help.

Informal contacts among *delegates* are also of great importance in furthering the learning process. To facilitate such contacts, meal times, coffee breaks, cocktail hours, and periods of recreation are kept as informal as possible and are scheduled to be as long as possible. Delegates are encouraged to review and work through what is going on in their groups and what they have heard in lectures; to work out in subgroups those problems which the total T-group could not solve; to explore in greater depth issues which have arisen in the group; to get other members to elaborate on feedback which was given initially in the group; to explore with others, who have similar jobs or come from similar organizations, the relevance of things learned to the job situation.

The focus during T-group meetings is on here-and-now group events; informal times provide an opportunity to talk about there-and-then back-home problems or more general issues. Informal contacts also provide important supports. The skeptic can seek out other skeptics and share his doubts about the value of the laboratory method; the enthusiast can seek out other enthusiasts; the person who is troubled by something said to him in the group can talk it over with someone whom he perceives as being supportive. Incidentally, in those laboratories where the physical facilities require delegates to share rooms, it is found that the late evening bull sessions among roommates are one of the most meaningful of these informal contacts.

Outcomes of the Laboratory

As the laboratory draws to a close, a variety of reactions among the delegates is noticed. There are those for whom the opportunity to concentrate on themselves and their own problems has been so meaningful and so releasing that they are genuinely reluctant to see the experience end. They feel they have become better acquainted with themselves. They may not be sure how this will affect them on the job or at home, but they are sure that the experience has been very worth while.

There are others who feel they have had a revelation as to what makes other people and groups work. They have had the opportunity, for the first time perhaps, to study the reactions of others and to observe how a group must struggle with the diversity of its human resources. Sometimes such insights lead to sharply changed attitudes toward groups and group action. Outright hostility toward any form of committee often changes into a more sensitive understanding of groups, and into recognition that groups can only be effective if allowed to mature and work through their initial problems.

There are some delegates for whom the most meaningful experience has been that they have been accepted and liked by the other group members. They go back home with a renewed sense of confidence in themselves. There are others for whom the experience has been primarily disturbing because they may have discovered that they were not as persuasive, clever, or powerful as they had assumed. They will go home with more questions about themselves than they had brought, and many of these questions will remain unanswered for some time after the laboratory.

Still others will see in the laboratory some gimmicks and devices for use in back-home groups, and will attempt to utilize these in spite of entreaties from staff not to take the laboratory method as a model of how to run a work group or a business. For some of these "alumni," the gimmicks will fail; they may then turn against the laboratory method feeling it to be a fraud, without recognizing their own misuse of the method.

Some delegates will cherish the fact that the laboratory provided a two-week period during which they could leave behind their work and family and ruminate about basic issues of life. For them, it offered a retreat and an opportunity to revitalize themselves. Some delegates will find that among their fellow T-group members, roommates, or other contacts, they can now count several close friends with whom they will maintain a relationship in the future. Some of these friendships may be more intimate than any they have in their back-home situation.

Some delegates will suffer intensely during the entire laboratory period because, from their point of view, very little was actually accomplished; they will go home puzzled, confused, and still skeptical.

All delegates, whether they are aware of it or not, go home with greater skills as group observers and diagnosticians, and with greater sensitivity to the complexity of interpersonal relationships. Whether they *utilize* this increased sensitivity constructively or not depends upon them, but there is little doubt that they have acquired it. All delegates become familiar with a new approach to learning—utilizing their own experience and learning from it. All delegates finally understand why it was so difficult for others to tell them what the laboratory would be about. As they think back over their own experiences, they realize how personal and unique these have been and how difficult it will be to tell others what has transpired.

We have attempted to provide a description of a laboratory, but have given little of the assumptions, values, theory, or issues which underlie laboratory training. An overview of these issues is our next task in Chapter 3.

3

Overview of Laboratory Training

The first three chapters which comprise Part I of this volume are designed to provide an overview of laboratory training, so that subsequent material can be more easily rendered and understood. In Chapter 1 we placed laboratory training in its socio-cultural setting and provided a framework of its origins and present status. Chapter 2 was primarily descriptive, mindful of the fact that there is no adequate substitute for the experience itself. We hoped to give the reader a feel for some of the complexity and vicissitudes of laboratory training by walking through, so to speak, a typical schedule of a two-week laboratory. Now we would like to discuss, in greater detail than was possible before, the basic elements of laboratory training.[1]

In order to probe more deeply into laboratory training and to clarify its basic character, we propose to discuss (1) its underlying assumptions, (2) its values and "meta-goals," (3) its goals and outcomes, (4) some of the necessary conditions for learning in a laboratory, (5) two models of learning which have been proposed, and (6) several laboratory components which exert a major influence on learning outcomes.

Underlying Assumptions of Laboratory Training

Laboratory Training Is Anchored in the Behavioral Sciences[2]

Laboratory training has its roots in the behavioral sciences. It grew out of a vision of an *applied* behavioral science: a store of knowledge

---

[1] For another discussion of some of these same issues, see Bradford et al. (1964), especially Chapter 2.

[2] It should be kept in mind that these are assumptions and are not always scrupulously adhered to in practice. In this respect they may resemble ideals more than practice.

which could be utilized to realize certain socially desirable goals. And most of the founders of laboratory training were trained in and influenced by the empirically oriented, newly developing social sciences.

The best example of this assumption was developed and formulated by Kurt Lewin, one of the founders and moving spirits of laboratory training. The idea was simple enough: to base action on carefully collected and analyzed data. The central idea of this process, called "action-research," is that action should be based on as many reliable (scientifically validated) data as available. Then, once action is taken, continual checks should be made on the results of the action (feedback) and these data should be evaluated before further action steps are taken.

Thus it is with laboratory training. Wherever possible, valid data are used to influence action, and action, itself, creates still more data for evaluation.

Laboratory Training Is Based on Intervention

But data and scientific findings, while necessary conditions, do not go far enough. Understanding, interpreting, and explaining stop short of action, of intervention, and laboratory training is directed toward intervention and change. Intervention is not only a requirement for bringing about action, it may, at times, be crucial for producing the necessary valid data. Kurt Lewin once said that "If you want to understand how something really works, try changing it." Integrating knowledge and intelligent action under appropriate conditions comprise the assumptions of intervention.

Laboratory Training Must Affect Social Role

Laboratory training is distinguished from other educational methods by its concern with its relevance to other social systems, most particularly those from which the delegates have come. It shows this concern in its attempt to influence the delegate in terms of his *social roles,* i.e., his profession, his organizational activities.

For example, in psychotherapy there is a contract for the cure of the patient, which is gauged by the doctor and the patient within the confines of the clinic. In traditional classroom teaching the implied contract is for the acquisition of new knowledge by the student; within the confines of this classroom, success is gauged by the teacher, and, occasionally, the student. In both of these cases the social role of the learner has only an obscure relationship to the learning process:

In laboratory training, on the other hand, the contract is based on social learning and is gauged by the individual and the groups in the laboratory, as well as the individual's interpersonal performance in his social roles *outside of* the laboratory situation.

In other words, most educational methods are evaluated by criteria which are really only relevant to the student-teacher relationship and not to the external world and the social roles of the individual. Laboratory training is distinguished by its emphasis on the socially relevant aspects of behavior and stresses connections between the delegate and those reference groups which are most important to him. This means that a predicted change in behavior is more of a value in laboratory training than either the abstract cognitive functions of classroom education, or the concrete emotional experiences of psychological therapy. Not to overgeneralize, laboratory training does encompass cognitive and affective functions and, just as certainly, education and psychotherapy are related to social roles. But the difference in emphasis is unmistakable. While society is the ultimate benefactor in all cases, laboratory training is more concerned with society as client than most educational methods.

These three assumptions: (1) anchorage in the applied behavioral sciences, (2) intervention, and (3) relevance to social role comprise the underlying structure of laboratory training. Let us now proceed to the question of values.

The Values and "Meta-Goals" of Laboratory Training

Two main value-systems influence laboratory training. They are highly related, general, and vague, and therefore are susceptible to easy distortion. Yet they are undoubtedly powerful and pervasive in determining the course of laboratory training and its outcomes. We should point out, also, that the values we elucidate are seldom *fully* realized in practice. Rather, they represent a set of dimly perceived ideals, frequently tacit, occasionally ignored, or even violated. Nevertheless, they do serve as guides to action.

The first set of values evolves out of *science* and can best be understood if we concentrate on the mores, ethos, and attitudes of science and not on its findings. So we will be concerned with an attitude—an orientation toward truth and discovery, which we will term a "spirit of inquiry"—when we discuss the value of science.

The second set of values that determines significantly the course of laboratory training we refer to as "democratic." When discussing democracy we find it easier, certainly less risky, to say what we do *not* mean than what we do mean by democratic values.[3] Most of all we do *not* mean those doubtful terms permissiveness or *laissez-faire* which, more and more, are coming to imply tender-minded naiveté or the indulgences of pseudo-democratic social systems. What we have in mind when we use the term democracy is a climate of beliefs governing behavior that people affirm by deeds as well as words.

Earlier, we referred to these twin values of science and democracy as meta-goals. Before going on to discuss them, it might be useful to clarify this latter term. We use meta-goals as a synonym *for* values to indicate that they determine the course of laboratory training (and various staff decisions) and also represent its latent goals. That is, to a large extent, they represent the unspoken, but enormously influential, goals and outcomes of laboratory training. To be more specific, while the values of science and democracy are almost never explicitly *stated* (or necessarily understood) in terms of desired outcomes of laboratory training, they frequently are the learnings assimilated and internalized by the delegates (often tacitly or unconsciously). In short, the meta-goals not only influence laboratory culture, they also help in affecting the outcomes of laboratory training.[4]

"Everything the child learns in school,. he forgets," goes an old French maxim, "but the education remains." In a similar sense we are using the term meta-goals interchangeably with values: to get at the essence of laboratory training, the "education which remains" and which tacitly guides the staff. Let us now turn directly to them: first, to the values of science.

The Values of Science

A Spirit of Inquiry. The first meta-goal or value is an attitude of inquiry most often associated with science. It is a complex of human behavior and adjustment that has been summed up as the spirit of inquiry and includes many elements, only two of which are considered here. The first may be called the hypothetical spirit, the feeling for tentativeness and caution, the respect for probable error. The second ingredient is experimentalism, the willingness to expose ideas to empirical testing, to procedures, to action.

The exigencies of the laboratory situation help to create this orientation in the participants, for the ambiguous and unstructured situation creates a need to define and organize the environment. In addi-

---

[3] For a recent discussion of democracy, see P. Slater and W. Bennis (1964).
[4] For a similar analysis, see C. Argyris (1962), Chapter 6.

tion, the delegates are prodded and rewarded by staff members to question old and to try new behaviors; the delegates are reinforced by concepts to probe, to look at data and realities, to ask "why."

In laboratory training, all experienced behavior is subject to questioning and examination, limited only by the threshold of tolerance to truth and new ideas.

Expanded Consciousness and Choice. Closely related to the spirit of inquiry is the meta-goal of expanded consciousness and sense of choice. To a great extent, laboratory training is structured to achieve these effects. For example, delegates are usually transplanted from a culture where things are routine and taken without question into a culture which deroutinizes and upsets expectations, particularly when the delegates are urged to observe and understand group interactions. Laboratory training is a device that deroutinizes and restructures, that slows down and lifts up for analysis processes usually taken for granted.

The main impulse for this restructuring—or unfreezing, as we refer to it later on—comes about because the ordinary control mechanisms which automatically govern most of our social behavior are decisively absent in laboratory training. There are no built-in devices for regulating behavior such as *Roberts Rules of Order,* chairmen, or designated authority. Nor is there any tradition or convention for making decisions or guiding the goals or activities of the group. Thus, there is a great deal of ambiguity and confusion regarding norms and expectations for appropriate behavior.

This unfreezing, then, tends to create a need for the delegates to find things out for themselves, to create order, to establish identities, norms and a sense of community. In fact, we can look at laboratory training as the formation of a community—except, unlike most communities, the constituent members are present (and analyzing) at its birth.

Laboratory training, then, realizes its meta-goal of expanded consciousness and choice by way of a complicated process. This process consists of (1) extracting participants from their day-to-day preoccupations, (2) cultural insulation, (3) deroutinization. Parallel to, and combined with, this unfreezing process is an emphasis on awareness, sensitivity, and diagnosis. All of these factors combine to create conditions which encourage the delegate to think about his behavior, to expand his consciousness of human phenomena, and to think about how he chooses to behave. (We will have more to say about the process of unfreezing later on in this chapter and in Part IV which concerns theory.)

Authenticity in Interpersonal Relations. Another meta-goal of laboratory training concerns authenticity in interpersonal relations. Implied is a relationship that enables each party to feel free to be himself. This relationship, in turn, implies more open communication that makes it more possible for delegates and staff to communicate feelings and ideas authentically—and for others to reciprocate in kind. In other words, the value of authenticity encourages individuals to be themselves and to communicate inwardly with themselves and outwardly with others as freely as possible. A line from King Lear sums up this particular meta-goal: "Speak what we feel, not what we ought to say. . . ." [5]

The Values of Democracy

The second set of values or meta-goals that plays an important role in shaping the direction and outcomes of laboratory training is what we referred to earlier as democratic. We said that it was difficult to express democratic values simply. In attempting to be more specific, we have settled on two core elements in the value system of democracy: (1) collaboration and (2) conflict resolution through rational means.

Collaboration. A spirit of collaboration pervades laboratory training. The traditional authoritarian student teacher relationship is minimized insofar as possible and the participation, involvement, self-control of the delegate are encouraged. We do not mean that the staff does not try to manipulate the learning environment and the delegate to some extent. As we shall see in Part IV, the staff is heavily involved in influencing the delegate. But we do mean that the staff is committed to and works toward a relationship with the delegate based on trust and confidence.

This collaborative relationship is developed in a number of ways. The delegate is free—and is encouraged—to question (and reject, if desired) all inputs from the staff or other delegates. Self-control, rather than unilateral authority of the staff, is vigorously sanctioned; delegates are viewed by the staff as free agents, autonomous volunteers in the learning process. At the same time, the staff avoids, as much as possible, patterns of dependence and counter-dependence with the dele-

---

[5] It may not be obvious why we included authenticity among the values of science. We included it here because we think it bears a direct relationship to one of the moral imperatives of science, honesty and openness in the methods and results of a person's work. For an excellent discussion of the concept of authenticity, see Argyris (1962, Chapter 1).

gates.[6] In short, the *interdependence* of the delegate and staff in the learning process is emphasized and acted upon. As the laboratory proceeds, more and more joint planning between delegates and staff is undertaken.

Conflict Resolution through Rational Means. Another core element in the consideration of democratic values concerns the management and resolution of conflict. Insofar as laboratory training is concerned, this means that there is a problem-solving orientation to conflict rather than the more traditional approaches based on bargains, power plays, suppression, or compromise.

What does a problem-solving orientation or conflict mean?[7] First, it implies that if conflict does exist, it must be recognized and confronted as such instead of being denied, suppressed, or compromised. Then, once recognized, conflict must be managed and resolved through understanding its causes and consequences fully and then bringing to light all data relevant to further understanding. Finally, the conflict must be resolved by consulting with all relevant individuals and groups and by exploring under conditions of trust and confidence all the possible alternatives for a solution. If these conditions are satisfied, then we can say that conflict resolution was managed and resolved through rational means.

These two values, science and democracy, however awkwardly defined and obscurely manifested, have an unmistakable impact on laboratory training. There is little doubt that they play a large part in the countless decisions that go into the operation of a laboratory as well as the kinds of learnings that delegates retain.

And yet, before going on, two qualifications must be made so that the reader does not gain a false impression. First, a warning should be repeated that was implied earlier: these values are ideals, models, ideal types. They are empirically imaginable but rarely fully achieved. In the realm of scientific values, particularly, we have often observed important discrepancies between value and practice. Even more distressing, at times, is the seeming lack of awareness that an important

---

[6] For the moment, let us define counter-dependence as the reverse mirror image of dependence; it simply betrays dependence through a rebellious veneer. The best example is the adolescent boy who claims that "father doesn't influence me a bit. I just do the opposite of whatever he asks of me." See Bennis and Shepard (1956) for a full discussion of this concept.

[7] See R. R. Blake, H. A. Shepard, and J. S. Mouton (1964) for a full discussion of problem-solving.

meta-goal (such as a spirit of inquiry) is being ignored or violated.[8]

Second, we want to stress again the meta-goal of *choice*. Perhaps we have not stressed this enough with respect to our own enunciation of the meta-goals. We are not advocating the wholesale and undiscriminating reliance on the foregoing meta-goals; nor does laboratory training exemplify them. We are recommending their application when *appropriate* and under the right conditions. Take the value of authenticity in interpersonal relationships, for example. There may be many conditions when exercising authenticity would be inappropriate or even dysfunctional. When is authenticity appropriate? Under what conditions? When, with what individuals, engaged in what kinds of role relationships, involved in what kinds of tasks, and for what reasons? All of these are valid considerations and must be examined. *Choice, regarding the implementation of the values, is the overarching and fundamental value.*

Goals and Outcomes of Laboratory Training

There are at least three ways to think about goals and outcomes of laboratory training. We have just discussed meta-goals, which the staff rarely articulates, but which shape the stated goals. The second set of goals is that which the staff *does* recognize and transmit to the delegates. Finally, we must consider what the delegate *actually* learns and carries away with him, regardless of staff purposes and/or values. We are calling the second set, *goals*, and the third set, *outcomes*. Let us take them up in order.

Goals

There seems to be general agreement about the goals of the laboratory training. The take-home booklets, the promotional material, the opening lectures of laboratories generally reflect this consensus. And while there are some variations of the stated goals, depending on the staff and delegate composition (e.g. a laboratory for school administrators or nurses or juvenile court judges), they usually include objectives such as these: (1) self-insight, or some variation of learning related to increased self-knowledge, (2) understanding the conditions which inhibit or facilitate group functioning, (3) understanding interpersonal operations in groups, and (4) developing skills for diagnosing individual, group, and organizational behavior.

Quite often an outline of these objectives is presented to delegates

---

[8] More will be said about this in Chapter 18.

at the opening session. In Table 3–1 we have duplicated a chart that is typical of many presented during the orientation session.

Table 3–1 Learning Understandings, Insights, and Skills

Self	Group	Social Organization and Functioning
1. Our feelings and motivations	1. Finding our place in a group:	1. Finding our place in the organization
2. Consequences of behavior in others	a. Reduction of anxieties	2. Diagnosing social organizational problems
3. Hearing others, accepting feedback, and communicating with other persons	b. Finding need satisfactions	3. Inventing, constructing, and adapting group norms, standards, laws
4. Skills of appropriate interactions with other persons	c. Finding place in influence structure	4. Diagnosing problems between and among units in the organization
5. Skills for continuous learning	d. Meeting expectations of others	5. Working as a member in the organization:
	2. Gaining understandings of group behavior	a. Finding and filling appropriate roles
	3. Gaining diagnostic skills	b. Applying problem-solving methods
	4. Gaining skills of appropriate member action on:	c. Maintaining oneself as a constructive member of the organization
	a. Task problems	
	b. Maintenance problems	

Outcomes

In our discussion, so far, we have been concerned with goals almost primarily in terms of the staff's expected or desired outcomes as a result of laboratory training experience. Neither the goals nor the meta-goals take into account either unanticipated outcomes or actual outcomes that result from laboratory training. The fact of the matter is that some delegates do not learn, others learn something, but not necessarily what the staff had in mind, and still others learn an unusual variety and combination of things.[9]

What is needed now is an analytic framework for all the possible outcomes delegates may, in fact, learn. Thus, if we consider delegate needs, organizational problems, staff goals, and meta-goals, we can classify outcomes as follows:

---

[9] In Part III, we will report and discuss some laboratory training outcome research.

Self—

1. Increased *awareness* of own feelings and reactions, and own impact on others.
2. Increased *awareness* of feelings and reactions of others, and their impact on self.
3. Increased *awareness* of dynamics of group action.
4. *Changed attitudes* toward self, others, and groups; i.e., more respect for, tolerance for, and faith in self, others, and groups.
5. Increased *interpersonal competence;* i.e., skill in handling interpersonal and group relationships toward more productive and satisfying relationships.

Role—

6. Increased *awareness* of own organizational role, organizational dynamics, dynamics of larger social systems, and dynamics of the change process in self, small groups, and organizations.
7. *Changed attitudes* toward own role, role of others, and organizational relationships; i.e., more respect for and willingness to deal with others with whom one is interdependent, greater willingness to achieve collaborative relationships with others based on mutual trust.
8. Increased *interpersonal competence* in handling organizational role relationships with superiors, peers, and subordinates.

Organi-
zation—

9. Increased *awareness* of, *changed attitudes* toward, and increased *interpersonal competence* about specific organizational problems existing in groups or units which are interdependent.
10. *Organizational improvement* through the training of relationships or groups rather than isolated individuals.

Let us underline several things that our classification scheme alerts us to. First, notice that the goals lie in three fundamental dimensions. The first involves the *level of learning:* whether it is merely awareness or understanding, whether it reaches the level of attitude change, or whether it reaches the level of behavior and greater competence. The second dimension involves the *reference point of the learning,* whether it involves the person in general, the person in relationship to others in a group setting, the person in an organizational role, or higher order units like role relationships, group relationships, and total organizations. The third dimension, which is not spelled out here but is implicit, concerns the *ultimate client* for laboratory training, whether it is the individual delegate or some larger unit like an organization or subunit of a social system.

We will go into a detailed analysis of goals and outcomes in Chapter 4 of this volume. For now, let us say just this. Learning about oneself in general and oneself in an organization role overlaps to some extent, but it makes a difference whether the laboratory is primarily organized to focus on one aspect or the other. This distinction will be a recurring one throughout this volume. When the person's particular organization and its particular problems become the focus of laboratory training, the client concept shifts or broadens from the individual learner to the organization or unit of organization that becomes involved in the training effort. Particularly in recent years, we have seen an increasing use of the laboratory method within a unit of an organization where clearly the primary goal is organizational improvement and where the learning of individual members of the organization is less pivotal to the total laboratory training effort. Once the individuals have increased their awareness, changed some of their attitudes, and acquired somewhat greater interpersonal competence, the focus of laboratory training shifts to improving *relationships* among individuals and groups. In any case, the pivot of the training activities—i.e., who is the ultimate client—will be an issue we will be returning to in Part II.

Necessary Conditions for Learning in Laboratory Training

Now that we have reviewed some of the possible outcomes of laboratory training, let us examine some of the conditions present that create these learning outcomes. We should say, to begin with, that our knowledge of the forces that influence the outcomes of laboratory training is relatively limited and undeveloped. Part of the problem stems from conventional learning . theories, such as those academic psychology provide or, say, those of psychoanalytic theory. They seem inadequate for our purposes: the former because of its oversimplified assumptions and mechanical operations, and the latter, because of its more restrictive focus.

We will attempt to fill some of this theoretical void in Part IV of this volume where we discuss learning theory in some detail. To prepare for that discussion, some of the basic conditions present in laboratory training that facilitate learning will now be presented.

Here-and-Now Focus

At the heart of laboratory training is the notion of the here-and-now. If this is understood, then we will have gone a long way in imparting the basis of laboratory training's character.

The here-and-now approach to learning means that the focus of examination in laboratory training is the *experienced behavior* of the delegates, nothing more or less. This focus represents the basic ingredient of laboratory training and the essence of the contract between the trainer and the delegates. This means that the context of inquiry for laboratory training is circumscribed by the data generated by the individuals in interaction with each other: their *common* experience.

Some examples might help: If a group member brings up, in the T-group, a back-home problem, say, a difficult work or community problem, the topic is either transformed into a group problem or is changed so that it has relevance for the group in this present setting. Or, if a group member goes to the blackboard to list the important elements in leadership, then the group—often aided by the trainer—attempts to examine whether or not by going to the blackboard the person was exercising leadership and in what way. The group might even discuss whether the elements of leadership listed on the blackboard have any relationship to the behavior occurring in the group. Or, take a group discussing the pros and cons of conformity in an intellectual way. If the group tackles an examination of its *own* problems of conformity, we can say that it is waking to the here-and-now mode. All of these examples stress the idea that the primary basis of learning is rooted in the data generated and exposed by the social encounters confronting the group members in the present.

The emphasis on here-and-now influences every aspect of laboratory training, not just the T-group. For example, the various exercises employed, like the Inter-group Conflict described in Chapter 2, rely on the analysis of experienced behavior. Even in general lecture sessions the lecturer will often draw on his interaction with the delegates to emphasize a point.

In other words, here-and-now learning is based on experiences which are shared, public, immediate, direct, first-hand, unconceptualized, and self-acknowledged. Compare this with the conventional ways of learning: through experiences which are vicarious, detached, incomplete, sanitary, overly intellectual and protective, frequently imposed by an authority, and often irrelevant. While the here-and-now orientation is not an official monopoly of laboratory training, it is perhaps its main distinguishing feature.[10]

One final example, from G. B. Shaw's *St. Joan* (1924), will enable us to dramatize the here-and-now approach as well as to elucidate some of its implications for learning. In the Epilogue to *St. Joan* all the characters who witnessed her sacrificial burning at Rouen gather twenty-five years later. They are discussing the execution, still vivid in their memories. The character who concerns us most in what follows

---

[10] Psychotherapists employ the here-and-now focus in the "analysis of the resistance" and with respect to transference phenomena; educators also use it, but perhaps less frequently, in "role-playing" and in other ways.

is Chaplain John de Stogumber, a cleric, whose hatred and fear helped to bring about Joan's demise:

JOAN: Poor old John! What brought thee to this state?

DE STOGUMBER: I tell my folks they must be very careful. I say to them, "If you only saw what you think about you would think quite differently about it. It would give you a great shock. Oh, a great shock." And they all say "Yes, parson: we all know you are a kind man, and would not harm a fly." That is a great comfort to me. For I am not cruel by nature, you know.

SOLDIER: Who said you were?

DE STOGUMBER: Well, you see, I did a very cruel thing once because I did not know what cruelty was like. I had not seen it, you know. That is the great thing: you must see it. And then you are redeemed and saved.

CAUCHON: Were not the sufferings of our Lord Christ enough for you?

DE STOGUMBER: No. Oh no: not at all. I had seen them in pictures, and read of them in books, and been greatly moved by them, as I thought. But it was no use: it was not our Lord that redeemed me, but a young woman whom I saw actually burned to death. It was dreadful: oh, most dreadful. But it saved me. I have been a different man ever since . . . .

What do this striking example and the previous ones tell us about learning in the here-and-now? First of all, they point out that concepts *follow* experience, and that concepts about human behavior can be best understood when they are accompanied by an emotional experience. Second, they show that learning is based on *direct and personal* experience and not upon vicarious and distant experience. Third, they tell us that the here-and-now provides a reference point of *reality*, i.e., *concrete behavior* to which concepts, words, ideals can be related and compared. De Stogumber never really "knew" what cruelty or kindness meant until *he* caused it, saw it, acknowledged it, felt it through Joan's burning. He then could assess the discrepancy between the abstract ideal and his concrete behavior. We cannot overstress this last point because so much learning in laboratory training starts from the recognition of discrepancies or incongruity between the brute reality of experience, objectified through behavior and feelings, and concept or ideal.[11]

Perhaps this is why we have placed the here-and-now orientation as one of the main cornerstones of laboratory training. It is through this

---

[11] The epistemological problems here are difficult. However we are essentially trying to make the same distinction about learning that William James made years ago, the distinction between an abstract process of reflective thinking and the knowledge gained from direct experience of fact and situation. *"Knowledge about"* is the former and is easier, according to James, to put into symbols, words, graphs, maps. *"Knowledge-of-acquaintance"* is derived from experience and is hard to transmit except by example, imitation, and trial-and-error.

orientation that individuals learn to distinguish appearance from reality, to become aware of the difference between feeling and intellect.

Feedback

One of Kurt Lewin's great contributions grew out of his concern with the idea of providing valid data on the improvement of performance in social learning. He extended this idea to practically every social avenue we can think of: to action researchers trying to improve the operation of a business or social-work agency, to supervisors trying to improve their managerial relationships, to parents trying to improve their relationships to their children and so forth. A short-hand term for this process of providing timely and valid data is feedback, a term, borrowed originally from electrical engineers, that described messages about deviations from a desired goal.[12]

Like the principle of the here-and-now, the idea of feedback is simple, even obvious. Practically all of our learning is based on the idea of obtaining information about our performance and then determining how far our progress deviates from some desired goal. Thus, we have report cards, advice columns, performance appraisals, man-to-man talks, evaluations, as well as more subtle ways to gain some idea of "how we're doing."

Feedback serves some covert purposes as well; for example, confirmations or disconfirmations about various realities concerning ourselves, or external events. Norbert Wiener remarked once: "I never know what I said until I hear the response to it." This is not the statement of an "other-directed" man, but a matter-of-fact statement about the need for cues and information about constructing realities, most of all about the reality we call "selfhood."

As an aside in this discussion of feedback, we would venture that the demand for and popularity of laboratory training today betray an important flaw in our society, namely, the lack of adequate and trustworthy mechanisms of feedback built into our social institutions. Bosses cannot talk or level with employees, wives with husbands, children with parents, students with teachers, and so forth. A number of pathetic symptoms of this communication gap can be seen in our contemporary society: intergroup strife of all kinds, divorce rates, the ubiquity of emotional problems, and what political scientists call "pluralistic ignorance," a malignancy born out of the absence of information about

---

[12] It is no accident that Lewin, who popularized this phrase for the behavioral sciences, was teaching at M.I.T. during this period of time.

what others think—or a distorted version of this information—leading to absurd action or impotent despair.[13]

This is not to say that feedback will remedy all social problems. It is only to say that feedback can be used to establish more valid realities. This is basically what we mean by feedback: a social mechanism for establishing reality.

Feedback is an essential ingredient of all laboratory training activities. Without it, the idea of here-and-now becomes sterile; with it, laboratory training can open up new channels of communication about the nature of human behavior and most of all, about the connection between appearances and reality.

In order for a communication to qualify as feedback, what conditions should be met? [14] First, feedback should be based on data generated from the here-and-now. This is a check on distortion as well as a valid boundary for distinguishing laboratory training from psychotherapy or traditional educational practices. Second, feedback should be as contiguous in time to the experience as possible. (Of course, choice must be exercised here. If the feedback follows the event too closely it may be met by a high degree of defensiveness on the part of the recipient.) The point here is that feedback should be data based and should rest on experiences that were commonly shared and public. Third, other things being equal, as many sources as possible should be employed to check and control feedback. For example, if group member A reports an impression about group member B, as many sources as there are group members can verify, question, contradict, modify, and gradually reach consensus—and, hopefully, reality—regarding the feedback to A.

We have made the important qualifications of "other things being equal." In doing so, we were attempting to indicate that there are times when reaching consensual validation may be impossible, unrealistic, or even misleading. George Bernard Shaw one said that "Fifty million Frenchmen cannot be right!" Similarly, there are times when unrealistic impressions and distorted images are reported to group members and supported with innocent unanimity by all. Scapegoating is one example of this. Ascertaining reality and continually

---

[13] Like the town in Kansas that "drinks wet and votes dry" each year for fear that nobody else drinks; or the town in Maryland where Republicans have given up voting because it is "a Democratic town"; yet, according to a recent poll, more Republicans than Democrats reside there, but don't vote because they "know" it is hopeless; i.e., "it is a Democratic town."

[14] For another discussion of giving feedback in groups, see Argyris (1962).

checking on its accuracy provides one of the most important and difficult activities in laboratory training—and there are no easy or foolproof methods for arriving at Truth.[15]

To return to our original question, what are the criteria for valid feedback? We can state the following tentatively: feedback should be based on publicly observed and experienced behavior, sufficiently contiguous in time and space, and modified through all the data sources available. These conditions shape the process of feedback, a mechanism that helps the group to establish reality.

Unfreezing

A third condition for learning in laboratory training is unfreezing. Unfreezing is a graceless term that implies that a period of *un*learning or "being shook up"—to use teenage slang—must take place before learning can be initiated. The impoverishment of terms that describe the process of unfreezing betrays both its complexity and our lack of total comprehension about its elements. In any case, its processes can be observed in almost any enterprise where *new* behaviors are required and have to be internalized, from the quarantine period in the army to regression in psychoanalysis, from the pledge period of the fraternity to the honeymoon in marriage.

Unfreezing is an umbrella term, taken from Lewinian change theory and adopted by us to encompass a *complex process initiated to create a desire to learn*.[16] First of all, unfreezing includes the idea of *contrast* whereby things that people take for granted in their ordinary life become absent or changed. In other words, an attempt is made to make the familiar strange. The T-group is a good example of this. All delegates coming to a laboratory have been in groups before, in fact, they have probably spent the bulk of their lives in them. But in the T-group, the idea of a group becomes real because the customary way groups behave no longer holds true.

By removing the familiar props and mechanisms from the T-groups, by violating the expectations of the delegates, the rug is pulled out from under foot, so to speak, causing individuals to search and explore the environment for new solutions. The old proverb: "Fish discover

---

[15] The epistemological questions we have ignored or chosen to avoid are enormously important and beyond our competence; they touch on the foundations of ascertaining the reliability and validity of *knowing*.

[16] A much more detailed discussion and analysis of unfreezing is provided in Part IV.

water the last" is related to this process. It rests on the assertion that curiosity and consciousness are born out of contrast.

Another aspect of the unfreezing process is represented by the *ambiguity of the situation*. The goals are unclear, the training staff provides minimal cues, the reward system is nonexistent, certainly, not very visible. The general absence of expectations creates an unstructured, i.e., ambiguous, situation. This serves to upset old routines and behavioral grooves and to open up new possibilities for the delegates.

A third factor in unfreezing is *disconfirmation*, in which participants of laboratory training hear and receive cues about their own behavior which may not jibe with their usual perceptions about themselves. Quite frequently individuals screen themselves off from realities, surround themselves with voices that confirm their own illusions about self, or pretend to act without knowledge of others' perceptions. In a laboratory setting, devoid of power relationships and previous ties, people are urged to speak what they feel and see. A situation is then created where individuals are confronted with, and possibly discomposed by, disconfirming cues.

Contrast serves to induce curiosity, ambiguity serves to create a vigilance (sometimes an anxious one) about inward and external realities, and disconfirmation aims to deroutinize stereotyped behaviors. These three processes comprise the mechanism of unfreezing, a complex adjustment that leads to a desire to learn about human behavior and, most of all, about oneself.

Psychological Safety[17]

In order for unfreezing to lead to an increased desire to learn rather than to a heightened anxiety, where the individual is immobilized or impervious to new inputs, an environment must be created with maximum psychological safety. This is a difficult and paradoxical task for, with one hand, the laboratory culture is trying to unfreeze and increase tensions, and, with the other hand, it is providing an atmosphere where one can take chances (which experimentalism implies) without fear and with sufficient protection.

How does laboratory training accomplish the twin goals of psychological safety and unfreezing? First of all, the laboratory is a learning

---

[17] In Part IV, we will be developing a model of learning that includes psychological safety as a part of the unfreezing phase. For the present, we present them as separate categories.

environment which is cut off from the more serious aspects of society's activities, and is a place where a person can behave in a "cultural island" and make mistakes without dire consequences either to him-himself or society. Second, the laboratory builds into its normative structure a high valuation on inquiry, experimentalism, "sticking-one's-neck-out-without-reprisals" attitude as distinguished from "playing-it-safe." Thus a climate is built which encourages provisional tries and which tolerates failure without retaliation, renunciation, or guilt.

But most important in developing a culture of psychological safety is the power of the T-group itself. For restoring the equilibrium of its members, for reducing threat, there is no substitute for the group. We are always amazed at this supportive and ameliorative strength of the group in freeing its members for creative and courageous acts. Even more amazing is how our society fantasies about the solely negative power of the group, whether it be toward conformity or destructive-ness or what. The point remains: the main source of psychological safety for the individual delegate is his sense of support and strength earned in and somehow borrowed from his T-group.

Observant Participation

One of the most difficult tasks for delegates of laboratory training to master is that of observing as well as acting, of diagnosing as well as behaving. We hasten to add that integrating knowledge and action is not only a Herculean task in the laboratory; it is equally difficult in real life where false separations are frequently made between the world of action and the world of analysis. To be detached without losing commitment is the aim of laboratory training (as well, we suppose, of education in general).

The tension between action and scrutiny typically becomes one of the main issues in laboratory training, where, during the early days, most delegates become discontented and even anxious about the undue emphasis they feel is placed on the process of observation and analysis. The emphasis is heavy, but the reaction is based on past experiences where action-for-action's sake was the norm. Even more important than past experiences is the suspension of conventional activities with *tangible* effects, like producing things or writing papers or managing and engineering complicated situations The anxiety caused by the initial unfreezing phase of the laboratory coupled with the lack of action outlets causes a good deal of frustration. Often the spirit of inquiry as exemplified by staff questions seems to the delegates as punishment and evaluation.[18] And in fact, in one important way it is. Deferring action until adequate analysis is undertaken tends to intensify anxiety through sealing off the usual "acting-out" mechanisms for warding off anxiety.

Camus once wrote: "My greatest wish: to remain lucid in ecstasy." Similarly, the goal of observant participation—to preserve detachment without forfeiting action—is of heroic proportion and rarely fully achieved.

Cognitive Maps

Much of the behavior generated by laboratory training can be characterized by the words *emotional* and *perceptual*. Equally important for learning, and, in fact, the *basis* for the affective component is a framework for *thinking* about the experiences. The term cognitive map is frequently used in laboratory training to refer to this intellectual framework. Of course, there is not one cognitive map, but many, for linking and ordering the variegated experiences the delegates encounter.

Theory inputs are important for a number of reasons aside from the obvious relief they afford delegates and staff from the intensive interpersonal round of activities. First of all, cognitive maps may help to supply a mastery over phenomena that previously perplexed the delegate. Quite often delegates experience events that, up to the point of conceptualization, are only vaguely sensed and felt. Rendering the dimly sensed feeling into words, into concepts, often helps to make the experience more understandable and hence manageable. There is a powerful sense of mastery in being able to make finer discriminations in one's emotional spectrum and to verbalize these discriminations. Hopefully, this will lead to better choices.

Another reason for the cognitive inputs has to do with building a culture. Cultures are built on a common language for shared experiences. Quite often, it happens that some concepts and theories create a cohesion through their shared comprehension.

Finally, theory material is crucial in providing a linkage not only between experience and concept but also between the cultural island of the laboratory and back-home responsibilities. So particularly where

---

[18] Early in the laboratory, the staff member can merely ask: "What's going on now?", a question that is heard by delegates as punishing, chastising, or downright rude depending on his frame of mind. It is rarely perceived as a simple request to gather data on the process of interaction in the here-and-now.

action steps are involved, cognitive material must be introduced in order to help with this transfer of learning from the laboratory to back-home.

In general, there is no set solution to the problem of how many or what kind of theory inputs should be given. Many staffs argue fervently on this issue and one of the main conflicts dividing staff trainers is the amount and presentation of cognitive material given. Some trainers favor practically no cognitive material, others desire a rather large portion. The decision about the quantity and type of theory material to be used is usually made on the basis of needs of the delegate population, the importance of conceptualizing the experience, the need for linking the material to action steps, and the inclinations of the staff.[19]

In any case, however it is presented, an intellectual structure is important, not only for the learning of the delegate but as a precaution against obscurantism and cultish practices and values.

These are the six conditions which comprise the basis for laboratory training: here-and-now, feedback, unfreezing, psychological safety, observant participation, and cognitive maps. It is not an exhaustive list of the basic components of laboratory training, but it does provide the necessary groundwork for our theoretical treatment in Part IV. Let us go on to examine more closely the learning process itself and its dynamics.

Two Models of the Learning Processes and Dynamics of Laboratory Training

The conditions for bringing about the processes and dynamics we have just reviewed are complicated. So are the processes themselves. In order to simplify these processes, we would like to present two rough models:

Dilemma-Invention Model

Blake (1960a) has constructed what he calls a "dilemma-invention

---

[19] Lectures and theory sessions can have certain hidden causes too. Occasionally they may be used by staff for their own needs: to gain prestige or exhibit intellectuality. For their part, delegates occasionally use lecturers as scapegoats, as ego ideals, and role models.

—feedback-generalization"model to describe the processes of laboratory training. In Table 3–2, a step-by-step description of this process and its comparison to the traditional classroom is shown.

Table 3–2 Two Approaches to Learning

Classroom Method	Laboratory Method
1. Teacher tells—demonstrates.	1. Delegates face a dilemma created by trainer or by trainer and delegates together.
2. Students listen, practice, drill according to the coaching of the teacher.	2. Delegates act to solve dilemma by experimenting, *inventing*, and discovering.
3. Teacher tests students.	3. Delegates do *feedback* evaluation of their own actions and of reactions by others.
4. Teacher accepts, rejects the students via grading.	4. Delegates and trainer *generalize*, theorize, formulate hypotheses, retest and recycle into next learning phase; i.e., into new dilemmas.

This model reveals a number of interesting contrasts to conventional classroom learning processes. For example, the main source of energy for learning in laboratory training is the dilemma created by the situation, in this case the unknown and ambiguous characteristics of the learning experience. It has been said that man is a dilemma-seeking and dilemma-solving organism and in laboratory training this certainly appears to be the case. Notice, also, that the role of authority is understressed and is put into the background by situational needs.

As a result of the dilemma and subsequent invention and discovery phase (and the behavior generated by the search), the delegates can now examine their experience and give feedback to one another. Finally in the last phase, generalizations and theory are sought in order to make sense of the experience. The cycle then begins again when new dilemmas are generated that fuel the group for more invention and further discovery.

Learner Change Model

Miles (1957, 1960) has developed a somewhat more complicated model, but one that tends to accentuate similar processes:

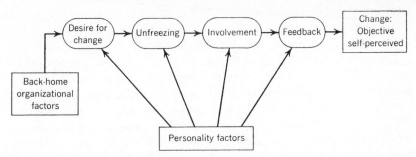

Figure 3-1 Antecedents of Learner Change at the Laboratory (Miles, 1960).

At the Laboratory. This model (Figure 3-1) emphasizes four processes in a sequential manner. The delegate must (1) *desire change* in the area of human relations; (2) *unfreeze* old behavior patterns; (3) *become involved in* the laboratory process; (4) *receive feedback* on his role and performance so that he can assimilate new ways of behaving.[20]

In Figure 3-1 we observe the changes that a delegate can undergo during the course of a laboratory experience. In order to account for changes that may take place in the back-home organizational setting, Miles has developed the model shown in Figure 3-2.

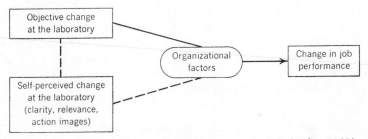

Figure 3-2 Antecedents of Learner Change on the Job (Miles, 1960).

Back on the Job. In Figure 3-2, we present a schematic diagram of the forces which play on the amount of learning the delegate transfers to his back-home organizational unit. (This is an extremely significant problem and will be treated both more intensively and empirically in Part II of this volume.) According to Miles, the best possible predictor of actual change on the job is objectively measured change at the laboratory. In addition, the learnings must be clear to the delegate, relevant to the job, and must involve action steps, things he can do

---

[20] Miles also asserts that personality factors (such as ego strength, flexibility, and need for affiliations) influence the learning process and outcome.

back on the job. Organizational factors must also be considered in order to route the course of learnings from the cultural island of the laboratory experience to the organization.

Let us now review some of the important elements in the laboratory method of learning. First, there is a *sequence or phasing* of learning going from some, vaguely defined, sense of unfreezing to cognitive mastery. Second, there *are both cognitive and affective responses* induced by the situation, what appear to be close approximations to what is meant by insight. This is an important characteristic of laboratory training, we believe, because it is one of the few learning methods which tries to integrate the intellectual and emotional functions of man. Third, the *sources of energy spring* not from authoritarian or conventional forces but *from the tension aroused by the situation itself*. This is not to say that authority plays no role in the learning; it does. But it implies that other group members plus the situation itself induce powerful forces for learning as well.

Fourth, as a result of the unfreezing there is a good deal of *unlearning;* i.e., a good deal of attention is devoted to interpersonal matters which the delegate now finds annoying in himself or guilt inducing or distasteful or disconfirming to his ideal self. Fifth, the process of *feedback* is involved; that is, systems of data exchange about interpersonal phenomena are developed and employed in the groups. Sixth, the data are generated and analyzed *by the delegates;* data are not imposed from other sources. Finally, there is a *self-generated momentum* to the training. Once launched, it seems to have a life of its own, generated by the complexities of the experience and the ever-changing nature of the phenomena.

Major Components that Influence Learning Outcomes

In describing laboratory training in this detail there is always a risk of exaggerating one factor out of proportion to make a point. One aspect that seems almost impossible to exaggerate is the variety and admixture of training activities in a typical laboratory.

So many forces interact and blend together to produce laboratory training that it may be wise at this juncture to isolate and examine some of the main *control mechanisms* in the learning process, i.e., the forces which play a major role in learning and shaping events in laboratory training. There are five we shall take up in order: (1) the laboratory culture, (2) the laboratory design, (3) the laboratory staff, (4) groups and various social encounters, and (5) the individual delegate. (We will return to all of these in Part IV).

Laboratory Culture

First we have to reckon with the idea of *culture,* the set of values and symbols that tinctures the day-to-day activities at a laboratory. A great deal has been made of the cultural island and quite often the residential laboratory is considered by staff as the one immutable ingredient that should not be compromised if laboratory training is to remain what it is. In any case, it is believed crucial for the delegates and staff to be insulated from the regular pressures of everyday existence so that the culture can be developed quickly and allowed to grow without outside contamination.[21]

It is probably no accident that the first laboratory at Bethel, Maine, took place in a remote, country setting. And Arden House, located at the very top of a small mountain, is sometimes compared to The Magic Mountain where time stood still and introspection ruled. These place-names, Bethel and Arden House, have even become the label for the laboratory experience, objectifying the culture of laboratory training. So we hear people say, "I've been to Arden House," or "I've been to Bethel," as if that conveys the essence of laboratory training. Perhaps it does.

In any case, culture intrudes in many ways, some subtle and almost imperceptible, some crude and visible. For example, there may be a community room where delegates and staff gather to exchange stories and lore, to sing, to chatter, to drink beer. People room together and share meals together. There is a community newspaper. Rituals emerge. A shared language is developed. One day feels like one month and chronological time seems unrelated to psychological time. Above all, still inexplicably, *a sense of community* forms, possibly out of confronting and sharing in the crisis of a community participating in its own birth.

Laboratory Design

Still another control mechanism in shaping laboratory training is the *laboratory design.* In Part II of this volume we will discuss a variety of designs and the rationales behind them. For the time being let us say that they have a substantial effect in guiding training activities.

A laboratory design represents a blueprint of the most significant

---

[21] Quite often outside newspapers go unread and radio and TV stations go unattended. It is as if the community is taking on a life of its own, with all the provincialism of a small village.

decisions in the life of a laboratory. Its significance can be confirmed by the hours and energy staff members invest in it. A laboratory design encompasses such decisions as the sequence of activities, the amount of time spent on T-groups as opposed to exercises, the size of groups, the placement and kind of cognitive inputs, the composition and size of groups and staffing. Laboratory design also includes some less obvious matters such as decisions about how recreation periods are utilized, how research and data collection are used, how coffee periods and meals are integrated into training purposes. It is fair to say that the culture of a laboratory is shaped more consciously by its design than any other single factor.[22]

Laboratory Staff

We have said very little so far about the *staff*, the laboratory trainers. They are typically drawn from universities throughout the world and usually, though not always, possess membership as a Fellow or Associate in the National Training Laboratories. Their experience and training usually combine a twin concern for social practice and social science. If anything, they can be characterized as "clinical social scientists," insofar as they work as laboratory trainers.[23] The staff is an extremely important force in the laboratory training process; their values, competence, and collaboration are crucial for the success of the laboratory.

Groups and Social Encounters

A fourth mechanism for shaping laboratory training activities is membership in the various groups. Foremost, of course, is the T-group, the group which ordinarily becomes what in one laboratory is called the "home-base" group. The T-group has attained a certain status in laboratory activities because of its intensity and duration and most of all because of its rich, emotional impact on the delegates.

But recently the T-group and its singular status has begun to be

---

[22] Paradoxically, delegates not infrequently remember laboratories as a succession of T-groups strung together over a two-week period. As an afterthought they may remember a lecture or two. Delegates, in their first exposure to laboratory training, can rarely identify more than the crude elements of laboratory design, and, like good background music for movies, the less visible it becomes, the better.

[23] It is a difficult group to generalize about; many conduct basic research and others are concerned with the integration of theory and practice. In Appendix 1, further information about staff can be found.

challenged by other kinds of group composition. For example, some laboratory designs have featured dyads, two person groups that meet for a half-hour or full hour every day. Tannenbaum, in Part II of this book, describes a variety of social encounters (clans, dyads, and tribes) which experiment with different size groups ranging from the full-scale total community down to two person groups. What is happening to laboratory training is that a number of trainers have begun to experiment with different styles, compositions, and numbers of delegates and are showing that these different size groups can produce distinct learning outcomes. For example, some individuals apparently learn more easily and more quickly in a two person group, others flower in a larger group. More research is required before we can come to any conclusions about the appropriate size of groups, but there is no question that a variety of experiences should be provided.

Individual Delegate

Finally, we must mention the *individual delegate* as an extremely powerful factor in the laboratory experience, perhaps the ultimate one. We still know very little regarding the learning capacities of delegates, what makes good ones and, even more critically, how to screen out those individuals who do not profit from the experience. We need to know far more than we do now regarding the characteristics of the delegate and the benefits he will gain from laboratory training. For example, what about the meaning of social role in learning? Does a man's position in an organization have anything to do with his experience in laboratory training? How does age figure into learning? What about previous experience in the case of laboratory alumni? How important is voluntarism or the desire to learn? Are there any ways of guaranteeing that individuals attend on their own volition, and does this make any difference? What about the cognitive functions of the delegate? How bright should he be, or does that make any difference? What about tolerance of ambiguity as a variable in predicting success at a laboratory? What about personality and the motivational properties of the individual? Does ego strength determine the success of the experience? What about level of anxiety and other personality characteristics? Can they be ascertained before the individual comes to the laboratory, and how will testing or interviewing be construed? Is it true that those who most need the experience are the least likely to attend a laboratory?

These are only some of the questions concerning the population characteristics of the delegates that need to be answered through research before we can speak with confidence about the extent to which delegate characteristics determine laboratory experience. We can say that the individual delegate is an important, but incompletely understood, agent in the total learning process.

❂   ❂   ❂

We have tried, in this section of the book, to present for the reader a compact and elementary view of laboratory training. We hope we have not imposed our own orientation, so that the reader can meet this material on his terms. In the rest of the book we shall become more specific and concrete when we discuss the uses of laboratory training in Part II, more empirical when we discuss research in Part III, and more abstract and restrictive when we present our theory in Part IV.

THE USES OF
LABORATORY TRAINING

In this part of the book we are addressing the reader who is concerned about the range of applications of laboratory training and the kinds of criteria by which he should determine whether or not it is applicable to a particular kind of problem. Chapter 4 outlines some of the major variables in terms of which the reader can differentiate between the kinds of laboratories and illustrates the various applications of laboratory training in terms of these variables. Chapters 5, 6, 7, 8, and 9 were contributed by various of our colleagues who are involved in some of the most innovative applications of laboratory training. In these chapters, we are deliberately seeking applications which explore the limits, which go beyond the conventionally defined uses of laboratory training. Finally, in Chapter 10, we present some of the major considerations which are involved in deciding whether or not laboratory training is appropriate for a particular organizational problem. We discuss there the whole strategy of change, the requirements needed for the change agent, and the conditions which must be met before the change agent can appropriately suggest laboratory training as a possible learning program. Also included are several cases where laboratory training failed. These cases highlight the importance of some of the criteria which should be considered.

4

Variations in Laboratory Training

The laboratory method of human relations training has been used in a variety of contexts. Because this method is a philosophy of learning, it is not limited to certain settings or populations. Rather, the group of people who approach human relations training from the laboratory point of view adapt the method in terms of the needs and givens of the situation in which the training is to be done. Each situation is approached with the question of what kind of laboratory design would be most useful in that situation at that particular time. Only rarely do laboratory staffs find themselves using packaged designs.

For example, at Bethel or Arden House, heterogeneous groups of delegates convene for one or two weeks to concentrate intensively on *personal* learning; in another setting, a top management team spends a week to ten days in examining their *work relationships* to each other; a lab convenes to *improve communications* between the several power groups of a community or to *improve the intergroup relationships* between a headquarters organization and its field branches. It would be almost impossible to list all the different activities which have gone on under the label of laboratory training. We can, however, identify certain basic variables in terms of which laboratory training experiences differ and give examples of programs to illustrate the differences.

Basic Variables for Categorizing Types of Laboratory Training

1. The goals of the laboratory.
2. The characteristics of the delegate population.
3. The nature of the sponsorship of the laboratory and the implied contract with the delegate.

4. The location of the laboratory and its degree of isolation from work or family.
5. The length of the laboratory.
6. The characteristics of the training staff, its size, and the staff/ delegate ratio.
7. The nature of the training design.

The Goals of the Laboratory

We discussed laboratory goals and outcomes in Chapter 3. Let us review this discussion, refocusing on the basic dimensions under-lying these goals. The specific goals in any given laboratory are the resultant of (1) the general learning theory underlying the laboratory method, (2) the basic values of laboratory training as expressed in its meta-goals (p. 30), and (3) the organizational problems or dele-gate needs which brought the laboratory into existence in the first place. We emphasize this multiple causality because the specific laboratory goals usually are not identical with what the organization

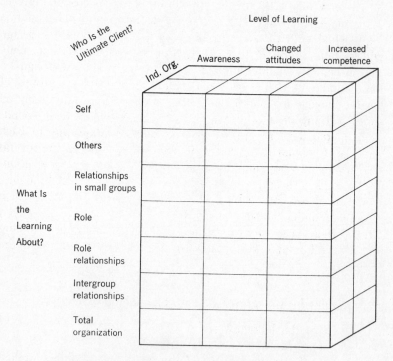

Figure 4–1 A Scheme for Classifying Laboratory Goals.

CAMROSE LUTHERAN COLLEGE
LIBRARY

or client group started with as its needs or goals, nor are they simply the meta-goals in disguise. Rather, they are usually a creative compromise reached collaboratively between the representatives of the client population or organization and the laboratory planners.

The dimensions which we identified as underlying laboratory outcomes can now also be used to classify goals (see Figure 4-1).

1. Who is the ultimate client—the individual or some social system from which he comes?
2. What is the learning to be focused on—self, relationships, role, group, intergroup, or organizational phenomena?
3. What is the level of learning to be reached—increased awareness, changed attitudes, or increased competence?

Dimension 1 refers to the important difference between laboratories which are organized to help individual delegates learn and grow as people and those which are organized to influence an entire organization or some subunit of it. Although both kinds work through individual delegates, the ultimate client in one case is the delegate, while in the other case it is the social system from which the delegate is drawn. As we will see, this difference has many implications for training design, implied contract with the delegate, laboratory staffing, and location.

Dimension 2 refers to the content focus of the laboratory. Training experiences can be organized to focus on the person himself, his feelings, his reactions to others, and his impact on others. They can also be organized to focus on how relationships between people and small groups operate, or on the dynamics of being a role occupant, e.g., what does it mean to be a manager or a teacher or a nurse? Finally, training experiences can center on the dynamics of social systems, how groups are organized and relate to each other, and on the dynamics of organizations or communities.

Dimension 3 is the most difficult to describe clearly. It implies a hierarchy of learning levels. We are making the assumption that stable behavioral change in the direction of greater competence implies some change in underlying attitudes about self, relations to other people, groups, role and system. Improved competence is therefore a deeper or more extensive level of learning than attitude change. But attitude change implies some recognition of a problem, some awareness of what is happening inside oneself, in others, and in groups. Attitude change, therefore, is a deeper level of learning than increased awareness. In this sense, we identify this dimension as involving the level of learning.

We will illustrate laboratory varieties primarily in terms of Dimension 2, the learning focus. On one end of the continuum, some laboratories emphasize personal learning to the relative exclusion of attention to organizational or role relationships. This emphasis is reflected in a relatively greater proportion of the total laboratory time being devoted to T-groups, the selection of a training staff particularly committed to personal learning models, and the use of theory which focuses primarily on personal learning. Such laboratories are alleged to go deeper into personal and interpersonal emotional dynamics (see Chapter 6).

At the other extreme, we have training designed to influence organizational performance. For example, Blake, Mouton, and Blansfield (1962) ran a laboratory in which a district group of the U.S. Internal Revenue Service was seeking improved relationships and communication with the regional headquarters group (and vice versa). The groups were brought together for a six-day laboratory during which the major activity concerned each group's developing its image of itself within the organization, its image of the other group, and the sorts of problems which were perceived to emanate from the other group. A training design was developed to help each group communicate its images to the other in such a manner as to enable themselves to *learn* from this report rather than to react punitively.[1]

Several kinds of laboratory training fall between these two extremes. First, there are laboratories designed for homogeneous occupational groups but heterogeneous with respect to the particular organizations or levels within them from which delegates are drawn. For example, at Bethel each summer for the past several years, there has been a laboratory for school executives. These are concerned with individual learning but they also focus on increased awareness of organizational dynamics (school system and community) and changed attitudes toward the occupational role performed. This shift in laboratory goals influences the training design, the kind of staff employed, and the length of the laboratory.

Laboratory goals may also be influenced by the nature of the sponsorship and the implied contract between delegate and staff. Laboratories which are primarily organized for a particular occupational group may formally or informally derive their financial and

---

[1] There is little doubt that individual delegates learned at the personal level, but this must be considered a by-product of the laboratory rather than something which was intended as its primary goal. The focus of the laboratory was clearly on organizational relationships and how these could be improved.

other types of support from this occupational group. This, in turn, implies that the training should be specifically geared to this group rather than being a standard training package. The staff chosen for the school executives laboratory will often include people who have done significant research on school systems or who have special knowledge about the school executive role. Industrially oriented laboratories, like the Management Work Conferences conducted by NTL at Arden House, New York, will have on their staff a number of organization theorists or researchers who have studied and written about industrial management problems.

Another type of laboratory which falls between the two extreme types is exemplified by the Workshop for College Leadership which has been offered for the past four years to teams of administrators, faculty, and students from college campuses, and the annual laboratory for Community Leadership which draws individuals and teams from community action groups. These laboratories involve heterogeneous groups of delegates from different colleges or communities, but are homogeneous in involving entire teams from given colleges or communities. The primary goal of these laboratories is personal learning for the individual delegates. But, the presence of teams also facilitates emphasis on relationship training and building core groups which might in the long run exert influences toward organization improvement on each campus or more corrective community action.

This broader set of goals is reflected primarily in the design of the laboratory. Increased emphasis is given to self-study within each college or community team, diagnosis of back-home problem areas, and the development of strategies for dealing with the back-home problems. Such problems may include improving faculty-student relationships in the classroom (to lead to more meaningful learning), reorganizing certain administrative relationships in the college organization (to improve the learning climate), improving relationships between community organizations, and the like.

Another example to illustrate variations in goals is the program recently initiated under a grant from the National Institutes of Health for the National Council of Juvenile Court Judges. The Council hired NTL to develop two types of laboratory experience, a series of regional institutes which are in effect one-week laboratories, and a series of local work conferences in different parts of the country which focus more specifically on the work relationships of the judge with other members of the rehabilitation team.

The one-week laboratories are attended only by judges who have volunteered. They have as their goals (1) increased awareness of the judge's role vis-à-vis social workers, probation officers, and others who make up the rehabilitation team; (2) changed attitudes on the part of the judges toward their own role and the role of others; and (3) increased interpersonal competence in dealing with the other members of the team.

The local work conferences involve the entire team in laboratory activities and are designed to focus primarily on improving relationships between judges, social workers, probation officers, and other members of the team. The laboratory also serves as a vehicle for some specific goals like providing the judges with increased knowledge of the emotional dynamics of juvenile delinquency, specific legal training (provided by a lawyer added to the staff), and knowledge of the sociology of delinquency and community disorganization.

Our final example illustrates a somewhat unique kind of application of laboratory training. Dr. Weldon Moffitt of the Extension Division of the University of Utah, with the cooperation of the Welfare Department in Salt Lake City, undertook to meet twice a week with a group of chronically unemployed males. The men probably came because they felt they had to in order to collect their welfare checks, but, as the group began to meet to discuss their common problem of chronic unemployment, the men found intrinsic satisfaction in being able to share their problem with each other and to have a professional social psychologist take an interest in them. The early group meetings were marked by strong hostility toward Moffitt, in part because the men felt he was judging them negatively (which he feels he may have been doing unconsciously). But, as the men were able to communicate their side of the story to him and establish a good relationship with him, this hostility was replaced by dependence and genuine respect.

The initial goal of this effort, according to Moffitt, was to help the men in overcoming the problem of chronic unemployment. At the outset, however, it was not at all clear *why* they were chronically unemployed. In the group discussions, factors came to light that became more specific goals of training. For example, many men were so frightened of a job application interview that they would not even attempt one. Systematic role playing of such interviews helped greatly to reduce these fears and build the competence needed to deal with them. Specific laboratory goals emerged only as the laboratory training got under way.

Summary. Several general points emerge from a consideration of these examples: (1) Most laboratories have multiple goals which can be roughly arranged in a hierarchy of importance but which also interact with each other to such an extent that it is often difficult to judge exactly where the primary emphasis lies. (2) The goals of a laboratory take on meaning only as they are translated into a particular set of decisions about what kind of training staff to have, what kind of training experience to consider, and what specific training design to use. Consequently, as we discuss these variables, we will by implication always be referring back to laboratory goals. (3) Different training experiences do differ substantially in their goals, and, as laboratory training activities in this country and abroad are perused, little evidence is found for any stereotype. The T-group is not always used and personal learning for the delegate is not always a primary goal.

Characteristics of the Delegate Population

Some of the important differences between laboratories derive from differences in the characteristics of the delegate population. Sometimes these characteristics define the goals of the laboratory, as in the case of occupational homogeneity or heterogeneity, but in other instances they merely affect the training design, as in the case of the age, background, intelligence level, and prior experience of the delegate with laboratory training. Obviously we cannot specify all of the possible characteristics which may make a difference, but we can classify these characteristics broadly into those which are personal and those which are role related or organizationally relevant:

A. *Personal characteristics*
   1. Age
   2. Sex
   3. Intelligence
   4. Personality
   5. Readiness to learn

B. *Role or organizationally relevant characteristics*
   1. Occupation
   2. Rank or position
   3. Connection to other roles or positions
   4. Specific problems facing members of that organization

In addition to these characteristics, we must also consider the homogeneity or heterogeneity of the delegate population *as a whole*, in terms of any of the above characteristics. Laboratories have varied in their mixture of delegates with respect to age, sex, intelligence, and readiness to learn. Personality has been systematically varied to a lesser extent only because of the difficulties of measuring it. More importantly, laboratories have varied in the degree of occupational heterogeneity, in the degree to which they have mixed rank levels, and in the degree to which they have maximized or minimized organizational connections between delegates.

In terms of this variable, we can identify five types of laboratory: (1) *general human relations laboratories*—occupationally and/or organizationally heterogeneous; (2) *in-company human relations training for a diagonal slice of the organization*—from the same organization, but heterogeneous in terms of rank and organizational connections; (3) *in-company training for a horizontal slice*—same as above but homogeneous with respect to rank; (4) *family group training*—training for an entire department cutting across several rank levels; and (5) *team training*—training for a work group which is interdependent and small enough to be able to operate more or less as a face-to-face group.

Sometimes the *characteristics of the delegate population are initially fixed* and a training staff is brought together to design an experience which will be meaningful to that particular population. We have many examples of companies deciding to provide laboratory training to some portion of the organization, either a family group, team, or larger unit. Perhaps the best known effort along these lines was Esso Standard Oil Company's program introducing laboratory training for all the management and technical personnel of each of its refineries.[2] These were large groups of delegates ranging widely in age, readiness to learn, and occupational orientation within the organization (line vs. staff, technical vs. managerial). Because of the size and heterogeneity of the population, the laboratories tended toward the traditional human relations type and delegates were selected (in groups of 20 to 25) to be as far removed from each other organizationally as possible (in most instances diagonal slices of the organization). The laboratory goals were more toward personal learning and less toward learning about role and organization.

---

[2] Parenthetically, this program illustrates the degree to which laboratory training tends toward innovation and resists standardization. The four refineries involved in the overall program used designs that differed in length, number of T-groups, presence of a trainer in the T-group session (one refinery used instrumented laboratories as developed by Blake and Shepard) and placement of the basic laboratory in a larger program of organization improvement. See Chapters 7 and 8 for a description of instrumented training and Blake's model of organization improvement.

Several colleges, notably Lesley College and the University of Maine, have launched family training for specific groups of faculty members to improve departmental and interdepartmental relationships.

A third example of a fixed population is the one-week laboratory for Sloan Fellows at M.I.T.'s School of Management, held during the first week of their academic program. Its purposes are multiple—to ease the transition from the high activity industrial setting to the slower paced academic setting, to provide an opportunity for common concerns and anxieties about the approaching academic year to get aired, to develop in the Sloans a spirit of inquiry and an experimental approach to the learning process, to develop a climate of support and cooperation in the Sloan group, and to introduce opportunities for personal learning as a prelude to learning about organizational phenomena covered later in the year. However, the population of Sloans is not chosen in terms of these goals. It tends to be very heterogeneous with respect to readiness for personal learning and prior laboratory experience.[3]

At the other extreme, many laboratories do *not* start with fixed populations. Rather, they *select* their delegates in terms of fairly rigid requirements, e.g., the delegates may have had to have a previous laboratory experience, may have to be diagnosed in some way as having achieved a state of readiness to learn, may have to occupy certain organizational positions, may have to be of a particular occupational group, or may have to fulfill minimum educational requirements.

Two examples would be: (1) the Organization Development Program, an alumni program, developed by an NTL committee, for directors of management development activities who were presumed to be already in influential change agent roles in their organizations; and (2) NTL's Social Science Intern Program, which is intended for capable social scientists who have genuine promise as laboratory trainers.

When each of these programs was developed some years ago, it was not even clear whether a potential delegate population existed or whether the program would attract a potentially available population. In the case of the Organization Development Program, fewer delegates were found than were sought; in the case of the Intern program, there were far more applicants than could be accommodated.

---

[3] The Sloan laboratory raises the problem of voluntarism. All Sloans are asked to participate in the laboratory. For a discussion of this issue, see Chapter 10.

Both of these programs involved a more intensive experience taking place over a longer period of time than the typical laboratory. In the case of the Organization Development Program, the goal was clearly defined to help each delegate obtain a better understanding of his own role as an agent of change, to change his attitudes toward his own role if necessary, and to increase his interpersonal competence in his role. To this end, the program was designed to be one year long, consisting of an initial 10-day laboratory followed by three three-day work sessions roughly four months apart.

Each delegate was to work on a back-home project during the course of the year, using the other delegates and staff as consultants on the project. Theory sessions and training activities focused on the dynamics of the change process: how to initiate and manage change in organizations, how to evaluate change efforts, how to build and maintain a helping or consulting role, and so forth. The kinds of projects chosen varied with the personal needs of the delegate and the kinds of problems his organization faced at the time. One delegate devoted his year to developing and implementing a strategy for introducing laboratory training into his highly conservative organization (which meant figuring out how to change the negative stereotypes of several top executives in the organization about the nature of laboratory training); another delegate devoted himself to the development of some answers to the question "after Bethel, what?" to deal with the problem in his organization of a great many people being sent haphazardly (so it seemed) to laboratories without any plan for utilizing their learning in the organization; another spent his year organizing a self-study survey of organizational problems in the several units of multiunit hospital; and one delegate tackled the question of developing criteria for the management needs of the 1970's so that management development programs in his organization would begin to build for the future.

As is evident from the range and scope of these projects, the position of the delegates in his organization, his readiness to be an effective agent of change, and his potential skills as a change agent were crucial requirements for effective learning in the training program.

In the case of the Intern Program, we have an instance where the selection of delegates had to reflect the multiple goals of NTL which were: (1) to bring new blood into the network of people competent to do laboratory training (a detailed description of this network is given in Appendix I); (2) to stimulate research on laboratory training by bringing into the program young social scientists already committed to research and acquainting them with the problems involved; (3) to improve the status of laboratory training within the academic community by bringing into the trainer network individuals of sound academic and research background; and (4) to improve the overall quality of laboratory training by selecting as interns only those individuals who could meet the above criteria, and demonstrate readiness to learn laboratory trainer skills. Individuals were sought who would possess a personality and character structure consistent with the responsibility which the laboratory trainer assumes vis-à-vis his clients, and who would reflect an interest in bridging the gap between action and research.

Applicants were recruited through a brochure which went to the existing trainer network asking the network to nominate from among their acquaintances likely prospects for the program. Applications, letters of reference, a personal interview where possible, and general academic standing were all taken into account in selecting individuals for the program.

The program itself is partially supported by the National Institutes of Health who provide a grant sufficient to pay a reasonable stipend to each of 10 interns for the program, the formal part of which lasts eight to ten weeks during the summer. The program includes several phases; the first is being a regular delegate in a human relations laboratory. This phase is followed by a three-week intensive training period of the entire intern group. This is followed by one or two apprentice assignments as junior staff in a regular laboratory under the supervision of a senior staff member. Each intern who is able to handle training assignments at an acceptable level of competence continues to be utilized during the following year in a junior staff role in a variety of NTL programs, following which he becomes a regular member of the trainer network.

Most of the general human relations laboratories or those designed for a large occupational group like the Community Leadership laboratories or the Arden House Management Work Conferences have some requirements for acceptance as a delegate, but these requirements are not as stringent as those of the programs just described. The procedure for the most part is simple. The applicant gives his name, title or position, name of organization, age, sex, whether or not he is an official representative of the organization, whether or not he is a member of a team, and answers to the following questions—"describe briefly your job by listing your major responsibilities and the individuals and groups with whom you work"; "what are the major goals you are working toward on the job"; and "what obstacles confront you in your work and how do you hope to eliminate them?"

This short application form hardly suffices for obtaining much personal information about a delegate, but it provides a basis for weeding out the person who is obviously interested only in personal therapy (for whom the laboratory training would be inappropriate) or who has personal problems which make it likely that he may not benefit from the laboratory. In questionable cases, the NTL central office group responsible for selection will write or telephone acquaintances or former alumni in that organization in order to obtain a more complete picture of the reasons why the person has applied. If it appears that he wants something other than what the training offers, he is likely to be rejected.

The selection procedure for these heterogeneous laboratories also takes into account age, type of organization, type of job within the organization, and so forth, in order to obtain maximum heterogeneity with respect to these variables. As team training has become more prevalent, there is increasing encouragement for organizations to send teams, but if one organization wishes to send several teams while another organization has only one, the latter may be admitted to obtain greater heterogeneity. With respect to certain variables such as age or rank, there have developed informal standards of the limits of desirable heterogeneity. For example, the Management Work Conferences have tended to attract mostly middle level management. If a vice president or president applies, he may be encouraged to attend one of the conferences for higher level executives unless he particularly wishes to attend the middle level one.

Summary. An examination of the variety of laboratory training activities reveals that the characteristics of the delegate population are highly variable, just as are its goals. Who the delegates are depends upon who initiates and sponsors the laboratory, the type of training which is to be conducted, and the types of goals to be achieved by the training. Delegates to laboratories have ranged in age from late teens to the seventies and eighties; they have come from industry, community organizations, school systems, colleges, state and national government organizations, political party organizations, hospitals, religious organizations and schools for missionaries, the American Red Cross and other welfare and charitable groups, the YMCA, YWCA, Boy Scouts, Camp Fire Girls, and a variety of other occupational groups and organizations. The growth of laboratory training in several countries of Europe, Asia, Africa, and South America promises to expand still further this variety of client populations (Miles, 1962).[4]

The Nature of the Sponsorship of the Laboratory Experience and the Implied Contract with the Delegate

There are two basic patterns of laboratory sponsorship. Each implies a somewhat different informal contract with the delegate:

1. *NTL or other training center sponsorship.*[5] Delegates are essentially self-selected, pay tuition for the program, and contract for a learning experience which is described in published brochures, course descriptions or the like.

2. *Organization or occupational association sponsorship.* Delegates are selected or encouraged to attend by an organization or association, generally do not personally pay tuition for the program, and contract for a learning experience which includes what is described in brochures, and *training which is primarily in the interest of the organization or association* (the latter may not be openly described).

The differences between these two patterns can best be clarified through two extreme examples. The typical human relations laboratory sponsored by NTL or one of a number of university based human relations training centers offers a certain kind of learning experience to volunteers from a large potential population. Each delegate, whether his organization reimburses him or not, pays his own tuition, and is entitled to a learning experience in accord with what the published brochure states. From the point of view of the staff, the

---

[4] A great deal of laboratory training has recently been generated in Western Europe. Although most of the countries in Western Europe have developed active and viable programs in laboratory training, not until 1962 did a multination organization of these programs emerge. Then, at Lausanne, Switzerland, trainers from Belgium, Holland, England, Austria, France, Norway, Germany, and the United States planned a European organization in many ways parallel to NTL. Since July 1962, formal meetings of this Association have convened at Leiden and Paris. The rate of activities is increasing, and multinational staffing of laboratories is growing.

[5] Interuniversity training centers drawing staffs from many sources have been formed on the West Coast (Western Training Laboratories) and in the Rocky Mountain states (Intermountain Laboratories), and are in the process of formation in other parts of the country. In addition, a number of universities have their own human relations centers or programs, e.g., UCLA, Boston University, New York University, George Washington University, and Temple University.

experience is clearly for the delegate's personal benefit and only remotely connected to benefits the back-home organization may derive.

The other pattern is best exemplified by the use of laboratory training as part of a particular organization's self-improvement program. For example, one large company has as its long-run goal the training of autonomous work teams. In order to get the individual members of the work teams ready for team training, the decision was made to hold a series of one-week general human relations laboratories for heterogeneous groups of managers within the company. The company has stated its expectation that eventually all management personnel will attend the laboratory program, but has left the timing to the individual departments and people within them.

To staff the laboratories, the company has hired members of the NTL network, described to them its overall organization improvement plan, *and its specific problems in implementing the plan,* i.e., some of the reasons for having the laboratories in the first place. The crucial factors which make this pattern different from the other are that the company, rather than a training center, is hiring the trainers, and that the company is explicitly or implicitly communicating to the trainers what some of the training goals *should be,* i.e., amelioration of some of its specific human relations problems. This pattern affects the implied contract with the delegate because of the likelihood that neither the company nor the training staff will be completely open with him about the specific nature of the organizational problems which are being worked on in the laboratory. The delegate, on the other hand, is contracting for what the published brochure, company literature, his boss, or the training department has told him; the training staff has actually contracted *with the company* for some additional learning goals which the delegate may be unaware of.

For example, there may be traditions operating in the company which dictate that one communicates with superiors and subordinates minimally and only within the context of formal authority and the immediate task at hand; that line groups are more important to the organization than staff groups; that feelings have no place in the world of work and must be suppressed in oneself and ignored in others. The person or group in charge of initiating the laboratory may perceive these traditions as standing in the way of good team work and may decide, with the help of consultation, that a series of general laboratories would aid in exposing and re-evaluating such traditions. But, neither they nor the training staff would state to the delegate group that one of the primary purposes of the laboratory was such a re-evaluation.[6]

In the case of the NTL or training center sponsored laboratory, implicit goals may also be present which are not, at the outset, shared with the delegates. But, the reason for the failure to share them could, in most cases, be traced to the professional judgment of the staff that the delegate either would not understand or would not benefit from this knowledge. For example, a training design could be created which emphasizes certain content areas, like problems of giving and receiving help, because of a staff diagnosis that the occupational group most heavily represented in the laboratory has particular problems in this area. Such a decision might be defended as having been made on the staff's own initiative in terms of its own professional judgment. In the organizational sponsorship case, the staff may be accepting a diagnosis from the organization and thereby obligating itself to work on certain problems which were initiated *by the organization*.[7]

For a human relations trainer with a set of professional standards, the problem becomes one of finding a balance in his obligations to the organization which hires him and the delegate who shows up at the laboratory, without jeopardizing the delegate's self-interest. In most of the organization programs which have utilized members of the NTL network of trainers or others with comparable social science background and training experience, the staff has put great emphasis on protecting the individual delegate—sometimes to the point of refusing to accept as legitimate laboratory goals any of the organizational problems which may have stimulated the laboratories. Nevertheless, the dual contractual obligation remains as a potential source

---

[6] In the case of the Esso program in the Baton Rouge refinery, there was a specific problem of lack of communication and mutual negative stereotyping between first-line supervisors and technical personnel, such as the engineering groups. Each laboratory saw the removal of this communication barrier as one of its primary but *implicit* purposes.

[7] We have belabored this distinction because many of the more subtle ethical and professional problems of laboratory training are connected with it. The suspicions of the delegate in the organizationally sponsored laboratory that the staff will report their evaluations of him back to his boss, the accusation by Baritz and others that social scientists have become "servants of power" because they are primarily hired by top management to fulfill top management goals (Baritz, 1960), and, the accusation by Odiorne and others that laboratories often seduce unwitting participants into emotional bloodbaths (Odiorne, 1963) are all related to this issue of the unwritten implicit contract with the delegate. We will treat these ethical issues in greater detail in Chapters 10 and 18.

of tension and misunderstanding, both for the delegate and the organization.

The Location of the Laboratory and Degree of Isolation from Work and Family

Several different types of laboratory training can be distinguished in terms of this variable:

1. *Total residential.* Delegate is removed from job and family.
2. *Partial residential.* Delegate is removed from job but not necessarily from family.
3. *Nonresidential, full-time.* Delegate attends laboratory during working hours but lives at home and maintains work contacts.
4. *Nonresidential, part-time.* Delegate attends training session for several hours per day, several days per week but maintains his normal work routine at other times.

Residential Laboratories

The laboratory in Chapter 2 serves as a good example of a *total residential* laboratory, e.g., the Management Work Conferences conducted at Arden House, Harriman, N.Y., on the top of a mountain some 50 miles north of New York City. Most delegates do not leave such locations for the entire two-week period.

Specific advantages of the total residential program are that the delegates have more opportunity, psychologically, to concentrate on the training course and to let themselves go. They do not have to maintain the image they have built up on their job and with their co-workers or even with their family. This freedom encourages analysis and experimentation with new ways of behaving. The psychological climate resembles that of a retreat and, for many delegates, the benefits are similar to what a religious retreat could afford them.

In planning a general human relations laboratory, the staff usually seeks a site which will facilitate a total residential program. Even if organizational problems are to be worked on, as in laboratories in which teams are present, it is desirable to separate delegates from the day-to-day pressures of job and family in order that maximum learning may occur. Hence, it is almost taken for granted among the staff that, if it is at all possible, a total residential setting is to be sought.[8]

---

[8] In examining the role of the laboratory culture and social structure as a force for learning, we will elaborate on the advantages and disadvantages of the total residential setting (see Part IV).

Partial Residential Laboratories

An example of a *partial residential* setting is Bethel, Maine, where many delegates bring their families and where recreational possibilities inevitably draw the delegates' attention to other matters for some proportion of the laboratory time. As was described in Chapter 2, the use of informal time for learning purposes is highly desirable. If this time is spent with others who are either unacquainted with or unsympathetic to the laboratory training experience, or who represent the old values, the delegate is put into a strained situation which may make it more difficult for him to take full advantage of the learning opportunities. To offset this risk in the laboratories run at Bethel, an effort is made to acquaint the families of the delegates with the laboratory program through special activities designed for wives and teenagers, or by encouraging wives to attend the laboratory as well.

The issue of degree of isolation applies not only to delegates but to staff as well. If staff coordination is an important ingredient of a well integrated laboratory design, it becomes important for the staff to spend a considerable amount of time together so as to keep their own channels of communication open. The larger the staff group the more important this becomes. Staff members do not usually bring families to places like Arden House. In the Bethel setting, some strains are created for those staff members who find themselves in conflict between wanting to devote time to family and time to contacts with other staff members.

Whether the presence of families in the laboratory community aids or hinders learning is not at all clear. One finds, among staff members, strong proponents of the position that the staff should be required to leave their families at home while working on a laboratory. Others argue strongly that it is good for the staff member to get away periodically from the supersaturated learning environment which the residential laboratory tends to become. We suspect that the ultimate answer to this question cannot be found without a more detailed examination of the inter-relationship of laboratory goals, design, and outcomes. The degree to which it is most beneficial for a laboratory to take a total residential form is heavily dependent on the nature of the laboratory goals.

Nonresidential Laboratory Training

The *nonresidential* laboratory is best exemplified by laboratory training which occurs as part of a larger educational enterprise in a university setting or in a company. A good example of a *nonresidential, full-time* laboratory is the Sloan program previously discussed. This laboratory meets for five and a half days, from 9-5, and the delegates go home each evening. After the laboratory, they enter regular courses in the Masters' Degree program. In contrast, examples of the *nonresidential, part-time* laboratory are the sensitivity training courses offered to undergraduates or graduate students at a number of universities. The class meets two or three times a week for one and a half to two hours and combines, within that time, T-group activity, theory presentation, exercises, and whatever other components are designed into the course. Some companies have adopted this form of training and have their executives spend one or two afternoons per week on laboratory training activities of various kinds.

The effectiveness of the nonresidential program must be assessed in terms of the training goals, the nature of the delegate population, the total number of sessions available, and the kind of staff. Not too many years ago, it was believed that the kind of learning which people experienced in T-groups could only occur in a residential setting. Eventually, several people began to experiment with other forms of training and discovered that certain kinds of emotional learning were possible in settings very different from residential laboratories. In our own experience with college students, it has become clear that certain laboratory phenomena can and others cannot be reproduced in a part-time nonresidential training experience. It is harder, but not impossible, to establish the appropriate climate necessary for effective laboratory training and meaningful learning in the nonresidential setting.

Summary

The issue of the laboratory setting appears to be reduced to the following points: (1) the residential laboratory, total or partial, provides a more integrated, intensive learning experience; (2) if the needs of the delegate population preclude the use of a residential laboratory a great deal of meaningful laboratory training can still be accomplished in a nonresidential setting, but a more careful diagnosis of the state of readiness of the population must be taken and the training design more carefully planned; (3) in general, the nonresidential laboratory offers less freedom to the staff in terms of training design possibilities but, on the other hand, probably stimulates more creative innovations. Some of these innovations will be explored in the section on training design variations.

The Length of the Laboratory Training Experience

The length of a training experience can be assessed only in reference to whether it is residential or not. Residential laboratories have ranged from three days to three weeks, with an occasional program of four weeks duration or longer. Most, nowadays, are one or two weeks in length. Nonresidential laboratories may consist of anywhere from 10 to 25 sessions or more.

Residential Laboratories

Most of the regular human relations laboratories for heterogeneous populations or for given occupational groups run for two weeks. The laboratories at Bethel were three weeks in duration until several years ago when the decision was made to experiment with two-week laboratories. The obvious advantage of the shorter one was that more delegates found it possible to attend, particularly those from organizations which could only release an employee for a two-week period. While the research results are not completely analyzed, it was observed in a follow-up study that, in some of the laboratories, the three-week to two-week reduction was not significantly related to the amount of learning. In other laboratories it was found that less was learned in the shorter laboratory. Most of the laboratories run by companies for their own personnel have gone from two-week to one-week programs in recent years, the reason again being that more people could be comfortably released from their jobs for a one-week period.

Problems in Assessing the Impact of Length. Several formidable problems prevent a reliable assessment of the relative impact of laboratories of different length. One problem derives from the fact that in the move from three to two weeks, the training staff typically filled the two-week design with about as many training activities as had been contained in the three-week laboratory. It was mostly the free time that was reduced, leaving delegates with much more of a feeling of high-paced, intense training while affording them less time to ruminate and consolidate what they learned. But, it is not clear how much effect this reduction has had on the amount or quality of learning. On the other hand, it has brought some advantages. Not the least of these is the economic one of enlarging the potential delegate population. Another one is the possibility of improving staff quality by attracting a wider range of staff.

Another problem in assessing the impact of laboratories of different lengths, and this applies particularly to the one-week vs. two-week laboratory, is that the training goals shift as the staff has less time to fill. Personal learning goals can usually be accomplished in a one-week laboratory, but if organizational or role-related problems are to be explored as well, more than one week is necessary. Most training staffs feel that if personal learning is to be an important goal, there must be a minimum of 9 or 10 T-group sessions. If the laboratory is one week long therefore, not much time is left for exercises or other activities.[9]

A third problem in assessing differential training impact stems from the change which is occurring in training philosophy. The emphasis is now moving toward repeated exposure to laboratory training rather than a single more intensive exposure. Increasingly, organizations are considering the initial one-week laboratory as a kind of appreciation training which will get the participant acquainted with the learning possibilities, and which will personally open him up somewhat. The intention is then to follow up later with an additional laboratory experience of three days to one week in duration during which specific organizational relationship problems can be tackled.

This pattern has been successfully used by Stop & Shop, Inc., of Boston, who have used for store managers and zone staff two one-week laboratories separated by a one-month interval. The first week was entirely devoted to learning about self and group; the second week was devoted entirely to organizational problems. During the second week, a wider range of people were brought into the laboratory to work with the original delegates on organizational problems. A similar pattern is being used by Hotel Corporation of America who have a series of one-week laboratories for heterogeneous cross-sections of the organization, followed by intensive team training of the management group of a given hotel.

At a number of university centers, notably UCLA, *continuing* human relations training is directed not toward organizational problems but toward greater personal learning and self-actualization (see Chapter 6). Selected alumni of a one- or two-week regular laboratory experience are brought back into a group which meets once a week for nine weeks plus a weekend and a mid-Saturday session (Tannenbaum and Bu-

---

[9] Some exercises can be adapted to the reduced session, one example being the intergroup competition exercise which has been reduced in total length from three three-hour blocks of time to one two-hour block and one three-hour block while still retaining many of the same learning possibilities. Such reductions have made it possible to provide in one week a fair approximation of the range of training activities which were available in a two-week laboratory. Here, as with the nonresidential laboratory, necessity has been the mother of invention. For a more detailed discussion of the design problems of one-week laboratories, see Chapter 5.

gental, 1963). NTL also has, for many years, sponsored alumni programs which, although varying in purpose, provide a second two-week experience to alumni.

As a final point, we mention that, in even less time than one week, it has been possible for training staffs to generate programs which have had unmistakeable learning impact on the participants. The three-day laboratory has been used for some time (Bradford, Lippitt, and Gibb, 1956) with considerable success. By full use of the three days, it is possible to work in nine sessions of the T-group plus some theory. This is more than enough to get the learning process started and to communicate to the delegate what the laboratory approach consists of.

The most recent example of the use of a three-day laboratory has been M.I.T.'s introduction of such an experience into the 12-week program for Senior Executives, a group of 20 to 25 higher level managers. The entire program is residential and the laboratory is introduced during the first weekend. Following the laboratory experience, the entire group is exposed to a regular course on organizational psychology along with other business courses.[10]

Another example is a focused training experience for the New York Area Training Conference of the Panel of Americans.[11] In order to improve techniques of panel presentation and response to audience questions, particularly under stress conditions, a program was designed which ran from Friday night to Sunday noon. The program included reference group meetings (similar to T-groups), panel presentation exercises and other activities designed to achieve the training goals.

In summary, the issue of how long a residential laboratory should be for optimum learning remains very much a matter of opinion and professional judgment. There is not as yet enough research evidence to warrant drawing any firm conclusions. Even the question of how many T-group sessions there should be is a matter that is worked out on the basis of staff members' experience and judgment rather than on systematic research evidence.

Nonresidential Laboratories

The number of sessions held in the nonresidential experience is highly variable and often depends on factors other than the training

---

[10] Since the writing of this chapter, the laboratory has become five days long because the program could accommodate that much time and the staff felt that the learning gains from five days did exceed those from three days.

[11] This training program was reported to us by Roger Harrison.

design. If the laboratory is run as part of a regular course, the number of sessions will be determined by the usual number of times the course meets. If it includes T-groups, it has generally been found that, in the nonresidential setting, it takes the T-group somewhat longer to get started, a fact which argues for a design which includes more than 10 T-group sessions, if possible. In some courses, the number of meetings is as high as 25 or 30, but not all of them will be T-group sessions.[12]

Recently, we have attempted to reintroduce[13] laboratory training into the regular graduate program in the M.I.T. School of Management by adapting Blake's instrumented training laboratory[14] to the particular course structure available in our program. T-groups met once a week for the entire semester, approximately fifteen weeks, and were supplemented by theory sessions, exercises, and other training activities. Courses similar to this one have been used, for a number of years, at the University of Texas, Boston University, and other colleges.

One final comment needs to be made about the length of the laboratory training experience. It has been the observation of most staff members that groups pace themselves according to their knowledge of how long the training experience will be. Thus, groups in the one-week laboratory seem to advance more quickly than those in the two-week; however, increasing the length of the laboratory does not necessarily mean that the T-group will go farther or deeper. We do not know of any experiments where a group was given *unexpected* extra time to determine whether this would aid further learning or result merely in a learning plateau. It is safe to assume that, within broad limits, the training design and the goals and skill of the staff have more to do with the direction and depth of learning than the length of the laboratory experience per se. Length has its major effect in setting boundaries, not in affecting the learning process directly.

---

[12] Of course, the goals of the laboratory, size of the staff, length of the sessions, and other forces will influence the rate of group development also.

[13] Bennis and Shepard taught an elective course for M.S. students of Industrial Management from 1953 to 1956 in which alternate sessions each week were devoted to T-groups and theory sessions.

[14] A complete description of the instrumented training laboratory approach can be found in Morton's description of the use of such a laboratory with a hospital population (see Chapter 7).

Characteristics of the Training Staff and Staff/Delegate Ratio

There are a number of characteristics of staff members that influence the character of the laboratory training.
These are:

1. The underlying philosophy of training and the specific training theory of the staff member (trainer).
2. The professional background and prior experience of the trainer.
3. The personality of the trainer and his training style.
4. The rank or status of the trainer in his professional group and within the training organization.
5. The overall competence of the trainer.

Staff Characteristics

As the reader may surmise, the issue of staff characteristics is one of the most important and also one of the most difficult to unscramble in terms of what we actually know versus what our own biases and prejudices lead us to believe. The most obvious generalization which one can make is that the staff members' training theories, personalities, backgrounds, and experiences will influence the goals and training design of the laboratory. By personality, we mean those personal characteristics which, on the one hand, give the trainer certain distinctive competencies and, on the other hand, set limits to the kinds of situations he can handle.

With some exceptions, most staff members have strong preferences for working in certain kinds of training designs and resist other designs which they lack faith in, which demand of them competencies they may feel they lack, or which they know will make them uncomfortable.[15] To the extent that the original organizer of the laboratory knows this and knows the personal biases of possible staff members, he will implement his own conception of training goals and designs by initially hiring staff members who are perceived to share such goals and design concepts with him.

A source of variation in laboratory training which is *nonfunctional* is *excessive heterogeneity* in staff philosophy, personality, status, and/ or competence. This happens more regularly in large laboratories

---

[15] Of course, it is important to distinguish between preference based on experience and preference or avoidance based on the staff member's own anxiety induced by a certain kind of laboratory.

which are staffed more on the basis of availability than compatibility. Such incompatibility often results in a relatively less integrated training design and a greater degree of staff tension which is implicitly or explicitly communicated to the delegates.

For example, at one large human relations laboratory, there was strong disagreement among the staff concerning the value of composing new groups on the basis of personality test information gathered on the first day. The underlying issue concerned training theory and staff member personalities, in that some staff members sensed that the use of such tests would make the whole laboratory focus so much on personal learning and self-actualization that they would become personally uncomfortable. Some staff members admitted that they would not be comfortable in responding to any inquiries by delegates as to their test scores; others asserted that the professional ethics of the American Psychological Association forbid giving out test scores without providing adequate consultation opportunities. The issue was fought out at various levels during staff planning sessions and was finally resolved in the direction of using the personality tests as a basis for composing new groups.

The effects of the lack of design integration did not become evident until the second week of the laboratory. It was discovered, at that time, that there were indeed very different conceptions, among the staff members who had new groups, on how feedback would be given to these groups concerning the basis of their composition. The total staff group finally decided that no *individual* feedback would be given and that the staff member who had originally proposed the tests should give each *group* feedback (tell each group on what basis it had been composed) in a large general session.

Some staff members felt that this session did not go well, and that part of the reason was the somewhat confusing mandate that had been given to the presenter (the original test proponent). According to some staff, the presenter actually went beyond what the group had wished him to do (but more in line with his own needs) and aroused further tension among the total staff. Whether this tension communicated itself to the delegates, and whether it reduced the learning potential of the laboratory is, of course, difficult to determine. What could be observed was a relatively greater amount of staff energy expended on resolving internal planning conflicts than on diagnosing and meeting delegate needs.

Usually disagreements in training theory and personality conflicts can be resolved rationally because of the staff's commitment to its own training theory. Such a resolution, however, requires adequate planning time and certain minimum levels of competence, maturity, and flexibility in the training staff. The major dilemma for staff groups is often the recognition that heterogeneity may produce not only the possibility of a less integrated laboratory, but also a rare opportunity for staff members to learn new approaches and grow in their own competence. As we have spelled out in Chapter 3, part of the overall ethic of laboratory trainers is that conflict can be genuinely worked through toward creative synthesis and need not be suppressed or compromised.

Variations in experience and competence among staff members pose another type of problem for the total laboratory. Such variations are inevitable in a growing profession because potentially good staff members must be given training opportunities in order to develop their competence and to gain experience. Yet, because of their lesser experience, such staff members often create problems during laboratory planning. First, they often preoccupy the staff group with issues which may be of lesser importance to the total design, e.g., how to get maximum learning opportunities for themselves. Second, they subtly influence the staff toward safe and conservative designs, i.e., designs in which the junior staff will be less anxious.

Within the T-groups, there is the problem of working out how the senior and junior trainers present themselves to the delegates and what kind of role differentiation occurs between them in their style of intervention. Because of the needs of the junior staff to discuss with the senior trainer what went on in the group, the staff becomes less available to the delegates.

In some cases, this particular problem can be resolved by finding a delegate population that is willing to be trained by a less experienced group or that is perceived to be willing to tolerate the tensions which this kind of training creates. The best example of such a resolution occurred in the laboratory run at Frostburg, Maryland, for the Montgomery County school system in 1960 and 1961.

The Montgomery County group wanted a laboratory for its own personnel, but was forced to operate on a very tight budget and a very restricted time schedule. The timing was such that an *intern* training staff, who had just completed the eight weeks of intensive training at Bethel, along with one or two senior staff could be made available. With such a staff, the school system could plan a reasonably large laboratory with minimum staffing expense (interns were paid a minimal amount because they were still officially in training). This pattern worked to the mutual advantage of Montgomery County and the intern program because a good quality laboratory was provided which gave the interns a far more realistic and intensive experience than they would have obtained by entering a regular laboratory as junior staff members.

Staff Size and Staff/Delegate Ratio

Laboratories vary considerably in the total size of the staff and in the staff/delegate ratio. We have already mentioned that one problem of the larger staff is the likelihood of heterogeneity which requires more planning time and the expenditure of more effort to achieve an integrated design. The largest laboratories we know of are composed of approximately 100 delegates and from 10 to 20 trainers, depending on the number of interns or junior staff. At the other extreme, there are laboratories of 20 to 30 delegates which operate with two or three staff members. Occasionally, a single staff member will work with a single group, but experience indicates that the kind of planning required to generate a good training design and the kind of emotional support which a staff member needs to cope with his own feelings during the training program argue for at least two staff members, even in the small laboratory.

If the training design calls for T-groups in which a staff member is to be present, there must be at least one staff member for every 10 to 15 delegates.[16] Most laboratories add one or two staff members beyond these minimum needs. If the delegate population is so large that staffing T-groups becomes a problem, the planner may move toward an instrumented training laboratory which can be run by two staff members for as many as 100 delegates, if adequate data processing facilities are available. The best examples of this pattern have been in large undergraduate courses where teaching loads, lack of funds, and lack of available trained staff generally have militated against trainer led T-groups.

As the staff/delegate ratio increases, the training design is generally affected in subtle ways. For example, most staff members wish to be involved in a T-group. As the number of Staff goes up, there is greater likelihood that T-groups will have co-trainers, which, in turn, presents new learning opportunities, yet greater coordination

---

[16] Ten to 15 members seems to be an optimum size based on trainer feelings. There is no hard evidence to support these assumptions but the argument is made that the group must be (1) large enough to provide heterogeneous resources, (2) large enough to allow the shy member to be silent without being conspicuous, yet (3) small enough to allow everyone to participate freely.

problems. As the number of staff members goes up, there is also a greater opportunity to design complex exercises for the total laboratory community by having subgroups of the staff concentrate entirely on one part of the design. In most large human relations laboratory staffs, the theory sessions as well as the exercises are coordinated by different subgroups. The advantage of such subgrouping is to cut down the amount of planning time of the whole staff, but the danger of developing uncoordinated training designs is correspondingly greater.

In the three-week laboratories, there was a tradition of T-groups in the morning and exercises in the afternoon, with different staffs being responsible for the different parts. This arrangement often aroused tension because the morning staff was considered to be of higher status and more competent. In the two-week designs, there were generally fewer exercises, which resulted in less staff division and in greater integration of training designs.

Summary

There are few general laboratory patterns related to the size of staff or the staff/delegate ratio. Laboratories can be found that illustrate almost all combinations, within very broad limits from a minimum of two staff members to a maximum of twenty. Staff/delegate ratios have varied from 2/100 to 1/7. The size of staff and the staff/delegate ratio have consequences for the nature of the training design, the degree to which the staff is likely to be integrated, and the degree to which the staff is likely to be free of tension. There are no ready generalizations about the necessary and sufficient conditions for an integrated training design, however.

The Training Design

It is commonly believed that training laboratories follow a fairly standard pattern, and that there are packaged training designs available which could be implemented by a staff at short notice. This stereotype is wrong in two important respects, both reflecting the whole underlying philosophy of laboratory training. *First,* a genuine value is attached to innovation. If the pattern of laboratory designs over the years is studied, a tremendous change and development is found in them, particularly in response to the different training goals and different laboratory populations which have developed. *Second,* it is found that for a laboratory staff to function effectively during the period of training, it is very important that they understand and are fully committed to the training design. Such commitment and understanding can come about only if the staff implements a design which they themselves have created. Even if a given laboratory is being run for the twentieth time, the staff brought together to run it will generally start from the beginning in developing its own design. They will utilize past designs as a point of reference, but will in no sense be bound to use any part of the designs unless they themselves wish to.[17]

In short laboratories with a few degrees of freedom, where the same staff is being brought together for a second or third time, and where that staff has previously hammered out the particular design they are using, one sometimes sees a particular design being repeated with a minimum of replanning. But such designs are still the staff's own designs, psychologically. Under most circumstances, the designing of the laboratory proves to be a challenging and rewarding task which staffs enter into eagerly.

Variations in training designs are tremendous and difficult to describe, partly because there is not as yet available a clear theory of laboratory training in terms of which one could classify training designs. Given this problem, it appears most practical to approach the variations in terms of the kinds of questions which laboratory staffs themselves face as they begin to plan a design.

By the time the staff convenes for a residential laboratory experience, there are usually certain givens within which they have to work. The setting is probably already selected, the delegate population is already known, and the length of the laboratory is decided. For most laboratories the training goals are also partly specified at the outset, though the planning staff can add to them or modify them if they feel strongly. Beyond these givens, the staff is generally allowed a maximum of freedom to create a training design that suits them. Enough staff planning time is provided, generally two to four full days, to enable them to construct a design prior to the opening of the laboratory.

Staff Issues in Initial Laboratory Designing

When the laboratory staff comes together to plan, the first question it generally asks is "what are our various theories of training and what

---

[17] One important exception has been instrumented laboratory training as developed by Blake and Shepard. The early instrumented laboratories were highly standardized, as are Blake's recent training designs built around the management grid (see Chapter 8).

kinds of favorite laboratory components do we have?" In collecting data for this question, the staff may, explicitly or implicitly, be developing their own group by getting acquainted, feeling each other out, discussing their differences, and, if necessary, examining the here-and-now process of their own group. In other words, the staff attempts, as much as possible, to operate in their own group by the same training philosophy as they attempt to communicate to delegates in the laboratory. Time pressures and emotional resistances sometimes partially block this endeavor, but the group generally maximizes its efforts to be open and to build its effectiveness.

Out of the general question of different points of view toward training and favorite components emerges an explicit or implicit list of the sorts of components which will be considered in building the laboratory. At this point, a blank schedule may be put on the blackboard and tentative activities filled in. This process is guided by a number of questions, which recur in most training settings, concerning the basic components of the laboratory design.

Questions About Basic Design Components

1. *T-groups*
   a. whether to have them or not
   b. how many meetings to have
   c. placement in the schedule
   d. whether to schedule any activity into the T-groups or not
   e. how large to make them
2. *Theory or information sessions*
   a. whether to have them or not
   b. topics and content areas to be covered
   c. placement in the schedule, particularly in relation to the T-groups
   d. style of presentation—straight lecture or audience participation
   e. length
   f. assignment of topics to particular staff members
3. *Exercises or focused activities*
   a. whether to have any or not
   b. which exercises to have
   c. placement in schedule
   d. particular design to be used in the exercise
   e. assignment of staff responsibility for planning and staffing the exercises

4. *Supplementary activities*
   a. two-man groups before or after T-groups
   b. consultation groups on back-home problems
   c. seminars
   d. activities to be encouraged during free time, e.g., use of library, contacts with staff, etc.
   e. diaries
   f. use of questionnaires, tests, or rating scales on which feedback is given individually or to groups
   g. new groups, a second T-group or task group or some other new group experience
5. *Assignment of delegates to groups*
   a. selection criteria to use—age, sex, occupation, organization, team membership, previous training experience, personality characteristics (as inferred from prior observations, questionnaires, or tests), delegate preferences
   b. which criteria to use for which group assignments—T-group, new groups, consultation groups, dyads, exercises
   c. how heterogeneous to make groups
6. *Research activities*
   a. purpose of research project
   b. degree of opportunity to use research activity for training purposes
   c. amount and nature of feedback to delegates
7. *Deployment of staff resources*
   a. who should work in T-groups and should there be single or co-trainers; if co-trainers who should be paired with whom
   b. should there be a separate T-group and exercise staff or an integrated staff; if separate, who should work on exercises
   c. are there special staff skills or resources which should be utilized in special activities
8. *Staff work needed in support of the design*
   a. what is needed
   b. who should do it
   c. how should it be done

As the reader peruses the above outline of questions about which a laboratory staff must make some sort of decision, he may well wonder how the laboratory gets off the ground at all. When staffs are deeply embroiled in an issue, such as whether to have a particular exercise or not, they sometimes wonder also. The fascinating thing is that staffs do manage to process all of these issues in time and also construct reasonably integrated training designs. The process of planning is not a neat sequence of decision steps. Rather, a series of major decisions will first be made to get a *concept* of a design. Decisions on the various specific aspects of it, then, will follow more easily. In talking about training design variations, we will deal more with the general concepts than with all the varieties of the specific components.

Designs for Personal Learning

Thinking back to our discussion of goals, we have, at one extreme, the laboratory that is designed primarily for *personal* learning. Once the staff accepts this as a primary goal, a series of consequences almost automatically follow: the design will have to be built around T-groups, T-groups will have to be bunched at the beginning of the laboratory, and theories and exercises will have to be primarily supportive of T-group learning.

For example in one management work conference the staff decided to maximize self-directed learning by allowing a maximum of free time. Almost every afternoon was completely unscheduled but an excellent library on psychology, philosophy, and religion was provided. Theory sessions were held on the problems of self-directed learning, personal choice of values, and philosophy of life; a bulletin board was provided for exchanging information on preferences for seminar themes; the laboratory was held in a setting (Arden House) in which solitude, pairing, or meeting in larger groups was maximally available. The staff made a concerted effort to encourage rather than direct the delegates genuinely to explore their own learning needs and desires. This meant that almost all exercises and training activities which involved the delegate in a regimented situation were ruled out. Instead, reading was encouraged and films such as *Twelve Angry Men, The Seventh Seal,* and *Patterns* were shown.

Many of the laboratories conducted by the Western Training Laboratories (combining staff resources from the Los Angeles and San Francisco areas) have been the most creative in stimulating deeper and more extensive self-actualization training. If this is clearly the goal, one immediate consequence which becomes important is that more attention is placed on the initial selection and screening of delegates so as to insure that those who attend the laboratory know what they are contracting for, and have the readiness and openness to benefit from such an experience.

If the delegates have been carefully selected, the staff can plan training experiences in and around the T-group that stimulate self-exposure and self-expression to a greater degree than the typical laboratory does. The theory sessions are likely to be devoted to problems of creativity, emotional expression, and self-actualization. Individuals and groups may be asked to create something—a picture, poem, cartoon, or skit. The training staff will put fewer informal boundaries on the content to be discussed in the T-groups, allowing the content to become more personal and deep while still adhering to here-and-now data.

More varied, unstructured, interpersonal experiences are provided by scheduling meetings for groups of different size. In a recent design, groups were built on a dyad-clan-tribe model, with the tribe being made up of the whole laboratory of 10-15 people, while clans were half T-groups, or 5-7 man units (Tannenbaum and Bugental, 1963). The emphasis of the training is on the delegate's becoming more familiar with his own strengths and weaknesses, his areas of flexibility and his areas of rigidity, and his responses to the experiences in different size groups. The question constantly before the laboratory is how to make better use of those resources which the person possesses, and how to accept realistically his limitations.

If new groupings are used in the laboratory, they may be constructed on the basis of personality test data. People are put together who are either similar or dissimilar on certain dimensions. In a general session, the consequences of such compatibility or incompatibility for group functioning are then discussed. The use of the tests and the ensuing discussions of personality dimensions supports the individualistic personality focus of the laboratory.

Some additional training devices to support this focus can be listed: (1) a period of silence of varying length preceding the first regular meeting of the T-group in which members are asked, to assess silently, their relationship to each other in any way which seems meaningful to them; (2) the writing out by members of initial impressions of others and the feelings which these others have created in them; (3) the showing of a film like The Eye of the Beholder which emphasizes how the same events are perceived differently by different people as a function of their own motives and personalities; (4) writing out, as part of the orientation to sensitivity training, some of the most potent personal feelings which delegates have experienced in their interpersonal encounters and which they keep hidden from other people; (5) public reading of some of these responses by a staff member who keeps them anonymous but is often able to show how similar the responses of different people are; (6) a general session on the language of emotions dramatizing visual, auditory, verbal, and nonverbal means of emotional expression, and so on (Tannenbaum, Weschler, and Massarik, 1961; Weschler, Massarik, and Tannenbaum, 1962).

Designs for Role and Organizational Learning

As laboratory goals shift to incorporate awareness of organizational phenomena and attitude changes toward own and others' *role*, the design of the laboratory changes in a number of significant ways. *First*, the number of T-groups is likely to be cut down to one a day, after the initial few days. *Second*, theory sessions will deal with individual and small group material supportive of the T-group in the early days, but will progressively shift toward organizational content from the middle of the laboratory on. *Third*, exercises which have proven to be highly successful in highlighting organizational phenomena will be introduced in the middle or latter half of the laboratory. *Fourth*, more attention will be given to seminars and other activities which utilize staff specialities and interests in organizational problems. *Fifth*, there will be provided, through exercises, theory sessions, consultation groups, etc., an increased emphasis on the process of giving and receiving help on back-home problems, on the theory of change, and on the skills necessary to initiate and manage change effectively. In dealing with the theory of change, the emphasis will shift from understanding *oneself* as an instrument of change to understanding the *social environment* which is to be changed.

Activities which focus the delegate intensively on himself and his feelings are likely to be omitted. If there are new groups, the learning emphasis in them may be shifted slightly from an examination of the personal implications of reactions to a new group, to the problems of multiple membership, which have clear back-home counterparts. Personality tests are less likely to be used as a basis for constructing groups, and the keeping of personal diaries is less likely to be encouraged. Implicit in these decisions is the assumption that the laboratory and the T-group already focus an individual heavily on himself. Unless it is a primary goal to push such a personal emphasis to the extreme, it is assumed that the laboratory can afford to bring in other activities without undermining personal learning.

If the laboratory includes particular occupational groups, such as community leaders, Juvenile Court Judges, or school executives, there will, in addition to the above general emphasis on organizational phenomena, be an increased emphasis on theory and exercises which deal specifically with the problems of that occupational group. For example, in one school executive laboratory, there were seminars on classroom grouping of students, staff freedom and administrative control, blocks and helps to classroom learning, and improvement of faculty meetings. An outside expert was brought in to hold several seminars on the role of the superintendent; a general session on human relations and educational achievement was held in the form of a mock Senate hearing; and, a general session dealing with the challenge of social science to education was presented late in the laboratory (Miles, 1960b). In the Judges' laboratories, a lawyer is included in the staff to discuss particular legal problems of the Juvenile Courts. The community laboratory will sometimes hold a large exercise in the form of a simulated community. Consultation groups may go to work on particular problems dealing with the occupation represented.

Those laboratories which involve *teams* from organizations require another major design variation which has to do with the constructive utilization of the teams. The best examples of such laboratories are the College Leadership and Community Leadership laboratories held at Bethel. When the staff designs the laboratory, a number of key decisions must be made concerning the types of groups to have and the allocation of team members to such groups. Most of these laboratories use T-groups to further the goal of personal learning. To maximize heterogeneity of membership in the T-group, teams will be broken up such that no team member is in the same T-group as his other team members. However, an equally important goal is to train the teams as teams so as to provide both nuclei of strength for the initiation of organization improvement programs back home, and to enable team members to reinforce in each other what they have learned. This requires training the group in the direction of improved team relationships and building into the team skills of initiating and managing change in a larger social system. The team may be encouraged to bring up actual back-home problems, diagnose the forces operating, generate strategies of change, and test ideas of implementation. Observations of its own group process and a diagnosis of its own effectiveness are likely to be interwoven with the actual problem oriented work to facilitate learning about itself and how it can become more effective as a team.

If the primary purpose of the laboratory is to improve relationships between teams, the activities will emphasize even more heavily how each team manages its internal and external relations, how it views itself and the other team, how it communicates about itself and interprets communication from the other. Blake's laboratory for the headquarters and field units of the Internal Revenue Service which was previously cited serves as a good example.

In all cases, it is analysis of here-and-now data which is the prime source of learning. But, the training design will influence heavily what sort of data are generated and which data are focused upon in the welter of available data.

Split Designs

As laboratories take on a greater variety of goals, they become more complex in design. Integration of the components begins to be an ever more important issue. Activities which facilitate team learning may also make it difficult for delegates to focus on their own personal learning. Or, more likely, if the delegate becomes highly involved in personal learning, he may be quite unwilling to shift gears and begin to consider organizational or back-home problems. It is sometimes too hard to concentrate both on becoming a better person and on becoming more effective in one's organizational role.

It is largely in response to these design strains that some programs have split the personal learning from the team training segment. In such instances, two one-week programs separated by a period of time or a personally oriented residential laboratory followed by a series of three-day family or team training laboratories, at the place of work, are used. Another format is one in which the organization uses regular NTL sponsored human relations laboratories to give their members an initial, personal learning experience, followed by a family or team training design tailored to the particular needs of the company.

Split designs make it possible for the delegate to test his personal learning experiences back on the job prior to the second laboratory exposure. A useful design element in the second can then be a reconvening of the T-group to discuss what problems of implementation the delegates faced in the back-home situation. Sharing with each other experiences of where personal learning had been most and least meaningful then paves the way for deeper levels of learning.

The split design also makes it possible to insert seminars, focused exercises, or other training activities into the back-home context prior to the next laboratory exposure. In the Organization Development Laboratory previously discussed the experiences of the delegates in attempting to implement the project they had developed in the first laboratory served as the main agenda for the subsequent three-day laboratory. During the three days, the staff helped the group to relate experiences, rediagnose, retest strategy, and develop new action steps if new ones were needed. In the three-day laboratory some months hence, the group again examined interim experiences and started a new problem solving cycle.

Other Design Variations: The Instrumented Laboratory

An important design variation, along a somewhat different dimension, is the instrumented training laboratory developed by Blake and Shepard (see Chapter 7 for a more detailed description). It became apparent to both of them that the typical T-group was influenced by the particular personality, training philosophy, and style of the trainer. Furthermore, in many situations, it was desirable to have training groups even though there were insufficient staff resources. These reasons, along with considerations of economy and the dependence of delegates on staff, led to the development of the instrumented laboratory built around a trainerless T-group.

The instrumented laboratory includes most of the same components as the general, but it adds systematic and frequent formal data collection as a central ingredient of the design. Facilities for rapid processing of the data have to be available in order that the delegates can obtain feedback on their own collective reactions to events in the laboratory as soon after they happen as possible. Much of the learning then revolves around the attempt to understand the reactions as revealed by the data in terms of what is going on in the group. This cycle of data collection, processing, feedback, and analysis of results is used for each T-group meeting, for determining the outcome of focused exercises, for obtaining personal feedback (each member is asked to rate the other ones on set scales), and for consolidating what has been learned.

The primary functions of staff members are to design and administer the laboratory, give theory sessions, collect and analyze the group and exercise data, and help the delegate group draw generalizations from their experiences. One or two staff members can run a laboratory of as many as eight to ten groups if the data collection and analysis procedures are properly designed for IBM mark sense or punch card equipment.

Work-Problem Centered Laboratories

Some training designs explicitly emphasize the day-to-day work problems of the delegate group and de-emphasize personal learning or even here-and-now group data unless the group itself brings such data into the discussion. In this category would be family group and team training with the focus on "how can we do our job more effectively," or "what are the barriers preventing more effective job performance."

Such designs may be used if the initial diagnosis of the delegate population reveals (1) that the group could learn best from focusing directly on work problems, or (2) that as a group, they are not ready for the kind of learning opportunity which residential laboratories make available, or (3) that they would not volunteer for such a laboratory, if given the opportunity, because they do not themselves recognize some of the problems which exist in the work relationships.

In the latter two cases, the company may employ one or two staff members to work with a family group or work team for the explicit purpose of assessing the barriers they encounter in doing their job and developing approaches toward overcoming these barriers. The trainer may have the implicit aim of gradually getting the group ready to look at their own interactions. By minimizing process interventions early in the life of the group, he allows this readiness to develop at its own pace. He helps the group collect data on how to do their job more effectively and attempts to build group strength by suggesting procedures on agenda building, problem solving, and decision making.

A focus for looking at their own group may be introduced in a variety of ways. One of the commonest is simply to ask the group, after a number of sessions, how they feel about their own progress as a group and what suggestions they might have for proceeding more effectively. As members begin to share observations and reactions, the trainer may add some of his own observations and thereby legitimize this kind of discussion. Most groups find a discussion of their own process fascinating and pursue it with vigor once the door is opened to this possibility. As the group becomes more comfortable with this level of analysis, the trainer may gradually begin to raise the issue (if the group itself has not already done so) of the relationship between their own process and the main agenda of how to create more effective on-the-job relationships. At this point, the group may become a modified T-group in its group process emphasis, but retain its ultimate goal of better work relationships.

A great deal of discussion has occurred over the years with respect to the question of whether superiors and subordinates could or should be placed into the same T-group. It had been observed in those T-groups where the experiment was done, that initially there was more resistance, but once a mutual trust was developed, it was possible for such groups to learn effectively, particularly if the boss was willing to open up some of his own feelings to the group. In the kind of family group just described, superiors and subordinates, sometimes across three levels, have been put into the same group. The initial emphasis in these groups on how to get the job done more effectively provides an opportunity for group members to feel each other out and make calculated decisions as to how much they will trust each other. If several members, particularly the higher ranking ones, cannot be trusted, the group may never move beyond a there-and-then job discussion. The trainer, in this instance, supports the group in its avoidance of dangerous interpersonal material. However, he may suggest that the one or more key members attend some outside training program as preparation for further work with the group. Such a decision, particularly if the company treats it mechanistically and insensitively, can have disastrous consequences for both the individuals and the organization improvement program and, therefore, is fraught with ethical dilemmas for the trainer. He certainly does not wish to precipitate a decision to send a particular man to a training laboratory under circumstances where the man might view this as a punishment for his own ineffectiveness. If the man is in a strategic or highly placed position, it may be better to suspend the program until such time as he is better prepared for it.

If, on the other hand, the higher ranking members of the team or family group are able to be open and to elicit trust, it is often possible for the group to move as far and farther than typical T-groups. It can utilize not only the data generated in the group meetings, but also the data which have been generated over the years in the working relationships. The possibilities for consolidation of learning and actual attitude and behavior change are, therefore, much greater in such groups once the initial resistance has been overcome. From a training design point of view, such programs tend to be minimally planned at the outset and constantly replanned as new data from the groups become available. They require an innovative and flexible staff who can invent the right activity for the right time. A relatively greater responsibility for good initial selection of *groups* is also involved. Rather than ending up with a group which is blocked by one or two members, it may be better to initiate the program with groups in which all members are considered to be ready for this level of learning. Unfortunately, this often results in learning opportunities being given to those individuals and groups who are perhaps least in need of them. We still lack a good theory and skill technology of how to build learning readiness in people and groups who do not already have it (see Chapter 10 for a further discussion of this issue).

Summary

We have not treated all the questions which have to be faced in constructing a laboratory design, but this was not our intention. Once a concept of a laboratory emerges in terms of (1) the major goals to be achieved, (2) the kind of delegate population to be trained, (3) a concept of whether the ultimate client is to be the individual or the organization, and (4) a notion of the level of learning to be achieved, many of the specific design questions answer themselves. Therefore, we have limited our discussion to broad variations in design. We have tried to point out that such major variations revolve around the above questions. The resulting designs reflect the different concepts in terms of how many T-group sessions, their placement in the laboratory, the composition of T-groups, the number and kind of focused exercises and supplementary activities, the tasks assigned to groups, and the deployment of staff resources.[18]

Overall Summary and Conclusions

We have attempted to discuss variations in laboratory training in terms of several key variables: (1) the goals of the training; (2) the nature of the delegate population; (3) the nature of the sponsorship of the laboratory; (4) the setting; (5) the length; (6) staff characteristics, size, and ratio to delegates; and (7) the training design.

As must be evident to the reader from the above discussion, these elements are highly inter-related and are focused around the three basic dimensions which define laboratory goals—the focus of the learning (self, group, role, organization), the level of learning (awareness, attitude change, increased interpersonal competence), and the ultimate client (the person or the organization). Throughout our above discussion, we have been faced with major differences resulting from the nature of the ultimate client and the focus of learning.

We have placed relatively less emphasis on laboratory variations which reflect different *levels* of learning. This is partly because this

---

[18] If the reader wishes to pursue further the question of design variation, he should refer to Chapter 5 and also should request, from the National Training Laboratories, copies of the proceedings of different laboratories run over the years. Each laboratory keeps a record of its design and these designs are available upon request.

variable has remained more implicit in training designs, and partly because our subsequent theoretical discussion will treat it more explicitly. Certainly there are important differences between laboratories which emphasize only awareness, those which attempt to induce attitude change, and those which seek improved interpersonal competence. But, we are not as yet very clear in our theorizing about the relationship of level of learning to the other variables we have considered.

By way of conclusion, we wish to underline the tremendous variety of laboratory training situations which can be identified. Our examples barely scratch the surface. Important work has been done with 4-H clubs, with ships crews, with political party workers, with labor unions, with teen-agers, with faculty groups, with mental hospital attendants, missionary groups, psychiatric residents, and so on. Companies such as Esso Standard, Pacific Finance, Space Technology Laboratory, Aluminum Company of Canada, U. S. Rubber, Hotel Corporation of America, General Electric, IBM, Eli Lilly, Hydro-Electric Commission of Ontario, Beltone, and many others have made laboratory training an essential part of their management development and organization improvement efforts. Increasingly, laboratory efforts have been tried in national or local government agencies such as the Internal Revenue Service, the Peace Corps, AID, and the.Public Health Service.

Experiments have been conducted with very short and very long laboratories. Different delegate composition has been tried all the way from training a top management team to training foremen. Staff characteristics have been varied from using group oriented psychiatrists on one extreme, to using intelligent sensitive nonprofessionals or graduate students at the other extreme. Training design innovations are going on constantly to the point where it is difficult to keep up with them.

The single most valid conclusion which can be drawn about varieties of laboratory training is that at the present stage of the development of laboratory training, the varieties exceed our capacity to systematize and classify them into neat pigeonholes. There is little need to worry that laboratory training is stagnating or becoming packaged.

A Note on the Following Five Chapters

Chapters 5 through 9 were contributed by various of our colleagues. We asked them to provide us with material such as these chapters cover to fulfill the following purposes: (1) to illustrate more fully the variations in laboratory goals, design, and target population; (2) to give the reader a feel for some of the developments at the frontier of training; and (3) to provide the reader with a variety of conceptualizations about laboratory training as a supplement and counterpoint to our own theory presented later.

In order to fulfill these aims, we have deliberately left the contributed pieces intact. We wished to preserve their integrity and unique style, even if this created some discontinuities from chapter to chapter. The reader should be aware that each of the authors is developing laboratory methods in directions which to him make the most sense, even though, from another point of view, such developments may seem unrealistic, silly, or poorly conceptualized. But, because they are at the frontier, some of these developments are more advanced in practice than they are in underlying theory. They illustrate the commitment of laboratory trainers to innovation.

The reader who wishes to explore some of the further varieties of laboratory training is invited to peruse the next five chapters. If the reader wishes to continue with our own conceptualization and discussion, he should go on to Chapter 10.

5

The Design of One-Week Laboratories

ROGER HARRISON AND BARRY OSHRY

The one-week training laboratory poses interesting problems in laboratory design because its length forces the staff to make difficult choices. These are common choices which must be made in any laboratory design, but they are probably sharper in the one-week laboratory than in any other. For example, two-week designs permit a good deal of movement between concentrated T-groups and more structured exercises dealing with intergroup and organizational processes. Short weekend or four-day experiences practically limit one to sampling some aspect of laboratory training.

The one-week design is marginal in some respects. On the one hand, it is possible for a happily mixed group to have a very rich experience in the time allotted. On the other hand, if the group moves slowly, the staff and participants often end up by feeling that if they had spent just a little more time, the rewards in terms of personal learning through the exchange of reactions to one another's behavior in the group could have been much greater. Knowing this in advance, even while not quite trusting these "just a little more time and it would have been great" feelings, there is pressure to crowd as much T-group time into the experience as possible, to the exclusion of organizational concerns.

The authors recently conducted three one-week laboratories for the Small Aircraft Engine Department of the General Electric Com-

NOTE. In this chapter, Harrison and Oshry provide an interesting discussion of how they went about developing an integrated and innovative design for a *short* laboratory, one lasting only five days. Not all of the underlying premises or theory which led to the design decisions are presented in the chapter because of lack of space. The reader should note the manner in which the design was adapted to accommodate the particular training goals and the short time available. This chapter is a revised version of a paper which appeared in *NTL Subscription Series*, No. 5, 1964, and is published here with the permission of NTL.

pany in Lynn, Massachusetts.[1] Because these laboratories were repeated with virtually the same staff and similar kinds of participants, this project offered a unique opportunity to build an integrated design and, through experimentation, to improve upon the design in each succeeding laboratory. The purpose of this paper is to share the results of some designs which were developed in our attempts to resolve conflicts among competing training goals.

The Participants and Staff

Each laboratory was attended by 20–24 middle managers with varying functions within the department. The ages, educational background, and distribution of functions of the participants were similar to those attending other open laboratories conducted for managers. However, a larger proportion of the General Electric managers were technically trained, and a number of them managed highly technical functions. Further, while participants were selected to be organizationally unrelated, some close work relationships invariably turned up in the T-groups.

The staff in each laboratory consisted of the authors plus two members from the personnel function in the department, each of whom had had various laboratory experiences, including T-group co-training functions.

The Training Goals

The major goals were as follows:

1. To provide participants with a sufficiently full and complete T-group experience to permit significant increases in self-awareness and understanding of one's impact on others.

2. To provide a laboratory experience in competition and of conflicting resolution, which would simulate as closely as possible the real life negotiation of differences between groups.

3. To provide the opportunity to develop a conceptual framework for understanding group and interpersonal processes and to provide opportunities for practice in the diagnosis of process in ongoing groups.

[1] We wish to acknowledge the significant contributions to this study of the following Small Aircraft Engine Department personnel: D. R. Lester, who made the project possible; R. W. Haskell, who served as liaison and training staff; Bruce Deem and Roger Hebert, who joined us as training staff. We also wish to thank the Boston University Human Relations Center, under whose auspices this project was conducted.

The Design Problem

The basic problem seemed to us to be how to provide meaningful intergroup experiences and conceptual structure without interrupting or overdiluting the emotional flow of the T-group experience. The conflict seemed most acute in integrating the intergroup exercise into the laboratory. In our experience, the artificial tasks which are usually imposed upon a T-group in intergroup exercises often break the flow of increasing concern with interpersonal relationships in the group. For the goals of the development of interpersonal concern and a climate for feedback, the intergroup exercises in which we had participated seemed often to be interludes rather than integrated experiences. While these may, in a longer laboratory, furnish useful tension relief, in designing the one-week experience we felt considerable pressure to have every topic of conversation in the T-group be as potentially relevant as possible for involvement in and understanding of the group process and interpersonal relationships among the members.

We felt similar pressures in the scheduling of theory sessions by the staff. Every T-group trainer has experienced the annoyance of breaking his group for a previously scheduled theory session which he feels is irrelevant to the important concerns in his own T-group. Further, one has only to observe the planning of a Bethel laboratory to realize how difficult staffs find it to predict in advance what theory content will be appropriate for *most* of the participants at any given time.

Finally, we were interested in exploring ways in which T-group development could be facilitated. We felt that the tendency to increase the proportion of time in T-groups as the laboratory gets shorter has its limits. We had observed that when groups are pushed to develop too fast, they seem to react by spending increasing amounts of time in flight to back-home topics and other less personal issues.

The Design Elements

Major design features of the laboratories were decided upon in the first laboratory. Then various forms of the elements were experimented with in the remaining two designs. The basic elements were present in each design, and where they differed in detail we shall usually describe the later design. The elements were as follows:

Element A. The first element was intended to increase the flexibility of the staff in providing conceptual input about group and interpersonal process, and to fit the particular input separately to the needs of each of the two T-groups. We decided to eliminate general theory sessions entirely. To permit flexible and timely conceptual input, we tried to structure the role of the "outside" trainer (the authors) in the T-group to include brief lectures on theory, as well as long, discursive interventions intended to provide conceptual structure for what was happening in the group at the time. The "inside" (or General Electric) trainer in each group usually balanced this more pedantic training model by intervening on a level closer to that of group member, modeling the expression of feelings, the giving and receiving of feedback, and other kinds of effective member behavior. This is not to imply a clear division of labor; there were more similarities in role than differences. Where there was a role difference, however, it was in the structuring, conceptualizing function of the outside trainers.

This design element was not new, but it is not ordinarily used in such an extreme form. In general, we felt this model permitted us to capitalize much more than usual on group events to illustrate concepts. We concluded that we had gained more in flexibility and immediate relevance of theory than we had lost.

However, this design has its own problems. It requires that the trainer self-consciously accept a high degree of responsibility for conceptualization, and that he be articulate in communicating concepts extemporaneously. We met these requirements better as we gained experience, but in the first laboratory there seemed to be more than the usual number of complaints about confusion and lack of structure. This was not true of succeeding laboratories.

The model works least well when the group or a subgroup is involved in a highly counterdependent or dependent relationship with the trainer. During periods of controversy about the trainer's role, conceptual inputs may often be responded to primarily in terms of feelings about authority. During counterdependent phases of a group, it sometimes requires some courage to intervene with conceptual material, knowing the intervention will serve as the occasion for another attack by members.

Element B. In place of the traditional morning theory session, we had an extra forty-five minutes to an hour for additional T-group time. We used this extra morning time to introduce a second design element, *the split T-group.*

We had observed that frequently T-groups change more in their productivity and emotional climate *between* sessions than they do *during* a session. We had seen groups spend a whole session in some flight activity, or in fruitlessly trying to resolve a difficult issue, only to come back the next session ready to work or to try a fresh approach. Our hypothesis was that, within limits, the *number* of T-group sessions has more effect on the progress of a group than the *amount of time* spent in session. We felt free to schedule T-groups of an hour or an hour and a quarter if by so doing we could multiply the number of sessions. We generally had two of these shorter sessions in the morning, and longer two-hour sessions in the afternoon and evening.

We did not fully explore the limits of the short T-group. Our design permitted us to have four T-group sessions in a normal day. We do not know what would be the effect of scheduling five sessions during the same total time, for example, or of reducing all four of the sessions to, say, one hour, and using the remaining time for other learning activities. We do feel that such experimentation would be reasonable and worthwhile because we were unable to distinguish the quality or productivity of our different length sessions. Within the limits we used, a T-group session seemed to be a T-group session.

Element C. A major design concern was to integrate externally applied task requirements into the natural life and concerns of the T-group. We believe that the development of the T-group with highly work oriented members is aided by providing situations where the members can spontaneously produce their normal work behavior in a laboratory setting, under conditions of time pressures, productivity and quality considerations. Essentially, this means assigning the T-group a task, to be completed at a certain time, where the quality of the job done will be subjected to some realistic test.

The rationale for the introduction of tasks rests on the premise that the training laboratory should, for maximum personal learning, provide the member opportunities to behave in accordance with his own image of himself. Through natural action and feedback from others, he can assess his effectiveness as a group member and his impact on others. For a participant whose image of himself is significantly determined by his work relationships, the T-group with no task requirements may never become a real place, and he may never feel real enough in it to link his behavior or learning there with his self-image and behavior in his everyday world.

Nevertheless, we felt some distaste for the externally imposed tasks as we knew them, because of their frequently artificial and trivial nature. We thought that for a task to be considered truly integrated with the T-group experience, the quality of the product should have a clear and testable impact on the progress and success of the individual, the T-group, and/or the laboratory of which it is a part.

The only design we know which met this requirement was Hjelholt and Miles' (1963) laboratory in Denmark, in which T-groups developed plans for the design of the last part of their laboratory. They then negotiated with one another to arrive at a final plan and carried out the training design they had decided upon. This model fitted our requirements perfectly; however, it had originally been used with highly sophisticated participants towards the end of a longer than usual laboratory. Our task was to adapt the model to a one-week laboratory for participants who come relatively unequipped with social science concepts.

This design task proved to be both difficult and anxiety provoking for the staff. If we gave the participants responsibility for design assignments beyond their competence, then not only were *they* exposed to a failure experience, but *we* also were committed to and responsible for carrying out a bad design. If we reduced the size of the design job to where the consequences of failure were insignificant, then the task also became trivial and insignificant.

We were not satisfied with all our accomplishments in this area. In the process of learning, we had to suffer through one bad design, and we assigned one or two other tasks which erred on the trivial side. However, the hoped for advantages of the integrated task assignment in involving the participants in *real work* and in thereby producing spontaneously natural work behavior more than justified the risks and failures.

We feel that our aims were best met in the intergroup exercise of the third laboratory, assigned to each T-group on Tuesday evening. The group had two hours to develop a design for two one-and-a-half hour sessions on Thursday. The objective for each group was to produce a design in which the groups would make use of each other to enhance the richness and variety of learning experiences in the laboratory. The groups could choose one or a combination of joint learning models: (1) an N-group design, in which individuals would be assigned to the new groups on the basis of personal characteristics, values, or behavior patterns they had shown so far in the laboratory; (2) an intergroup observation design, in which one group would observe another working as a T-group or on a task.

One group planned an N-group design, and the other preferred an intergroup observation. The result of negotiation between them was an intergroup observation, with each T-group remaining intact. The exercise produced more effective observation and more receptivity to feedback between the groups than any either of us had previously seen. We attributed some of the unusual effectiveness of the exercise to the effects of participation in increasing commitment to the decision. Probably defensiveness between the groups was also decreased by the intergroup negotiation design, which is described below.

In summary, this task design had in it the major elements we have come to value in designing work experiences for T-groups. (1) The content of the task focused the work of the group on questions of process and behavior in the group; (2) the decisions to be made were of a scope which would be adequately conceptualized by the participants. The groups had the resources to make a good decision; (3) the final decision was actually carried out, permitting evaluation of the quality of work accomplished; (4) the responsibility of the groups was for a significant but not major part of the total laboratory design, thus limiting the consequences of failure. The risk of failure was further reduced by limiting the choices that could be made in solving the problem to a range of possibilities which the staff had previously decided had potential training value.

Element D. The final design element involved extending the usual T-group model to the study of intergroup phenomena. Our question was: Can we help participants learn more about intergroup phenomena *in much the same way* as we help them learn about interpersonal phenomena. In moving toward an intergroup design, we were working with a T-group model involving the following elements:

1. *An interpersonal dilemma.* Participants with differing interpersonal styles are brought together in a group; they are told to live with one another and, in the process, to learn about the consequences of their interpersonal styles for their relationships with others.

2. *Free choice.* The structure is such that participants can freely choose how they will interact with one another. There are no assigned rules.

3. *Awareness of choice.* In the process, participants are helped to see that their behavior is not entirely determined by the requirements of the situation, but that they are in fact choosing to act one way rather than another. The staff role is to help them see the implications of their chosen behavior for their own feelings and for the feelings and reactions of others.

4. *Experimentation and change.* As the process unfolds, and as participants become more aware of the choices they are continually making and of the implications of these choices, it then becomes possible for them to make new choices, to experiment with new styles of interpersonal behavior, to become aware of the implications of these new styles, and to choose again.

The T-group model, then, is a continuing cycle of free choice, greater awareness of choice, experimentation and change (new choice).

In our intergroup design, we attempted to extend these same T-group features to the study of intergroup interaction. These considerations led to an intergroup model with the following characteristics:

1. *An intergroup dilemma.* Two or more groups are given a problem to solve which is of such a nature that their freely chosen solutions will be in significant conflict. That is, the solutions will differ in such a way that if one is followed, the other will have to be substantially altered. The groups are given the task of resolving the conflict and, in so doing, of learning about the processes of intergroup interaction.

2. *Free choice.* The groups are asked to negotiate a joint solution which they will then carry out. The negotiation is carried out under conditions which permit both collaboration and competition.

3. *Awareness of choice.* However the participants structure the situation, the staff intervenes to help them examine and conceptualize the process, and experience feedback as to the impact of their behavior on one another. Significant choice-points are examined *as they occur* in the problem solving process.

4. *Experimentation and change.* Participants are provided a setting and consultative help in diagnosing the barriers to communication, planning new approaches and testing them. The exercise is carried out until a range of approaches have been tried and evaluated, enabling the participants to experience both the negative consequences of competition and the complex demands required for effective collaborative action. It then becomes possible for participants to engage in a continuing cycle of making new choices, experimenting with new styles, evaluating the consequences of these, and choosing again.

In fact, we came close to this model only in the last of the three laboratories. The task given each group on Tuesday evening was to plan the training for two sessions as described above in the section on task design. The entire Wednesday morning of three hours was devoted to the negotiation session, in which differences in the two plans were to be resolved. The session began with a forty-minute public negotiation between representatives of the two groups. Representatives were permitted to consult with their groups at will.

The inside staff members supervised this session, while we observed and planned for a later transition to collaboration. We kept a record of examples of competitive behavior. Around these examples, we built a short lecture intended to illustrate the differences between competitive and collaborative strategies and to point up the circular process by which initial competitive behavior reduces trust and openness and leads to increased competition.

Following the twenty-minute lecture, each group was given fifteen minutes to diagnose publicly how it had contributed to the development of competition, while the other group observed. The staff intervened to keep the discussion by each group focused on its own behavior and to keep the discussion off the faults and failings of the other group.

We decided to follow diagnosis by breaking the entire laboratory up into five-man problem-solving groups (three from one group, two from the other) which would then report back a collaborative solution by way of a representative. These representatives were to negotiate the final solution. There was considerable sentiment against this plan in the groups. Vocal members argued that this method would just produce more solutions to which subgroups would develop commitment, thus increasing competition. They proposed that the two T-groups decide the issues in a general session of all participants.

We reasoned that since the most competitive members supported this proposal, commitment to arriving at a joint decision would be enhanced by permitting the participants to develop their own problem solving arrangements. After some debate, a committee was selected to work out a solution, and all agreed to go along with their decision.

There was a general feeling of success by staff and participants over this exercise and over the plan which the committee developed. We felt that the opportunity to diagnose and try to work out of a competitive situation had given the participants a considerably better understanding of competition and collaboration than in previous competition exercises we had conducted.

We felt rather lucky that things turned out as well as they did. We realize that we know much less about creating conditions for collaboration than we do about stimulating competitive behavior. While we are satisfied with the basic model, we feel the need for much experimentation with the design of settings to follow the diagnostic part of the exercise and to bring collaborative victory out of competitive defeat.

6

Sensitivity Training and Being Motivation

J. F. T. BUGENTAL AND
ROBERT TANNENBAUM

From the first, participants in sensitivity training have asked for additional related experiences. A variety of formal and informal programs have been attempted to meet the need. A modest but consistent proportion of trainees are known to have entered individual or group therapy of one kind or another. Some groups have been formed on the participants' initiative to carry on after the end of the regular program. Several advanced or continuing programs have been conducted at the training laboratories. In general, these programs have tried to continue from the basic model of the original program, with some relatively minor variations.

In the fall of 1961 an effort was made to design a program which would place primary emphasis on the constructive or self-actualizing processes in the personality as contrasted with the more pathologic or growth-resistive. In general, the orientation parallels the difference Maslow makes between D– (or Deficiency–) motivation and B– (or Being–) motivation (1962). Said differently, much of the typical sensitivity-training program and most of psychotherapy have been concerned with exposing and (hopefully) overcoming those forces within individuals which limit their abilities to fully realize their potentialities.

NOTE. In this condensed version of a paper previously published in the *Journal of Humanistic Psychology*, Spring, 1963, pp. 76–85, Bugental and Tannenbaum describe a sensitivity training laboratory which pushes to the extreme the goal of personal learning, ignoring role and organizational issues unless the participant himself brings them up. It is of most interest in describing various of the techniques the authors and their colleagues have developed to help people gain a deeper awareness of themselves and their relationships to others.

107

The notion upon which plans for a new continuing sensitivity training were developed was that it might be possible to aid people already reasonably healthy in their functioning to develop their potentialities more directly. An analogy might clarify this point: it is as though we had traditionally focused our efforts to help sprinters by demonstrating to them how bulky clothing, poor starting posture, and bad breathing habits have slowed them. Now we propose to concentrate on helping them build stronger leg muscles, gain more spring in their starts, and achieve a better pacing of their energy expenditure. As the analogy should make evident, there is no implication that one approach is superior to the other, only that each deserves attention, and thus far one has tended to outweigh the other.

By late winter of 1962 the discussions had progressed to the point where we felt we wanted to try some of our ideas in practice. Accordingly, a group was recruited and the two present writers were designated to serve as its trainers.

A general announcement of the program was sent to participants who had completed sensitivity training or the Western Training Laboratory in recent years, and about 30 applications were received. Selection from these was made in terms of the following criteria.

Participant Selection. While ideally the program should seek participants free of psychopathology, this is admittedly unrealistic. Instead, it is desirable to screen candidates to rule out grosser evidences of emotional and social disturbance and then to examine the extent to which each approximates the ideal in the following ways:

1. Functional excellence in:
   a. vocation
   b. marriage
   c. friendship relations
2. An observing and curious ego, manifesting a desire for further self-exploration and greater self-actualization
3. Adequate tolerance for psychic stress, e.g., from:
   a. ambiguity
   b. intrapsychic conflict
   c. interpersonal conflict
   d. uncertainty and risk
4. Motivation for group interaction

A group of twelve was chosen, chiefly on the basis of assessments provided by former trainers, modified by an effort to get heterogeneity related to sex, variety of backgrounds, differing professions, and so forth. The group consisted of ten men and two women, with an average age of 44 years. They averaged a little more than 17 years of education, i.e., near the master's level. Eight were married, four widowed or divorced. Four had had psychotherapy, but only one of these had had an intensive experience. Occupationally they were in the professional and managerial ranks, with about an equal number in each.

Early in the life of the group, each participant was given a mimeographed statement which read as follows:

Horizons Unlimited and Limited

Our perspective for Advanced Sensitivity Training is that of gaining an expanded range of possibilities for each of us. It is our conviction that each of us gets embedded in presuppositions about the way each of us is and about the way the world is and that these presuppositions—which may or may not be accurate—serve to delimit our views of what is possible. It has seemed to us, therefore, that a very fundamental mission Advanced Sensitivity Training can perform is to help us develop awareness of and skill in the way in which we can:

a. discover the presuppositions about outer and inner worlds within which we tend to limit our operations,
b. test those presuppositions to see whether they are indeed intrinsic, necessary, and reality-founded,
c. evaluate those which are not intrinsic to determine whether they serve us usefully or not, and
d. try out setting aside those limitations which we find to be neither intrinsic nor useful; i.e., operate in new and freer ways.

A second part of our (the trainers') perspective for Advanced Sensitivity Training grows out of the manner in which you have been selected for this group: insofar as possible, each of you is deemed to be a person of reasonable maturity, personal and social effectiveness, and possessed of some degree of creativeness. (It is recognized that each of us—group members and trainers alike—is far from the ultimate or even the optimum in each of these ways. Nevertheless, it is reasonably certain that each of us has these qualities in some measure, no matter how much we may each recognize the ways in which we do not manifest them.)

From the composition of our group, then, grows the second hypothesis about how we may best serve each other. This takes the following form: We are of the opinion that the pooled motivations and the combined creativities of all of us can best be consulted to guide us in the sorts of activities we want to undertake at any particular point in the life of our group. We, the trainers, do not feel that we have the wisdom or the experience to predetermine what sort of procedure will best serve the group on the third or eleventh or any other particular session.

This is not to say that we have no ideas about activities in which we might usefully engage. We do. But we invite—more, we recognize the implicit necessity of—the group to take a mature role in determining its own life. To this end, we have brought together in these materials a number of thoughts we have developed about this program, about the kinds of goals or end-products it may hopefully achieve for each of us, about the types of conditions which might facilitate our attainment of the goals, and about some of the forms of group activity which might be used by us to achieve our goals.

In setting these forth in this manner, we must recognize a reality: The group (including the trainers) is responsible for itself; each of us must exercise his personal and joint responsibility if any degree of "self-actualization" is to be achieved. Further, we are approaching a relatively uncharted frontier about which we as yet know little. Thus, we will inevitably extend this list as we exercise our ingenuity in finding further and more effective ways to make the total Advanced Sensitivity Training experience a productive one for each of us.

What has been said so far tends to be cast in terms of overcoming limitations. This effort is certainly worthwhile and one thing we hope this experience can facilitate. However, a third part of our perspective as trainers has to do with our belief that much may be gained from developing the positive, the creative, the "growth-edge-ful" in its own right. (Let us hasten to make explicit that we mean neither Couéism nor Pollyanaism.) To the extent that we can be skillful in recognizing that which is positive, enriching and meaningful in ourselves and our experiences, and to the extent that we can be effective in nurturing and expanding such processes, we are convinced that we shall be forwarding the purposes for which we are all in Advanced Sensitivity Training.

Some of Our Hopes

We hope that this joint venture will help each of us make personal progress along at least the following paths:

1. Experiencing personal outcomes in ways we have previously assumed to be unattainable for ourselves.
2. Experiencing our relatedness to all men as personally enriching and as potentially enhancing to them and to us.
3. Experiencing our individual uniqueness with its potential for personal satisfaction and creativity, and recognizing (but seeking not to be limited by) the fear of being different.
4. Being able to distinguish between the realistic limits (both within ourselves and without) on our own functioning and growth and those which are unrealistic (neurotic), and to be able to free ourselves from the latter.
5. Being able to recognize and to utilize an increased number of alternatives as we face the omnipresent necessity to make choices.
6. Gaining respect for the use of feelings and moods, fantasy and speculation, tenderness and concern, sharing.

Some Possible Facilitating Conditions

We believe that the attitudes which we each bring to the group will be fundamental in determining the degree to which we are able to make of the group an effective tool for our purposes. Some of the attitudes which we feel will be most helpful include:

1. Seeking an ever-increasing awareness of one's own feelings at each moment.

2. Accepting as fully as possible and assuming responsibility for personal feelings of which we are aware.
3. Sharing with the group as much of what we are aware of as may be possible at any point, and constantly striving to increase the degree to which we can so share.
4. Being willing constantly to consider and experiment with the feasibility of alternative ideas and methods in order to move toward new possibilities and new experience.
5. Being willing to live dangerously, facing the personal risks of satisfaction, success and adequacy as well as of embarrassment, exposure, and failure.
6. Accepting and valuing for ourselves and others the realities of being human.
7. Being willing to accept our own difficulties in fully being everything implied by the above.

Some Possible Methods or Procedures

We present the following ideas only as starters. The range of possibilities available to us is extensive, and many of the most productive probably yet remain to be created.

1. Using the basic sensitivity training group for the purpose of sharing and exploring, but with an emphasis on the goals of this advanced program.
2. Focusing on our hopes and aspirations, and on the means for their realization.
3. Making force-field analyses: i.e., examining the facilitating and constraining forces related to possible new behaviors.
4. Sharing the existing creative products of our personal lives—paintings, writings, films, designs, pottery, theories, artistry, wood or metal work, sewing and knitting, etc.
5. Engaging in spontaneous creative or expressive activity—producing a play, writing poetry, singing, composing a melody, producing a product, painting, conducting an orchestra, etc.
6. Confronting existential moments—birth, fear, stress, elation, death, helplessness, success, exhaustion, etc. (arranging for visits or activities to make this possible.)
7. Utilizing a visiting resource person; e.g., a specialist in dance therapy or an artist.
8. Maintaining diaries to capture and preserve our developing experiences and insights.
9. Utilizing questionnaires or other instruments to collect relevant data and to provide feedback.
10. Utilizing a "what if . . . " technique; i.e., making the assumption that certain usual constraints on one's behavior are not present and experiencing what it might be like if one were able to avoid such constraints.
11. Experiencing and conducting experiments in extrasensory perception.

Findings from Trial Program

Our experiences in the program cannot be detailed here. Instead we will report some of our tentative learnings and briefly indicate some next steps. First, we will examine some disappointments:

1. We were much too ambitious in our conceptualization of the program. Although beginnings were made toward our goals, their attainment still remained very distant at the program's conclusion.

2. Our hope to select a group freer than usual of the deterrents of psychic disturbance was vain. The group was a fairly typical selection of twelve functional, reasonably socially effective people who nevertheless were beset by a clear range of emotional interferences with their functioning.

3. We, as trainers, were severely handicapped in attempting to give primary emphasis to positive forces in the participants' personalities by our own unresolved neurotic components and by our years of training and experience which have been largely in the frame of reference of psychopathology and dealing with deficiency motivations. Time and again we found ourselves most active in the familiar ways of pointing to interferences and distortions and least effective in facilitating growth, venturing, and creativity.

4. The participants, as faithful products of their culture and personal histories, seemed to be more ready to recognize and deal with that which was negative and pathologic within themselves and unsure and self-conscious about the positive and creative.[1]

On the more encouraging side, several observations may be made:

1. The participants showed a real readiness to adopt a more open approach and thus to experiment with group activities in a way that beginning sensitivity-training groups frequently resist. Moreover, they reported some carryover of this attitude to their outside lives.

2. Some individuals in the group felt they had experienced major insights or changes of outlook which they thought would have profound effects on their lives. For example, one wrote:

For me, the sessions have been the most frightening, frustrating, soul searching, exhilarating, rewarding experiences of my life. I just cannot adequately express my feelings about this. I sincerely believe that these past few weeks have altered the future course of my life. My past efforts in the field of human relations have been directed toward becoming more effective in my relations with other people. While this is a worthy goal, I failed to realize that I must first learn to get along with myself. I doubt that I will ever be 100% successful in this, but I have made a good start.

---

[1] One may be drawn to speculate how pervasive in all phases of our individual and group living is a whole outlook arising from our centuries of preoccupation with contending with deficiency problems.

3. The possibility of using more active participation around projects or procedures was demonstrated as useful, but it required more planning and effective guidance in some instances than we gave.

4. One observation, in accord with many made in other settings, was that the relations among pairs of individuals in the group were of especial potency. Similarly, the opportunity for one part of the group to watch another part at work on a problem was frequently highly productive (Clark, 1963; Tannenbaum and Bugental, 1963).

Follow-up Session

Approximately nine months after the completion of the program, a reunion meeting was held. Ten of the twelve participants returned and told of their experiences in the interim. The most frequent reports were:

1. The experience was remembered with a kind of nostalgia and warmth. Several were very explicit in saying how much they missed having the opportunities for such open communication and genuine acceptance.

2. The most frequently mentioned gain from the program was an increased willingness to experiment in living, to take a chance (interpersonally), to attempt some things which previously they had hesitated about doing because of fears of not being adequate. Some examples offered included making new friendships, expressing opinions in discussions, trying a creative project.

3. Closely linked with the willingness to live more experimentally was a report by several of decreased fears of failure or being different, and of performing more spontaneously.

4. About half of the group expressed a feeling of pronounced need for some program which would provide "booster shots" of spaced reinforcements for the orientation of the program. In one way and another it was made clear that to live more in terms of being motivation is difficult in our culture and that the participants felt their gains slipping away and old patterns reasserting themselves.

7

The Uses of the Laboratory
Method in a Psychiatric Hospital

SECTION A: The Patient Training Laboratory

An Adaptation of the Instrumented Training Laboratory

by Robert B. Morton

Although the idea of adapting the human relations laboratory training methods to a patient population was considered to be a logical step from its use with an industrial population, the need for trainers in each development group made such an adaptation impractical. A major breakthrough occurred with the advent of the instrumented laboratory, which does not require a trainer to be present in the group (Blake and Mouton et al. (1962).

The first Patient's Training Laboratory came about through the influence of the Southwestern Training Laboratory, the author's association with Jane S. Mouton and Robert R. Blake, who served as consultants, and the local support of the Houston Veterans Adminis-

NOTE. In this chapter, Morton describes what is perhaps one of the most important and creative adaptations of laboratory training we have witnessed to date. Using the instrumented laboratory technology as first developed by Blake and Shepard, Morton and his colleagues have designed and successfully implemented a laboratory training program for hospitalized mental patients. Not only is this a fascinating chronicle of how the laboratory was run, but the chapter provides a useful elaboration of the training theory which underlies the approach of Blake and others. This chapter also has a good section on the evaluation of training outcomes.

tration Hospital.[1] It was conducted at the Houston Veterans Administration Hospital, Houston, Texas, in May of 1961.

Goals and Rationale

The laboratory method of learning is used to bring about change by establishing conditions whereby the participants are forced to test their assumptions regarding interpersonal, intragroup, and intergroup relations. Abstractions regarding intrapersonal dynamics, felt to be deterrents to learning, are treated as irrelevant (Sanford, 1962). The goal of the laboratory is "learning how to learn." Whereas the most common professional approach to change in personal behavior is through the route of analysis of conflict and the development of insight, here emphasis is placed on the learning resulting from analysis of objective consequences of here-and-now behavior. Objective forces which impinge on perceptions of self, situation, and others are examined and become part of the data that provide the basis for change. Of equal importance for change is the effort to establish a climate where previously existing patterns of behavior can be tested and their effectiveness or ineffectiveness ascertained.

Certain conditions seem to be essential for change in laboratory training, even though when found in other clinical methods they usually are treated as tangential. The first condition is the establishment and the maintenance of an experimental climate wherein the participants begin to invent and try out new patterns of behavior. In contrast, many of the clinical methods of change give support to the patient who explores his most abstract feelings and attempts to relate these feelings to his supposedly significant past. Second, in a laboratory it is essential that support be given for attention to here-and-now behavior. The groups very rapidly develop the norm of support for the persons who deal with here-and-now problems and create new ways of behaving in response to these problems. Third, the groups must assume the responsibility of analyzing the consequences of their behavior and feeding back the resulting data under conditions of learning. Fourth, just as George W. Fairweather (1961) has found that he can-

[1] Special recognition is acknowledged to Ina Boyd, M.D., Assistant Chief of Psychiatry, who carried the legal responsibility for the patients, Lee D. Cady, M.D., Manager, and Hugh Vickerstaff, Assistant Manager, who provided administrative and financial support for the project, and Alex D. Pokorny, M.D., Chief of Psychiatry, whose support withstood the criticism of his own professional group. Jay Hall and Martha Williams, graduate students from the University of Texas, assisted as trainers.

not explain cohesive, decision-making groups with psychotics if a professional leader is present, it appears that the absence of a trainer is essential in the laboratory training groups if the individual members are to develop levels of responsibility necessary for more rapid and significant learning. Even the most permissive psychotherapist is at times sharing the responsibility for his group's behavior by providing or setting the norms with his "noncommittal" responses. In this sharing he cannot escape the reinforcing of dependency.

The basic rationale for change in the instrumented laboratory is the Dilemma-Invention–Feedback-Generalization theory of learning (Blake and Mouton, 1961b).

Dilemma

Dilemmas are created by the staff, but only to a minimal degree. Most are created by the participants themselves. These dilemmas not only provide most of the content for the Development Groups (D-groups) but also provide the cues for the lecturettes, the exercises, the role problems, and problems for the consultation groups. (Each of these is but one of the methods utilized to achieve learning in the laboratory, and each will be described later.) Each successive day is a new experiment or series of experiments designed to explore the learning possibilities involved in the problems the groups have developed or in problems that have been provided by the staff.

Invention

As in all groups, solutions to early dilemmas are attempted by formal or habitual patterns of behavior. The need to invent does not appear until it becomes apparent that these habitual patterns of behavior are not effective. It is at this point that the participant becomes aware of his own dilemma. Anxiety mounts. Under usual conditions he may regress to more secure patterns of behavior, but, if the climate is supportive, he may begin examining personal assumptions which underlie his behavior. Analysis of the forces operative in the dilemma begins, and the basis for search thinking, creative, or inventive behavior develops. New concepts acquired from the lecturettes and from the utilization of group measuring instruments provide additional resources for the individual in the analysis of his, as well as his group's behavior. As problems of status, cohesion, and intragroup and intergroup competition develop, the behavioral relationships become more complex and more significantly related to the problems of living. In the atmosphere of an experimental laboratory and under the care of a supportive, cohesive group, trials with new patterns of behavior are attempted. Experimentation quickly becomes the norm. Inventions, whether on an individual basis, a group basis, or by the group for the benefit of a single member, are then given support.

First, personal experiments usually develop around talking. The usually silent member tries talking. A talkative one tests silent behavior, and often to his surprise learns that the group progresses smoothly without his domination. More complex inventions are developed by the groups. In one instance a member became transiently psychotic. He ran away from the ward and was found by the hospital chauffeur six blocks from the hospital, walking to his home about 500 miles away. He returned to the hospital but was unwilling to remain in the program. He was ventilating about events which had occurred eight years before, rejection by a girl, and his last job. We agreed with him that he could transfer to a closed ward, but when arrangements were made for his transfer he could not be found. He was discovered later back in his group. His group had perceived the situation as a group dilemma. In response to this dilemma they brought him back and elected him temporary chairman. From this time on he was an effective member of the group. Five months after discharge he reported he was working, for the first time in eight years, as an effective member of society.

Feedback

Behavioral inventions are not by themselves sufficient for learning; another step, feedback, is necessary for change to occur. The many cultural blocks to feedback, however, have to be rendered ineffective. Giving of feedback is legitimized by the use of buzz groups which meet immediately following each exercise. Here the members talk over the experimental instructions under which they were behaving and compare their thoughts, reactions, and feelings under each of the conditions of the exercises. The giving of feedback is supported by the staff in the manner with which they deal with the discussion following lecturettes. Feedback is made the responsibility of each participant by requiring him to scale his own behavior on the degree to which he "leveled" in his D-group. The D-group scores of these behavioral measures are computed and discussed by the group at the conclusion of each session. Questions raised in an attempt to account for variances in scores often provide the basis for more critical and incisive feedback. They also often provide the basis for more dilemmas. Consultation groups provide the loci for feedback which is too threatening or too sensitive to reveal in the larger D-group. From the inputs of the buzz groups, the exercises, the D-group scales, and the consultation groups, the norm of feedback comes to be incorporated into the D-group value system.

Generalization

Once a new pattern of behavior has been attempted and feedback from supportive but leveling associates is received, the participant is ready to attempt the pattern of behavior in a new setting. The generalization of learning from the psychotherapy setting to the real life situation has always been most difficult to achieve. This is still a major problem with the instrumented laboratory, but some methodologies are being constructed. Two methods are emphasized specifically for the accomplishment of generalization or "application" as it is referred to by the participants. First, it is understood from the beginning between participant and staff that the participant will leave the hospital on the weekend, if at all feasible. The purpose is to keep the participant as closely in contact with his back-home problem as possible. To our surprise the participants utilized the weekend situations to experiment with their new learnings. These personal experiments were reported in the diaries, which all participants maintained. Follow-up interviews in the homes, which are being conducted at the time of this writing, confirm these reports.

Role playing,[2] the second method utilized to enhance generalization, is the dominant activity of the fourth week. Theory, methods, and techniques which were learned during the earlier part of the laboratory are tried out in roles involving back-home type problems. For example, the problem of the consequences of power in decision making is interjected into the laboratory through two exercises. Power in two-person relations is introduced in a work problem. The problems of a worker and his boss and power are studied in an intergroup competition exercise (Blake, 1960; Blake and Mouton, 1961a; Morton, Rothaus, and Hanson, 1961b). Although both of these are back-home type problems, they are introduced in the laboratory to develop knowledge of the effects of behavior under different conditions of power. Role playing is then further utilized as a method of learning by application of the newly acquired knowledge to problems of family living. These problems concern the disciplining of children,

---

[2] Dr. Philip Worchel, who also served as a consultant from the University of Texas, was especially helpful in this area.

family budget, and harmonious family living. For this exercise, groups of women are brought in to represent the housewife's point of view. Nursing students, dietetic interns, staff, and volunteers have served in this capacity.

Adapting the Laboratory Method to a Hospital Population

Distinct problems were anticipated in the adaptation of the laboratory method of change to hospital patients. Our first anticipated problem was: "Could the laboratory method be adapted to this population?" The laboratory method had been developed primarily with professional, management, and supervisory personnel, and with college students. Several of the exercises had been tested in the training program of the hospital janitorial and kitchen personnel. Even though the verbal and writing skills of some of these personnel were not highly developed, and a few possessed as little as fourth grade formal education, they participated meaningfully and acquired significant learning. Additional evidence that the laboratory methods could be applied to a psychiatric population was provided by Dr. George A. Wiggins, a psychiatrist of the Houston Veterans Administration Psychiatric Service and a graduate of the Southwestern Training Laboratory. He had incorporated some of the laboratory methods in his psychiatric program and had established psychotherapy groups without a therapist present. The patients were instructed to talk only about their problems, in sessions which were recorded. At frequent intervals, members of the group would report to Dr. Wiggins or ask for consultation regarding the dilemmas which arose in the group. It was Dr. Wiggins' impression that these groups dealt with more significant problems and progressed more rapidly than any other group he had conducted or observed.

Another anticipated problem was that people come to hospitals expecting to be treated as patients. Could they assume the role of learners? The idea of being a patient carries certain assumptions regarding responsibility, authority, disease process, and, for those who have had previous hospitalization, the "proper" treatment. In the laboratory all of these personal assumptions are tested and found to be erroneous or unnecessary.

For many of the participants, the laboratory is their first experience with authority that does not control them. To those who have had numerous hospitalizations, this "negligence" on the part of authority is characterized as criminal neglect. The many contrived, as well as real, aches, plans, and plots which appear, especially early in the laboratory, are attempts to force the staff to bring its authority to bear in the patients' problems and decision making. The staff avoids as far as possible all professional contacts with members of families except when there is some social work problem in the home. Case histories and testing for the purpose of diagnosing are never sought.

Third, the history of the patient care indicated that we could not expect patients to assume responsibility for their behavior. The patients are first faced with the necessity of taking responsibility in the initial interview when the choice of entering the laboratory program is left up to them. They also have to assume responsibility for their own behavior on the ward. In many of the most permissive open wards, a ward government substitutes for staff responsibility in the problem of control, but it still carries the sanction of the chain of command. The ward organization of the laboratories, however, has never been more than a means of conducting a planning forum that arranges the participants' responsibility for their own behavior and the maintenance of the ward during the weekend. No staff personnel are available on weekends, but only once in the first five laboratories was one called to make a decision regarding a patient's behavior.

Since the initial interview lasts only five minutes or less, many prospects for the laboratory feel that proper attention given in previous therapies is not being given here to the significant events of their past. If they persist in their attempts to draw the attention of the staff to these kinds of data, they are told that such details are not considered important for change. Consequences of the assumption of historical causality create many dilemmas during the early part of the training.

A fourth problem was: "would the severe neurotic, near psychotic, or psychotic in remission accept and continue through this training program?" In an industrial laboratory when the dilemmas begin to pile up, we see many evasive tactics utilized by people who have not learned anything about themselves for years. Sometimes the tension and anxiety build up to the point where it is felt with considerable confidence that the only reason they stay is their fear of the implications back at the company if they should leave early. The hospital population is, for the most part, without such stable or compelling social anchorages. Many of the participants are characterized by their impulsive behavior. The frustration tolerance is low and sustained goal directed behavior extremely limited. To date, however, more than 300 persons have completed the training, and less than two percent have left without the support of the staff.

Selection of Participants

When we looked back over the hospital records of the first laboratory, it appeared that we used very few criteria in our selection. The participants had to be able to read and write at an estimated level of fourth grade skill. Those who were completely fixed on somatic complaints were eliminated; however, approximately 40 percent of those selected emphasized somatic complaints predominantly. The one positive criterion was that the individual must conceptualize, to some degree, that he was in the hospital because of some problem or problems of an interpersonal nature. Often this was reduced to the point where in the initial interview the question would be asked, "You have no troubles with anyone?" The patient's answer would be, "No." Then the question would be, "Well, did you have any trouble with your wife when she divorced you?" If the answer was, "Well, some," then such recognition was considered as meeting the criterion.

There were 21 participants in the first laboratory. The majority suffered from what are called anxiety reactions, although there were many with somatic complaints and some with depressive features. Several had diagnoses of character disorders, but the general instability evident in the lives of almost all indicates such problems in varying degrees. Eleven of the men reported significant problems with alcohol. During the laboratory two became transiently psychotic. The duration of significant difficulties ranged from five months to eighteen years, the average approximately six years. Only one of the participants could be considered acute.

Half the group had no prior hospitalization, although two had received private psychiatric treatment. Four had two previous hospitalizations. Five had from more than two hospitalizations to almost continuous hospitalization for several years. Three were in state hospitals over an extended period of time.

The age range was from 25 to 46 years, the average 36. Twenty of the participants were Caucasian, one was Negro, three were Latin American. The educational range was from sixth grade to college graduate. Thirteen did not complete high school, three had high school only, three had some college, and two were college graduates.

The level of work varied from the most unskilled type, and this predominated, to safety engineer. Eleven of the group had no extended employment. Two more had no employment stability in recent years. Eight were on the same job for four to fifteen years. Twelve were unemployed on entering the hospital, and nine were employed and returning to the same job.

Seventeen were married when they entered the hospital. With four of these, divorce was threatened at the time of entering or staying in the hospital. The other four were divorced. Many of the marriages were quite stormy, although of some years' duration. Twelve of the men had only one marriage, seven were married twice, and two had multiple marriages, one three and the other five.

Having completed the first laboratory successfully, we modified our criteria for selection and accepted more chronic and less well-integrated patients. For the second laboratory, we selected a well known chronic patient for each of the groups. We wanted to test (1) whether such a person could gain significant learning, and (2) whether such a person could be integrated into a cohesive group. All four that fit our criteria of greater chronicity successfully completed the training. Although we have not heard from two of them, the other two have been working since discharge from the hospital.

By the time of the fourth laboratory we accepted patients in relatively large numbers from the closed wards. These persons entered the hospital as psychotic and were considered in remission. All successfully completed the training except one, who had to be returned to the closed ward. As experience was gained, the range of patients and problems was extended. Whereas the first laboratory was made up predominantly from the open-ward waiting lists, now the laboratories include participants from the open and closed neurospychiatric wards, neurology, physical medicine, and rehabilitation, as well as psychosomatic patients from medicine and surgery.

Organization of the Training Laboratory

The laboratory is organized around the D-groups. All other activities are planned to provide data to be utilized in the D-groups that in turn give the individual member a chance to explore the laboratory data for an increased understanding of his problems and the level of skill with which he attempts solutions.

A laboratory has either three or four D-groups. At least three D-groups are needed to conduct the exercises. It is possible to have more groups than four, but the difficulties of planning as well as the difficulties of the staff's being aware of all that is taking place militate against a larger number of groups. Each group consists of seven to nine members. When a group drops to less than seven members, it loses the value of heterogeneity and tends to become too cohesive.

When the group exceeds nine, the pecking order becomes more pronounced, the more reticent become less active and the power struggle for control becomes more divisive.

These groups have been referred to as leaderless groups. This is not at all the situation. There is no staff person present in the D-groups and staff influence by personal action rather than through the design of the laboratory is avoided insofar as possible. The groups are, however, never without someone, one of the participants, to provide the leadership functions.

The groups are organized as heterogeneously as possible. Dimensions such as chronicity of illness, work record, education, intelligence, degree of somatization, alcoholism, race, age, marital experiences, interviewer's prediction of potential for change, and degree of distractibility are considered in the assignment to groups.

The staff serve as resource people dealing with the problems of establishing a climate whereby the participants can learn to utilize their own resources in the solutions of their problems. This is achieved primarily by the staff being resource persons in methodology rather than experts in the content of participants' problems. They direct their attention to questions of methods, scaling, concepts, and general principles. They avoid becoming involved in the specific content or problems of the D-groups or in the individual's relations outside of the laboratory. All such problems are referred back to the D-group through the person who approached the staff member.

The First Week

The first week activities of the laboratory were designed to develop cohesive groups and to introduce the skills, techniques, and concepts for diagnosing the processes of intragroup behavior. In this activity the self-concept of being a patient rapidly yields to that of becoming a learner. The skill of scaling behavior requires that each person not only be a participant in his group, but that he also be an observer. If his scaling is too deviant from the group's, it becomes necessary for him to justify to the group the basis for his observation. This justification often proves to be learning for the group as well as for him. If the scale values fall below the group expectancy, deviants find it necessary to account for their failure to contribute to the group work. Such analysis leads to dilemmas. The more the members attempt to solve the dilemmas by old habits and patterns of behavior, the greater the dilemmas the groups develop for themselves. In the search thinking, which so far has always developed, attention begins to be directed to the concepts of the instruments. Ideas gathered from the lecturettes begin to be tested. Alternative approaches sometimes suggested in the exercises, at other times collected from the experiments of individuals, are tried out. Small but significant experimentation in personal behavior develops.

Orientation

To accomplish the design of the first week, the first three days are directed toward orientation to the laboratory approach to change, and toward learning to become a participant-observer. The orientation is accomplished by engaging the participants in the full activities of the program immediately. The program begins with a lecturette on the naturalness of learning through lifegroups and on the utilization of the groups in the laboratory as a method of learning.

Usually the first two D-groups are given a general but not too compelling agenda topic. The implicit assumptions of the participants based on their past experience and expectancies, are so controlling that the assigned topics are set aside, usually on the basis of a self-authorized decision, and the groups behave in the manner of past experience in group or individual psychotherapy. This in turn leads the group into another minority-made decision; the decision that each participant should take his turn and tell his life history. Invariably the first few to tell their histories are those who are competing to establish themselves at the top of the pecking order. The decision to hear everyone's life history becomes strongly entrenched by the time the third person has taken his turn. By this time the D-group has developed a first-class dilemma. Most members have become bored. Those who have not had their turn are annoyed at the delays. Very little listening occurs. Some are beginning to fear the inevitable experience of talking about themselves and are wishing they could somehow get out of their dilemma. Those who have had their turn begin to act like therapists, as another means of dominating the group. The rank ordering of talkativeness (Scale 2) by the members of all other members of the D-group, including themselves, gives feedback which is direct and easily validated. This rank ordering of the amount of talking, from the most talkative to the least talkative, provides one of the most easily utilized behaviors with which to learn scaling. Such scaling also facilitates the development of the role of participant-observer. Talkativeness is also the area in which the greatest number of personally and privately developed experiments are initiated. Some participants, facing resistance and rejection because of their monopoly of the group's time, experiment with reduced participation. Some, who find they have not fulfilled the group's expectancy, experiment with increased participation.

Coffee breaks also provide a chance for orientation. The staff has coffee in the assembly room with the participants. It is through the coffee time that the peer status of participant and staff is most strongly reinforced. During the first few days, the participants attempt to exploit this opportunity by bringing their psychiatric and somatic complaints to the staff. All such approaches to the psychiatrists are referred to the nursing assistant, who in turn refers the participant to sick call. If the nursing assistant feels there is need for immediate attention, he talks to the nurse, who exercises her judgment.

The principal statement of the theoretical orientation of training, the dilemma–invention–feedback–generalization theory of learning, appears in the first lecture. Lectures and lecturettes are differentiated in terms of their length, specificity, and complexity. The lectures are general statements of theory, the systematic integration of a number of concepts, or a synthesis of the dynamics which are occurring in the behavior of the groups. Lectures occur at crucial times throughout training: when there is a need to unfreeze behavior, give direction and rationale, and assist in the clarification of objectives. The lecturettes are usually introductions to single dimensions, concepts, or techniques. Thus they tend to be less than twenty minutes in duration.

In the patients laboratory we very carefully avoid "talking down" to the participant. Concepts are always presented in the most accepted behavioral language, never translated into popular language. The responsibility for understanding belongs to the individual. The groups prove to be a testing ground for understanding.

The last specifically designed activity for orientation is the recreation time. In contrast to most hospital recreational therapies, where the recreation is prescribed by the physician, the recreational therapist meets with the groups. He describes the activities, and the conditions under which the activities are available. The participants are responsible for their own involvement. Under this arrangement, persons known to the recreational therapist, by way of previous hospitalizations, have taken part in activities in which they never before engaged.

Learning to be a Participant-Observer

The second learning, to become an observer of one's own participation, continues throughout the laboratory. The primary methods of achieving this learning are the scales, diaries, and exercises. The scales,

Table 7-1 First Week

	Sunday	Monday	Tuesday	Wednesday	Thursday	Friday	Saturday
8–8:30				Sick call			
8:30–9		Lecturette 1ᵃ	Exercise 2: Labeling	Lecturette 3: Task functions	Lecturette 4: Maintenance functions	Vignette 1c; Procedures used in decision making	Free time
9–9:30		D-group 1 Topic: Getting acquainted	Coffee	Coffee		Scales 11ᵉ introduced	Weekend passes and recreation activities available
9:30–10		General assembly: Introduction: Scalesᵇ	Feedback: Data exercise 2	D-group 5	Vignette 1a: Maintenance functions		
10–10:30		Coffee	D-group 3 No topics assigned after D-group 2		Coffee	Coffee	
10:30–11		General assemblyᶜ Staff introduced		Scales 1,2,3, and 5	D-group 6ᶠ	D-group 8	
11–11:30		Lecture 1: Dilemma invention — feedback-generalization, theory of learning	Scales 1 and 2	New scales introduced 4,8,9ᵉ	Scales 2,3,4,5, 8,9ᵍ	Scales 3,4,5,7,8, 9,11.	
11:30–12				General assembly Recreation facilities		Lecturette 6: Consultation skills	

126

			Noon		
12–1					
1–1:30	Exercise 1: Bean jar	Lecturette 2[d] D-group 4 Scales: 1 and 2	Free time	Lecturette 5: Process analysis	Consultation groups 1: What have I learned?
1:30–2	Coffee			Vignette 1b: Process analysis	Coffee
2–2:30	D-group 2 Topic: What can I do for the group?	New Scales* introduced: 3 and 4	Recreation activities available	Scale 7* introduced	D-group 9
2:30–3	Scales: 1 Interest	Coffee		Coffee	
3–3:30	2 Talkativeness			D-group 7	
3:30–4		Exercise 3: For procedure for analysis of D-group data		Scales* 3,4,5,7, 8, and 9	Scales 3,4,5,7,8, 9, and 11
4–4:30	Introduction of diaries				Lecturette 8: Wrap-up of the week
4:30–7			Diaries		
7–					

Note: Footnotes/or Table 7-1 appear on page 128.

Footnotes for Table 7-1

[a] Lecturette 1: Living, Learning, and Working in Groups.

[b] The staff is always present at coffee breaks and mixes freely with the participants.

[c] Scales are introduced following the first D-group. The participants individually complete the scales. The group statistically analyzes the data and plots the results on the appropriate wall chart. Hereafter, new charts are added as needed and are completed at the close of each D-group meeting.

[d] Lecturette 2: Procedures for decision making.

[e] Scales: Mon.

Scale 1 Interest

Scale 2 Talkativeness

Scale 3 Group atmosphere

Scale 4 How do I feel about the group?

Scale 5 Did I get help as needed?

Scale 6 "Here-and-now" versus "there and then"

Scale 7 Content versus process

Scale 8 Was I leveling?

Scale 9 How clear are the group goals?

Scale 10 Agenda items

Scale 11 Decision-making procedures used

Scale 12 What type of organization did the group adopt?

[f] Usually by this time some group dilemma has developed which requires the entire collaboration of all the groups before a solution can be developed. The laboratory schedule is always modified to meet these dilemmas.

[g] Interest scale is dropped. It is used primarily to introduce the technique of scaling.

[h] Talkativeness scale is dropped. It is used to introduce the scaling method of rank order as well as to deal with a significant problem.

exercises, concepts, lecturettes, and techniques of the first few days, however, are kept as denotable as possible. The exercises are relatively simple, and the data so concrete as to be perceived as self-evident. The degree of complexity increases as the laboratory progresses.

Scales

The scales of the first few days also direct attention to behavior which is either quite denotable (Scale 1—Interest) or quite familiar to the participant (Scale 2—Talkativeness). As the program progresses, not only do the methods of scaling become more complex, but the dimensions become more complex and the concepts less familiar or even unknown to the participants.

The impact of the scales on learning to become a participant-observer is both great and varied. The almost immediate learning observed to take place is the beginning of thinking in terms of degrees of "more or less than" rather than in terms of "kinds or categories." The scaling forces the participant to analyze carefully and to sharply delineate his observations and activities. This learning later facilitates the search thinking necessary in the solving of dilemmas. The data · feedback from the scales may be ego enhancing, deflating, or even devastating, but the scales provide a method of solving a participant's need to see himself as others see him. When these revelations are tied to observable behavior and to the conditions under which the behavior occurred, some of the important principles for modifying behavior are present.

Through the scales new concepts are introduced, first used, and later developed into working assets. Almost unnoticed is the impact on learning to listen. When the participant knows he is going to have to scale aspects of behavior in his group, he listens for the significant events which affect the scaling. When he knows his behavior is influencing the scale values, he is listening with his "third" ear, under a pressure he usually does not experience.

Diaries

Diaries are introduced on the first day of the training. It was felt that the diaries would bring about a situation where each person would have to think through the day's experiences, formulate them a little more clearly, perhaps, and in so doing more clearly define the experiences in which he was involved. It was also hoped that through this action some relations between the learnings in the laboratory and back-home problems might develop. Not only have these two things occurred for a large number of persons, but the diary provides a record which is used individually as a measure of change and a research instrument for measuring change through the training.

Exercises

A first exercise, the Bean Jar, is used to demonstrate the availability of many alternative ways of solving a simple problem. Each group, in general assembly, is given a jar of beans and is told to invent as many methods as it can for determining the number of beans in the jar. Ten minutes are used for instructing, fifteen minutes for searching for solutions, and ten minutes for reporting and discussing the implications. Every effort is made to prevent the groups from focusing on intergroup or even intragroup dynamics at this time. The goal is a simple demonstration of the idea that when the habitual pattern of behavior (counting) is blocked, many other alternatives are available.

A second exercise, Labeling, is used to demonstrate how set or emotional bias affects judgment. A single set of statements is given to each member of the group. The instructions to the participants are that they privately are to express their degree of agreement or disagreement with each statement. The group with negatively valued labels consistently expresses significantly more disagreement than the group having a neutral value label as well as significantly greater disagreement than the group having a positive value label. The learning developed in the discussion of the data following the exercise is how personally and subtly judgment is affected by preconceptions, prejudices, or set ideas.

Ward Government Dilemma

By the middle of the week, groups begin to talk about the need for having some kind of ward meeting. The ward personnel have imposed no rules, regulations, or directions other than attendance at all meetings. Problems develop as a result of the lack of regulations, when members fail to meet their individual responsibilities to themselves and to others. The first response is to ask the staff for regulations. This, of course, is refused, and the problem is given back to the group. Although it has often been the experience in many ward government programs that the patients devise rules and regulations more harsh, restrictive, and punitive than those that would be imposed by the hospital staff, such regulations have never been the experience in the training laboratory. What has nearly always occurred is the agreement that such behavior is the responsibility of individuals, but if the individual does not meet his responsibility, then his D-group should consider the problem. On a few occasions a president or chairman is elected and given the job of overseer to report back to the group. The almost total absence of acting out behavior and of trespassing on the rules which are imposed on the rest of the hospital attests to the degree to which the participants accept their responsibility.

Another dilemma which tests their willingness to accept responsibility is the weekend in the hospital. The ward is established without provisions for a nursing staff on the weekends. The Veterans Administration has a regulation which prohibits persons from being on a ward without nursing personnel in attendance.[3] On the first week-end all who do not take leave from the hospital are transferred to a regularly organized ward. The loss of responsibility for his own behavior always creates in the individual the desire to remain on his own ward during the following weekends. Once the groups have made the decision to be responsible for themselves and the ward, their decision is accepted by the staff. Exceedingly few individuals during the first 14 months of operation have failed to abide by their commitment. No group has failed to carry out its weekend obligations.

Midweek Dilemma

By the middle of the first week many dilemmas are created. These are almost completely unintentional and are accomplished without the individuals' awareness of the contribution each has made. Everyone is aware of the problems, and each is rapidly becoming aware that regardless of what he does the situation gets worse. Clinical and behavioral evidences of anxiety increase. The problems of the staff at this time are to build techniques of support into the group, to provide additional concepts and related skills for analyzing the current problems, and to facilitate the growth of group cohesion and intragroup support. Much of this is accomplished through D-group vignettes. For example, a lecturette, "Maintenance Functions," presents the kinds of functions a group needs to maintain itself as an effective problem-solving group. Following the lecturette, one of the groups volunteers to conduct a short D-group meeting (vignette) before the other groups. During the vignette, members of the group keep a record of the maintenance

[3] We are extremely grateful to Miss Martha Mack, Chief of Nursing, for her trust in her own staff and her willingness to experiment with ward control and responsibility.

functions which are provided by its members. At the same time the observing groups also keep their records. At the close of the vignette the participants' data are then presented and discussed. Discrepancies between the data from the two sources provide indices for further clarification and learning by the participants. During the discussion the concepts of the D-group scales are applied, producing evidence of their usefulness in areas of behavior outside of their own D-group.

Each group, in succession, conducts a vignette, testing out some new concept, method or proposition. In this testing many of the problems within the group become clarified. New reference points are discovered which add stability to the group, and learning which has been acquired in one group gets transferred to the others.

Consultation Groups

A last technique that is introduced during the first week is the consultation group. The D-groups are broken into smaller groups of either three or four members. This provides an opportunity to reduce the competition of numbers, which permits some individual members to be more supportive. Others become less restrained. Ideas that get lost in the competition for time in the larger group are given greater consideration. Tests of confidentiality are undertaken in these small groups which would not be accepted in the larger ones. The pressures to conform are also reduced; ideas which the member hesitates to express for fear of the kind of reception he might receive become aired.

The method of consultation groups is introduced in the first Friday afternoon, before the weekend break. Two goals are sought: One, the introduction of another method, and, two, an attempt to have the participants assemble and make available to each other the learnings that have been acquired during the week. It also provides for those going home for the weekend a clearer statement of what has been occurring during the week. Each week, the learnings of the week are a problem for Friday's consultation groups.

Final Activity

The final programmed activity of each week is a lecturette, by a staff member, covering the week's experiences. Usually it is a brief statement of the dilemma-invention relationships and an evaluation of the progress the groups have made in their learnings. A prediction is given regarding the expectancies of the next week. This, as do all the other lecturettes, ends with a brief question and answer period. As in the other discussion sessions, questions which do not generalize from the problem under discussion are referred back to the D-group.

The Second Week

The primary controlling goal of the second week is the building of group membership. The additional goals, obtainable only if strong cohesive groups are achieved, are: (1) the development of skills in maintenance functions; (2) the increase of the individual's exploration of his personal assumptions regarding here-and-now behavior; (3) the increase of skills for observing more complex behavior; (4) the increase of skills for giving, receiving, and testing feedback data; and (5) the learning of the dynamics and consequences of intragroup conflict and development.

The interactions of the participants increase in intensity and degree of complexity. Lecturettes become less frequent but are directed to problems of greater complexity and generalization. Whereas, during the first week the scaling of behavior progresses from simple and more easily denotable behavior (talkativeness) to personal actions (was I leveling?), during the second week scaling of personal sensitivity (feelings of responsibility, hostility), group sensitiveness (adequacy of function, teamness), and methods of organization (organic, mechanical, or bull) are added. The exercises during the first week are built around as simple an interaction as possible to emphasize the methods of observation and the acquisition of data by which one can acquire feedback. The exercises of the second week are designed to involve the participants in all the complexities of the problem of group relationships and to direct their observations to many of the significant variables which affect their relations with others.

The second week starts off with major personal dilemmas which develop from the weekend. By the end of the first week the self-concept as a patient has significantly diminished. Physical complaints and frequencies of reporting to sick call are reduced. The concept of a learner's learning to solve problems is developing. Group members begin to refer to each other as students and to ward activities as classes. On return home during the first weekend, however, members of the family, friends, and neighbors all respond to the participant not as a a learner learning how to solve problems but as a patient being treated for his illness. Those who remain at the hospital are transferred to a regular hospital ward. There they find that they no longer are treated as responsible for their own decisions but rather are forced into con-

Table 7-2 Second Week

	Sunday	Monday	Tuesday	Wednesday	Thursday	Friday	Saturday
8–8:30	Free time			Free time			Free time
8:30–9		Lecturette 9[a]	Exercise 5 contd. Data feedback and theory	Lecture 10: Circular behavior	Exercise 3 Decision making in groups	Exercise 7 Conformity and deviation	Weekend passes and recreation activities available
9–9:30		Coffee					
9:30–10		D-group 10 Scale 6 and 10 introduced and used with scales 3,4,5,7,8,9.	Coffee				
10–10:30			D-group 11 Scales 3 to 10	Consultation Groups 2 contd. Personal feedback from behavior items scale			
10:30–11							
11–11:30		Exercise 4 Tape listening	Vignette 2 a, b, and c. Scale 11 Type of group organizations	D-group 13		D-group 15	
11:30–12				No scales		All scales	

134

			Noon		
12–1					
1–1:30	Consultation groups 2 Topic: Problems I am having in the D-group	Consultation groups 2 contd. Fill in behavior items scale	Free time	Exercise 6 contd. data feedback and theory	Consultation groups 3 Topic: What have I learned thus far?
1:30–2			Recreation time available		
2–2:30				Coffee	Coffee
2:30–3	Exercise 5	D-group 12		D-group 14	Lecturette 11 Wrap-up of week and review D, E, F, G
3–3:30					
3:30–4					
4–4:30		All scales		All scales	
4:30–7			Free time		
7–			Diaries		

• Individual versus Group Goals.

formity to the rules, which reinforces their dependency on the decisions of others.

On Monday of the second week, the physical complaints, reporting to sick call, and the requests for private interviews with the staff reach their highest frequencies. These personal dilemmas are, insofar as possible, referred to the D-groups for consideration. The building of group membership is enhanced each time the group contributes to the solution of some problem. The more the members find help, support, or inventions within their group, the greater is their identification, as well as cohesion, with the group. The greater the strength of these anchorages the greater is the venturesomeness in personal and group experimentation. The second week's program attempts to exploit this identification, cohesion, and group membership to increase the freedom for testing personal assumptions, investigating the efficiency of habitual approaches to problems, and experimenting with new approaches to solving problems.

The lecturette of Monday morning is oriented toward assisting in the recovery from the weekend experiences. The nature of personal goals, which have been reinforced over the weekend, is reviewed as in conflict with the goals of the laboratory method of training.

Tape Listening Exercise

The D-group tape listening exercise provides training in the skills of listening. It also provides a basis for comparing how the members see themselves at this time with how they perceived themselves in D-groups of the previous week. Instructions are provided to listen for the occurrences of task and maintenance functions and to discuss those places where such functions were needed but not provided.

Application of Consultative Skills

We are now ready to apply the consultative skills learned in the first week to more significant problems. The participants are asked to prepare a list of problems that are present in their group. After each has prepared his list he meets with a consultation group consisting of some of the members of his D-group. Each then tells of one of the problems he has listed, and the consultation group discusses experiments it might perform to develop solutions for the problem. At the close of this session carbon copies of the original lists are collected. The staff, using these lists as source material, develops the Group Member Evaluation Form. This form lists from twenty to thirty behavioral items (see Table 7-3). It includes, for example, behavioral items of (1) control (tends to dominate the group), (2) maintenance function (shows interest in people and their ideas), (3) conflict creation (annoys others), (4) task functions (summarizes where group stands), (5) support of others (helps others express their ideas and feelings), (6) flight behavior (runs away when faced with a problem), and (7) skill in interpersonal relations (knows when to talk and when to listen).

In preparation for the next consultation group, each person rates every member of his D-group, including himself, on each of the items, using a one to nine-point scale—from never applicable to always applicable.

Table 7–3 Group Member Evaluation Items (Items Used in the First Patient Training Laboratory)

1. Levels with other members
2. Contributes to the group
3. Expresses self clearly and concisely
4. Summarizes where group stands on an issue
5. Contributes without shutting the gate on others
6. Helps get to the meat of issues
7. Annoys others
8. Yields to group pressures—conforms
9. Sets himself apart from the group
10. Is hard-headed, sticks to his point regardless of feedback
11. Provides helpful feedback to group members
12. Listens with understanding to what others say
13. Takes lead in selecting topics
14. Helps members express their ideas and feelings
15. Shows interest in people and their ideas
16. Shows lack of concern in learning from feedback
17. Knows when to talk and when to listen
18. Helps other feel at ease
19. Helps group to stay on target
20. Runs away when faced with a problem (goes into flight)
21. Puts group goals above personal needs
22. More ready to fight than work out problems
23. Shows that he likes us
24. Blocks the group's development
25. Likes to wander off the topic
26. Dominates and imposes his will on the group
27. Takes responsibility for moving group along

After the ratings by each member, the staff compiles the data so that each participant receives his personal ratings. The returned data sheet contains the participant's self-rating, the ratings by each of the other members of his D-group, unidentified, and his mean rating by his group. This feedback provides him with data of how he sees himself, as well as a range of how others see him. Each is given an opportunity to study the ratings. He then meets with his consultation group to explore the implications, and seeks clarification by asking for examples of behavior which led to the rating. This feedback leads to the search for alternatives and assistance in the solution of problems that are revealed.

The consultation group at one and the same time forces the individual to test some of his assumptions about his behavior as well as the behavior of the others. It provides feedback as to how he is behaving in the group as well as an evaluation from others regarding his behavior. It is often at this point that the individual drops his defensiveness and first presents his hypothesis that some of his problems are of his own doing. He can test the validity of his own observations as compared with those of others by asking for the behavioral instances which provide the basis for the rating that was given. Each individual controls the area and the level of feedback at which he works by asking the questions he wishes to have discussed. The staff attempts to create an atmosphere within which, when dilemmas develop, the participants will attempt to develop experiments for testing alternative behaviors rather than attempt to solve the problems by abstract there-and-then discussions.

The utilization of the smaller groups makes it possible to bring more sensitive problems and feelings into discussion. This facilitates the introduction of the more difficult problems into the D-group meetings.

The learnings in these consultation groups are not limited to content. Not only does the participant receive feedback regarding his behavior, and a testing of his interpretation of the behavior of others, he also receives training in the giving and the receiving of help. In the smaller consultation group it is much easier to give and receive support in discussing a sensitive or difficult area or problem than it is in the larger D-group. Since competition of time is reduced, the person talking is not under as much pressure to talk and can learn the helpful role of listening and giving support.

Power Spectrum Exercise

The exercises of this period of the laboratory are introduced when it is felt that the skills of scaling behavior and of interacting under experimental directions have been acquired. The Power Spectrum exercise, using problems of work relations, is designed to demonstrate different consequences of making decisions under various degrees of power. The participants are divided into two groups, supervisor and subordinate. Differences of opinion are established by having the participants, individually, establish a rank order of the solutions for each problem. The pairs then come together and attempt to establish a joint list, under several experimental conditions.

Under Condition A the supervisor takes the role of a hard-nosed boss, who feels he knows better than anyone else what is correct, and who has the right to insist on his point of view. Condition B calls for the boss to establish a role of participation or collaboration. In Condition C the supervisor attempts to establish a supportive climate, with the subordinate taking greater responsibility for the decision making. The results from the first four training laboratories involving 94 participants are shown in Table 7-4.

Table 7-4 Power Spectrum Exercise (Combined Data from First Four Laboratories, $N = 94$)

| | Experimental Condition | | | | | |
| | A | | B | | C | |
	Sup.	Sub.	Sup.	Sub.	Sup.	Sub.
Leadership	7.8	3.6	5.3	5.5	3.2	5.8
Satisfaction	6.9	5.2	7.4	7.7	6.3	7.6
Agreement	6.7	4.5	7.8	7.5	8.7	7.4
Adequacy	7.3	6.5	8.2	7.3	7.3	7.1
Compliance/ Resistance	7.2	5.3	7.9	7.8	8.3	7.8
Quality of List	7.3	5.4	7.3	7.5	6.1	6.9
Responsibility	8.3	5.7	7.2	7.1	5.1	6.6
Teamness	6.6	5.2	7.2	7.5	5.8	6.7

As in data collected in industrial training laboratories, the combined scores under the conditions of collaboration, Condition B, are all of positive value and higher than the combined scores under either Condition A or C. Of interest is the discrepancy between the scores when one partner has significantly greater power than the other. Under Condition A when the supervisor has the power or exacts greater control, the supervisor reports greater satisfaction, agreement, adequacy of partner, compliance, quality of list, feeling of responsibility, and teamness than his subordinate reports.

Group Decision Making

The next exercise, Decision Making in Groups, is introduced, at a time when intragroup cohesion is at a high point, to compare the efficiency of individual decision making with the efficiency of the group. The film *Twelve Angry Men* is utilized as the source of data. Factors such as knowledge, influence in the group, perception of positive influence, status, and sensitivity are studied in relation to the decisions made by the group. If the exerting of influence on a group causes the group to produce an incorrect decision, the inclination to consider the opinions of others is strengthened. If the person who had the correct knowledge failed to bring his resources to bear for a more adequate decision, he feels responsible to his group to participate more actively.

Conformity and Deviation

The third exercise of this period is an experiment in Conformity and Deviation. The groups are divided into triads, with one in the triad designated as the leader, and are assigned a problem with a number of alternative solutions. In the conformity situation no instructions are given other than to come to an agreement on one of the alternate solutions to the assigned problem. Usually the alternatives vary to such a degree that there is little difficulty in reaching a group agreement. In the deviation situation, however, the leader is instructed to take an extremely deviant position. Conflict develops, and when the conflict persists the leader is rejected by the other members of the triad.

Table 7–5 Conformity and Deviation (Combined Data from First Three Laboratories, $N = 71$)

	No Deviant	With Deviant
Satisfaction	7.2	5.6
Friendly/Hostile	6.5	2.7
Goodness of Group	7.3	5.7
Group* Atmosphere	Cooperative	Competitive
	Rewarding	Fight
	Work	Tense
	Competitive	Work

* Words are listed in order of frequency when 50% or more of the groups checked the word as descriptive of the interaction.

The presence of the deviant in the group reduces the satisfaction, increases the hostility, reduces the goodness of the group, and creates an atmosphere of work under conditions of competition, tenseness, and fight. The support situation in conformity is seen as competitive and work but cooperative and rewarding.

By the middle of the second week, feelings of personal inadequacy are high. Dilemmas within the group are increasing in complexity. It appears that as soon as one problem becomes solved, two more, each more complex, have developed. It is at this point that most of the transient psychotic episodes have occurred. In order to help stabilize behavior we introduce a lecture based on Lippitt's concept of circular behavior using examples from laboratory behavior as illustrations. The concepts of mix between perception and objective reality as the stimulus to behavior, skilled and unskilled responses, the perceptual screen of the receiver, and the validation and invalidation of one's assumptions through his own perceptual screen are presented as a working frame of reference for evaluating one's own as well as other's behavior.

The second week is concluded with consultation groups analyzing what the groups have learned to date and with a brief synthesis of the progress they have made in relation to the dilemma-invention–feedback-generalization paradigm of learning.

The Third Week

The third week has two primary learning goals. One is an understanding of the forces which impinge on the behavior of an individual at any choice point. The other is the dynamics of intergroup conflict and methods of resolution.

Personal Experimentation

Carbon copies of the participants' diaries are turned in to the staff and are read regularly by one of the nursing aides for significant remarks. One of the data which he looks for is personal experimentation either in the groups or elsewhere. Usually one of the diaries from the Sunday evening before the third week will reveal some instances of personal experimentation with some problem in the back-home situation. The most widely reported experimentation is with the wife in some decision making situation. Instead of approaching the decision making in their habitual pattern, they report trying out some of the learning from the power spectrum. The reports in the diaries, as well as through other channels of communication, are taken by the staff as evidences of generalizations from the laboratory learning.

The third week starts with a general assembly to explore these

Table 7-6 Third Week

	Sunday	Monday	Tuesday	Wednesday	Thursday	Friday	Saturday
8–8:30	Free time	General assembly: Testing for involvement	D-group 17	Feedback data exercise 6	Exercise 10	Exercise 10	Free time
8:30–9	Weekend passes and Recreation activities available	Coffee		Coffee	Intergroup competition	Concluded	Weekend passes and recreation activities available
9–9:30		D-group 16		D-group 19	(Coffee during exercise)	Data and theory session	
9:30–10							
10–10:30			All scales			Coffee	
10:30–11			Coffee			D-group 20	
11–11:30		All scales	Lecturette 14 Process analysis	All scales		All scales	
11:30–12		Lecturette 12 Level of aspiration	Exercise 9	Free time			
12–1				Noon			
1–1:30		Lecturette 13 Force field analysis	Exercise 9 contd Process analysis	Free time	Exercise 10 contd	Lecturette 15 Reference groups	
1:30–2		Exercise 8 Force field analysis *Twelve Angry Men*				D-group 21	
2–2:30		(Coffee during exercise)	Coffee		(Coffee during exercise)	No scales	
2:30–3			D-group 18			Coffee	
3–3:30						Role playing 1 Back-home relations	
3:30–4							
4–4:30		No scales	No scales			Wrap-up of week	
4:30–7							
7–				Diaries			

personal experiments in an open discussion. For those who have experimented, the discussion provides a means of asking questions, of checking assumptions, and of being rewarded (recognition) for trying out some of the hypotheses generated in the training. When success is reported, some who have been more skeptical of the value of the methods of the laboratory begin to be reassured. Some, of course, report attempts at experimentation which are not so successful. These, too, are recognized, analyzed by the groups, and left open for further discussion in the D-groups.

Whereas the earlier lecturettes are mostly confined to specific problems or concepts, during this third week they deal with general theoretical positions related to the exercises. To reduce the effectiveness of the assumption of the participants that they were the victims of their drives, instincts, childhood background, or any of the other rationalizations that they generally utilize to release themselves from responsibility for their behavior, the lecturette "Level of Aspiration" and the lecturette and exercise "Force-Field Analysis" are introduced. The film *Twelve Angry Men* is used for the force-field exercise. After the lecturette on force-field analysis, a few examples—smoking and length of women's skirts—are analyzed. Participants are then divided into trios and assigned a jury member, whose behavior is then analyzed by force-field analysis. The film is stopped just prior to the third vote. The trios meet, make their analysis, and then make a report of their analysis in general assembly. Quite frequently the analysis is so complete that the order of change of the juryman's vote from guilty to not guilty is correctly predicted. In all instances this method of analysis has resulted in less error of prediction than is achieved by either the individuals or the groups.

To further study the forces which influence behavior and to increase skill in the analysis of group processes, the film is rerun. The instructions this time are, "When you see some kind of behavior which helps you understand or predict some other behavior which will occur later, stop the film and discuss what you perceive and its significance in relation to the future behavior."

Intergroup Competition

Concomitantly with these exercises, the data from the scales indicate that the D-groups are reaching a significant level of behavior which includes concern for process of group functioning as well as content. The content is consistently and primarily here-and-now rather than there-and-then. The atmosphere is reported as work, tense, rewarding, and helpful. Leveling is high, and each group thinks of itself as being the best and of having reached an organic level of organization. It is at this point of cohesion and group identification that a problem of inter-group competition is introduced.

Whereas the learning from this exercise in industrial laboratories is directed to the dynamics of win-lose conflict between departments, between union and management, and in social struggles, the learnings in the patient laboratory are directed to the dynamics of win-lose con-flict in family, community, work, and social relations. The devotion to prejudices and their consequences in social action are also reviewed. The methods of resolution—voting, representation, personal appeal and arbitration—which are habitually utilized are built into the exercise. These are analyzed along with the forces which contribute to their effectiveness or ineffectiveness.

The exercise and lecturette "Reference Groups" serve as a follow-up and generalization from the learning in the intergroup exercise. The film *Our Invisible Committee* is used to investigate how membership in different groups affects the values and behavior of a person when he copes with some other, often seemingly unrelated, problem.

Role Playing

The final activity of the third week is the introduction of the last methodology of the laboratory—role playing. During the final week this is the most extensively used method and is utilized to facilitate generalization of learning from the laboratory to back home. The intro-duction at this point is to help the participants describe back home what has been taking place at the hospital. It also helps them integrate their learnings. The roles are established for the participant with a friend and relative inquiring about his hospitalization.

Following this role playing is the summary of the week. Usually a relatively high degree of anxiety is present at this time; so the summary also includes a statement of the expectation of what the next week will bring.

The Fourth Week—Application Studies

The fourth week of the laboratory is a period of testing the learn-ings of the previous three weeks for generalization to the back-home problems. The goal is to help individuals integrate these learnings into a rationale for approaching problems: i.e., a rationale for learning how to learn to solve problems as opposed to the accumulation of a series of techniques or solutions for application to problems. The program of this last week is designed to link in problems of personal behavior, to learn how to apply tests to assumptions regarding behavior, and to learn to apply the concepts, theories, and techniques which have been acquired during the training.

Personal and Back-Home Problems

The participants return to the laboratory from their third weekend with two kinds of vivid experiences. Some report success in experimenting with new patterns of behavior. Others have run into the skepticism of their families and community regarding their leaving the hospital so soon. For most this is the shortest stay they have had in a psychiatric hospital. Since in the future they will have to deal with the problems of family and social skepticism, we start the week with a D-group meeting, in which, with a group of peers, the participants are free to discuss the events of the weekend and the problems of their return to their community.

All the lecturettes of the week are oriented to the tieing-in of the back-home problems. Role playing is introduced as a method of practicing alternative patterns of behaving, of appraising the feelings of another person, and of testing alternative ideas in search of solutions to a problem.

The lecturettes "Self-Concept" and "Changing Roles in Family and Work Relations" are used as a means of emphasizing the tieing-in of personal problems. The final lecture "Learning to Learn" is a restatement of the Dilemma-Invention–Feedback-Generalization paradigm. It attempts to provide a statement of the rationale for the learnings of the laboratory. Primarily, however, it is an integrated frame of reference within which we attempt to provide a workable orientation of learning how to learn from experience.

Role playing, without being identified as such, was introduced in the beginning of the participation in behavioral experiments. The learnings in the experiments were, however, directed primarily to general principles. At this time role playing is introduced as a significant method of experimenting with the alternative personal hypotheses or inventions a person creates in response to his dilemmas. Prior to the first role playing of the fourth week, participants are asked to list their personal dilemmas in the D-group. From these lists they select the problems they wish to experiment with in role playing. Once they select a problem, they speculate regarding the conditions which have given· rise to the problem. Persons are assigned to carry out the conditions con-

Table 7–7 Fourth Week

	Sunday	Monday	Tuesday	Wednesday	Thursday	Friday	Saturday
8–8:30	Free time	D-group 22	Lecturette 17 Self concept	Lecturette 18 Changing roles in family relations	D-group 25	Lecture 10 Learning to learn	Free time
8:30–9	Weekend passes and recreation activities available					Coffee	Weekend passes and recreation activities available
9–9:30			Coffee	Exercise 11		D-group 26	
9:30–10		All scales	Role playing 3	Power spectrum in family relations	All scales		
10–10:30		Coffee	(Alter ego)	(Data feedback)	Coffee	No scales	
10:30–11		Lecturette 16 Role playing			Role playing 4 Back-home problems	Role playing 5 Absent member	
11–11:30							
11:30–12		Role playing 2					

	Role playing 2	Consultation group 4	Noon	Exercise 12	Role playing 6
12–1					
1–1:30	Role playing 2 (Problems in the group)	Consultation group 4	Free time	Exercise 12 Introduction to change: Traits versus problems	Role playing 6 Work problem: Mental health versus learning to adjust
1:30–2	Coffee	(Fill-in data)			
2–2:30	D-group 23	Coffee		Coffee	Coffee
2:30–3		D-group 24		Consultation groups 4 contd	D-group 27
3–3:30					
3:30–4					
4–4:30	All scales	No scales		Feedback	No scales
4:30–7			Diaries		
7–					

147

sidered to be significant, and the role playing starts. Immediately after the role playing, a period of analysis provides an opportunity for clarification of individual assumptions and/or interpretations, as well as providing ideas of application to be tested.

The role of the alter-ego facilitates acquisition of sensitivity to the probability that one person may not be viewing the situation in the same manner as another. One problem which often gets involved in this role playing is the problem of a third person attempting to resolve a difference between two others.

Changing of Roles in Family Relations

A most realistic application of role playing is achieved in the exercise in the changing of roles in family relations. One of the earliest exercises was the power spectrum in work relations, in which one half took the role of supervisor and the other half the role of subordinate. In this exercise, the participants take the role of the father in the household. The role of the wife is taken by women from various hospital organizations or students from the hospital intern training program. The problem is the distribution of decision-making power in family problems. The role instructions are assigned to the men under the conditions "A," "B," and "C," as in the previous power spectrum exercise. The exercise is followed by buzz groups, data feedback, and discussion of the theoretical implications of the data.

Table 7-8 Power Spectrum in Family Relations $N=94$ Male Laboratory Participants and 94 Female Visitors

	A		B		C	
	Men	Women	Men	Women	Men	Women
Who Controlled	7.8	6.0	5.3	5.4	3.0	5.0
Satisfaction	6.9	5.2	7.8	8.1	6.7	6.5
Agreement	7.4	4.1	5.7	6.9	5.9	7.3
Adequacy	6.5	5.7	8.4	8.3	7.9	6.8
Responsibility	7.8	4.8	7.2	6.9	4.5	7.2
Teamness	5.0	4.4	7.6	7.6	6.4	5.8

As in the power spectrum exercise using work relations problems, there is greater combined satisfaction, agreement, perceived adequacy of partner, sense of responsibility, and feeling of teamness under experimental condition "B" (participation) than under conditions "A" or "C." Also where one person shows significantly greater controlling (the men under conditions "A," the women under condition "C"), that person perceives significantly greater agreement than his partner and also feels more responsible than his partner.

Problem of Seeking Employment

Back-home dilemmas are now listed and provide the source material for the rest of the role playing. The final role task is study of the problem of seeking employment following discharge from the hospital. Roles are taken as an applicant presenting himself for work, first, as a former mental patient and, second, in the role of a person who has been to the hospital and had training in problems of adjustment. Ratings are made on employability on a three point scale. The results through three laboratories show 81% of the observers with a more favorable attitude toward the problem-centered self-description. Only 13% are more favorable toward the mental illness concept. An analysis of variance of this data produces an F of 45.49 and is significant beyond the .001 level (Rothaus and Morton, 1962).

Group Member Evaluation

While attention in the laboratory is being directed to the role playing exercises, attention is also being focused on the problems of the individual, through the Consultation Groups. During the early part of the week, each member again rates himself and the other members on the Group Evaluation form. The data are compiled and again fed back to the individuals who in turn meet in consultation groups for analysis, clarification, and feedback. These ratings are usually more valid than the ratings of the previous Group Member Evaluation and thus facilitate understanding and make clearer the areas where change is needed. This also provides feedback in the areas in which change has been accomplished.

The final hours of the laboratory are spent in a D-group.

Results

As this paper is being prepared a follow-up study of post-hospitalization is being conducted. Interviews and questionnaires are being used to obtain data from the former participants and significant others, such as employer, wife, or another member of the family. The data will be compared with data from a control group of patients who were selected as being capable of responding to therapeutic intervention. The control group was processed through the same admission procedures as the laboratory participants. Although the collection and analysis of the data have not been completed, one finding is very much in evidence. The average hospital stay of the laboratory participants is thirty days, whereas the average hospital stay for the control group is ninety days. Clinical evaluation of the interviews reveals that the laboratory participants are doing at least as well as the members of the control group.

Pre- and post-test data for the first laboratory were analyzed and presented to support the continuation of the laboratory program (Morton, 1961). The results for the 21 participants follow.

Changes in Projective Data

The Holtzman Ink Blot Test (Holtzman et al., 1961), administered in an AB-BA sequence, as interpreted by S. E. Cleveland (1961)[4] is as follows:

"Overall the preliminary results suggest that participation in the training laboratory produces neither dramatic cure nor disastrous breakdown in psychiatric patients. There is no significant shift in their fantasy life. Mainly this concerns an awakening of human interest. That this awakening sphere takes form also as an increase in hostile, angry, even destructive feelings and thought is not necessarily negative or a bad turn of events. These patients are habitual repressors and deniers of emotional feeling. Increase and arousal of strong emotions may represent an acceptance of personal problems and increased awareness of existence of psychological factors and increased acceptance of human problems. This interpretation is supported by additional findings of no increase in pathology or in anxiety together with slight decrease in somatic fixations. In other words, the arousal of human and emotional interests and feeling does not appear to be accompanied by any increase in regressive trends nor in an anxiety level; while at the same time there is a loosening of physical preoccupation and somatic ties."

Changes in Somatic Data

Under the direction of Aileen Schaefer, Ward Nurse, all somatic complaints were recorded. The number of complaints decreased progressively from the first part of each week to the last part as well as from the first of the training period to the last. Even the impending discharge from the hospital did not result in any increase in somatic complaints. A comparison was made of the number of complaints of the first ten laboratory days with the last ten, using the Mann-Whitney U

---

[4] Dr. S. E. Cleveland, now Chief Psychologist, Veterans Administration Hospital, Houston, Texas.

Test. The differences in the ranks of the frequences of complaints is significantly less for the last ten days ($p < .02$).

Changes in Diary Data

The daily diaries were analyzed using the Discomfort-Relief system of analysis of personal data (Mower, Hunt, and Kogan, 1953). The mean weekly DRQ's based on the diaries were compared by means of an analysis of variance (Rothaus and Morton, 1961). The differences among the means were found to be significant at an .01 level of confidence. Further analysis of the differences among the means was made by employing Duncan's multiple range test for correlated means. The mean DRQ for the first week (46.50) differed significantly from the means of the fourth (17.30) and fifth weeks (22.60), at the .01 level of confidence. The results indicate a marked decline in the proportion of unhappy, uncomfortable, and disturbed content in the diaries during the last two weeks of the laboratory.

Changes in Psychiatric Evaluation

All participants were given a psychiatric evaluation prior to and following the training program. The participants were seen by the same psychiatrist for both evaluations. Part of their evaluation was the Lorr Personal Audit (Lorr et al., 1962) interview inventory. Significant positive changes occurred on eight of the interview rating items. No significant negative changes occurred.

To summarize the impressions of the interviewers, the patients appeared to be less tense ($p < .02$), depressed ($p < .02$), apprehensive ($p < .001$), and self-recriminating ($p < .05$) on the second evaluation. They made fewer somatic complaints ($p < .05$) and expressed fewer dependency needs ($p < .01$) and greater responsibility ($p < .001$) for their own behavior. The psychiatrists' overall evaluation of difference in adjustment was significant at an .01 level.

Post Hospital Work Record

The final bit of evidence presently available is in the post hospital work record. The average period of unemployment prior to hospitalization was eight years. As mentioned earlier, eleven of the group had had no extended employment, and two more had had no stability in recent years. Sixteen of the twenty-one participants of the first laboratory have been heard from. Only one of the sixteen has not been employed at all. Twelve have been employed regularly. Three have changed jobs and are working or are expecting to return to work.

SECTION B: Follow-up Evaluation of Human Relations Training for Psychiatric Patients

by D. L. Johnson, P. G. Hanson, P. Rothaus, R. B. Morton, F. A. Lyle, and R. Moyer

The Human Relations Training Laboratory for psychiatric patients, also known as the Patient Training Laboratory, was established at the Houston VA Hospital in May, 1961 as a new and experimental approach to the treatment of behavior problems. In departing from traditional psychiatric treatment modes, the Patient Training Laboratory borrowed concepts and techniques from social psychology and industrial management training. The introduction of a new approach to the problems of psychiatric patients immediately raises the question of whether the newer and unorthodox approach offers significant advantages over conventional therapies. The present paper presents an evaluation of the effectiveness of human relations training as a therapeutic modality.

An earlier study (Rothaus, Morton, Johnson, Cleveland, and Lyle, 1963) reported a partial assessment of the training program. Patients were used as their own controls and studied through the use of interview rating scales, psychological testing, ward behavior observation, and diary analysis. Research findings indicated significant reductions in the amounts of depression and dependency in psychiatric patients, as well as a reawakening of interest in interpersonal relationships. Three clear-cut limitations of this exploratory study are apparent. First of all, changes from pre- to post-testing could answer only limited questions about the effectiveness of the program; there was a distinct need for a post-hospitalization follow-up study. Second, the effects of the program were considered solely for the first group of patients processed through the training program, thus introducing the ever-present danger of a Hawthorne effect. Finally, there was a clear-cut need for comparison with a different treatment program drawing subjects (Ss) from the same patient population.

152

The research reported here attempts to supplement and enlarge upon the findings of the earlier study. A decision was made to compare the Patient Training Laboratory, which is group-oriented, with a group therapy treatment ward operated in a more conventional manner (Bloom, Boyd, and Kaplan, 1962). To be accepted as a valued addition to the currently existing means available for changing behavior, the Patient Training Laboratory should meet predetermined standards at least as well as the more conventional group therapy program, which is recognized as successful and is held in high esteem by both staff and patients.

Procedure

Patient Training Laboratory and Group Therapy Program

Miles (1961), and Shepard and Bennis (1956) have cited certain general distinctions between human relations training and group therapy. Group therapy is characterized by its dealing with patients and illness and with the inner reasons or "why" of behavior. Human relations training is described as more oriented toward normal behavioral functioning, and as more concerned with the development of social skills (the more external "hows" of social functioning). In the specific hospital setting where the group therapy and Patient Training Laboratory programs were conducted, other distinctions exist.

Time limits. Individuals participate in the training laboratory for a definite, preset period of time. Each Patient Training Laboratory session is four weeks long. Furthermore, the Patient Training Laboratory groups are closed; a group of men begins together and completes the session together. Group therapy, by contrast, is usually for an indefinite length of time and the groups are open-ended, adding new members when others terminate the group.

Type of leadership. Patient Training Laboratory groups are self-directed, that is, the participants meet in daily sessions without the presence of any staff or professionally trained personnel. Traditional group therapy has as a leader a professionally trained therapist. Functions ordinarily served by the therapist are carried out in the Patient Training Laboratory sessions by the participants, all receiving group sensitivity training. This training is supplemented by the use of rating scales that focus attention on group process and by specially designed exercises that promote group discussion and encourage problem-solving exploration.

Time orientation. The Patient Training Laboratory places more emphasis on here-and-now problems than does traditional group therapy, which tends to be past-oriented. The difference here is one of degree. Many group therapists do emphasize here-and-now problems, but, in comparison with the Patient Training Laboratory, most group therapy is past-oriented.

Intensity of group experience. The Patient Training Laboratory is designed to occupy the participant's exclusive attention throughout the four-week training period. Nearly all exercises, lectures, and other ward activities are carefully scheduled to focus attention on the development group itself. Group therapy, in contrast, ordinarily takes place as a relatively isolated event in the patient's day. His other time is spent in occupational therapy or in recreational activities, and often with groups of men who are not closely associated with his own therapy group. Thus, the group therapy patient's attention may be diverted from the group experience rather than continually redirected to it.

Similarities between the Two Programs

Similarities in the Patient Training Laboratory and group therapy programs are noteworthy, but difficult to assess. The architecture of the two wards was similar. Both programs shared common hospital facilities, i.e., library, dining hall, recreation, and medical laboratory services. Norms governing patient behavior were similar. Weekend passes were essentially the same for both groups. Ward governments functioned in a democratic milieu in both programs.

Follow-up Studies

Two follow-up studies compared the programs. In the first, a *field interview* was conducted by a trained interviewer[1] who contacted both the discharged veteran and a significant other—a wife or near blood relative living with the veteran at least thirty days prior to the follow-up date. Interviews were usually conducted in the home. The study included men who had taken part in the first three Patient Training Laboratories and group therapy patients who had completed their program at about the same time.

---

[1] The authors were assisted in the project by William Booker, graduate student, who carried out the interviews, Catherine Bentinck, M.S.W., who supervised the interview procedures, and Barbara Meek and Lucille Hart, who located subjects and obtained information for the mailed questionnaire study.

The format of the interviews was extensive and identical to that being employed in a larger Veterans Administration follow-up study conducted by the Psychiatric Evaluation Project. For practical reasons interviews were limited to men within the Houston metropolitan area. All interviews were conducted in the tenth month after the veteran's discharge date. Appointments were made by phone or by letter if no phone number was available. If an interview appointment could not be made in the tenth month following discharge, the veteran was dropped from the interview schedule.

The second follow-up study involved veterans in the fourth through twelfth Patient Training Laboratories and group therapy patients completing treatment at the same time who were studied through a seven-page *mailed questionnaire* sent to all veterans regardless of their geographical residence. As in the field study, the mailed questionnaire was sent out during the tenth month after the veteran's discharge. If the veteran failed to respond to the mailed questionnaire, three follow-up letters at ten-day intervals were sent soliciting his cooperation. If there was no response to the third attempt and if he could not be reached by telephone, the veteran was dropped from the study.

Both studies obtained information on rehospitalization, employment, psychological well-being, physical well-being, social participation, estimated benefit derived from the hospital treatment, and length of time the patients stayed on each treatment ward. However, the wording of questions and the manner in which they were collected were sufficiently different in the field study and the questionnaire to render it inadvisable to pool the data. The mailed questionnaire also obtained information about the patient's view of how he had changed as a result of treatment. The two follow-up studies are reported separately.

Scoring

The following definitions were used in coding aspects of the narrative data of both the field interview and questionnaire into statistically treatable responses:

Rehospitalization. A S was considered rehospitalized if he was admitted to a hospital for psychiatric treatment and remained at least five days. The S's own statement on this was checked against hospital records for veracity.

Employment. A S was classified as employed if he was currently being paid for at least ten hours' work a week. Full-time college students were considered employed.

Alcohol. Trouble with alcohol was classified on a three-point scale ranging from (1) "No problem with drinking," and (2) "Some trouble with drinking," to (3) "Drinking an extremely serious problem."

On the questionnaire, further scale scores were obtained as follows:

Psychological Symptoms. The S's psychological well-being was assessed through three scales. In the first, he checked the extent of his trouble ("Much trouble," "Some trouble," or "No trouble") with the following eight symptoms: dizziness or nausea, bad dreams or nightmares, confused thinking, shakiness or trembling, feelings of anger, feelings of jealousy, feelings of being misunderstood, and worry. Scoring 0, 1, or 2 according to the degree of difficulty reported, a Psychological Symptom Score was obtained. The highest possible score was 16.

Four additional five-point scales checked by the S dealt with anxiety, depression, tiredness, and insomnia. A high score indicated poor adjustment on each of these scales.

Ss also responded to the following question on a five-point scale: "How does your general condition *now* (your feelings, satisfactions, attitudes, and so forth) compare with the way you felt *before* entering the hospital treatment program?"

Somatic Symptoms. Trouble with physical symptoms was reported by checking whether the S had "Much trouble," "Some trouble," or "No trouble" for twelve different body regions. A Somatic Sympton Score was obtained through pooling for each S. The highest possible score was 24, a high score indicating high symptomatic distress.

The S's assessment of change in his physical condition was also indicated by his response to the following question: "How does your physical health *now* compare with your health *before* entering the hospital treatment program?" Responses were in terms of "Much better," "Better," "Same," "Worse," and "Much worse."

Social Participation and Adjustment. The field interview collected two kinds of information about social participation: (1) Feelings of being socially withdrawn during the past week were reported on a three-point scale; (2) a measure of social activity was obtained with a twenty-five item activity check list. Ss checked the number of activities engaged in during the past week.

On the mailed questionnaire, the following two items of information were collected: (1) The S's feeling of being a part of his community was measured by a five-point "community alienation" scale, a high score indicating a strong feeling of alienation; (2) patients who were married at the time of the follow-up (75 men in Patient Training Laboratory and 45 men in group therapy) were asked to describe their relationships with their wives. Responses were categorized as satisfactory or unsatisfactory.

Perception of Change. Finally, patients were asked: "Do you feel that you have changed in any significant way as a result of the hospital program?" Their responses were classified as follows: No response, no change reported, yes, changed, unelaborated; yes, changed, physical terms only, e.g., "The medicine helped; I'm not as nervous," yes, changed, intrapersonal, e.g., "I'm more self-confident," yes, changed, interpersonal, e.g., "I talk with my wife more about my problems."

Subjects

The majority of patients for the Patient Training Laboratory and group therapy programs were transfers from the Houston VA Hospital open psychiatric admitting ward; the rest were transfers from closed wards or direct admissions to the hospital. Both programs preferred patients who were not currently psychotic and had some awareness of the psychological basis of their difficulties, coupled with a motivation to change. Only literate subjects were included in the study.

In some instances, group therapy patients had been sent to the Patient Training Laboratory to complete their hospital program. In others, Patient Training Laboratory participants showing a need for additional help had been sent to the group therapy program. In all, there were 64 such patients, of whom 64% responded to the follow-up request. These patients are omitted from this report.

The field interview sample consisted of 27 Patient Training Laboratory and 33 group therapy patients, or 54% and 60% respectively of the discharged patients from each program living or known to be in the Houston metropolitan area. The mailed questionnaire sample was considerably larger. Completed questionnaires were returned by 114 Patient Training Laboratory and 76 group therapy patients, or 67% and 70% of those solicited. The percentage of patients contacted and of contacted patients who completed the follow-ups did not differ significantly for the two programs.

Comparison was made of demographic variables of Patient Training Laboratory and group therapy patients who were the Ss of the field interview and questionnaire follow-up studies (Table 7-9).

Table 7–9 Demographic and Psychiatric Characteristics of Training Laboratory and Group Therapy Patients

Demographic and Psychiatric Characteristics	Patient Training Laboratory		Group Therapy	
	Field interview study (N = 27)	Mailed questionnaire study (N = 114)	Field interview study (N = 33)	Mailed questionnaire study (N = 76)
Mean age	37.4	39.2	11.4	38.0
Mean years of education	10.6	10.6	36.8	10.3
Per cent married	48.0	67.9	64.0	67.6
Per cent in occupational categories				
Professional and semi-professional	0.0	0.8	3.0	2.6
Administrative and owners	11.1	7.1	9.0	6.6
Skilled	55.5	46.0	42.4	48.7
Semiskilled	22.2	31.9	36.4	31.6
Unskilled	11.1	14.2	9.0	10.5
Per cent white	88.9	88.6	97.0	89.5
Per cent in diagnostic categories				
Anxiety or depressive reaction	77.7	71.9	69.7	69.7
Schizophrenic	3.8	12.3	12.1	9.2
Personality and character disorders	3.8	3.5	6.1	1.3
Other psychiatric	14.8	12.3	12.1	19.7
Number of times previously hospitalized, by per cents				
None	25.9	50.0	27.3	40.8
Once	33.3	24.6	21.2	30.3
More than once	40.8	25.4	51.5	28.9

Table 7–9 indicates only small differences in the population characteristics of Patient Training Laboratory and group therapy Ss. None of these differences was statistically significant. Accordingly, it is felt that the groups were reasonably comparable or well-matched on a variety of important background variables at the time they originally entered the hospital for treatment.

Finally, a separate comparison was made of the demographic characteristics of the men who did not return questionnaires with those who did. Responders and nonresponders showed no significant differences on the demographic variables. Accordingly, this report assumes that responders and nonresponders constitute the same population and that responders are representative of the total population.

Results

Field Interview

On none of the measures of post-hospital success, adjustment, or comfort did the Patient Training Laboratory and group therapy groups (Table 7–10) show any significant difference[2] either in the interview data from the veteran or from the significant other person in his life (Table 7–11).

Table 7–10 Differences between Training Laboratory and Group Therapy Patients on the Field Interview: Self-Reports

Follow-up Variables	Patient Training Laboratory (N = 27)	Group Therapy (N = 33)	Level of Significance
Rehospitalization			
Rehospitalized	22.2%	21.2%	NS
Employment			
Current employment			
Employed	48.1%	57.6%	NS
Unemployed	51.9%	42.4%	
Mean number months			
employed	5.93	4.70	NS
Psychological status			
Anxiety			
Little or none	51.9%	57.6%	
Moderate	40.7%	27.3%	NS
Marked	7.4%	15.1%	
Tired, adynamic			
Little or none	70.4%	57.6%	
Moderate	29.6%	42.4%	NS
Marked	0.0%	0.0%	
Difficulty in sleeping			
None	59.3%	51.5%	
Moderate	25.9%	42.4%	NS
Marked	14.8%	6.1%	
Depression			
Little or none	55.6%	57.6%	
Moderate	44.4%	36.3%	NS
Marked	0.0%	6.1%	

---

[2] The statistical tests used throughout were t-tests and chi-squares.

Table 7–10 (*continued*)

Follow-up Variables	Patient Training Laboratory ($N = 27$)	Group Therapy ($N = 33$)	Level of Significance
Mental disturbance			
Little or none	63.0%	54.6%	
Moderate	29.6%	39.4%	NS
Marked	7.4%	3.0%	
No response	0.0%	3.0%	
Problems with alcohol			
Serious	14.8%	18.2%	
Mild	25.5%	6.1%	NS
None	59.3%	75.7%	
Physical symptomatology			
None	74.1%	42.4%	
Moderate	18.5%	36.4%	NS
Marked	7.4%	21.2%	
Social participation			
Feeling of being socially withdrawn during past week			
Little or none	63.0%	57.6%	
Moderate	33.3%	36.4%	NS
Marked	3.7%	3.0%	
No response	–	3.0%	
Mean number of social activities performed during past week			
(Total possible = 25)	10.62	9.94	NS
Attitude toward hospitalization			
Did hospitalization help?			
Yes	85.2%	84.8%	NS
No	14.8%	15.2%	
Was hospitalization			
Too long	25.9%	21.2%	
Just right	37.0%	42.4%	
Not long enough	33.3%	33.3%	
No response	3.7%	3.0%	
Length of hospitalization			
Mean number of days on treatment ward	36.70	66.76	$p < .01$

Only two findings were suggestive. Patient Training Laboratory patients were employed a mean of 5.92 months during the nine-month follow-up period, whereas group therapy patients were employed 4.70 months ($p > .10$). But more group therapy patients were actually employed at the time of the follow-up (57.6% as compared to 48.1% for the Patient Training Laboratory). Another suggestive finding was that Patient Training Laboratory respondents tended ($p < .10$) to report fewer physical troubles.

Table 7–11 Differences between Training Laboratory and Group Therapy Patients on the Field Interview: Reports by the Significant Others

Follow-up Variables	Patient Training Laboratory (N = 26)	Group Therapy (N = 28)	Level of Significance
Change in patient's mental condition			
Improved	65.4%	71.9%	
Same	23.1%	9.4%	NS
Worse	11.5%	18.8%	
Mental disturbance			
Little or none	30.8%	42.9%	
Moderate	57.7%	50.0%	
Marked	11.5%	7.1%	
Trouble with alcohol			
None	61.5%	65.5%	
Mild	11.5%	13.8%	NS
Serious	26.9%	20.7%	

The only variable on which the two groups differed significantly was the length of time spent in the hospital. The Patient Training Laboratory group was on the study ward 36.70 days and in the hospital 50.93 days, whereas the group therapy patients were on their ward 66.76 days and in the hospital 86.17 days. In other words, group therapy patients were in their treatment program 30.06 days longer and in the hospital 35.24 days longer than Patient Training Laboratory patients ($p < .01$).

The Mailed Questionnaire

The two groups did not differ significantly in number of men who were *rehospitalized* (Table 7–12). Rehospitalization percentages were 16.2 for the Patient Training Laboratory and 26.1 for group therapy.

Significantly more of the Patient Training Laboratory than the group therapy were *employed* nine months after leaving the study program. While only 50% of the group therapy patients were employed, 65.8% of the Patient Training Laboratory held down remunerative jobs ($\chi^2 = 5.27$, $df = 1$, $p < .05$). Furthermore, the Patient Training Laboratory patients were employed a significantly greater amount of the time— 5.70 months as compared with 4.17 months for the group therapy program ($t = 3.04$, $df = 189$, $p < .001$).

Although data were not available on the prehospitalization employment of the groups, it was possible to find out whether or not the

Table 7–12 Differences between Training Laboratory and Group Therapy Patients on the Mailed Questionnaire Study

Follow-up Variables	Patient Training Laboratory ($N = 114$)	Group Therapy ($N = 76$)	Level of Significance
Rehospitalization			
Rehospitalized	16.2%	26.1%	NS
Employment			
Employed at time of follow-up	65.8%	50.0%	$p < .05$
Mean number of months employed during follow-up period	5.70	4.17	$p < .001$
Employment status after hospitalization			
Employed			
Returned to formerly held job	29.8%	28.9%	NS
Obtained new job	35.1%	21.1%	
Unemployed now			
Returned to formerly held job	4.4%	9.2%	
Obtained new job	18.4%	18.4%	NS
No employment	12.3%	22.4%	
Psychological status			
Mean Psychological Symptom Score	6.14	6.22	NS
Mean psychological ratings			
Anxiety	2.13	2.36	NS
Depression	1.93	2.07	NS
Tiredness	2.12	2.21	NS
Insomnia	1.90	1.92	NS

Follow-up Variables	Patient Training Laboratory ($N = 114$)	Group Therapy ($N = 76$)	Level of Significance
General condition *now* compared with pre-hospitalization			
Better	59.0%	57.0%	
Same	31.0%	38.0%	NS
Worse	10.0%	5.0%	
Problems with alcohol			
Reporting serious trouble	5.2%	2.6%	
Reporting possible problem	37.8%	29.0%	NS
Reporting no problem	57.0%	68.4%	
Physical symptomatology			
Mean Somatic Symptom Score	5.69	4.45	$p < .05$
Physical health *now* compared with pre-hospitalization			
Better	38.0%	46.0%	
Same	49.0%	40.0%	NS
Worse	13.0%	14.0%	
Social adjustment			
Mean Community Alienation Score	2.04	1.69	NS
Marital relationship described favorably	69.3%	66.7%	NS
Perception of change			
Did hospital program effect change?			
No, or no response	39.4%	42.1%	NS
Yes	60.5%	57.9%	
Unelaborated	7.0%	11.8%	
Physical treatment	7.0%	6.6%	
Self-development	21.9%	28.9%	
Interpersonal	24.6%	10.5%	$p < .05$
Length of stay			
Mean number of days on research ward	36.56	52.29	$p < .001$
Mean number of days in hospital after leaving research ward, but prior to discharge	11.91	7.42	NS
Mean number of days in hospital during follow-up period, if rehospitalized	10.32	19.78	NS

veteran returned to his old job, obtained a new one, or did not work at all. From Table 7–12 it is apparent that the two groups were alike in the number of men who returned to their previous employment and remained at this job. This was true of 30% of each group. Another 4.3% of the Patient Training Laboratory and 9.2% of the group therapy patients returned to a previously held job, but were unemployed at the time of the follow-up. The greatest difference between the groups appeared in the category, "obtained a new job and remained employed." Thirty-five per cent of the Patient Training Laboratory and only 21% of the group therapy were in this category. Obtaining a new job and being unemployed at the time of the follow-up was the situation for 18% of each group. Twelve per cent of the Patient Training Laboratory and 22% of the group therapy held no job at all during the follow-up period. Apparently, the differences between the groups on the employment variable were due to hospital experiences rather than to any pre-hospitalization claims on jobs or job-holding ability.

The measures of *psychological status* yielded highly similar results for both groups. On the Psychological Symptom Scale the Patient Training Laboratory patients reported a mean symptom score of 6.14, the group therapy patients a mean score of 6.22. As seen in Table 7–12, the scores for anxiety, depression, tiredness, and insomnia were nearly identical for the two groups. Patients in both groups reported about the same amount of change in their general condition as a result of hospitalization. Slightly more than half of both groups reported improvement. Nor did the groups differ in the degree to which drinking was a current problem. Of the Patient Training Laboratory sample, 11.4% reported serious problems with alcohol, 57.0% stated they had *no* problem with alcohol, and the remaining 31.6% admitted having some trouble with drinking. The group therapy group reported 3.9% had serious drinking problems, 68.4% had *no* problems, and 27.6% had some problems with alcohol.

The Patient Training Laboratory reported significantly more *physical distress* on the Somatic Symptom Scale than did the group therapy patients, with mean symptom scores of 5.69 and 4.45 ($t = 2.06$, $df = 189$, $p < .05$). In response to the question, "How does your physical health *now* compare with your health *before* entering the hospital," there was a tendency for the group therapy group to report feeling better. Although this is consistent with the findings that the group therapy group reported fewer physical symptoms, the difference between the groups was not statistically reliable.

No differences appeared in the reports of Patient Training Laboratory or group therapy patients about their social and interpersonal adjustment, e.g., on the feelings of community alienation scale, or in their marital relationships.

The two groups were quite similar in the over-all proportions of discharged patients who felt they had changed as a result of the hospital programs (66.7% for Patient Training Laboratory veterans and 61.5% for group therapy patients). The groups differed, however, in their reports of how they changed. Of the 61 Patient Training Laboratory patients who gave positive reports and who elaborated on how they changed, 8 offered physical explanations, 25 intrapersonal, and 28 interpersonal explanations. Of the 35 group therapy patients responding positively, 5 cited physical changes, 22 remarked on intrapersonal gains, but only 8 mentioned interpersonal gains. In other words, both groups emphasized psychological far more than physical gains, but the emphasis for the programs was different; a significantly higher proportion of Patient Training Laboratory patients stressed interpersonal gains, or conversely, a greater proportion of group therapy patients stressed intrapersonal accomplishments ($\chi^2 = 5.34$, $df = 1$, $p < .05$).

Finally, as in the field interview study, the Patient Training Laboratory patients were in psychiatric treatment for a briefer period of time —36.56 days as compared to 52.29 days for the group therapy patients $p < .001$). As might be expected, the variance for the group therapy patients was much greater since that program adapted the length of stay to fit the apparent needs of each patient. Nearly all Patient Training Laboratory participants stayed on their ward between 30 and 45 days; only 6 men stayed longer than 45 days. While many group therapy patients stayed about 30 days, 32 stayed more than 45 days, and one man remained 250 days.

Discussion

The somewhat disparate results yielded by the two follow-up studies make their interpretation ambiguous and require that the two research techniques be evaluated before appraising the comparative effectiveness of the two treatment approaches. This point is perhaps obvious since the results show that there were no significant differences between groups in the field interview, but that there were significant differences in several of the areas tapped by the mailed questionnaire.

The field interview offered distinct advantages in the assessment of subjective matters in that information was obtained by a trained interviewer from both the veteran and another person significant to him. The mailed questionnaire, on the other hand, obtained only the veteran's own self-report, subject as it may have been to his own biases and lacking the confirmation of another's point of view. It seems that, other things being equal, the field interview is superior, at least for such subjective data as that on psychological well-being or even for evaluating the extent of trouble with alcohol. For objective information—rehospitalization, employment, and number of days in the hospital—such differences between the research techniques did not matter.

The second consideration in appraising the techniques has to do with the size and representativeness of the samples. Here, there would seem to be clear advantages for the mailed questionnaire. It resulted in a much larger sample, and, perhaps even more important, it made it possible to gather information from former patients who were living away from the near vicinity of the hospital. The field interview was confined by practicalities to the Houston metropolitan area; unfortunately, this may have introduced a bias toward poorer post-hospital performance in that the most available Ss were those who were rehospitalized at the time of the follow-up. It is true that these most available patients were just as likely to have been contacted by the mailed questionnaire, but the generally larger sample provided a more widespread base. With these considerations in mind, it seems possible to regard the field interview as a pilot study and the mailed questionnaire as the main body of research.

An overview of the results of the larger sample (the mailed questionnaire) strongly suggests that the major advantage of the Patient Training Laboratory over the group therapy group is economic. The period of hospitalization for the Patient Training Laboratory group was shorter, more of them were employed during the follow-up period, and, of those who were employed in both groups, the Patient Training Laboratory men worked for a longer period of time. Each of these points needs further amplification. It is probable that the Patient Training Laboratory's advantages in the employment area are due to a greater emphasis placed on vocational matters during the training session. Discussion sessions were held with representatives of the Texas Employment Commission (Hanson, Rothaus, Cleveland, Johnson and McCall, 1964; Rothaus. Hanson, Cleveland, and Johnson, 1963). In addition, participants were trained through lectures, discussions, and role playing in ways of approaching employers about jobs. While specific information about this is lacking, it is likely that these techniques have had some impact, resulting in greater motivation for employment by the Patient Training Laboratory group, together with the acquisition of skills necessary to obtain and hold jobs. The results showed a tendency for more Patient Training Laboratory men to obtain new employment.

The finding that Patient Training Laboratory men stayed in the hospital a shorter period of time takes on meaning only when considered in the context of the other follow-up results. That is, a hospital could admit and discharge patients at a very high rate and show a low average length of stay, but, unless the shorter-stay patients did at least as well as longer treatment programs (as measured by follow-up criteria), no real advantage could be claimed. The Patient Training Laboratory experiment has shown that it is possible to shorten length of stay without sacrificing effectiveness of treatment. In all follow-up areas but one, the Patient Training Laboratory men did at least as well (and in those areas mentioned above, better) as the group therapy men. The one area of exception as that of physical symptoms in which the Patient Training Laboratory men reported a greater number of complaints. This difference may be a function of less attention given to chronic illness due to the shorter stay, a lesser emphasis on medical treatment in the training laboratory, greater initial physical symptomatology in the Patient Training Laboratory group, or any combination of these factors. This finding needs further study.

One other economic advantage of the Patient Training Laboratory is its ability to function with a smaller staff. This advantage is highly significant in view of the current manpower shortages in the mental health field. Although the Patient Training Laboratory requires a trained staff, their attendance is not necessary at all group meetings, thus freeing them to work with a greater number of patients. In human relations training in a psychiatric setting, the problems of patients are sufficiently severe to require the staff's careful acquaintance with individuals and awareness of each group's development. Whereas these demands limit the number of groups that can be worked with at one time, it is possible to work effectively with larger numbers of patients using a Patient Training Laboratory approach. A further saving in staff size in the Patient Training Laboratory results from the fact that no nursing service is provided on the ward during weekends or holidays. The participants govern the ward themselves and attend sick call on another ward if they become ill.

The absence of differences between the groups on the psychological well-being measures may be made more understandable by comparing these results with findings reported by Stone, Frank, Nash, and Imber (1961). For their sample of individual psychotherapy patients, followed for a period of five years, "improvement in discomfort occurred rather early, whereas improvement in social effectiveness . . . occurred less rapidly." They mention specifically that symptoms of anxiety and depression were alleviated rather rapidly. One conclusion can be drawn from the study by Stone, et al.—that regardless of what type treatment program has been utilized, the specific time at which changes are measured after hospitalization may be more important than any differences between programs. That is, the differences between short and long-time effects of any program may be greater than the differences between such programs. Measures such as anxiety and depression may be unreliable as indications of psychological well-being because of the multifarious effects of the many stresses occurring after hospitalization. If this is correct, serious doubt is cast on the use of such measures as anxiety and depression ratings in evaluating treatment programs. This means that more of the emphasis in the follow-up studies should be placed on such social effectiveness measures as employment or objective ratings of social participation. These measures would be less easily influenced by transitory difficulties arising in the individual's everyday life and would, perhaps, more nearly reflect his ability to weather these psychological storms.

In evaluating the effectiveness of the treatment program, Stone et al. (1961) have another point which is pertinent to the present study. They suggest that "a more nearly valid evaluation of different forms of psychotherapy might be in terms of their ability to accelerate improvement." They reason that since data suggest that various forms of treatment are indistinguishable after a lengthy period of time, the treatment of choice is the one that produces the greatest improvement most rapidly. According to these criteria, the Patient Training Laboratory results would be judged more satisfactory than those obtained by the group therapy. While there are significant differences in favor of the Patient Training Laboratory group at the time of the nine-month follow-up period, it seems quite likely, in view of the experience of other studies, that after three to five years these differences will disappear and the effectiveness of the groups will be indistinguishable. Should the two approaches then show equal effectiveness, the Patient Training Laboratory group would still have achieved equivalent results in a shorter period of time and at less expense.

8

A 9,9 Approach for Increasing

Organizational Productivity

ROBERT R. BLAKE AND

JANE SRYGLEY MOUTON

Factories are important building blocks in a production profit economy. From them come many of the important elements of modern
living. Their operations contribute many of the material comforts of
living. They also are an important source of salaries and dividends
that sustain family living and taxes that support government, education and needed welfare. The significance of smooth-running and
efficient factories in the operation of our society would be difficult to
overemphasize.

But not all factories are smooth-running and able to solve human
problems of production in an age of rapid technological change. For
instance, a factory may be faced with many problems of varying
severity. Its production is not high as compared with its competitors.
Its wage rates are out of line and profit margins razor thin. Departments that need to cooperate to get the job done are in conflict. Organization members have ideas that can improve the efficiency of
the operation, but they do not get used. Communication failures con-

NOTE. In this chapter, Blake and Mouton take us to the other end of our continuum
of learning goals, from personal learning to the problems of organizational change.
Blake has been one of the foremost innovators in adapting laboratory methods for
the resolution of intergroup and organizational problems. In this chapter, he and
Jane Mouton outline their approach and indicate how different training methods fit
into it.

The training methods described in this paper are not those commonly employed
in the T-group laboratory. Rather they are concerned with Grid team training of
the character pictured in *The Managerial Grid,* Houston, Texas: Gulf Publishing
Co., 1964.

cerned with the routine of day-by-day operations occur throughout the organization—up, down and laterally. Wage earners feel themselves to be "numbers," insecure people who, as they age, are becoming surplus due to technological and other advances. Foremen who have come up through the ranks are portraits of men of low morale, partly because people who are technically trained are replacing them, but also because those above them show careless disregard for their thoughts, feelings and attitudes. Higher management makes a decision today but reverses itself tomorrow. Union and management relations are in continuous conflict.

Let us go further. It might be said that this factory, faced with such difficulties, has been unable to solve its human problems of production. Its ability to survive in our competitive economic system is in serious doubt. To invest more money in modernizing its equipment or to build new equipment under these conditions would be risky. The operation of this factory presents a dismal picture. Perhaps the situation facing this factory is not common, but the difficulties it encounters are by no means exceptional. Not all factories are confronted with this wide range of symptoms of human failure, but in many a factory one or more of these problems is disturbingly visible.

The question is, "Under what conditions might the operation of this factory be shifted to attain higher production, to achieve union and management relations where the two groups are working together towards accomplishing common goals, to attain effective coordination between departments, to make better utilization of the ideas available to it, and so on?"

A Six-Phase Approach to Organization Improvement

The way to attain organizational improvement described here is *not* based on treating symptoms, such as union and management antagonism or low production. Rather, it is based on a correction of underlying causes of problems that come to the surface as union-management conflict, and so forth.

The primary goal is to change *patterns* of relationships between people and groups or between a group and the organization so that more effective problem-solving and greater production effort can occur throughout the entire organization. After this has been achieved, it can be expected that there will be an improvement in the *actual* operation of the factory—through detecting and correcting technical failures, making better economic or business decisions, doing a better job of conducting union and management affairs, or getting greater production.

The approach involves six successive phases. In these is considered the achievement of production requirements through mature interpersonal relationships that are integrated around the production purposes of the organization.

A learning program based on behavioral science laboratory experiments is the first phase. The program consists of a series of learning sessions in which all managerial members (and operational personnel, where feasible) examine theories of human behavior and participate in controlled experiments to test these theories. There also is face-to-face feedback in which each organization member learns how he and others are reacting to the experiments and to one another. Each participant is provided the opportunity to examine and to study a variety of alternatives for dealing with people in connection with production.

Team training, in the second phase, involves direct interpersonal feedback among actual work group members. These are people who have boss-subordinate relationships and who are on the same level in a work group. The aim is to examine and to resolve problems of communication, control, and decision making among those whose work requires unity of effort and close cooperation.

A third phase is similar to the second phase. There, however, the problems which are faced and resolved are between groups. This horizontal linking includes people from the same organizational level but from different groups who come into contact with each other in day-to-day activities. They are people who can accomplish their own production goals best when those from other units with whom they work are meshing their efforts with them in a coordinated way.

The entire managerial force sets broad organizational improvement goals in the fourth phase. The fifth phase is designed to bring about, in a concrete way, the organizational goals which were set in phase four and to correct the faulty problem-solving actions that were discovered in the earlier phases.

Once the strategy of problem solving and production improvement has been learned, the goal is to insure that it will be applied continuously until it becomes a stable way of organization life. Thus, the sixth and final phase is a stabilization period. Its aim is to insure that changes already achieved are maintained and that they have become firmly embedded into organizational operations.

The phases described are pictured as successive steps. In actual practice, various phases may occur simultaneously in different parts of the organization, or, depending on circumstances, a different order than that described may occur. The point to be emphasized is that greatest insurance that an organization improvement effort will be successful is possible when all of the phases described are included.

In a large industrial plant employing 3,000-5,000, the completion of these phases may require from three to five years, or even longer. The length of time depends on the intensity of the effort applied, the seriousness of the problems confronting the organization, and the degree of improvement sought.

Phase 1: Learning to Apply Behavioral Science Theory of Solving Problems of Work in a Human Laboratory

The program, designed to bring about the desired changes in an organization, begins with a series of learning sessions. The purpose is to focus attention of organizational members on how work is accomplished best through involving people in attaining production (Blake and Mouton, 1962a; Blake, Mouton, and Bidwell, 1962a). The aim is for managers to study and to understand behavioral science theory and research findings sufficiently well, and in such a concrete and personal way, that intuitive assumptions underlying habitual behavior can be replaced by sound managerial approaches for getting work done in a manner that arouses mutual confidence and respect. This is the purpose of Phase 1.

Many issues are examined, but two are dealt with in detail. One is concerned with power in supervision. Examined are the different ways in which power can be exercised in directing, controlling and coordinating the efforts of people engaged in production. The effects on production that are likely to result when different managerial approaches are used also are assessed.

The other issue deals with managing the conflict which is produced when people have different views of how to get work done. Issues examined include how to avoid win-lose competition and destructive conflict which works against organizational performance goals, and how to manage problem-solving situations where deliberation, debate and interplay of ideas are essential to obtaining maximum effective effort.

The framework of ideas employed in studying such problems in a behavioral science laboratory is quite complex. A brief description of the framework may help to orient the general approach. It is called *The Managerial Grid.*

The Managerial Grid

The Managerial Grid, Figure 8-1, identifies a variety of theories of managerial behavior. These theories are based on two ingredients.

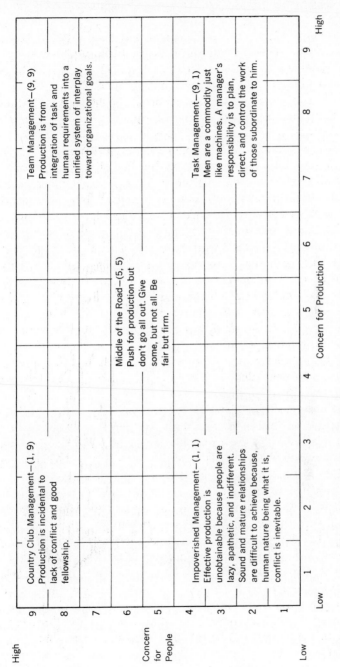

Figure 8-1 The Managerial Grid.

One is *concern for production*. The other is *concern for human relationships*.

Before going on, a word of explanation is needed about "concern for." This is not meant to indicate *how much* production is obtained, nor is it intended to reflect the degree to which human relationship needs actually are met. Rather, emphasis here is placed on the *degree* of "concern for," because action is rooted in basic attitudes. Here, what is significant is how much a supervisor is *concerned* about *production* and how much about *human relationships*.

The words *production* or *human relationships* cover a range of considerations. Attitudes toward production, for example, may be assessed through the number of creative ideas that applied research turns into useful products, procedures or processes, quality and thoroughness of staff services, workload and efficiency measurement, or units of output. Production is not limited to *things*. Its proper meaning covers whatever it is that people are engaged in accomplishing. In a similar fashion, human aspects of interaction cover a variety of different concerns. Included are concern for degree of personal commitment to completing a job for which one is responsible, accountability based on trust rather than force, self-esteem or the personal worth of an individual, desire for a sense of security in work, social relations or friendships with co-workers, and so forth. As will be seen, *concern for production* and *concern for people* are expressed in vastly different ways, depending on the specific manner in which these two concerns are joined together.

The *Managerial Grid* shows these two concerns and possible interactions between them. The horizontal axis indicates concern for production while the vertical axis indicates concern for people. Each is expressed in a nine-point scale. The number 1 in each instance represents the minimum. The number 9 represents the maximum.

There are 11 managerial theories which may be shown on this grid. Emphasis now will be placed on the corners and the mid-point. This will identify five theories. These extreme positions are seldom found in pure form, but they make clear cut examples to discuss, and then there are situations that approach rather closely one or the other of these positions. The other six theories will be examined later.

At the lower left corner of the Grid is the 1,1 style. This has the minimum of both *concern for production* and *concern for people*. Going up the Grid from the 1,1 style to the upper left corner is found the 1,9 style. Here there is maximum concern for people but minimum for production. In the lower right corner is 9,1. This style has a maximum concern for production and a mimimum concern for human relationships. In the upper right corner is the 9,9 style, which has a maximum concern for both human relationships and production. Then, in the center is the 5,5 style, which is middle of the road in both kinds of concern. Each of these five key managerial orientations is studied intensively in the Behavioral Science Laboratory. Perhaps the flavor of learning will be clarified by saying that each participant is aided to discuss which of these five is his own dominant theory, which is his second, or back-up theory, and so on.

The Laboratory Instructors

Through using methods of laboratory learning now available, line personnel, rather than academic behavioral scientists, serve as the faculty for each of the laboratory sessions. The advantages in doing so are several, but it is important to mention at least two.

One is that line members gain the opportunity to learn some of the skills required in effective teaching. Many would maintain that teaching skills are a critical characteristic of good managing, because a skillful manager is one who is able to aid others in learning strategies for solving problems effectively.

The second is that, when organization members take responsibility for such teaching, they also feel increased responsibility for seeing to it that the learning is *used in work*.

Phase 1 has a dual purpose. One purpose it serves is to motivate or to trigger, to create an awareness of and a readiness to dig into the human problems of production. Its other purpose is to provide a framework for thinking about managerial actions which can be used to replace intuitive and common sense rules of thumb that are widely, though not necessarily effectively, used to guide behavior (Blake and Mouton, 1961b).

The Behavioral Science Laboratory phase is not intended to contribute directly to operational improvement. Nevertheless, to insure maximum concreteness, key experiments in the laboratory learning phase are focused on diagnosing causes and cures for organizational problems. Problems studied may range in scope from matters such as "How to improve union-management relations," to "Identifying actions to be taken to improve plant P/L." By using problems of this sort as the basis for key experiments, organization members already are engaged, in a preliminary way, in exploring the kinds of issues which become central in Phase 3. Indeed, dramatic organization improvement comes about, even during Phase 1, when organization members are able to place a clear focus on issues which previously were vague and fuzzy and discussed only under informal conditions where no actions towards solving them were intended. Completion of this human laboratory sets the stage for the next phases.

Phase 2: Team Training

During Phase 1, organization members have developed greater awareness of barriers to improving production-human relations interactions and have some insight as to how to eliminate such barriers in order to attain heightened productivity/efficiency/satisfaction. However, the general principles and concepts and the direct interpersonal learning in Phase 1 best result in concrete implementation in daily work, when additional phases specifically designed to help in their application are introduced.

The second phase involves using the background knowledge gained from laboratory learning to take another step. The second step is for organizational members to apply learnings directly in analyzing their *own work group operations* on a tailor-made basis. The underlying reasons for doing so include the following considerations.

Significance of the Work Team

The fundamental building block of an organization is the *team*. Any given organization team is composed of those who work together to discharge that part of the total organization's work for which they share responsibility. Such teams have the basic elements of all groups. Included are a power system, group standards, some degree of group unity and goals, and, most important, relations within an environment containing, among other things, other groups—above, beside and below them. Given the above, the major purpose of Phase 2 is to increase team effort. To do this requires intensive examination and improvement, as appropriate, in the communication, control and decision-making procedures of each team of the organization.

A sound way to accomplish such a result is through *team training*. This training starts, most desirably, with the top team composed of the plant manager and his immediate subordinates. Since each subordinate is the leader of another team, the same review is completed in each of their teams. Thus, the procedure goes on down through the organization.

Most organization members participate in training in both the work team of which they are members and in the work team of which they are bosses. Through team training, members can evaluate actual difficulties existing among themselves which appear on the surface as problems of communication, control, and decision making. At a deeper level, the issues examined are concerned with problems of power and authority, win-lose competitiveness considered from an interpersonal point of view, and learning to confront directly those things that need to be discussed in order to produce truly effective problem-solving action.

Instructor-Moderator Team Training

Organization instructors aid teams to come to grips with the problems of interpersonal and group operations. The instructor in this case is a "moderator" from another team. With respect to the team he is aiding, he is an "impartial outsider." Usually the instructor-moderator also has served as a faculty guide in Phase 1. In Phase 2 he intervenes, as appropriate, to focus attention on how interactions among the team members, as they are taking place in the here-and-now, may be preventing members from solving their more basic problems of productivity for which they shoulder team responsibility. After this kind of review and analysis of problems preventing or limiting team effectiveness has been completed, members shift attention to problems confronting them in day-by-day operations. By this time it is likely that barriers to effective cooperation in work will have been spotted and dealt with in a constructive fashion. Commitment for change and improvement based on open understanding and common agreement is a near certain result.

Key Role of the Top Team

Emphasis here is placed on training of the top team of the organization first. Lower levels follow. It might be argued that if the top team has learned to work effectively, problems confronting the organization can be solved. Then, further training would be unnecessary. This line of thinking is based on the idea that the top team is the one responsible for designing a total structure and for operating the entire organization. If the relationship and decision-making problems existing among members at this level had been successfully worked through, according to the argument, it should be that the operations required of lower levels could be directed effectively. The formulation above is heavily 9,1 in its assumptions.

It is doubtful that any top man or top team can introduce change as effectively *without* the understanding and involvement from subordinate units of the organization as *with* it. Top-team members rarely are able to discharge *either* responsibility effectively, by edict or by a command decision that is 9,1, or even by 9,9 discussion and talk-through with lower levels, *unless* lower levels have learned to work by the same rules of the game. Neither the absence of edict or command decision, nor the use of involvement and talk-through, by themselves, decreases the need of the top team to involve subordinate levels directly in planning and accomplishing organizational objectives. In other words, a change in problem-solving *method* by the top team, which is not understood by other groups, does not solve the problem of commitment or integration of people around production among different levels of the organization. Rather, it becomes necessary for the kind of training described here as useful for the top team, to be applied throughout the organization.

Vertical Linking

When team training is initiated at the top and continued on downward through the organization, vertical *linking*, which can improve control, communication, and decision-making between levels, also is aided. The critical role of vertical linking has been cited frequently (Likert, 1961). Since a subordinate in the top team is supervisor of the next level down, one by-product of a team effectiveness review is improving relationships up and down the organization.

In summary, the second phase involves members of various work teams of the organization coming to terms with one another and with their common work goals. But team training is only a second step. Additional critical phases need to be taken if conditions under which *total* organizational effort is integrated toward higher level of efficiency and satisfaction are to be achieved.

Phase 3: Horizontal Linking

In Phase 2, the emphasis is primarily on the work team and on connections between work teams in the up-down hierarchy. However, many contacts between people and many problems of communication, control and decision making extend beyond work team boundaries. They go out in horizontal directions by reaching, in an interdependent way, into operations that lie within the boundaries of other teams. Included here are problems of interteam cooperation, such as between a technical division and operations, operations and mechanical services, the research and development component and operations, on the one hand, and sales on the other; between various line units and staff services such as the personnel department, purchasing, and so on. Also of importance, is a sound problem-solving orientation between management organization and union organizations (Blake and Mouton, 1961c). Ordinarily, problems of coordination are seen to be the responsibility of the heads of the various components involved in coordinating these efforts. However, great strides toward organizational improvement are possible by improving, through training, the conditions of cooperation among those engaged in day-to-day contact (Blake and Mouton, 1962b). The focus of Phase 3 *is on improving intergroup problem solving.*

Interteam Exchange

The training procedure involves each team developing two word pictures. One is of itself. The second is of the other team. Usually this is done with two teams at a time. Each team, in the beginning, works independently of the other. The relationship which exists between the teams is described in sufficient detail to insure understanding when one team pictures itself to the other. In addition, performance problems between groups are identified and reasons for them evaluated. Concrete plans for solving them are sketched out against a timetable. The timetable increases the likelihood that performance improvement, which has been planned, actually is achieved.

Strengthening the Positions of Foreman

Another variety of horizontal linking involves building sound relationships among individuals on the same organizational level but from different work groups. An example are foremen who are confronted with similar problems of supervision and responsibility but who come from different departments. Because such a grouping involves people from different departments, even different regions, it is likely they have no clear procedure for solving basic difficulties shared in common. A frequent result is that foremen in one area resist taking actions for which they carry responsibility, because they "know" others in different areas will shirk responsibility for doing so.

The goal of horizontal linking is to create stronger bonds between individuals at the same level in a factory culture. When this goal is not achieved, change or correction is sought through edict or command decision. A common result is that the problem goes "underground." By this way described here, solutions to problems can be tackled on a concreted action basis by people who are of the same rank in the organization but who do not have the same boss.

The procedure is to work directly with the operating problems. Because of the large number of people who may share common responsibilities at any given level, particularly at lower echelons of supervision, it often is necessary to work through representatives, say two selected to speak for 12 to deliberate the problems facing all. Representatives then return to their own work groups and report the deliberations on a talk-through basis. Thereafter they reconvene to summarize their back-on-the-job group discussions to other representatives, and so on. The cycle is: representatives meeting and deliberating, reporting their discussion to those they represent, summarizing back-on-the-job group discussions with other representatives, developing a solution to a problem, which is widely supported by all the same level. This cycle may occur again and again. Frequency is determined by the nature and severity of problems confronting any given level. Such a cycle may occur many times in the building of sound and effective horizontal linkages among all members of an organization at the same level. It may be used to solve many different kinds of problems, such as early quitting, too much control, housekeeping, safety.

The significance of horizontal linking as a way to improve organizational effectiveness would be difficult to overemphasize. The reason is that frictions across groups and negative attitudes towards other groups are most likely to be corrected if everyone who is affected is involved. In this way, the cultural background and traditions of action—such as the culture existing among foremen—can be modernized and kept abreast of the changing needs of organization.

Phase 4: Setting Organization Improvement Goals

While in each of the three previous phases contributions to organization improvement may be achieved, these phases also provide a necessary background for approaching and solving broader and deeper problems of organizational effectiveness. For example, in Phase 1, organization improvement goals constitute the laboratory experiments. In Phase 2, goal setting for team improvement already has taken place. If done well, improvement plans have already been made and implemented. Problems of coordination between teams on a horizontal plane have been focused on and solved in Phase 3. Now, in Phase 4, problems that are everyone's responsibility, and that can be solved best by concerted organization-wide effort and dedication, are dealt with. In Phase 4, then, attention is on problems that can be solved best when the entire organization is committed to solving them.

Defining Organization-Wide Issues

The fourth phase is one that gives meaning to the concept of planned change. It provides a mechanism for insuring that changes sought after not only *are* planned, but also are carried through. This is done by the entire organizational force working to define the attainable goals and to commit themselves to their accomplishment. The reason for setting organization-wide improvement goals is that some problems are so pervasive that an effective solution for them must involve every organizational member in a decision-making way, particularly at managerial levels. Included as examples are such broad issues as the character of union and management relations, cost control, safety, or the degree of over-all productive effort being applied in daily work activities.

Setting concrete improvement goals *is* practical. Only when all organizational members who share responsibility for bringing change about have the opportunity to contribute their thinking to the definition of realistic and obtainable goals can best results be obtained.

Procedural Steps

Discussion units in this phase are composed of diagonal slices of the organization. Such groups, perhaps 15 persons in each, identify and talk through to understanding and agreement the areas of organizational life where improvement effort will likely produce positive results. After this has been done, it is possible to summarize broad areas of agreement that have occurred in group after group. These then become a basis for an intensive total organizational change effort.

The diagonal slice group is used when the goal setting is organization-wide. The reason is that each person is exposed to the attitudes and the feelings of others from different departments and different levels while at the same time having the opportunity to share his own view with them. When agreement has been obtained through organization-wide participation, involvement and commitment and understanding are felt more clearly by each person. In this way, the *total* organization can set a new direction or shift an old one, rather than one part of the organization attempting to pull or force other parts its way.

Phase 5: Implementing Planned Change—The Phase of Direct Intervention

Depending on the size of the organization and on the amount of effort applied, the phases involving the Behavioral Science Laboratory learning sessions (Phase 1), team training (Phase 2), horizontal linking (Phase 3), and the setting of organizational goals (Phase 4) may require two years or longer to complete. Accomplishing the changes planned in Phase 4 may take as much as two or more years.

While the goal setting of Phase 4 is effective in identifying areas and developing readiness in individuals to achieve change, this phase, by itself, is insufficient to insure that changes planned are brought about. The reason is that many changes may involve highly concrete, detailed, and, sometimes, highly complicated coordination of efforts. Needed, to provide a blueprint of concrete actions required and to keep the effort on course, are task forces that carry the responsibility for guiding effort as the many concrete steps required to achieve changes are taken. Such task forces are composed mainly from the line organization. Those enlisted as members are people who know the problem best. As a result, they may or may not be the individuals who are in formal positions of leadership in the hierarchical organization.

The task force, it should be emphasized, is an action group. As soon as the improvements, toward which they guide action, have been achieved, they are disbanded.

During Phase 5, it has often seemed desirable to support the planned change effort by having a monitor or moderator, a neutral who can participate throughout the organization to aid individuals, teams and even the organization as a whole to achieve the goals of Phase 4.

Phase 6: Stabilization and Replanning

The final phase is a period for stabilization and for planning new organizational development steps. Almost without regard to the effectiveness of the previous phases, the tendency is for the organization as a whole to slip back in some degree to old patterns and traditional ways of behaving. These are likely to be ones which require less skill and less effort to apply and which afford more comfort because they are second nature. A period of time, perhaps as long as a year or so, is desirable after the completion of the first five phases to identify throwback tendencies, to initiate corrective action, and to identify new areas within which further organizational improvement effort is indicated. As throwback effects are noticed and deliberately assessed, continuous practice of newer kinds of performance over a period of time can lead to the newer patterns becoming habitual. The aim is not to increase organizational effectiveness by setting new directions, although the stabilization period may be the beginning of a new cycle which accomplishes this result. The primary effort is toward insuring that the changes brought about in the earlier phases actually are able to withstand the pressures toward regression.

A 9,9 Approach for Organization Improvement

The title given this paper was, "A 9,9 Approach for Organization Improvement." Why was the approach to improvement described as 9,9? Four critical assumptions regarding how improvement comes about undergird the presentation.

The first is that concepts which can guide action are needed for individuals to feel confident in efforts to behave in new and more effective ways. The Managerial Grid is a framework of concepts which is well suited for this purpose.

The second is that a 9,9 approach to any organizational activity is built on achieving cooperation through understanding of the issues involved and agreement that efforts toward accomplishing them are worthwhile. Coaxing people, as in 1,9, using the stick and carrot approach of 5,5, or the command decision/edict of 9,1 are poor substitutes for facing conflict and working through differences and attaining commitment to action through understanding and agreement.

A third is that engaging in new behavior frequently requires skills of a sort that can be and are practiced in the Behavioral Science Laboratory sessions. Such skills reinforce the total effort, but, in addition, they also can aid individuals in doing jobs on those parts of their work which are routine.

A fourth consideration, which makes the present approach to organization improvement 9,9 is that this approach is geared toward involving all organization members, in a committed way, to achieve improvement objectives.

The general approach described here has been applied in two manufacturing establishments. The general conclusion from these studies is that substantial organization improvement is possible through the utilization of the method described here (Blake, Mouton, Barnes, and Griner, 1964).

9

Sensitivity Training
and Community Development

DONALD C. KLEIN

This chapter is a progress report of the application of a modified program of sensitivity training to a community development program in Milltown (pseudonym), a small, one-industry New England town. The project was initiated in 1961. It has involved the management of the only company in town, teams of citizens, as well as consultants and trainers from the National Training Laboratories (NTL), the mental health program of the Massachusetts General Hospital (1961–1962), and the Human Relations Center of Boston University (1962 to the present).

The components of the program have included:

1. Initial interviews with individual community leaders.
2. Development of an independent group devoted to community betterment.
3. Meetings with a management advisory group.
4. Participation of citizen teams in the NTL Community Leadership Workshop during two successive summers.
5. Consultation by outside behavioral science resources in relation to the work of the community improvement committee.

NOTE. In this chapter, Klein describes the use of laboratory training methods with even larger client systems than organizations, namely an entire community. Important work has been done by NTL and its network members in the area of community development and the improvement of community functioning. Klein, who is one of the leaders in this development, describes here a case which illustrates the possibilities as well as difficulties of working with larger social systems.

Acknowledgement is gratefully given for the help of Mr. Donald Ehat in the outlining of this report and initial formulation of certain sections.

The tap root of much of sensitivity training is the need for effective participation in the groups and organizations composing a democratic society. As it has evolved, sensitivity training has had a heavy emphasis upon either the development of the individual, the facilitation of face-to-face groups through more effective participation of their members, or the improvement of organizations' efforts to deal with their myriad interactional problems. To be sure, these individual, small group, and organizational issues are part of the substance of community life. They are at a different level of magnification, however, from a focus upon communication, decision making, and action patterns occurring within the community as a totality.

Educators, health workers, political scientists, extension workers, and others are becoming more involved in a somewhat amorphous— but nonetheless potent—field known as *community development*. As in the case of some other movements (e.g. mental health) its practitioners and policy makers are moving ahead under a banner that symbolizes different things to different people. Community development has been viewed from many different contexts. These include a concern with emerging nations, with helping in the transition from a peasant to industrial society, with an attack upon economically underdeveloped or depressed areas, with the fostering of local leadership, with persuading local communities to merge their resources and talents for the greater good, and so on.

For the purposes of the program which this chapter describes, community development has been considered to encompass *work with community groups and entire communities for the purpose of assisting in the development of leadership skills, of fostering effective citizen participation in meeting economic, social, and civic needs, and of enabling optimal utilization of state and national resources from both government and voluntary bodies while strengthening local community initiative and autonomy.*

Shortly before the project was being considered, a modified sensitivity training labratory had been developed for community leaders, at Bethel, Maine. It was believed that the training could contribute to a community's development program through a five-fold impact on its participants:

1. Increasing their sense of community, by which was meant the readiness to view community events in terms of interacting forces and processes within a coherent whole.
2. Enlarging their definition of citizenship, by which was meant an increased ability to identify and respond to opportunities for effective participation in community events.

3. Enhancing their sensitivities and skills as citizen participants within groups and organizations.
4. Developing more sophistication and objectivity in their attempts to diagnose the forces and processes contributing to community problems.
5. Helping them to function more effectively as agents of change in situations where collaborative planning and effort is needed.

The community laboratory was initiated by NTL in 1960. Designed especially for paid and volunteer community workers, it has been concerned with understanding the community as a complex network of interaction between individuals and between groups, out of which social action comes. A continuing project committee has sought to find the most suitable mixture of the small group and community sociology fields.[1] A summary report of the 1962 program describes the training in the following manner:

The major elements in the design are:
Problem analysis sessions in which problems encountered by delegates in their own work are defined, possible causes explored, action alternatives clarified, and consequences of various alternatives assessed.
Sensitivity training sessions in which through a variety of procedures each involving thinking, doing, evaluating, and replanning, one may be able to increase his sensitivity to persons and to processes in groups.
General sessions or theory sessions in which ideas and research findings are presented to help clarify problem analysis and T-group experiences.
Special interest seminars and/or individual work and consultation in which problems can be worked through with the special resources of delegates and staff.

The report continues:

The combination of learning situations is ordered by the purpose of the laboratory and these more specific objectives:
Increasing understanding of the nature of the community, and of forces affecting communities.
Increased understanding of behavioral science theory, research findings, and methods as a way of increasing individual understanding and application.
Better understanding of the small group as the essential work unit in the community and of the factors influencing the effectivness of the small group.
More awareness of one's own behavior and its effect on individuals and groups—awareness of self as a part of the problem dealt with.
The training approach has been to emphasize simultaneously problem analysis (and the helping role since the community leader by definition is one

---

[1] The committee has been chaired by Dr. Edward Moe, now of the University of Utah Bureau of Community Affairs; John Glidewell, Washington University Social Science Institute; Weldon Moffitt, University of Utah; and Donald C. Klein.

engaged in giving and receiving help), sensitivity training (as a way to acquire understanding of one's self in one's problems and of forces operating in groups and in communities), and relevant theory.

In the theory sessions, the staff identified some of the forces at work in and on the community, significant dimensions of community analysis, promising models of community action, some of the problems of analyzing change, and problems of the consultant or the helper in the community. The problems of decision-making, community conflict, and power and influence were examined. And, ideas about the community in an age of rapid change were explored.

Communities are far more complex than organizations, for the most part. They confront those returning from training with less clear pathways whereby change can be achieved. Resistances to change are apt to be more formidable and yet less tangible.

For these reasons, NTL has encouraged participation by community *teams*. Community workers from the same agency have attended (e.g. urban renewal workers from a midwest city), as have groups composed of workers from several different agencies in the same locale (e.g. one group included a YMCA worker, an urban renewal specialist, and a group worker concerned with adolescent gangs). Two teams have attended from Milltown, including six citizens and one paid company public relations man.

A description of the community was written by the author following an initial series of visits in 1961. The following excerpts may help the reader form an impression of Milltown.

The community is small, with a concentration of power up to 1961 in the hands of a few persons, primarily the management of the single industry. The community is not impoverished; its inhabitants have a high income level, and health and welfare facilities are adequate to meet most needs.

Milltown's two thousand inhabitants are almost all dependent economically upon the mill located on the bank of a river, which it once needed for both power and transportation of raw materials. The town was established about 60 years ago by the company. Inhabitants include families of the workers who built the mill and many others who immigrated from elsewhere in the State and from Canada because of the chance for steady employment and high wages. The employees are members of several trade unions, which have never called a strike to enforce wage or other requests.

There is at present no other industry. Retail businesses are small and, for the most part, not highly successful. There are a few groceries, a fuel oil and hardware business, some restaurants, gasoline stations, and a women's clothing store. Other shops have gone out of business as residents turned to larger stores in a more cosmopolitan community nearby when automobiles and better roads combined to increase mobility. The inhabitants also turn to the larger community for hospital care, certain entertainment, and, in the case of the managerial group, for much of their social life.

In appearance the town is somewhat drab. Many houses are in need of paint. There are a few well-manicured lawns or homes with ambitious gardens or planting of trees and shrubs. However, many inhabitants own hunting cabins or camps on one of the many beautiful lakes or streams in the vicinity and during the summers spend much time away from the community.

A historical description of the Milltown project follows. The community problem was first brought to the attention of the National Training Laboratories late in 1960 when the newly appointed staff public relations man of the company came to ask for help in developing a program of encouraging community beautification. The mill, becoming increasingly dependent upon technical and management personnel with business and engineering training, had been facing increasing difficulty attracting qualified young men to such positions despite high salaries, an extremely low tax rate, and the possibility of occupying low rental and comfortable company-owned homes. New management had become aware of what was described as a deep reservoir of ill will towards the company for previous actions of a paternalistic and perhaps authoritarian kind in connection with community affairs. Citizens were suspicious of the company's intentions and did not believe that management was sincere in wishing their increased participation in town affairs. Residents were described as generally apathetic, unwilling to accept responsibility, uninterested in their town, unable to join together in any sustained action for organizational or community betterment.

Early in 1961 a meeting was held in Boston to consider the possibility of establishing a cooperative community development program which would involve the National Training Laboratories, the Massachusetts General Hospital (MGH) Department of Psychiatry, and the company. Among those attending were the president of the company and his staff public relations man, Mr. Smith (pseudonym), the latter being responsible for on-the-scene community organization efforts in Milltown, Curtis Mial, and Drs. John von Felsinger and Donald Klein of MGH.

From this meeting there came three objectives, which are excerpted from the memorandum of the meeting itself:

1. To assist the community . . . to initiate a long-range community improvement and development program. . . ;
2. To enable the citizens . . . to participate actively and responsibly in this community development project;
3. To assist the . . . Company, the only industry in the community, to participate effectively, supportively, and nonpaternalistically in this community program.

SENSITIVITY TRAINING AND COMMUNITY DEVELOPMENT 189

The Company contracted with NTL for:

1. A consultation service to enable the community to assess its needs and to make plans for initiating the long-range community development project. . . .

2. A leadership training service to assist citizens in the community, leaders in various organizations and institutions, and responsible personnel in the . . . Company to participate effectively and productively in this program.

NTL, in turn, secured the services of the author and the mental health group from the MGH to carry out the initial study and to consult with community leaders and company officials. From NTL the consultant on community action and leadership training was Mr. Mial.

In the light of the objectives, the consultants set up indices for evaluation of the program. It would be significant if:

1. The community group were able to stay together and develop effective working relationships.
2. There were reduction of mistrust and apathy within community relationships, particularly those between mill and town.
3. Participation in town government and community affairs were to occur among a higher percentage of the townspeople.
4. The area of concern of the community were extended so that citizens were able to see their community within the needs and interests of the larger geographic region of which it is a part.

At this meeting there was also suggested a three-step program which was projected through the following summer.

1. The author, with Mr. Smith's help, would carry out a preliminary fact-finding effort, talking to approximately a dozen community leaders about the town, its needs, and how they might be met. The results of the fact-finding would be shared with the leaders themselves, with top management, and with an advisory committee drawn from the next levels of management most directly connected with the mill and its operations.

2. Periodic meetings would be held with community leaders to explore possibilities of establishing a permanent committee to sponsor a long-range community development program. The company agreed to pay the costs for Mr. Smith's participation as a staff assistant to such a committee and to underwrite the participation of a team of citizens in the NTL Community Leadership Training Laboratory.

3. A reappraisal and planning meeting would be held following the summer to decide whether the basis for a continuing program

had emerged and, if so, to establish guidelines and responsibilities for its implementation.

Following the Boston meeting, Mr. Smith talked with key people in mill management to discuss the nature and objectives of the project and to secure names of people who might fit into the community leader category. An effort was made to include non-management people in the list, though it was recognized that there might be some initial biases.

Mr. Smith then contacted twelve people who seemed in his judgment to be most representative. He explained the project and secured their consent to be interviewed by the author. It was possible for him to spend between one and two hours with each of the twelve establishing a relationship and conducting his own interview. These discussions covered two broad areas: (1) what were some of the problems in mill-community relations and how had they developed over the years; (2) what could he and others do to develop better mill-community relations and to promote more effective community leadership outside management ranks.

The first visit by the author to Milltown took place in March. A meeting was held with the management advisory group, which included the vice-president for production, the vice-president for materials, and the vice-president for finance as well as their assistants. This group raised many questions about the project. Recognizing that they might feel criticized by the new president for the way they had handled community relations, the consultant attempted to generalize the problem, pointing out that communities elsewhere were facing similar problems. He also helped the group set up some ground rules for the project, chief among them being the rule of confidentiality. The group accepted the fact that Mr. Smith and the consultant would be feeding back only general information from the study and that no individuals would be quoted. By the end of the meeting several individuals were making their own observations about problems which existed and the group as a whole seemed to be interested in the success of the project.

During the same visit, the author and Mr. Smith, together with the new personnel officer of the company, met with the twelve community leaders, who by that time had been dubbed "The Twelve Apostles" by the others in the town. Mr. Smith explained why the company had a stake in community development and interpreted his own role. The author indicated why as a mental health specialist he was interested in the project and said that he would be willing to serve as a consultant to the community leaders' group if they so desired. He made it clear that he would assume responsibility as a professional to remain with the program only so long as he felt that all concerned were working for the interests of the community. The latter point was made in response to a frank question about how neutral the consultant could be if he were being paid by the company. The author added that he would accept his pay from the community leaders' group if a means were found.

The group included: (1) A long-time resident, former principal, and active leader in several women's clubs; (2) the wife of a company engineer, college-educated, organizer of the Parent-Teachers Organization, resident for 15 years; (3) the former head of the labor council, a mill employee and native of the town; (4) the Catholic priest; (5) the Methodist minister of four years; (6) a native of a nearby community and lower management employee of the mill; (7) the physician, Health Officer and company doctor who lives and practices in the town; (8) the principal of the high school and resident of a nearby community; (9) the chairman of the town council, manager of the small local power company; (10 a native of the community, union member, active in little leagues; (11) the magistrate, a mill employee and union member; (12) the plant engineer at middle management level, and part-time salesman of prefabricated homes.

The group agreed that many worthwhile projects sponsored by leaders and groups in the community have been frustrated by a variety of causes, running from indifference through suspicion of the company and the feeling that management penalized independent leadership that threatened to emerge. Much time was spent in rehearsing past grievances. The group then discussed ways in which management attitudes had apparently changed recently.

It was felt that the group should continue to meet. The consultant emphasized the need to build an effective team before taking action on any project. The group agreed that it should try to avoid the fate of other committees which had taken on projects, then failed with them. It was felt that two more people should be added to make the gathering more representative; these were a native and present chairman of the labor council, and a long-time resident, successful merchant who is generally seen as being completely independent of any community factions.

During March and April, the author completed interviews at their homes and places of business with fourteen community leaders plus, in some instances, their wives and, in one case, the son of a respondent. Cooperation generally was good, though a few people remained somewhat reticent throughout. A highly informal and open-ended interview was used. It covered the following areas:

1. The individual's perception of his own role in the community.
2. Major problems which the individual felt the community was facing, and had faced in the past; how these problems were being met and how they were met in the past.
3. Major residential groupings within the town (a map was used on which person traced area boundaries), and the individual's image of each of the areas, its composition, status in the town, etc.
4. Directions in which respondent believed the community development project should be moving.
5. Nature and degree of company participation in community affairs which the individual believed to be desirable.
6. Distribution of social status and power among residents (each person was asked to name up to ten people whom he would wish to involve in a community project in order to insure its general acceptance in the town).

The consultant was most interested to observe that under the impetus of the project's initiation certain of the leaders already were seizing opportunities for constructive community action. As an example, for the first time in the history of the town, a citizen's group had prepared and distributed to all voters a mimeographed description of the warrants to be taken up at the Town Meeting in late March. Attendance at the Town Meeting was far greater than in previous years.

By June, a verbal report, supported by a written summary, was given to the group of interviewees, to the management advisory group, and to the President of the company. This report summarized recent changes in the community, emphasized the existence of widespread fear and distrust towards mill management, and pointed up a community self-image of inadequacy. It concluded that town residents were deeply interested in their community, but were discouraged by their past inability to work together for common objectives. The report suggested that there was need for community leaders to take the time to develop stronger working relationships before tackling specific projects. The function of leadership training was emphasized.

During the late spring, the informal group of community leaders, originally known as the Twelve Apostles and now expanded to fourteen members, formed themselves into the Milltown Improvement Committee. This body turned its attention to an inventory of major needs in the community and offered itself to the company as an advisory group with regard to new projects in the community (e.g. housing) that the mill might be contemplating. Mr. Smith of the company was asked to continue to serve as a resource to the Committee and the author agreed to be a consultant.

In June, the Committee held a public meeting at which the new president of the company gave an address. He outlined the reasons why the company was promoting community leadership, emphasized the need for change in the town in order to recruit professional and management personnel, and pointed out the interdependence of Milltown and surrounding communities. Shortly after this, the company announced its new housing program whereby partial help would be given to home builders. The Committee also sent its first team of three members, plus Mr. Smith from the company, to the community leadership training laboratory at Bethel. The group included the former head of the labor council, the present chairman of the labor council, and the wife of the company engineer.

Upon the return of the team from the 1961 Bethel program, events moved rapidly. In the fall, the decision was made to continue company support for the program. Because of cost and distance factors, the MGH agreed to assume principal responsibility for continuing consultation to Mr. Smith and the community leaders.

The Committee turned its attention to the community's need for a planning board and a town planner. Steps were taken to bring this need to the voter's attention at the spring town meeting. Meanwhile, individual members of the Committee took a number of actions designed to stimulate community participation. The Chamber of Commerce was reactivated, as was the community council made up of delegates from all groups and organizations. Lists of candidates were recruited for town council, school committee, and other town offices. For the first time in town history, a town council was elected in March 1962 that did not include a member of top management.

To make itself more representative, the Committee replaced old members with new people from previously unrepresented groupings in the town. Replacements became necessary when three people left the group, dissatisfied with its progress, its emphasis upon "just talk" and its unwillingness to take all-out action on a single project.

Some members who stayed on also wished the group to take action and to have a definite project for which it could gain recognition by townspeople. A few people, including two of the Bethel participants, wished the Committee to devote itself largely to providing mutual support to its members and an opportunity for a frank exchange of views on a highly personal level. Still others preferred that the Committee serve the community primarily as a study rather than action group, looking into problem areas and needs and stimulating appropriate groups to work when needed on problems. For a variety of reasons including transportation difficulties, Mr. Smith's uncertainties about his own future role in the project, major shifts in management within the company, and dissension within the Committee, the consultant's services were not used intensively through the late winter and spring, 1962.

In early spring, Mr. Mial and the author together visited Milltown to talk with Mr. Smith and the Improvement Committee about the future of the program. Questions were raised about the nature of human relations training and its relationship to a community development program. Some of those who had not attended Bethel the summer before questioned the Milltown team's apparent preoccupation with process issues. They felt the team had not explained the training well and had not returned with concrete help for the Committee and the town.

Nonetheless, the second Milltown team attended the Community Leadership program in 1962. It included the original committee member who is active in little leagues and other youth activities, as well as two people not on the original committee: an electrician in the plant and the wife of one of the vice-presidents. Upon their return, the two men became involved in long-range planning for the physical development of the town, as members of the newly formed planning board. The female team member became increasingly involved in school matters and ended up on the school committee.

In the months which followed, the Committee considered a variety of issues of current and long-range interest to the town. For example, the extension of water and sewer lines to a new development of homes had been defeated at a regular town meeting; the matter was revived through the efforts of Committee members and the extension was passed at a special town meeting. The group also continued to support the efforts of the new Town Planning Board, for which it had worked originally, to cope with criticism about the speed at which it was moving in dealing with highly involved issues that never before had been confronted as town responsibilities.

By spring 1963, the Committee was discussing the issue of whether a new shopping center should be encouraged, and, if so, where it might best be located. The group worked hard to involve other townspeople in considering both placement and financing of the center. In the end the company decided to take action without reference to the Committee's involvement or the efforts of the Planning Board to establish a total long-range physical development plan for the town. At about the same time, the group received another disappointment when the team of public school administrators that had accepted its invitation to attend the 1963 Community Laboratory at Bethel moved to new jobs in other towns and were not available for the training experience.

By this time, the majority of the Committee agreed that it would be desirable to involve the entire community in an appraisal of town needs and resources. The decision was made to enlist citizen help in planning and conducting a community self-survey. Representatives of the Committee discussed the proposal with mill management and the author.[2] The company at this time considered a budget for the next year's program, and granted in advance a total sum to be administered by the Committee. The author, who in the fall of 1962 had joined the faculty of Boston University, was now Director of the University's Human Relations Center, an interdepartmental resource for the application of the behavioral sciences. When the grant was made, the Committee contracted with the Center for consultation in developing the self-survey, including use of the University's Computer Center for tabulation of data. According to present plans, data will be collected from each family unit by volunteer interviewers, the latter to be oriented for their task in a workshop developed by the survey consultant, Mr. Donald Ehat, a graduate fellow of the Human Relations Center. To communicate results to the town, a reporting program involving a workshop and one or more public meetings is planned. The workshop is intended as an extension of leadership training and as an opportunity for citizens to discuss their mutual concerns and to develop specific plans for action where indicated. The public meetings are intended as a means of stimulating general interest, understanding, and involvement. Through the survey, the Committee already has brought from forty to fifty more people into direct contact with its work.

Rather than sending another team to the Bethel program, the Committee is now considering the possibility of sponsoring its own leadership training program in Milltown, using NTL resources for the training faculty. No decision has been reached about whether or not to proceed with such a project and, if so, how best to synchronize it with the survey and its reporting sessions.

---

[2] Mr. Smith decided not to go on in this aspect of community relations work. It was decided to proceed without an on-the-scene staff person. This change presented some difficulties which are not taken up in this report.

Evaluation

In the spring of 1964, a team spent three days in Milltown[3] interviewing past and present Committee members and other citizens and gathering other data in an effort to develop a retrospective analysis of community change since 1960. Respondents reported the following (partial) list of developments:

(1) *Economic*: More people shopping in town because of the new shopping center; new shopping facilities (hardware store and laundromat).

(2) *Government*: Increased number at town meetings; new recreation committee; new planning board; school trustees increased from 3 to 5 members; town assumed responsibility for the library from the mill; labor and management people elected to town council; more people speaking out and voting; more people of greater variety of backgrounds in the town running for office.

(3) *Schools*: Changes in curriculum identified by respondents as improvements; more money for teachers' salaries; introduction of counseling and guidance person; more students finishing high school and going on to higher education.

(4) *Housing*: More interest in property; new section of homes developed; company's assistance plan for private home development.

There is no doubt that change has occurred in Milltown, but which of these changes would not have occurred if there had been no community development program, and which would not have occurred if there had been a different kind of program in which sensitivity training had not been a feature? There are no definitive answers to questions like this. The best we can do is offer participant observations about the processes which have occurred and professional judgments about apparent links between components of the program and observed outcomes.

Some degree of certainty can be offered in discussion of certain of the indices put forth at the beginning of the program:

It would be significant if the community group were able to stay together and develop effective working relationships. Despite many travails and a persistent feeling on the part of most members that the Committee had failed to become a sufficiently effective action arm of the community, the improvement group *has* maintained itself,

---

[3] Members of the team were Donald Ehat, Charles Ferguson, and Wendy Wyatt, graduate students in adult education or psychology, also associated with the Human Relations Center.

has been able to meet regularly, recruit new members, and develop an atmosphere of openness and frankness of communication rarely found in community organizations. However, the group has not been able to resolve a pervasive conflict between those with sensitivity training experience, who are seen by the opposition as wishing to be concerned only with process, and most of the rest of the Committee, who are seen by the others as valuing results and achievement to the exclusion of the welfare of group members.

It would be significant if there were reduction of mistrust and apathy within community relationships, particularly those between mill and town. There has been considerable amelioration of the pervasive, intense hostility and mistrust originally felt by citizens towards management. Few people now express the feeling "The mill always has run things; why should we do anything?" It is harder to gauge the extent of change in feelings and attitudes between factions outside the mill. However, disagreements now seem to be expressed more openly, and with less of a sense that long-standing bitterness is being rephrased and nurtured by the expression.

It would be significant if participation in town government and community affairs were to occur among a higher percentage of the townspeople. Marked change has occurred in citizen participation in town affairs. Attendance at annual town meetings has increased at least three-fold, although population has remained virtually constant. More candidates are running for public office, such as town council and school committee. The educational level of those who run and are elected is higher than before. A town planning board has been formed by vote of town meeting and the recreational and library programs for the community, once the responsibility of the mill, now have been placed under the aegis of appropriate town boards.

It would be significant if the area of concern of the community were extended so that citizens would be able to see their community within the needs and interests of the larger geographic region of which it is a part. At the outset of the program, Milltown residents felt that their community was on the losing side of implicit competition with an older, more established, larger, nearby town. The latter's stores are more diversified; it possesses more recreational facilities; its homes include many that are larger and more striking; its history and traditions go back to colonial days; its industry is more diversified. Moreover, Milltown is dependent upon its neighbor for the services of the general hospital, and both communities are part of the same school district. Milltown residents tended to feel that the other community's schools were favored by the administration, and there was some dissatisfaction with the decision to locate the hospital outside Milltown. There also was bitterness over the fact that many new management people chose to live in the other community, and that almost all Milltown people found it necessary or desirable to do a great deal of their shopping outside their own town.

At the time of the initial interviews with townspeople, there was a general feeling that Milltown must become more autonomous and less dependent upon its neighbor. Something must be done about improving shopping facilities, and, most important, housing must be improved and people encouraged to move into Milltown. Finally, there was an apparent unwillingness to become concerned with the needs and problems of the rival community, or for that matter, of the region itself. The problem was not that Milltown needed to join with its neighbors. The problem was that Milltown needed to stand on its own and become as good or as better as its neighbors in all respects.

Today there is still a great deal of localistic feeling in the town. It is expressed by resentment against the company when it hires workers from outside the community. It also is expressed by the feeling that too many newcomers are being hired for management positions, and that the community is changing too rapidly to suit residents of long standing. Nonetheless, there also appears to be a growing recognition of the inevitability of change and the need to adapt to it. And, a few citizen leaders are eager to participate in country-wide activities designed to improve the economic situation of the area and to extend the program of community development and leadership training beyond Milltown's boundaries. An example of this is the readiness on the part of a few members of the improvement committee to encourage participation of people from nearby towns in any leadership workshop which the committee itself may sponsor in Milltown during the months ahead.

Many of the changes probably would have occurred without the intervention of sensitivity training, consultation from the outside, and the deliberate development of a community committee. How could there not have been an increase of citizen participation when company management clearly signaled its intention to foster such initiative? And certain of the changes in shopping facilities and housing were the direct result of company action.

The program probably is best conceived as part of, rather than distinct from, a process of change that already was gathering momentum at the time of the arrival of new management. The interviews with key citizens manifested management's desire to establish two-way communication. The company obviously was investing time of its personnel (i.e. the public relations man) in the project. Consulting help at that point probably made a significant contribution since it assisted in the company's formulation of its reasons for seeking community improvement. The consultant's report itself became a meaningful communication to management. That it was heard was reflected in the president's talk the following week at an open meeting of townspeople.

It is difficult for all concerned, including the consultants, to gauge the contribution of sensitivity training as reflected in the behavior of individuals both inside and outside the committee. There is no doubt that the committee functions at a level of openness that is rarely found outside a T-group. Moreover, individual members appear to have been influenced and helped to learn by the feedback they have received. Finally, the committee has been able to provide frank and apparently accurate reflection of community sentiment that has guided the company in certain of its actions.

It is true that the members of the committee so far have been unable to integrate the needs of process and task-oriented subgroups. The recurrent theme "We never accomplish anything" reflects reality insofar as the accomplishment of specific projects by the total committee is concerned. However, it also may be a reflection of one of the basic concerns of the community—that its citizens really cannot be trusted to work together and follow through on projects. Sensitivity training is believed by the others to have blocked the development of task orientation. Perhaps, it is nearer the truth to say that both the process and task people so far have tended to avoid a commitment to action and the possibility of an unequivocal failure experience.

The consultants believe that sensitivity training has helped individual participants to function with greater effectiveness both in the Committee and in the community. Two of the six citizen participants at Bethel are now chairman and secretary of the Committee. All but one of the others are active in the group, and that one left Milltown because her husband was transferred by the company. Those who have been to Bethel have been elected to the town planning board and the school committee, and have reactivated existing groups such as the PTA. They have enabled the improvement committee to develop an awareness of its own processes and have helped create a situation in which many of the conflicts and cross-currents of the town have been able to be expressed without the total disruption of the group.

This report, like the process of change in Milltown, must perforce be open-ended. A complex case experience of this kind perhaps never can be fully assessed. However, the consultants have felt that despite the many difficulties the presumption of constructive intervention by the methods used is great enough to warrant attempts at replication elsewhere.

10

Principles and Strategies
in the Use of Laboratory Training
for Improving Social Systems

Introduction

In this part of the book, we have been examining the uses of laboratory training in improving social behavior. We have identified two main target or client systems for the laboratory training. One is the *individual*, his growth, interpersonal competence, and self-actualization. The other is a *social system*, usually a formal organization or some subsystem or part of it.

In this chapter we will focus on the *organization* as a change target. It is with social systems (and their subsystems) that the *strategic* problems of laboratory training become manifest and where it is so crucial to understand the fit between laboratory training values and organizational goals. Where the individual is concerned, the problem of learning or change is ostensibly simpler; he can reject or accept, learn or not, without undue perturbation. When it comes to using laboratory training to change organizational systems, the strategic problems become impressive and complex with seemingly untold unanticipated consequences and risks. We propose here to examine some of the issues and dilemmas surrounding the use of laboratory training in effecting organizational change with the hope that increased understanding will lead to more effective utilization.

An Issue: Yogis and Commisars. Let us take a short detour and discuss a general issue which lies behind the recent impetus to use laboratory training in improving social systems. We stated at the beginning of this chapter that the individual and social system represent the twin change objectives of laboratory training. In fact,

201

these goals reflect an interesting and ubiquitous tension—rarely stated as such, but always present—concerning the general direction of laboratory training. Over the years, since the beginning of laboratory training, the conflict has taken a variety of forms but its potency for arousing staff debates or arguments over training design or staff strategies has been monumental.

It is hard to state exactly what *the* issue is, but it is very reminiscent of Koestler's distinction between the Yogi and the Commisar, between those who turn *inward* for insight and nirvana and those who turn *outward* for social salvation. It is the difference between those who believe in the manipulation of external forces, such as legal, technological, economic, political factors and those who look to the personality, self-actualization or the individual for ultimate social improvement.

In the past eighteen years or so of laboratory training's existence, almost all training designs and strategies have, tacitly or explicitly, reflected this conflict. The debate takes different forms: sometimes it appears in the guise of theoretical preferences, such as Lewin vs. Freud or self-actualization vs. organizational improvement; sometimes the argument oscillates between utopianism and existential despair. Most often, it is argued in terms of : "Who is the client," the organization or the individual.

For the most part, the dialogue which the debate has generated has been useful insofar as it has lifted up for analysis certain crucial issues such as: (1) the problem of transfer of learning from the laboratory culture to other cultures, the durability of training effects of the individual *after* the laboratory; (2) the relationship between self-enhancement and organizational improvement, if any; (3) the ethical-normative-value issues of transporting laboratory values into the fabric of the organization. We are a long way from resolving any of these issues, but one fortunate outcome of the debate is the increase in research and the improvement in conceptualization that it has forced.[1]

One other outcome, less perceptible but equally real and hopeful, is a decrease in the polarization of the issue, a recognition from both sides of the influences of the other.[2] Yogis are getting better acquainted

---

[1] In this next part, Part III, we will review some of the recent research. The reader is invited to read the excellent summary of research reported by D. Stock in Bradford et al. (1964).

[2] See the chapter by K. D. Benne et al. (1964) for an excellent history and development of laboratory training.

with the matrix of organizational factors and Commisars are becoming interested in personality factors.

The shift in orientation from regarding solely the individual as the ultimate client to regarding the organization, or some other social unit, as the ultimate client is a fairly recent development. Before the late 1950's[3] laboratory training was generally confined to a cultural island where strangers gathered, underwent an intensive experience, and abruptly left—again, as strangers. It was difficult enough to evaluate the effects of the laboratory on the individual delegate; it was practically impossible to trace the effects on the organization. What data there were implied that the individual could not even maintain his own *self*-changes within the organization, much less modify it.

The predicament is real: How do you gain the advantages of a cultural island and still transfer competencies and values internalized at the laboratory? Put another way, we can ask: Can you insure lasting change of the individual without also changing the social fabric (norms, policies, values) of the organization.[4]

The predicament has been solved over the past several years, as the preceding chapters have indicated, by bringing laboratory training to the organization rather than the other way around. In other words, instead of sending individuals of a particular organization to a stranger laboratory, the organization has set up, in one form or another, its own program, or has sent teams.

But introducing laboratory training into the climate of a formal organization (such as a hospital or factory or university or ship) brings about a set of strategic questions and raises certain issues of social change. In this chapter, we will discuss the background and perspectives on the use of laboratory training for changing social systems and consider the elements that make for its successful adoption by social systems: the state of the target system or subsystem, the role and competence of the change agent, and the strategies of implementation. After presenting the elements that lead to success, we will discuss three cases of failure. This chapter then ends with some propositions about the uses of laboratory training in effecting social change.

---

[3] We use this date as a crude baseline because the influential work of Shepard and Blake at Esso (1960) started about 1958–59.

[4] In Chapter 17 we state our hypotheses about the effects of different laboratory characteristics on unfreezing, changing, and refreezing.

Background and Perspectives on the Use of Laborataory Training for Changing Social Systems

Why This Recent Impetus toward the Use of Laboratory Training for Organizational Improvement

Obviously, there are many causes to consider in the emergence of any social phenomenon. Similarly, in order to understand the use of laboratory training as an organizational instrument, many social forces must be mentioned. Labor supply, the professionalization of management, automation, the growing complexity of the enterprise, the large-scale and sprawling quality of organizations in conjunction with the need for better communication and decentralization, the improved education of the worker and the changing population characteristics of our work force, the network of boundaries and transactions which clogs up the turbulent environment of the organization and a host of other factors must be included even in a superficial survey.[5] For us, the crucial factor is the inadequacy of present day organizations to cope with the complexity of rapid change and problems of human collaboration. Adaptation and collaboration are two of the main problems confronting contemporary society, and our organizations will fail or succeed depending upon their mastery of these two tasks.

This is only a part of the explanation. The inadequacies of bureaucracy have been examined in detail by many organizational theorists for a number of years. And they have produced countless thoughtful suggestions and ideas about a new vision of social architecture which would be more in keeping with what is known about human motivation. *The point is that laboratory training provides the instrument whereby the normative goals and improvements set forth by organization theorists and practitioners of organizations can be achieved.*

Let us take some examples to clarify our meaning. Take the problem of *intergroup conflict*. There is an urgent need to understand the network of interdependencies which stems from the myriad of specialties and complexity of technologies. When we talk with managers of large-scale operations, they frequently mention intergroup conflict and collaboration as one of their main problems. From a theoretical viewpoint, Likert (1961) arrives at the same conclusion and suggests the importance of a "linking pin," a mechanism for integrating groups that are work related. *But how is this mechanism developed?*

---

[5] See Bennis (1963) for a more detailed discussion.

Or take the problem of *authority and leadership* in organizations. McGregor (1960), in particular, has focused in his writings on the archaic workings of authority systems in bureaucratic structures. What is now needed, asserts McGregor, are systems of collaboration, of colleagueship between superiors and subordinates, not the blind use of controls and coercions. What we now need is increased autonomy, not dependencies and counterdependencies. *But how are systems created and people changed so that bosses trust enough to give their subordinates more autonomy, and how can subordinates learn to trust so that they can rely on self-control and collaboration?*

Lewin (1947), Allport (1945), and others have, for some time, produced evidence and arguments which show that as individuals participate directly in the decisions that are relevant to their work and life, they develop a higher state of morale and implement the decisions more effectively. *But how do organizations develop better and more responsive mechanisms for participative management?*

One final example: Argyris (1962) and others have insisted that *interpersonal competence* is a necessary ingredient in the role of a manager. He must be able to size up a situation, be aware of human factors impinging on a situation and develop a diagnostic sensitivity as well as behavioral flexibility in dealing with human problems. *But how do managers and other practitioners develop this interpersonal competence?*

The point of these examples is this. Ever since the historic studies of Mayo and Roethlisberger at Western Electric, there have been many profitable revisions and suggestions developed to improve the operations of the human organization. We have mentioned some of these in the examples above: better systems of collaboration, of adaptation, of authority, greater interpersonal competence. There was no shortage of criticism or prescription. The problem was that there had been no organizational mechanism capable of implementing these suggestions. Laboratory training appeared at the time when formal organizations were most pressed for revision, for change. *It provided an instrument whereby these normative goals and revisions could be translated into practice.*

What Are the Conceptual Goals of Laboratory Training with Respect to Organizational Change

We have just been discussing the growth of laboratory training in terms of the needs and problems of the managers and practitioners, as they saw them. Now we want to shift our emphasis to the *change agents* who have collaborated with these target systems. What do they have in mind as change goals?

Before answering this question, it might be useful to say a few words about the idea of a change agent. In 1963 *The New York Times* ran a large, classified advertisement announcing a search for "Change-Agents." As far as we know, the advertisement marks the first time this awkward term has been used so popularly—or with such obvious recognition—to a lay public. It is a rather new term and is used in many different ways. We are using the term change agent to refer to a person or group, practitioners or social scientists, who are using the theory which underlies laboratory training in order to improve the functioning and effectiveness of organizations. Later on, we will go into more detail about change agentry, but for the moment we will return to our original question: What do they have in mind as change goals? [6]

Although each change agent has in mind a set of unique goals, based on his own theoretical position and competencies as well as the needs of the target system, roughly speaking there are some general aims which most change agents would agree to.[7] Argyris provides a graphic model which can serve us as an example. In Figure 10-1 he shows (at the far left) the value system which dominates modern organizations. These values, basically impersonal and task-oriented and denying humanistic and democratic values, lead to nonauthentic relationships. These nonauthentic relationships tend to be coercive, phony, static, unhelpful, and basically incomplete; that is, they do not permit the natural and free expression of feelings which often must accompany task efforts. These nonauthentic relationships, then, lead to a state which Argyris calls "decreased interpersonal competence," a result of the shallow and threatening state of the relationships. Finally, without effective interpersonal competence among the managerial class, the organization is a breeding ground for mistrust, intergroup conflict, conformity, rigidity, and so forth, which in turn lead to a decrease in whatever criteria the organization is using to measure their effectiveness.

This is the basic paradigm: Bureaucratic values tend to stress the rational, task aspects of the work and to ignore the basic human factors which relate to the task. Managers brought up in this system of values are badly cast to play the intricate human roles now required of them. Their ineptitude and anxieties lead to systems of

---

[6] For a full discussion of change agents, see Lippitt et al. (1958) and Bennis et al. (1961).

[7] For a more complete and detailed statement, see Bennis (1963).

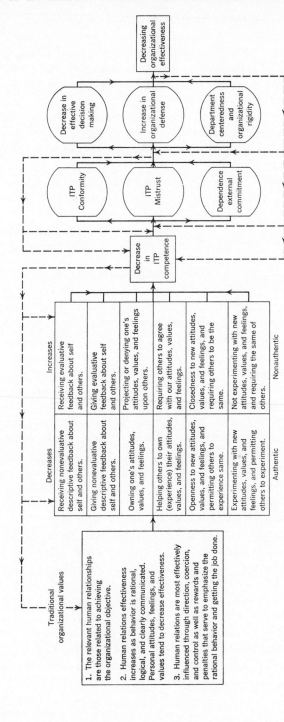

Figure 10–1 Model of Organizational Dynamics (Argyris, 1962, p. 43, ITP stands for interpersonal).

discord and defense which interfere with the problem-solving capacity of the organization. The aims of change agents then, are (1) to effect a change in values so that *human factors and feelings come to be considered as legitimate* and (2) to assist in *developing skills among managers in order to increase interpersonal competence.*

There are variations to this paradigm, to be sure, and we identified some of these in Chapters 3 and 4: For example, changed attitudes toward own role, role of others, and organizational relationships, or increased adaptibility of the organization to external stress. But basically, the variations show up more sharply in the *strategic models* employed to induce the change than they do in the conceptual goals. Let us turn to that now.

What Strategic Models for Inducing Change Are Used

This question has to do with the problem of *how*: How are change agents selected? How do they achieve their goals? How do they gain their influence and power? In order to get a foothold on these issues, let us pose two central questions: (1) Are the change agents internal or external to the target system, i.e., are they regular employees of the target system or not? (2) What is the basis of the change agent's power or ability to exert influence on the target system?

1. Change agents: internal or external? Whether or not the change agents are actual members of the target system is a crucial question to practitioners and students of organizational change. There are some who say that a significant change cannot occur without the impetus generated by the external agent (Lippitt et al., 1958; Seashore and Van Egmond, 1959). They argue that only a skilled outsider-consultant can provide the perspective, detachment, and energy so necessary to effect a true alteration of existing patterns. There are advocates of the internal model who take the opposite position. They argue that the insider possesses the intimate knowledge of the target system that the external change agent lacks. In addition, the internal change agent does not generate the suspicion and mistrust that the outsider often does. His acceptance and credibility are guaranteed, it is argued, by his organizational status.

2. The second question is: What is the source of the change agent's power? Generally speaking, he derives his power and influence from a combination of two sources: *expert* power and *line* power. As these terms suggest, the change agent is seen as possessing certain skills

and competencies (expert power) or he is seen as occupying a certain office or holding status in an organization which legitimizes his influence (line power).[8]

In our experience, the most common model used is the *external* change agent employing *expert* power. We call this the *Consultant* model because outside change agents are employed as consultants to the organization (usually, but not always, to the Personnel division) and attempt to help the target system build adequate laboratory training programs. In some cases, the consultants actually conduct laboratory training; in other cases, they coordinate laboratory training activities along with other consulting functions.

Perhaps an example of the Consultant model would help clarify its nature. The work of Shepard and other consultants at the Space Technology Laboratories is one of the best models of this approach. In this case, Shepard acts as consultant to the Director of Industrial Relations. In the course of their work together it was decided that career development (preparing managers for the future) was one of the most important problems facing the organization. After this, Shepard worked most intensively with the manager in charge of career development. The sequence of activities that followed all worked out with Shepard collaborating with this man and the Director of Industrial Relations, finally led to team training.[9]

At the other extreme from the Consultant model is the *Line* model, a strategy where the change agent is internal to the target system and possesses line power. A company president or any line leader who utilizes laboratory training would be an example of this. Alfred J. Marrow, the President of the Harwood Manufacturing Company, represents this approach. In Marrow's case, he works directly with the external consultants. Being a psychologist as well as entrepreneur, he conducts his own T-groups, participates in laboratories, and generally takes an active role in conducting and coordinating laboratory training in his organization. The President of Non-Linear Systems, Andrew Kaye, Hugh Harrison, President of Minnesota Mining, and Roger

---

[8] We have ignored some of the more personal and intangible elements which enter into questions of strategy, such as the change agent's personality, charisma, etc. These personal factors are rarely written about explicitly and only infrequently recognized. For these reasons, we do not feel confident in stressing anything but their *presence*.

[9] See Chris Argyris (1962) for a step-by-step analysis of the Consultant model. It is the clearest written account of this model.

Sonnabend, President of the Hotel Corporation of America, all, to some extent, exemplify the use of the Line model.[10]

A more popular model than the Line, but less so than the Consultant, is the *Staff* model as exemplified by Shepard while he was at Esso and, more recently, by Buchanan at Esso International. In this model, change agents are drawn directly from the headquarters' staff of the organization; for example, Shepard and his colleagues (some of whom were outside consultants) went to the Baton Rouge Refinery in 1959 and 1960 to conduct two-week residential laboratories for the entire managerial staff of the Refinery. The Staff model is similar to the Consultant model in that it emphasizes expert power, but similar to the Line in that its change agents are drawn from inside the target system.

A purer case of the internal change agent model was developed by Dwight Meader of the General Electric Company and is now used by that company in its "Business Effectiveness Program." In this case, change agents (called "catalysts") are trained by headquarters staff and outside consultants to go to a target system (a General Electric location) and live in as an internal change agent for however long as necessary to effect a change along the lines specified by the program. Some catalysts have been on location for as long as two years; others terminate after several months. What should be stressed here, for our analysis, is that the change agents are *paid by* and are considered regular employees of the target system itself.

Let us summarize now. Models implementing laboratory training for improving organizations can be viewed along two dimensions, internal vs. external and line vs. expert power. If the choice of change strategy is *internal*, then line or expert power can be utilized. The General Electric catalyst program is an example of the internal-expert model; the work of Alfred J. Marrow at Harwood is an example of the internal-line model. If the choice of the change strategy is *external*, then only one power alternative is open, that of expert, for line power must be drawn from sources internal to the target system. There are many examples of the external-expert model. We have already mentioned the work of Argyris, Beckhard, Blake, McGregor, Shepard, and others. It is probably the most widely used of the approaches we have singled out.

This classification we have developed for the uses of change strategies is crude, to be sure, and it ignores some of the more ingenious

---

[10] The extent to which these men actually conduct laboratory training varies. What is most characteristic of the Line model is that the top line management, rather than staff, takes the leadership in instituting laboratory training.

variations. But we would wager that over 90% of the change efforts utilizing laboratory training can be grouped in it. At the same time, however, new models are now being developed that may make this classification obsolete.

It seems increasingly clear to us that *combinations* and appropriate *sequencing* of these approaches may prove to be most useful. There are more and more signs, for example, that internal and external change agents, *in concert*, are more effective than either internal or external working alone. Moreover, all things being equal, a combination of line and expert power cannot help but be more effective than line or expert power working independently of each other. The evidence is far from conclusive at this point, but, from certain trends that we now see developing, new models for implementing organizational change will be used that rely on external *and* internal change agents in combination and using line *and* expert power. What this implies is a *team effort* involving a diverse set of skills, status, and roles in order to induce the organizational change. We believe this will prove to be the most useful strategy in the future.

Considerations for the Successful Adoption of Laboratory Training by Social Systems

In this section we will examine the conditions that facilitate the adoption of laboratory training by target systems. We will consider two: (1) the state of the target system or subsystem and (2) the role and competence of the change agent. Then we will discuss the interaction between the change agent and the target system in the strategy of implementation.

The State of the Target System or Subsystem[11]

In considering the state of the target system, a number of questions must be asked:

1. Are the learning goals of laboratory training appropriate?
2. Is the cultural state of the target system ready for laboratory training?
3. Are the key people involved?

---

[11] The boundaries of the target system which laboratory training affects may be a part (or subsystem) of the larger target system. For example, a target system like Aluminum Company of Canada has been directing the bulk of its laboratory training change program at one of its three main divisions. In the Esso change program, the refinery, a subsystem, became the chief target system. We will come back to this point later in our discussion of the strategy of implementation.

4. Are members of the target system adequately prepared and oriented to laboratory training?

5. Is voluntarism (regarding participation) insured?

1. *Are the learning goals of laboratory training appropriate?* To what extent do the goals and meta-goals relate to the effectiveness of the target system? We can think of many target systems where the answer to these questions may be negative, due to market, technological, and competitive conditions. Serious attention must be given, particularly in the early stages, to the appropriateness of laboratory training change goals for the particular target system. Later on we shall discuss some cases where laboratory training was obviously inappropriate in retrospect. A great deal of effort, at first, must be directed to diagnosing the target system's needs in relation to the anticipated outcomes of laboratory training. Are the outcomes relevant to the effectiveness of the target system? Is laboratory training timely, economical, congruent with the anticipated target system trends, and so forth? Later on, after discussing the cases where it failed, this question of appropriateness will again be raised.

2. *Is the cultural state of the target system ready for laboratory training?* What do we mean by "cultural readiness?" Each target system transmits and maintains a system of values that permeates the organization and is used as a basis for action and commitment. This does not mean that values are always adhered to, but it usually means that those who exemplify the values are rewarded and those who violate them are punished. Laboratory training also has a set of values which we outlined in Chapter 3, under the heading of meta-goals: we specified authenticity, choice, collaboration, and the expression of feelings among others. There is bound to be *some* value conflict between these values and the values of the target system, but situations should be avoided where the two sets of value systems clash extraordinarily.

The degree and range of value conflicts provide some of the best clues for diagnosing the cultural state of the target system. That is, if the discrepancy between laboratory training values and the target system's values can be realistically assessed, a fairly good idea about the target system's readiness can be obtained. Let us sample some of the most important dimensions of the cultural state.

The *legitimacy of interpersonal relationships*, both in terms of its effects on the work and the degree to which members of the target system view it as susceptible to change, is an important aspect of the target system's culture. In many target systems, interpersonal phenomena are not considered appropriate to discuss, germane to the task, or legitimate as a focus of inquiry. As Henry Ford once said about his own philosophy of management: "You just set the work before the men and have them do it." While this view is becoming slowly outdated by modern techniques of management, there are still many situations where interpersonal influence is regarded as invalid, illegitimate, or an invasion of privacy.

Another cultural variable which must be taken into account is the *control and authority system presently employed by the target system.* If it is too rigid and authoritarian, it may be too much at variance with the values of laboratory training.

The presence and intensity of conflict within the target system represents still another cultural factor which must be considered. It is difficult to generalize about conflict in terms of its relationship to the adoption of laboratory training. The impression we gain, however, is that it is best not to introduce laboratory training under conditions of intense conflict. In this case, the organization is under stress and may be *too* plastic; laboratory training may then be only a temporary dodge, become a tool in a power play, or be used later on as a convenient scapegoat. This is not to say that it may not be strategically employed during periods of conflict. It is only to say that the type, causes, and intensity of conflict must be examined in relationship to the laboratory training program.

The internal boundary system of the target system must be carefully examined in order to avoid situations where laboratory training values are internalized in one subpart of the system only to be rejected by and cause disruptions in an adjacent system.[12] In other words, the interdependence of the parts within the target system must be carefully scrutinized so that unanticipated changes in some parts of the system do not backfire or create negative repercussions in another part of the target system.

The last item to consider in assessing the cultural readiness of the target system is the most difficult to render in objective terms, and, yet, it is possibly the most important factor in estimating the probability of

---

[12] George Strauss and Alex Bavelas (1955) report an interesting example of this when a subunit of girls on an assembly line developed an ingenious and new method which increased their job satisfaction and improved their performance significantly. The only trouble was that it had repercussions on interdependent parts of the organization. The program eventually had to be stopped. Though we know of no such case, it will be interesting to identify sources of strain that laboratory training might create with the target system's *external* boundary system: suppliers, customers, government, employee sources, etc. It is doubtful that it would generate the same degree of strain as internal interdependencies, but it still bears examination.

success. *It has to do with the change agent's relationship with the target system,* in particular, the quality and potentiality of the relationship.

If the change agent believes that it is possible to establish a relationship with the target system based on a healthy, realistic understanding of his role and with realistic expectations regarding the change, then a change program may be indicated. But if the relationship is based on fantasy, on unrealistic hopes, on fear or worship or intimidation, then the change agent and/or the target system must seriously re-examine the basis for their joint work.[13]

We are suggesting that one of the best ways of diagnosing cultural readiness has to do with the way the target system reacts to and establishes a relationship with the change agent. The quality and vicissitudes of this encounter—insofar as it is a miniature replica of the intended change program—provide an important clue regarding the fate of the laboratory training change program.

What we mean by readiness is the degree of value conflict between laboratory training values and the target system's values in terms of: legitimacy of interpersonal phenomena, the range, depth, and intensity of conflicts and modes of conflict resolution, concepts of control and authority, the interdependence of parts of the target system, and the relationship between change agent and target system. Though they are difficult to measure precisely, thorough attention and rough assessment must be made before laboratory training can be introduced. Assuming that the cultural readiness of the target system has been carefully assessed and found to be appropriate, we must ask:

3. *Are the key people in the target system involved in or informed of the laboratory training program?* It can be disastrous if the people most affected by laboratory training are not involved, informed, or even advised of the program. To guarantee success, a great deal of energy and time must be devoted to assessing the extent to which the laboratory training is supported by the key people and the attitudes individuals generally hold regarding laboratory training.

4. *Are members of the target system adequately prepared and oriented to laboratory training?* The usual forms of *preparation* and *orien-*

---

[13] Let us be clear about this. We mean that if the change agent can *foresee* a healthy relationship in the future, he might well consider the laboratory training program. We do not think it is possible for the relationship to be totally trusting and realistic during the beginning phases of work. In any case, the main point we want to stress is the diagnostic validity of the relationship; the problems that inhere in that relationship are probably symptomatic of the problems to be encountered.

tation do not seem too effective for laboratory training, primarily because the word rarely conveys the sense of the experience. Laboratory training, if anything, is experience-based, and words, without an experimental referent, often tend to confuse and, in some cases, cause more apprehension than necessary.

Some introductory *experiences* often prepare and orient future participants adequately. We have tried a miniature laboratory (waggishly called by one of the participants an "instant laboratory") to simulate as accurately as we could the laboratory environment. In this case, an entire laboratory was compressed into one full day of training. In other situations we have executed a specific training exercise with some prospective delegates in order to give them a feel for the learning environment. In any case, we advocate some experience-based orientation in order to provide a reasonable facsimile of laboratory life.

Another alternative frequently used is seeding. Selected members of the client system attend stranger laboratories on their own. In this way, the organization can successfully build up a significant number of personnel who are familiar with laboratory training.

5. *To what extent is laboratory training viewed as voluntary by the participants?* We feel this is an important, perhaps crucial factor for the successful adoption of laboratory training by target systems. We think it is crucial not only for the obvious ethical reasons but also for realistic learning considerations. In order for a participant to profit the most, he must not feel coerced or pushed into the experience.[14] Involuntary attendance is particularly hard to avoid in those cases where the entire organization undergoes laboratory training and where there is a tacit rejection of those who refuse to attend. Still it is important for target systems to provide as much choice and voluntarism as possible, by providing the individuals with as much orientation as possible so that choice is meaningful and by minimizing organizational pressure to attend.

In this section, on the state of the target system, we have presented a series of factors to be taken into account in order to increase the probability of the successful adoption of laboratory training. In order to summarize this section as well as to make explicit the sequence of choices we have constructed a five-step model shown in Table 10-1.

---

[14] This often creates the dilemma of the people who most need the laboratory training experience resisting it and those who least need it volunteering for it. However unsatisfactory the resolution of this dilemma is, nothing would be gained and a lot possibly lost if people were captive to the experience.

Table 10-1 Five-Step Model for Diagnosing State of Target System

1. Are laboratory training change goals appropriate to target system?

   If yes, then:

   If *not, stop* and reconsider appropriateness of laboratory training.

2. Is the cultural state of target system prepared for laboratory training:
   a. Degree and type of value conflict?
   b. Legitimacy of interpersonal phenomena?
   c. Degree, range, intensity, resolution of conflict?
   d. Concepts of control, authority?
   e. Interdependence of target system?
   f. Relationship of trust and confidence between change agent and target system?

   If yes, then:

   If *not, stop* and examine areas where more preparation is needed or where value conflicts should be reduced.

3. Are key people involved and committed:

   If yes, then:

   If *not, stop* and examine ways to develop more commitment to program.

4. Are members of the target system adequately prepared and oriented to laboratory training?

   If yes, then:

   If *not, stop* and examine ways to develop more commitment to program.

5. Is voluntarism (regarding participation) insured?

   If *not, stop* and examine attitudes toward laboratory training: why people go or do not want to go to laboratories. After diagnosis, attempt to accurately indicate the place of laboratory training in career development.

The Role and Competence of the Change Agent

We mentioned earlier that the idea of change agentry, as we are using the term here, is very new. Because of its novelty, its fundamental outline is still emerging. Thus the role of the change agent is protean, changing, difficult to grasp, and practically impossible to generalize. However, it may be useful to make some tentative remarks about it in this section.

There are a number of things we would like to call attention to about the role of the change agent. We shall discuss each of them in more detail. The change agent's role must be construed in the following way. It is:

1. Professional
2. Marginal
3. Ambiguous
4. Insecure
5. Risky

The change agent is a *professional*. He counts heavily on a body of valid knowledge in order to realize his aims, under guidance of certain ethical principles, and with the client's interest, not his own, in mind. This last point should be emphasized; the change agent must defer his own personal gratification in his dealings with the target system, his client. Particularly in dealing with something as important as a large and complex organization—where the change agent's actions may affect thousands of individuals—he must continually check his own needs, motives, and wishes against the reality of the client's needs.[15]

The change agent is *marginal*. He does not have formal membership in the target system or with a band of colleagues working close by. Typically he works alone and his marginality can work to his advantage and to his discomfort. On the positive side, the marginality can enhance his detachment and perception; it can also create insecurity and an absence of mechanisms (like colleagues) for reality testing. In any case, both the target system and the change agent have to come to terms with the idea of marginality.[16]

---

[15] The change agent must be made painfully aware of some of the unconscious gratifications of his role too, so that these can be brought under control. We have in mind such fantasies as high-powered manipulation, an uncontrollable quest for power and omnipotence. See Chapter 18 for an elaboration of this point.

[16] In a recent case which we heard about, a change agent reported to work for his first day on the job and the plant manager requested him to do some work which seemed to be inappropriate for a change agent. It was work that one of the managers should have been doing. The change agent refused to carry out functions which properly belonged to management. In this case the manager could not come to terms with the marginal role of the change agent.

The role of the change agent is *ambiguous*. Essentially this means that the basic concept of the change agent is not widely understood and evokes a wide range of meaning. If one responds to the question, "What do you do?" with the answer, "I am a psychologist," it does not evoke the same bewilderment as the response, "I am a change agent." (In fact, the responder might be well advised not to answer in that vein.) The ambiguity of the role betrays its lack of legitimacy as well as credibility. It also involves certain risks such as drawing suspicion and hostility *because* of its ambiguity. On the other side, it can be helpful in providing the necessary latitude and breadth which more precisely defined roles do not allow.

The role of the change agent is *insecure*. This stems from a variety of causes: the precarious employment basis of the change agent (the fact that he may be the most expendable person under certain conditions); the lack of guidelines and adequate knowledge to guide many of his actions; the profound resistances which develop in attempting to change an organization. All of these factors tend to make the role insecure.

Related to the insecure elements in the change agent's role is the *risky* quality inherent in it, the risk not only to the target system but to the agent's professional status. As we shall see in the next section, the complexity of organizational change and some of its unanticipated consequences can lead to totally undesirable outcomes.

The *competence* of the change agent must encompass a wide range of knowledge including: (1) conceptual diagnostic knowledge cutting across the entire sector of the behavioral sciences; (2) theories and methods of organizational change; (3) knowledge of sources of help; (4) orientation to the ethical and evaluative functions of the change agent's role.

In addition to this intellectual grasp, the change agent must also possess (5) operational and relational skills: of listening, observing, identifying, and reporting of ability to form relationships and trust, of a high degree of behavioral flexibility. The change agent must be able (6) to use himself, to be in constant communication with himself and to recognize and come to terms with (as much as is humanly possible) his own motivations. Particularly in the diagnostic stages of the work, the change agent must observe how the target system deals with him. Quite often, as we mentioned earlier, the interface between the change agent and the target system is crucial for understanding and reaching a conclusion with respect to the state and readiness of the target system. In short, the change agent should be sensitive and mature.

Finally, the change agent should (7) act congruently (authentically), in accordance with the values (meta-goals) he is attempting to superimpose upon the target system's value system. The change agent must not impose democratic or humanistic values in an authoritarian or inhuman manner. If the change agent is concerned with creating more authenticity and collaboration, he must behave in ways that are in accord with these values. We say this not only for the obvious ethical reasons, but for deeper reasons as well. The fact of the matter is that so much of the change agent's influence grows out of his relationship with the target system and the extent to which he is emulated as a role model, that any significant discrepancies between the change agent's actions and his stated values cannot help but create resistance.

These are the requirements for the effective achievement of the change agent's role. We would not expect to find many such supermen among us, but we would expect this job description to be used as an aim.

Strategies of Implementation

We have examined the state of the target system and the role and competence of the change agent. Let us close this section by taking a look at some of the strategy questions which arise in connection with the interaction between the two. These can be stated as choice points, questions which ultimately have to be considered in any change endeavor and which can be decided only by a thorough examination of the target system.

1. First and perhaps the most important strategic question is: *Who is the client?* The organization? A particular T-group? The group or person who appointed and pays the change agent? An individual in stress? This is a hard question to answer and we would guess that the *salient* client shifts and oscillates among a host of different clients throughout the course of a laboratory training program. But the question itself should never be too far from the change agent's mind.

2. *Where is the point of entry?* That is, at what level of the organization should laboratory training be directed first? The top management group? Middle levels? Lower levels? There are some change agents, like Argyris (1962) and Blansfield (1962) who believe that change can only succeed if it starts at the top and percolates down, that in order for a real change to take place, the highest command must be the primary initiating force.

Others disagree with this strategy. They claim that change programs utilizing laboratory training can start at lower levels of the target system and still be successful. Furthermore, they argue, it is sometimes *preferable* to start the change at lower levels because in some situations, due to a variety of organizational conditions, starting at the top may be too risky.

To some extent, the problem of point of entry can be decided on the basis of the kind of model of change employed. If it is a *line* model, then the consequences of starting at the lower levels may be different than in a *consultant* or *staff* model. The kind of model used also pertains to our third question.

3. *Which systems are involved?* Obviously everyone cannot be trained at once. This raises the question of priorities and choice. Can training be isolated in certain components of the organization, leaving other components without it? Or should attempts be made to include segments of all subsystems of the target system in the initial stages of the program? In any case, a careful diagnosis needs to be undertaken in order to trace the most strategic circulation of effects throughout the total target system. In our experience, some of the most critical unanticipated consequences arose when a diagnosis of the interdependencies of the subsystems within the target system was not carefully worked out.

How to choose the point of entry and which systems to involve are important *and* related strategic questions. There is no simple guide line to apply in making these choices, except an intimate knowledge and diagnosis of the target system which we outlined above in Table 10-1, and a consideration of the model of change used. One final question must be raised.

4. *To what extent can the change agent involve the target system in planning and executing laboratory training?* In order to act in accordance with the values of laboratory training, the change agent should attempt to involve the target system in planning and goal setting for the change program. Sometimes this is easier said than done because the target system may not have the experience or expertise to collaborate realistically with the change agent. In any case, the change agent must attempt to make an adequate diagnosis of the extent to which the target system should be involved in the planning, goal setting, and execution of laboratory training.[17]

_____
[17] There is a dilemma here that is often commented upon by change agents and practitioners. How can systems of collaboration be established if one party to the encounter cannot adequately *choose* due to inexperience or lack of knowledge? Does coercion or faith have to be used during the very first phase of change? Can one start a democratic change program, for example, by ordering people to attend? Can a change agent insist that his client attend a laboratory so that collaboration, of a deep and enduring kind, can be achieved?

These are some of the main questions which come up and perplex change agents in initiating change programs. They do not exhaust the endless possibilities of problems. And until we have achieved perfect strategic comprehension of the target system in relationship to the change agent we will be beset by these and still other unanticipated problems.

Three Cases of Failure

In medical training, students and physicians are exposed quite regularly to an intriguing ordeal called the Clinical Pathology Conference in which a pathologist presents the autopsy of a patient and some expert is called in (in full view of all seated in the amphitheater) to diagnose the precise cause of the fatality. No equivalent teaching device exists in the behavioral sciences mainly because we are in a relatively early state of developing a practice.[18] Yet we thought it might be interesting to present several examples of failure or partial failure in order to dramatize and clarify different parts of this chapter. We hope these examples will help in formulating some principles which we propose in the next section.

What we propose to do is this: We will present three brief anecdotes or actual cases that have come to our attention in one way or another. (We have doctored and disguised the cases sufficiently so that no confidences will be endangered). The cases will be presented consecutively and without comment until the third and last one; then we will attempt to develop some principles from the case material.

Case 1: A Letter from a Government Training Center

This is a letter which came to one of the authors from a government training officer (Dr. A) connected with a large government training center. Laboratory training was started at the center several months before and since that time the following things happened: (1) the Director (Mr. Z) went to a two-week laboratory at Bethel, (2) about 250 government officials underwent a five-day laboratory at the center under Dr. A's leadership with other staff drawn from officials Dr. A had personally trained, and (3) Dr. A with the support of Mr. B (a strong advocate of laboratory training and second in command of the center) planned to set up a laboratory training experience for all 2,000

---

[18] There are other reasons as well: for example, the understandable secrecy regarding failures or mixed successes and the difficulty in attributing precise causality in these complex social change ventures.

officials stationed there. This letter arrived shortly after plans were laid out to train trainers in order to execute a massive design.

. . . I'm still behind on the reports on our lab training here, at least on the reports I'd like to get out.

Some of the little things that have cropped up. The Director who went to the *two* week lab away from here feels that those who have only gone through four or five days training here don't really have the capacity to talk to him.

Those members of the faculty who got the training late wonder why they were left to last. An "in" group and "out" group developed in the faculty. Some of the outs resented being trained by one of their peers. Some wanted to know: "How did you get to be a trainer?"

The head of our medical department told the Director that lab training type of training is dangerous.

The chief in Washington (over our Director!) asked someone in an aside: "What the hell is Dr. A doing giving that kind of training!"

A Grade 15 called in a Grade 12 scheduled to attend a five-day lab in April and said, not once but twice: "You don't have to go to this thing you know. I want you to understand it is entirely voluntary, you don't have to go unless you want to. . . What are you going to do if some younger official tells you he doesn't like the way you conduct yourself?"

One man comes up to me occasionally, looks around as if to make sure no one is watching, and then makes the sign of T with both hands.

The Director's deputy wrote a letter to Headquarters and asked for an evaluation of lab training. "If it's good for one, is it good for all?"

I received an informal request from a staff official in Headquarters asking me to answer about 12 objections commonly raised to lab training.

In short, a considerable number of anxieties have been raised. Some are intrigued, some are scared.

Two weeks elapsed and another letter arrived from Dr. A:

. . . We have unfortunately hit a snag. How serious it will be remains to be seen. Mr. B (Dr. A's main line support) has been transferred. This removed our chief advocate suddenly. Within a week the Director, Mr. Z, called in the Head of Curriculum and outlined how he wanted lab training put into the curriculum. A meeting was set up with me, the Director, and the Head of Curriculum.

(Up until this time we had been planning, with Mr. B's approval and backing, to put the training into one department and start in September. We proposed, if we could get the money, to get two outside trainers in for three weeks in August, to train this Department's staff. Someone from National Training Laboratories had been down and talked this over with the staff and I had manage to find a friend in Washington who said he would underwrite the program. We had not gotten down to the nuts and bolts of actually drawing up detailed plans for September, but that was the large outline.)

In the May 3rd meeting, Mr. Z started out by saying NTL didn't have any final answers to lab training and that his trainers at Arden House were quick to admit they didn't know all the answers. Thus, he said, we had a chance to strike out on our own and did not have to be bound by the fixed two-weeks approach pioneered by NTL. (Up to this time he was the only one who had been insisting on two weeks; we had been talking in terms of four and five days). Furthermore, we could not have officials foregoing their vacations in August, so any ideas about giving them three weeks of training couldn't be considered. Anyway, it didn't take much training because all his trainers did was sit there, they hardly opened their mouths during the two weeks. He would train the officials himself and he thought possibly one afternoon would be enough. What he proposed then was that after about six or seven weeks all the students be given one or two days to give each other feedback. This would be preceded by four or five lectures during the first week or so which would tell them what to be watching for. Keeping what they had observed in mind, they could then tell each other after the sixth week what they had observed. At the end of school, the students would be given another day or two days to give each other feedback. And so on. One or two of us tried to offer some comments or observations and were either cut off or ignored. As a consultant of sorts, I didn't feel quite up to exploring all the implications of his plan in front of the staff because I felt it was his prerogative to run the school as he wanted to.

Since that time various staff sections have been busy trying to pass on to other staff sections the job of trying to figure out what Mr. Z wants and making plans for his wishes. I've been invited to a meeting in the morning and will see what develops. I intend to talk to Mr. Z by himself after this if I can.

I'm curious to find out if he will tell me why he changed his mind, apparently, so suddenly and why he chose not to build on any of the data we had so painstakingly gathered. All this he just threw out of the window. And either just before or just after the May 3rd meeting he forwarded to Headquarters a report of the school activities in which he asked for funds for the August training I described.

We are unable to figure out whether Mr. B's leaving triggered the change, whether he is scared to try a four-day lab with students, whether he balks at paying the training price, whether he is irked at me, or just what the score is. But what makes it so hard to figure is that all the reports, letters, plans, etc., that he has seen and signed have nothing to do with what he has proposed. Some of what he says might be worked out into something quite useful, but in the meeting he brooked no comment—all he wanted was a rubber stamp.

I am not ready at this point to say the effort has failed because a lot of pressure has been building up in the past ten days. How much it will mean has yet to be disclosed. Certainly, at this moment the plans for the August training seem dead, although we may yet get the test in one Department rather than among 800 students. This really bugged me, trying something completely unknown and untested on 800 men.

Several weeks following this letter, Dr. A called to say that the Government Training Center had stopped its laboratory training and "had gone back to more traditional training methods."

Case 2: A Letter from Medical Services

This letter was sent as a confidential memorandum from the chief medical officer of a large manufacturing company to the Vice President of Personnel. A copy of this memo was sent to Dr. A, chief training officer for the company. Dr. A had been hiring consultants who use laboratory training quite regularly in their work for this company.

The medical division is concerned about the possibility of medical casualities from the T-group type of training program.

Dr. Jones says that T-group programs have greater likelihood of producing a higher percentage of disabling mental disturbances than do ordinary work situations.

The purpose of the Training Division is training.

The purpose of Medical Division is the prevention of illness and disability.

We feel the purpose of our Division warrants our scrutiny of any Company activity likely to be related to disabilities.

We recommended several months ago that the list of candidates for training sessions be passed before the local Company medical officer for his approval or comment regarding the names thereon. The suggestion is held impractical by some on the basis that the Company medical officers are not psychologically or psychiatrically oriented, have little knowledge or comprehension concerning the nature of the sessions and are not qualified to determine who are high risk candidates. It is my conviction that something along the following lines should be required by the Company, if for no other reason than the doubt surrounding the advisability of having therapy for medical conditions unsupervised by medical people:

a) Collaboration should start immediately to arrange a long weekend session in a suitable place, to be attended by the senior medical representative from each of our plants. Dr. A should prepare a clear statement of the purpose of these T-sessions, a clear statement of the procedure used in attempting to achieve the purpose, a clear statement on what these procedures demand from the individual, and a clear statement of the signs which the trainers use as indicators of impending disability, no matter how temporary. In addition, this working session should provide a sample experience for the doctors attending. The purpose of this session would be to take away any feeling that the local doctor was completely "clueless" regarding what is appearing to take on the shadowy form of a mystic cult; . . .

This case had a reasonably successful outcome. The chief medical officer himself attended a two-week laboratory at Bethel and shortly after his return organized a long weekend session that was led by two laboratory trainers, for all of his doctors, other key personnel and line officials. This 3-day weekend session was designed as a modified laboratory, and, according to the participants and the trainers, it accomplished its purposes: a better understanding of laboratory train-

ing by the doctors, and an improvement in the collaboration between medical and training divisions.

Case 3: The Undercover Change Agent

The following anecdote is based on interviews conducted with members of an organization in which laboratory training was tried and failed. The training endeavor was almost totally disastrous: the staff members conducting the laboratory training was fired, his colleague transferred; the director of training was ordered to stop all training connected with management development and to provide only technical training; the Vice President of Personnel resigned.

The company itself is a large retailing combine operating about fifteen department stores in the Midwest. The headquarters are located in Milwaukee and many of the branch stores are located in the conservative, German farming centers throughout Wisconsin and Minnesota. The company is family-owned and operated by the son of the founder, Mr. Hess.

The company committed itself to a considerable amount of executive training through its personnel department. Each year most of its managerial staff attended a one week course at a small hotel in the lake country near Milwaukee. For the most part, the human relations training was based on cases very like those collected and used at the Harvard Business School. These case courses were deemed very successful by management and by the participants.

Last year the company hired a new trainer (Mr. Jones) for their one week human relations training program. Before taking the job, Jones attended a two week laboratory and was deeply impressed by the experience. After several weeks of conducting case study discussions Jones asked his boss, the director of training, if they could try some laboratory training. The director of training did not understand it completely but said he would take the matter up with his boss, the Vice President of Personnel. The latter had only an inkling of what laboratory training was all about but passed on whatever he knew to the President. It was not at all clear who "cleared what with whom" or how much anyone understood about the idea of laboratory training, but, in any case, nine weeks of laboratory training took place with nine different groups, all at the lower echelons of management. During the ninth week the President arrived unannounced at the training site and demanded to be given entry into the T-groups. Jones refused at first but finally gave in to the President's orders.

Shortly after the President's return to Milwaukee, the training ceased and Jones was fired, etc. What had happened?

Leading up to the President's visit to the laboratory, which culminated in his storming into the resort hotel during the breakfast hour demanding entrance into the T-group, was a whole series of events. First of all, the President had heard about some "interesting" training going on, quite unlike what he had come to expect from case study discussions. He knew nothing about this "group dynamics business" and was angry at not being told about it. Second, rumors had come to his attention that some "hanky panky" was going on there. In fact, the Vice President of Buying had overheard a conversation between two of his assistant buyers that was reported to the President. One of the buyers had just returned from a one week laboratory and the other buyer was quizzing her about it. The conversation the Vice President reported to the President went something like this:

Buyer A: Oh, you just came back from Marlboro? (the training site)
Buyer B: Yes.
Buyer A: How was it?
Buyer B: This course was the deepest experience I have had in my life so far. . . Can you imagine, there was one man who took off his clothes completely!
Buyer A: A strip tease?
Buyer B: Uh huh.

Apparently, Buyer B was attempting to indicate to A the depth of the experience, the emotional revelations. In fact, what Buyer A passed on to her boss was that a literal strip tease took place at Marlboro. To this day there are some places in the company where this story is still believed.

There had been an attempted suicide by one of the participants in the training shortly after his return from the week at Marlboro.

Finally, whenever the President asked his Vice President of Personnel whether he visited Marlboro and whether he was aware of what was going on there, the Vice President said he did not really know what was going on and that he was advised by Mr. Jones to stay away. These events led to the President's surprise visit to Marlboro.

He arrived at Marlboro at breakfast in the third day of a week's program and demanded his entrance in the T-group. According to Jones:

I tried to dissuade him but to no avail. He insisted that he had the right. "If you have nothing to hide," he said, "then let me in. If you have something to hide, then I must find out." So he observed us for a two hour T-session. After the meeting I told him that it was hard to get a realistic picture of what goes on in T-groups. He noted this and smiled at my remarks and expressed astonishment about the lack of structure in the group.

After the meeting, while having coffee, he voiced a little surprise about my passive attitude and my not exercising leadership at all. I tried to explain to him how important this is, but I felt there was an enormous wall of prejudice I could not get behind.

Then I gave a lecture to the group on leadership drawing most of my material from McGregor's *The Human Side of Enterprise.* Then I asked the participants to organize the last day's training activities. . .

In the afternoon, right after their second T-group of the day, when people were on their feet, the President rose and told everyone to remain in their seats and then delivered a twenty minute speech. He first said that supervisory training was an important thing and that the company had already spent a lot of money on it. He thought the participants were getting something from the company which was not at all self-evident that a company would do for its people. Then he went on to say that these are critical times, that the competitive situation was worsening and that success would require the greatest effort of everybody. This could be achieved, he said, by working hard and by following the given orders without question—all the requisites, I thought, of a paternalistic management. He went on speaking then like a military leader. Then he referred to my short lecture on leadership and said that there was one point he did not agree with at all. (One of the participants asked if a subordinate always has to follow orders to the word. I gave a very qualified answer trying to show that there could be conditions for questioning a superior.) The President said that he most strongly wanted to emphasize that a subordinate had better follow orders—there was no question about that! Then he went into a monologue about leadership philosophy all of which ended up as a flat contradiction of the whole philosophy of the course. People were baffled by this sudden outbreak by the President and there was a certain amount of confusion about it. The participants realized that here were two exponents of two different philosophies. . . .

Here is the President's version of that fateful day!

They were discussing group relations, I guess. They were sitting in a circle and they would sit silent for awhile and they would ask: "What is your impression of me and what do others make of me? And I'd like to tell you what I think of you, Jane, or you, Jim." Then there would be silence, long silence and the pressure and tension would steadily mount and then it would explode and everyone would start talking at once about impressions people had of each other. They would "give feedback," they said. I don't know, I suppose that one can learn a lot about how one feels and sees, but I did not think that this kind of discussion was crucial for management training. Matter of fact, some of it seemed like communism to me; they've gone too far for me, too revolutionary!

Propositions about the Uses of Laboratory Training in Effecting Social Change

We have attempted to present the risks and promises of engineering social change in target systems via laboratory training. The three cases of failure, because of their dramatic aspects, should not blind us to the fact that these are the exception, not the rule. The other chapters in this section testify to that. On the other hand, abnormal as these three cases may be, it would be a mistake to regard them only for their pathological interest. What we would like to do now is consider both the successes and the failures and develop propositions about social change which are related to and clearly build upon the second section of this chapter concerning the considerations for the successful adoption of laboratory training by social systems.[19] *In Undertaking Any Planned Social Change Using Laboratory Training, the Core of the Target System Values Must Not Be Too Discrepant with the Laboratory Training Values.* Every target system has a core of values that characterizes it and determines a good deal of its decisions. Laboratory training, also, has a system of core values. We discussed these earlier in terms of legitimacy of interpersonal phenomena, concepts of control, and so forth. We stated then that the target system's values should be somewhat in accord with, or *potentially* congruent to, laboratory training values. Where the two systems of values are widely discrepant and rigid, and where the value system of the target cannot yield without vitally endangering the target system's core values, change induced by laboratory training will probably not succeed.

Let us be specific. In the case of the Government Training Center and the department store, it is obvious that the institutional base was perceived, by men in power, as seriously threatened. The values, the normative patterns, the set of shared expectations were all in flux due to the training endeavors of Dr. A and Mr. Jones.

Perhaps the central issue here concerns the definition of the word "training." *Webster's Dictionary* defines it as follows: "1. To subject oneself or be subjected to instruction, drilling, regular exercise, dieting, etc. 2. To form habits or impart proficiency teaching, drilling, etc." Most training affirms these definitions; training is a process whereby individuals learn the skills, attitudes, and orientation congruent to a particular role. Training, viewed this way, has a conservative connotation. It takes organizations as they are and attempts to shape individuals to them.

What we have been calling training is probably misnamed. For certainly a program that aims to change the very structure of the organization through modifying a role orientation[20] is not training

---

[19] These principles can encompass any planned social change, not only those directed by laboratory training.

[20] The meta-goals we outlined in Chapter 3 signify certain orientations toward role, for example, openness, collaboration. Contrast these role expectations with President Hess's expectations.

in the usual sense of this word. This is not only a semantic issue. Training, in its dictionary sense and in the way that most personnel managers use it and top management construes it, is viewed conservatively: fitting people to roles. Training in the sense that it was employed in these cases signifies a *fundamental* change, an alteration of the values, norms, and patterns of expectations. In this sense President Hess was completely correct in viewing laboratory training as "revolutionary" and General Z perfectly justified in going slowly on laboratory training at the military base. It is revolutionary to the extent that the core of institutional values that the leadership was striving to preserve was basically threatened by the laboratory training change programs.

Putting it a bit differently, most organizations agree to various training and development programs insofar as they strengthen the core of institutional values and insofar as they facilitate the functioning of the organization. When programs are seen as imperilling the institutional base, we can expect the strong resistance evinced in these cases.

But most social change programs, certainly laboratory training, attempt to alter institutional values. How, then, can the inevitable and powerful resistance be reduced?

In Undertaking Any Planned Social Change, Legitimacy for the Change Must Be Gained through Obtaining the Support of the Key People. This is not to say that laboratory training should start at the top; it does mean that a careful and deliberate effort must be made to gain acceptance by the top management group. Without this, the laboratory training is constantly in peril. Notice what happened when Mr. B (the top line official in the government center supporting laboratory training) was transferred: The program came apart at the seams. If Mr. B's successor had been well-briefed and oriented, and if Mr. Z were briefed and oriented, then the program might have had more resilience to shock. The same is true regarding the department store case: Nobody really seemed to know "what was up" except possibly Jones. And if the Vice President of Personnel had been able and competent to tell President Hess what was really going on at Marlboro, then it might not have been necessary for him to make the surprise trip.

In any case, efforts must be made to provide top management with as clear and realistic picture of laboratory training as possible. This is done not only as an acquaintance process but also as a test of top management's commitment toward the potential changes. If the commitment is weak at the top level, then a total re-evaluation of the strategy is required. It is far better to discover this early than late. In the case of the department store, partly out of fear and mostly from futility, the training staff worked surreptitiously, with the faint hope that the training effects would be accepted. The outcome produced an unstable situation where the lowest levels of management maintained values that were in conflict with top management. The tension created by this value conflict was reduced by removing its source, Jones, and restoring the old orientation.

Obtaining hierarchical acceptance, no matter how painstaking and difficult, provides at least some guarantee that management can understand, and hence, manage the change without undue tension.

In Undertaking Any Planned Social Change, the Process of Installing the Change Programs Must Be Congruent with the Process and Goals of Such Programs. We are talking here of a fairly simple, but crucial, matter. The change agent should know what he is doing and should act congruently and authentically. While we are not absolutely confident of this proposition holding in every situation (installing a totalitarian system, for example), we are sure that this is essential for a democratic change program. For reasons that appeared sensible at the time, Jones operated more as an undercover agent than as an agent of change. It is doubtful that he understood the consequences of his decisions: The fact that he viewed laboratory training as a simple substitute for the case method gives rise to this question. Were the goals and *meta-goals* of laboratory training clearly understood by the change agents?

It is not obvious that they were understood. Jones, in particular, violated to some degree the meta-goals: Authenticity was abandoned by the underground methods used to start the program. Action was taken without a spirit of inquiry, and the nature of the change program was far from a collaborative one. The way Dr. A dealt with Mr. Z and the way Mr. Jones dealt with President Hess were not examples of authentic and collaborative relationships.

Unanticipated consequences can jeopardize any change program. Only the omniscient can be blamed for those. But in the case of the department store, many of the consequences could have been foreseen and avoided—if Jones had used the processes of laboratory training in installing the change program. What we observed instead was the blind use of a tool in a way which contradicted its essence.

In Undertaking Any Planned Social Change, the Employment Security of the Change Agent Must Be Guaranteed. Blau (1961) points out that one of the prerequisites for adaptation in bureaucracy is the minimum employment security of the personnel. In terms of the brute reality of existence this means that most people would not risk their job in order to create change. Given the laboratory training approach to organizational change, minimum employment security is essential for the change agent, particularly if he is a member of the organization. The training staff must maintain their separateness from other company employees and must develop some discretion and autonomy insofar as training functions are concerned.

For Jones there was no real alternative but to let the President sit in; it was either that or dismissal. If a situation similar to that one occurred but the trainer had maximum employment security or was an outside consultant, employed temporarily by the company, possibly there would have been a different outcome.

In Undertaking Any Planned Social Change Utilizing Laboratory Training, the Voluntary Commitment of the Participants May Be a Crucial Factor in the Success of the Program. We have discussed this at some length earlier. But for emphasis we repeat that the difficulty of describing laboratory training through verbal orientation, plus the problematical aspects of organizational legitimacy to influence interpersonal behavior, lead to only one conclusion with respect to participant attendance at laboratories. This is that all delegates must undertake laboratory training in a completely voluntary spirit. It is highly doubtful that they will learn if this condition does not prevail.

In Undertaking Any Planned Social Change Utilizing Laboratory Training, the Legitimacy of Interpersonal Influence Must Be Potentially Acceptable. The spread and belief of the "strip-tease" rumor shows the desirability of an orientation for prospective participants. But it shows more than that. We must ask: How much and in what way can (should) an organization influence the personalities of its employees? It is not exactly obvious that interpersonal competence is correlated with effective role functioning; in some specific situations, there may be no, or an inverse, correlation. Indeed, the theoretical foundations of bureaucracy are based on *impersonality.* And even with the modern role conception of the modern manager—which includes social system management and responsibility—the prevailing norms of legitimacy of organizational influence must be explored and understood fully by the target system.

In Undertaking Any Planned Social Change, the Effects on the Adjacent and Interdependent Subsystems Relating to the Target System

Must Be Carefully Considered. All three cases demonstrate this principle, but perhaps none so dramatically as in the "Letter from Medical Division." Here we see so clearly how the reverberations and repercussions of laboratory training come back to haunt its creators unless the shock can be absorbed by their neighboring units. In this case, the company doctors could have easily absorbed the shock (as they later did after an orientation session) if they had been simply informed about and involved in laboratory training. They were irked because they were ignored and disturbed by perceived encroachment on their authority. But whether it is doctors or headquarters or colleagues or bosses, a complete diagnosis of the total effects on all relevant parts must be made before, not after, the training starts.

In Undertaking Any Planned Social Change, the State of Cultural Readiness Must Be Assessed. We emphasized this in the preceding section in terms of the internal state of the target system. Here we mean more. We have in mind the relationship between the organization and the wider society within which the target system is embedded. It would appear that Mr. Jones (and Dr. A, to some extent) failed to comprehend completely the normative structure they were attempting to alter. The values of President Hess· were known well in advance of the training failure, and he reflected the German cultural values of the farming communities his stores prospered in. Cultural readiness depends to some degree on the normative structure of the wider society; a clear diagnosis cannot be made without understanding these forces.

A Postscript on the Prospects for Democratic Social Change

The preceding eight principles provide only a partial view of the complex elements that enter into social change. This complexity, along with the drama of the failures, probably tends to make social change seem more hazardous than it need be. If we have tended to highlight the dilemmas and risks we do this with the hope that the recognition of these choice points when installing and maintaining similar change programs will enhance their effectiveness.

Ultimately, we believe, the forces for change in the direction of laboratory training's stated goals will gather more and more momentum in our society. There is some evidence for this belief already. But there are other environmental forces at work as well which portend even further acceleration of democratic processes (Slater and Bennis,

1964). There is a rapid rate of technological change, and there is a rapid infusion of professionals into organizations. These circumstances represent two of the most important factors in the outlook for change. And laboratory training, with its particular set of change goals, may provide an important instrument for building organizations where effective collaboration and adaptation can take place.

Part III

RESEARCH ON LABORATORY TRAINING OUTCOMES

This part of the book is written for the reader who wishes to know how one evaluates the impact of laboratory training, and what data have been obtained in studies of laboratory training. Because of the availability of other articles and books which deal with this problem in detail, we have not attempted to review the field. Rather, what we attempt to do is to provide an overview of kinds of evaluation research which are possible (Chapter 11), and then present two of the best studies we know, those of Miles (Chapter 12) and of Bunker (Chapter 13). This part of the book should be viewed, therefore, as providing a sample of what is possible if one wishes to evaluate laboratory training outcomes. In addition to these Chapters the reader is also referred to Section B of Chapter 7 for another example of evaluation research.

11

Research on Laboratory Training Outcomes

Much has been written about the uses of laboratory training and the theory which underlies these uses. In our next section, Part IV, we will add our own theoretical formulations about the learning process. The question remains, however, just how much hard evidence there is that laboratories make a difference. Is it sufficient evidence that organizations continue to use laboratory training and that people continue to attend laboratories? Obviously not. We need sound controlled observations which confirm that people who go through a laboratory training experience somehow come out differently after it. And, we need good research data that organizations who engage in laboratory training activities benefit from the effort and that the benefit is attributable to it.

We can say at the outset that the evidence is meager, largely because of the fantastic difficulties of doing valid evaluation research. Particularly lacking are systematic studies of organization change programs; these multiply the already considerable difficulties of research on individual delegates. The meagerness of evidence does not reflect lack of concern on the part of practitioners of laboratory training, but the actual difficulties of gathering data which have empirical validity. Two very general problems can be identified: (1) difficulties of achieving rigor of research design in a setting devoted to achieving practical change and learning goals; and (2) difficulties of gathering data in which we can have confidence as to their reliability and validity. Where human and organizational change is involved, it is difficult to determine what kinds of data we should gather that would reliably and validly reflect changes and learning.

In spite of these difficulties, the research effort has proceeded, making adaptations of design and data gathering as these were required by the exigencies of the situation. Those studies which have been done are encouraging. On the whole, results are positive and warrant the optimism we have about laboratory training. But vastly greater efforts will have to be made over the next decade before we can firmly say that laboratory training has been *proven* to be an effective method of personal learning and organizational change.

It should be noted that the difficulties of doing good evaluation research are not unique to laboratory training. Such difficulties are shared by all activities which are primarily concerned with inducing change, notably education and psychotherapy. It has been notoriously difficult to establish, for example, whether directive or participative teaching methods are more likely to be effective as educative methods. Virtually no valid studies exist which establish unequivocally that one method of conducting therapy is more effective than another. And so on.

There is no reason to believe that the practitioners of laboratory training are going to find it easier to solve the research problems than their colleagues in education and psychiatry. But we would hypothesize that those concerned are actually putting more effort and resources into evaluation of outcomes than either the profession of education or psychiatry.

Several factors account for this effort: (1) the practitioner of laboratory training usually has a background of training in the behavioral sciences and specific training in research; (2) there is less of a separation between the clinical and basic fields which constantly exposes laboratory training activities to other social scientists; the trainer is therefore more consistently under fire to justify what he is doing; (3) the ethics and professional standards of laboratory training itself demand that one should not expose people or organizations to forces which have uncertain and possibly deleterious outcomes. These and other forces create a constant and strong pressure to conduct research.

Types of Evaluation Research

Four basic patterns of evaluation research can be distinguished:

1. Integrated research-training design,
2. Before-after measures of delegates,
3. Measures of delegates only after the laboratory,
4. Informal observation, questionnaire administration, and interviews during and after the laboratory.

1. *Integrated Research-Training Designs.* By integrated research-training design, we mean that the laboratory design planners and re-

searchers have worked together from the outset to create a training design that will make it possible to gather the kind of research data that will provide good evaluation and be usable for training purposes.

This kind of research design has been the hardest to engineer for a variety of reasons. In the first place, the value of experimental control demanded by the research project often runs directly counter to the value of creating the best possible training experience. The researcher wants the training design to remain constant, while the trainer wants to adapt it as the laboratory proceeds, or to change it from one laboratory to the next. The researcher wishes to deprive half of the group of a potential learning experience in order to create a control group, while the trainer's ethics demand that he give the best possible experience to all delegates. In order to gather valid data, the researcher wishes to impose a standard testing situation coercively, while the trainer resists any attempt to coerce delegates.

The laboratories that have come closest to this kind of evaluation research have been instrumented ones. They have been standardized to a large degree in the first place, and much of the activity of the laboratory is centered on the gathering of data under more or less controlled conditions. Results obtained in such laboratories are typically in the form of changes in various criterion variables obtained during its course—member ratings of the amount of leveling, of clarity of group goals, feelings of belongingness, self-ratings along various dimensions, and the like. Most laboratories have been able to demonstrate significant changes on measures such as these.[1]

Integrated research-training designs have been conducted at UCLA under the auspices of the Western Training Laboratories (Weschler and Reisel, 1959), and more recently by NTL at Bethel and Arden House. Miles, Argyris, and Blake, among others, have made a concerted effort to build research designs into their training for organizational groups (Miles, et al., in press; Argyris, 1962; Blake and Mouton, 1963). These efforts represent a good beginning toward a full understanding of the changes which training produces and the mechanisms by which such changes occur. However, most research programs are still a long way from the kind of systematic variation of laboratory components which will be needed to understand the mechanisms of training more fully.

The main problems, other than trainer resistance, are: insufficient voluntary populations of delegates who are willing to be control populations of delegates for experimental designs and insufficient funds

---

[1] See Chapter 7 for one example.

and staff resources to conduct systematic studies with adequate control groups. It may also turn out that, as in the case of research on psychotherapy, we will have to develop double-blind research methods because so much of the training impact may be a function of the faith in the training method both on the part of staff members and delegates.

2. *Before-After Measurement Designs.* By a before-after design, we mean that the laboratory population is measured on certain variables prior to the laboratory and on these same variables near the end of or after the laboratory. Evaluation research of a before-after variety is sometimes used in company sponsored training programs. For example, Argyris (1962) studied a top management team's decision-making processes for several months prior to a laboratory experience, and then studied the same group's decision making for some weeks after. Substantial changes in the direction of greater effectiveness were reported.

The problems with implementing this type of research have been: (1) The difficulty of developing good performance indexes which could be reliably assessed both before and after, and (2) the choice of an appropriate control group. Once an organization decides on a laboratory training program, it is often too late to begin gathering the before measures. Such measures, even if possible to obtain, may be invalid if the potential delegates know why the measures are being taken. And, once an organization has embarked on an improvement program, it may be unwilling to deprive certain key people of the training experience merely for the sake of creating a control group.

Before-after designs are also more difficult to implement because the staff does not generally have access to the delegates prior to their entry into the laboratory. Efforts to mail evaluation instruments to delegates or to administer these on the first day of the laboratory are geared to overcoming this difficulty. But this procedure does not surmount the problem of obtaining *objective* performance measures to supplement the self-descriptions obtained on questionnaires. It is also difficult to assess the validity of data that are obtained from someone who has already volunteered for the laboratory experience. The very act of volunteering may already represent a considerable change of self-image.

Blake and Mouton (1963) report a before-after study to evaluate the effects of an idea laboratory in increasing the flow and utilization of ideas in an organization. By means of before-after interviews, questionnaires, and rating scales, they obtained positive changes in tendencies to appraise one's own performance, changes in managerial performance (better listening, greater readiness to face conflict, re-education of interpersonal frictions and blockages, and increased rejection of compromise as the basis for decision making), improved relations between regions and division and between superiors and subordinates. They also obtained increased awareness of and control over outworn traditions, precedents, and past practices, a better comprehension of where the problems of management are, and a greater variety of alternatives for developing solutions to these problems. These changes were observed in addition to the primary ones of increase in the production and utilization of ideas.

Another type of before-after design can best be exemplified by Burke and Bennis' (1961) study of changes of delegate self-images during the course of the laboratory. Instruments to elicit self-descriptions and descriptions of others were administered early and late. Significant changes in perceptions of self and of other group members were demonstrated.

3. *Designs Involving Only After Measures.* Because of the difficulty of designing before-after research, a number of studies have used only *post hoc* evaluations. Results of such designs are difficult to evaluate, hence they tend to be avoided by most researchers.

4. *Evaluation Data Gathered during the Laboratory.* The most common types of evaluation research are those which measure, interview, and observe delegates during and near the end of the laboratory without a systematic attempt to demonstrate before-after changes or to compare delegates with control populations. In this respect, the evaluation is more like a clinical evaluation depending on expert professional judgment than an objective empirical evaluation. This type of evaluation is in a real sense *not* research oriented. Its audience is the laboratory staff rather than the scientific community, and its purpose is to improve the training design, not to assess in detail changes in the delegate.

For example, at the end of one laboratory, all delegates were given a 50 item questionnaire, each question to be answered with a Yes or No. Sample items are:

Do you feel you were adequately oriented to the approaching laboratory experience?

There should have been more theory sessions.

More sessions on skills and techniques, even at the expense of groups time would be desirable.

I feel this has been a harmful experience.

I have felt at times that I was deliberately being brainwashed.

The primary effectivenes of the Laboratory is in individual insight and not in group development.

The overall evaluation was then presented in terms of the number of Yes and No responses to each of the items. As can be seen from the examples, the items were designed to determine how well the laboratory met its goals and to get reactions to the overall laboratory experience and the individual design components. The obvious problem with these types of data is that the enthusiastic delegate may heartily endorse the laboratory at the end of the experience, in spite of having learned very little by other criteria, such as changed behavior on the job. If specific information on a given training design is to be obtained, one should really get such evaluations for two or more designs, holding other things constant, and determine which design elicited the most favorable reactions. An open-ended item which reads, "My biggest objection to the Laboratory is _____," is sometimes used in an attempt to overcome the positive halo effect which delegates may experience at the end of a laboratory, but it is difficult to know how to interpret the responses given unless some comparison group is available.

Many laboratories combine the evaluation with the training by holding an exercise on the last day that encourages delegates to share reactions and comments on the laboratory experience. The staff may form a panel sitting before the delegate group, to share their own reactions as well. While this activity may be helpful in setting a proper mood for closing, it probably generates very little in the way of useful evaluation data in that the general atmosphere of the meeting usually militates against any objective or critical statements. More likely responses are positive testimonials, expressions of thanks, and the like.

Laboratory evaluations also are needed to give the staff a sense of closure and to make recommendations to future staffs. To accomplish this, the staff usually meets for an hour or two after or near the end of the laboratory to conduct its own evaluation. This session uses, as its prime data, the reactions and feelings of the staff members to the total design, supplemented by whatever delegate reactions one or more of them may have gathered.

Conclusion

It is our impression that in recent years, there has been an increasing push toward hard evaluation research of an integrated and before-after kind. As Miles' and Bunker's chapters will show, positive evidence is beginning to accumulate and research approaches are beginning to be formulated which will hopefully put the whole enterprise of laboratory training on a much more scientific foundation. It is likely that this new research will be more differentiated in terms of its goals and methods.

For example, we have pointed out that laboratory outcomes may be in the realm of awareness, attitude change, and interpersonal competence. Perhaps different research methodologies will be used depending on which of these is to be studied. There is also a growing technology of evaluation and action research which differs from the technology of basic and exploratory research (Chin, 1960). All of these trends should aid the long-run research effort.

12

Learning Processes and Outcomes

in Human Relations Training:

A Clinical-Experimental Study

MATTHEW B. MILES

Research on any form of treatment is classically difficult, unrewarding, and infrequent. When the product of a process is change in persons, the criterion problem is ordinarily a major one, whether the treatment occupies the domain of education, mental health, or social functioning. Goals are vaguely stated (partly because of ignorance, partly, it has been suggested, to protect the practitioner against charges of malpractice), and it is claimed that "real" change may not be assessable until long after the treatment has occurred. Even if goals are precisely and operationally defined, it often remains true that treatment programs themselves are difficult to describe accurately enough for later replication. Furthermore, test-treatment interaction is quite likely; subjects are easily sensitized by premeasures. Even more crudely, it is frequently difficult to locate anything like a meaningful control group, let alone establish its equivalence. Finally, Ns are usually small, and the treatment population is often biased through self-selection.

Thus it is not surprising that perhaps 95% of all treatment efforts go unstudied,[1] and that even the 5% typically show serious defects in design, measurement, or data analysis stemming from insufficient

NOTE. This paper, read at the Eastern Psychological Association Meetings, April 16–18, 1964, is based on research conducted by the author with Sanci K. Michael, Frederick L. Whitam, and Thomas M. Harris, and is reported more fully in a forthcoming monograph. It has previously been published in the *Journal of Applied Behavioral Science*, 1, Spring, 1965.
[1] This is probably conservative. A recent study (Johnson, 1964) showed that only ½ of 1 per cent of over 1,500 NDEA grants made in a large state for experimental educational programs—grants which *required* evaluation—were evaluated in any systematic manner.

attention to the problems alluded to above. Furthermore, methodological problems aside, most treatment studies have a central substantive weakness: being relatively atheoretical, they lead to no coherent additions to *either* science or practice. The variables presumed to *explain* the amounts of change in subjects are rarely specified, and change processes during treatment are hardly ever studied.

Yet these problems and dissatisfactions are not insuperable. The present study indicates some ways in which they can be realistically dealt with.[2] A population of persons, all occupying the same occupational role, was studied before, during, and after a human relations training laboratory. The aim was to assess precisely the contributions of personality to, organizational press of, and involvement in treatment processes in the final outcome. Major effort was put into the development of sensitive, durable criterion measures. Carefully selected control groups were employed. Most basically, perhaps, the explanation of learning outcomes during treatment was attempted via the specification of certain components of the treatment—variables thought to explain amounts and types of received change—within a reasonably systematic theoretical network. Finally, the attempt was made to exploit a small population intensively by the use of multiple measures and correlational methods.

Subjects. Thirty-four elementary school principals attending a two-week human relations training laboratory at Bethel, Maine, were used as the experimental population. Two control groups were used: a matched-pair group nominated by the experimental Ss, and a random group ($N = 148$) drawn from a national directory of principals. Comparisons across these groups, and with a national survey of elementary principals conducted by the NEA, indicated that the experimental group members, as might be expected from a self-selected population, had slightly more work experience, were more mobile, and had slightly more independence from their superiors, in comparison to samples of populations not appearing for training. The differences are not large, but the flavor, perhaps predictably, is one of cosmopolitanism rather than localism. Older women were also slightly over-represented.

Procedure. Criterion measures for the experimental group and the two control groups included the Ohio State Leader Behavior Descrip-

---

[2] See also the thorough discussion of these problems, and inventive solutions to them, offered by Hyman, Wright, and Hopkins (1962), using survey methods. For reviews of research on human relations training specifically, see Stock (1964) and Buchanan (1964).

tions Questionnaire, a peer nomination form, the Group Participation Scale (originally developed by Pepinsky et al. (1952) as a counseling criterion measure), and a perceived-change measure combining the views of S with his associates on the job. These were administered in a modified Solomon four-group design prior to, three months after, and eight months after the laboratory. At the laboratory itself a performance test, trainer ratings, and a self-perceived learning measure were also administered. The three variables underlying these instruments were labeled *sensitivity* (perceptiveness re social phenomena), *diagnostic ability* (use of relevant, appropriate explanatory categories in assessing social behavior of self and others), and *action skills* (effective intervention in social situations). The initial number of criterion measurements on each S was 38; combination and purification operations reduced this to 6. The problem of prediction and explanation was approached by hypothesizing that the learner's organizational position and situation, his personality, and his participation in the processes of treatment would all be relevant to his net change on the criterion variables.

Organizational measures included *security* (as measured by length of tenure in present job); *power* (as measured by number of teachers in the principal's school); *autonomy* (as measured by length of time between required reports to superior); and *perceived power* and *perceived adequacy of organizational functioning* (as measured by Likert scales). These variables were expected to condition the strength of desire for change prior to the treatment and to mediate the manifestations of treatment-caused change in the home organization afterward. Figures 12-1 and 12-2 indicate these predicted relationships graphically.

Participation (training-process) measures included: *desire for change, unfreezing* (reduction of defensiveness), *involvement,* and *received feedback.* These were expected to operate in a cumulative-sequential manner during the treatment (see Figure 12-2).

The personality variables measured were *ego strength, rigidity,* and *need affiliation.* These were *not* expected to predict criterion shifts—either during treatment or afterward—but to predict S's standing on the participation variables (see Figure 12-2). For example, an S high in ego strength and need affiliation would presumably be more likely to benefit from received feedback.

A total of 41 predictor variables was measured for each S; this was reduced to 19 via index construction. Data reduction and analysis were primarily accomplished through zero order, partial and multiple

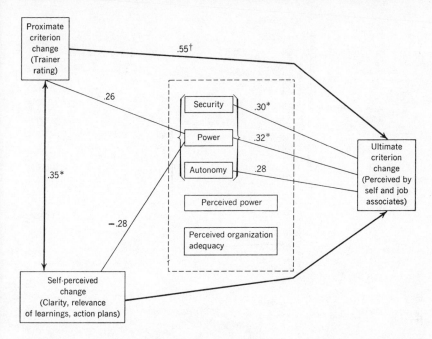

Figure 12–1   Predicted and Obtained Relationships among Criterion Measures and Mediating Organizational Variables. Heavy lines with arrows show predictions. Light lines show where significant (or near significant) relationships were found, but without prediction. Figures by lines of both sorts are obtained r's. $*p < .05$, $†p < .01$. Figures without asterisk or dagger approach significance.

correlation using the raw data and resulting indices, analysis of variance, and McQuitty-type cluster analysis.

Results. Criterion changes measured at the laboratory itself were examined via a multitrait-multimethod matrix, following Campbell and Fiske (1959); the three hypothesized underlying variables (sensitivity, diagnostic ability, and action skill) could not be discriminated across instruments (five different trainer and peer ratings). Thus a weighted "overall effectiveness" score drawn from trainer ratings was used as the basic proximate criterion. Seventy-six per cent of the experimental group showed gain over the two weeks of the treatment on this measure. These scores correlated .35 ($p < .05$) with an index of self-perceived learning (based on ratings of clarity and relevance to job, and number of actions anticipated following return to the job).

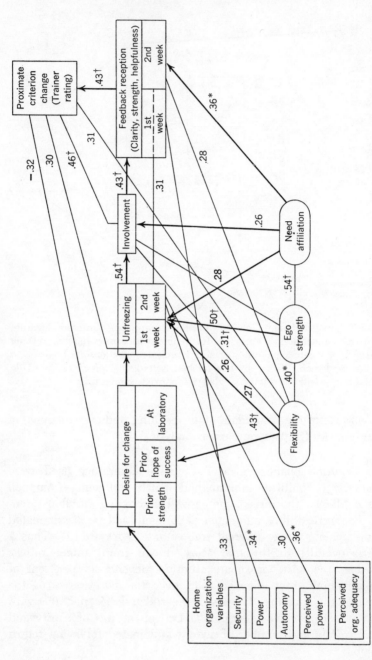

Figure 12–2 Predicted and Obtained Relationships among Organizational, Personality, Treatment Participation, and Criterion Variables. Heavy lines with arrows show predictions. Light lines show where significant (or near significant) relationships were found, but without prediction. Figures by lines of both sorts are obtained r's. *p < .05, †p < .01. Figures without asterisk or dagger approach significance.

The explanatory theory, as inspection of Figure 12-2 and Table 12-1 will indicate, was generally supported, with the exception of the first variable (desire for change), which as measured before the laboratory showed a negative relationship to gain. Ceiling effects and the apparent social desirability of professing a wish for change seemed to be at work.[3] Organizational factors, contrary to prediction, showed no significant correlation with desire for change.

However, the three remaining factors, unfreezing, involvement, and reception of feedback, did appear to operate roughly as hypothesized. A sequential arrangement is suggested by the fact that feedback and involvement are each more closely related to the immediately preceding variable than to any other in the supposed chain. There appears, in addition, to be a warm-up effect; the relationship between received feedback and gain does not appear until the second week, as if the treatment were beginning to take hold. However, a sequential-configural index of the last three participation variables proved no better (r of .51) a predictor of gain than a multiple R (.49).

As predicted, the personality variables did not correlate with gain during treatment, but did relate to some of the participation variables above. Ego strength appears to support unfreezing, early and late in the laboratory;[4] flexibility relates to unfreezing (1st week), and approaches significance with unfreezing (2nd week), involvement, and feedback (2nd week); and need affiliation is associated with reception of feedback (2nd week), approaching significance with unfreezing (2nd week) and involvement.

The analysis reported so far deals solely with measures internal to the treatment experience and has emphasized understanding of the effects of psychological components of the treatment on a proximate criterion measure (trainer ratings). Any evaluation study must also deal with the longer-term, more basic criterion problem.

Analysis of variance showed no experimental-control differences (and no test-treatment interaction) on the LBDQ, and on the Group Participation Scale (on which both E and C scores rose). In retrospect, the LBDQ in particular seems unsuitable as a change-measuring instrument, since each S's score comes from the summation of a number

---

[3] For example, female, older, and less flexible S's tended to have higher desire-for-change scores, yet tended to show less net change than male, younger, more flexible S's.

[4] Ego strength was also related (r's of .33 and .48) to the tendency to perceive feedback as pleasurable rather than painful. However, pleasure/pain is independent of the clarity, strength, and helpfulness of feedback, and of net gain as a result of the laboratory experience.

Table 12-1 Correlates of Change, during and after Treatment

	Change measure		
Personality Factors	Self-perceived, at laboratory	Trainer rating, at laboratory	Self and job associate-perceived, after laboratory
1. Ego strength (revised Barron)	.09	.09	.05
2. Flexibility (revised Barron)	.27	.31*	−.01
3. Need affiliation (French)	.30*	.22	.13
4. Personality index (comb. of 1, 2, 3)	.28	.26	.08
Age	−.41‡	−.17	.07
Sex (male)	.25	.45‡	.33*
Organizational factors			
1. Security (years as a principal)	−.23	−.09	.30*
2. Power (number of teachers)	−.17	.26	.32*
3. Autonomy (infreq. of mtgs. w. sup.)	−.15	−.04	−.03
4. Index combining 1, 2, 3	−.28	.03	.28
5. Perceived power of self in org.	.26	.11	−.06
6. Perceived flex. adequacy of org.	.06	.10	−.15
7. Index combining 5, 6	.18	.12	−.11
Participation factors			
1. Desire for change			
a. Prior need	−.03	−.32*	−.14
b. Prior anticipation of success	−.08	−.28	−.39†
c. During laboratory	−.15	−.03	−.15
2. Unfreezing			
a. First week	.10	.22	.08
b. Second week	.18	.30*	.33*
c. Index combining a and b	.16	.36†	.34†
3. Involvement	.17	.46‡	.25
4. Feedback reception			
a. First week (clear-strong-helpful)	.00	−.02	.04
b. First week (pleasurableness)	−.09	.10	.03
c. Second week (clear-strong-helpful)	.45‡	.43‡	.04
d. Second week (pleasurableness)	.27	.23	.12

Table 12–1 (*continued*)

| | Change measure | | |
Change during treatment	Self- perceived, at laboratory	Trainer rating, at laboratory	Self and job associate- perceived, after laboratory
1. Trainer rating	.35†	—	.55†
2. Self-perceived change	—	.35†	.06

* $p < .10$
† $p < .05$
‡ $p < .01$

For simplicity, these are two-tailed significance levels, since not all relationships were predicted.

(averaging 5) of his associates' scores; averaging effects occur and score stability is likely. The criterion measure developed by us was essentially primitive; both S and his associates were asked to describe any behavior changes which had occurred during the period under scrutiny, and extra scoring weight was given to "verified" changes— ones on which S and an associate, or two associates, agreed. The experimental-control differences on the eight-month post administration of this instrument are shown in Table 12-2. The various measures derived from the data indicate that experimental Ss appear to have changed with about three times as much frequency as control Ss, even when the base rate of control group change is allowed for.

A preliminary content analysis of the changes reported more frequently in E than C groups indicated that they fell mostly in the areas of increased sensitivity to others, equalitarian attitudes, skills of communication and leadership, and group and maintenance skills. Personal traits, such as "more considerate" and "relaxed," account for about a quarter of the reported changes in the E group, with organization-relevant changes (such as "delegates more") and group-relevant changes (such as "aids group decision-making") making up the remainder. This rough balance also occurred in the participants' self-reported learnings at the close of the treatment period,[5] and is congruent with the laboratory staff's statements of objectives.

---

[5] Bunker (1963) has since employed this measure in a study of the effects of six different training laboratories; similar experimental-control differences were found. The scoring method and the content analysis scheme have been considerably developed and refined; the measure now seems eminently suitable and usable for any treatment aiming at behavior change in S, including psychotherapy.

Table 12–2   Retrospective Changes in Behavior Reported by Self and Working Associates, Eight Months after Training Period

	Experi-mental Group (N = 34)	Matched Control Group (N = 29)		Random Control Group (N = 148)
Median change score*	3.5	1		1
Mean change score	4.4	1.2	†	1.7
S. D.	3.93	1.44		2.10
Per cent of Ss above base rate (score 2)	73	17	†	29
Per cent mentioning a behavior change in S:				
- Self	82	33	†	21‡
- Associates	30	10		12‡
Per cent of S's who have at least *two* associates mentioning a behavior change in S:	47	0	†	12
(Associate N)	178	140		155

* Score derived by totaling discrete changes mentioned, and adding 1 unit for each instance of associate-associate or self-associate agreement.
† Matched vs. random differences significant at .05 level. All E vs. C differences significant at .01.
‡ N is 34 randomly-selected subjects from the random control group.

This basic criterion measure gains added validity when we note that ratings of gain (the proximate criterion referred to above) made by the staff trainer who saw the participant longest and most intensively during the laboratory correlate .55 ($p < 01$) with it (Figure 12-1). Interestingly enough, the self-perceived measure of gain taken at the end of the treatment period shows no relationship with change on the job eight months later; apparently a competent professional sees behavior shifts which are not self-apparent to S.

It appears that some objective organizational factors may mediate to some extent between proximate and ultimate criterion changes. (Interestingly, *perceived* organizational factors seem not to have any mediatory effects). Table 12-1 and Figure 12-1 indicate that S's with high security (longer experience) are among the higher changers on the job ($r = .30$). If amounts of change during treatment are held constant by partial correlation, the relationship rises to .42. Figured the other way, the correlation of .55 between treatment and job change becomes .61 when the factor of security in organization is held constant. The factor of power (number of teachers in school) correlates .32 with change on the job, but this is reduced to .22 by holding treatment change constant. The treatment vs. job change correlation is relatively unaffected by power (.55 to .51). Partial correlations can conceal the nature of relationships; Table 12-3 gives some indication of how the mediation works. The majority of high changers during treatment who have high or moderate power and security at home also show high job change; low changers with low power and security change less when they return. And the middle group (high treatment changers with low organizational support, and low changers with high support) seem about equally likely for change on the job.

Table 12-3 Proximate and Ultimate Criterion Changes, as Mediated by Own Power and Security in Home Organization

		Ultimate criterion change (Self and job associate perceived)	
Proximate criterion change (Trainer rating)	Power/Security		
High	Moderate and high	2 / 2	10 / 9
High	Low	3 / 3	2 / 3
Low	Moderate and high	7 / 5	5 / 4
Low	Low	5 / 7	0 / 1

Finally, as predicted, personality variables did not show a relationship with change in job behavior of these subjects (Table 12-1).

Implications and Conclusions. The methodological problems of treatment studies can be overcome, given care in design, measurement, and data analysis. The main strategies employed in this study were those of careful criterion measurement and refinement, the use of a role-homogeneous population, the location of plausible control groups, the assessment of possible test-treatment interaction, the predictive analysis of components thought to cause change on criterion measures, and the use of large numbers of measures.[6]

Substantively, we have found valid experimental-control differences as a result of a human relations training experience; gains by Ss were primarily predicted by variables connected with S's actual participation in the treatment. The organizational variables studied had less impact on S's entrance to treatment than expected, but did appear to affect his subsequent use of his learnings on the job. The personality variables studied only seemed of importance insofar as they affected S's behavior during treatment.

---

[6] With so many relationships to be examined, the question of capitalizing on randomly-distributed significant correlations becomes important. A check on the *initial* (not reduced) matrix indicated that of the 595 relationships among the 27 nonconfounded predictors and 8 criteria, 54 reached the .05 level (two-tailed test) when 30 might have appeared by chance, and 23 reached the .01 level, when 6 might have by chance. The majority of these relationships had been predicted.

13

The Effect of Laboratory Education

upon Individual Behavior

DOUGLAS R. BUNKER

Training in awareness of self and social processes by laboratory methods has been going on for most of two decades. While current approaches are diverse and innovation is continuous, both the behavioral scientists who staff training laboratories and most of the managers, leaders, and educators who participate in them have in common an aspiration to promote more ·effective action in groups and organizations. In laboratory training, more than in most educational enterprises, increased intellectual understanding of the subject matter and altered attitudes are not enough. The aim, whether an individual or an intact organizational group is the unit in training, is to enable participants to make adaptive changes in their perceptions and behavior in their back-home organizational setting. From the theoretical perspective underlying this type of training, adaptive changes are likely to be those which improve self-understanding and the capacity for open, meaningful working relationships with others— relationships in which both collaboration and conflict can be rendered productive.

Inquiry into training processes and outcomes has paralleled the development of laboratory educational methodology (Stock, 1964; Durham and Gibb, 1960). Of the many studies which have investigated training laboratory phenomena, few have explored long-

NOTE. This article is drawn from research conducted by the author with Matthew B. Miles and Eric Knowles under the support of the National Training Laboratories, Washington, D.C. A monograph reporting the entire study in detail is in progress. (An earlier version of this paper has been reprinted as item 4, 1963, NTL Subscription Service).

range consequences in the work environment. One such investigation reported by Miles (1960a) was the point of departure for this study. In comparing a group of public school principals who had participated in a laboratory training workshop with both matched and random control groups of principals who had not, Miles, using an open-ended, perceived-change measure, found that experimentals were seen to have changed significantly more over a ten-month period than controls in sensitivity and behavioral skill. "Change," he writes, "was more apparent in organization and group-relevant behavior than in global attributes of the self" (Miles, 1960a). These results provide evidence that changes initiated in the laboratory setting can be applied over time in work relationships in the home organization. Similar results have been obtained from research on internal training programs reported by Argyris (1961) and the Personnel Research Department of a Canadian utility (Boyd and Elliss, 1962).

This study represents an effort to determine whether Miles' findings relative to behavior changes among school principals can be extended to an occupationally diverse, larger group of participants in training laboratories. A second purpose of this inquiry is to provide an empirical explication of the dimensions of change in on-the-job performance that might be associated with laboratory education. The focus of the inquiry is upon changes in individual behavior, but the research methods are designed to tap those types of change which are most visible and organizationally consequential.

Six separate educational conferences were selected to be evaluated. Although they were all conducted by the National Training Laboratories at Bethel, Maine, in the summers of 1960 and 1961, the staff of each conference was different, and the training design for each was unique in some respects. The three conferences conducted in the summer of 1960 were three weeks long, while those in 1961 were shortened to two weeks. In each summer, two of the programs were general human relations training laboratories, having a heterogeneous population including participants from industrial, governmental, religious, educational, medical, and social service organizations. The other program included each summer was a special session conducted for educational leaders, ranging from superintendents of school systems to assistant principals, and including a few senior classroom teachers. With staff, training design, and participant characteristics all varying, we should still recognize the invariant components of the educational situation which might be critical to the change induction.

The participants, though diverse, were for the most part self-selected —most having some at least tentatively favorable predisposition toward this type of educational experience. The training staffs overlapped somewhat, with a few staff members being involved in as many as three of the six conferences while others worked in only one.

Research Design and Methods

Miles (1960a) has correctly observed that laboratory training research shares problems with other kinds of treatment evaluation research in social science. These include the difficulty of obtaining comparable control groups, the problem of separating treatment effects from normal or base rate change and growth, and the perplexities involved in selecting a criterion which is at once measurable and operationally meaningful. Confronting these difficulties, we made efforts to deal with them in a way that would provide data with which we could assess the effects of laboratory training. Basic elements of the design were adaptations from Miles (1960a): A matched-pair control group was obtained by asking each experimental subject to nominate an appropriate control subject from his backhome setting, and an open-ended perceived-change questionnaire completed by several describers for each subject was the primary data source. The most important methodological innovation in this study is an objective coding scheme which increases scoring reliability and permits an assessment of the types of changes making up each subject's total change score.

Design for Data Collection

Because the focus of the inquiry was change on-the-job, participants were first asked to cooperate in the study eight to ten months after they had returned to the job setting. Beginning the collection of data after this much time had passed enabled us to tap whatever durable effects had survived the waning of immediate post-training enthusiasm and the erosive effects of organizational constraints. The separation of training and inquiry also had the advantage of reduced contamination of data from awareness of the training activity on the part of others in the organization who would be asked to provide change descriptions. At the same time, of course, the lag permitted a number of other events to intervene. Some of these (e.g., relocations and promotions) were reported, thus reducing the size of the research population; others (e.g., changes in organizational structure or participation in contaminating training activities), unknown to us, probably operated with mixed effects upon our criterion for both experimental and control subjects.

The general strategy was to obtain self-descriptions from both experimental and control subjects and, for each, an additional set of five to seven descriptions of observed behavior changes from peers, superiors, and subordinates. Control subjects were nominated by the experimentals on the basis of the following criteria: (1) identity or close similarity of organizational role to that of the participant; (2) no prior participation in the type of training program being evaluated; (3) openness or readiness, in the judgment of the nominator, to participate in laboratory training if the opportunity were offered. (This stipulation was added to reduce the probability that basic differences in orientation toward self and others might exist between members of the control and experimental groups). Describers were selected by asking all subjects to submit the names of 10 people with whom they had continuing working relationships which dated back at least 15 months. From these names seven people were randomly selected to receive questionnaires.

Criterion Development

The open-ended question for subjects took the following form: "Over a period of time, people may change in the ways they work with other people. Since May of 1960 (or 1961) do you believe you have changed your behavior in working with people in any specific ways as compared with the previous year? Yes____. No____. If 'Yes,' please describe." A similar item was used to elicit descriptions of subjects from their associates.

The great volume of verbal material contained in responses to these questions required that we employ an objective method of classifying and counting the responses so as to permit statistical comparisons. While our first inclination was to impose a previously used, theoretically meaningful set of categories upon the data, the notion of developing new categories inductively and thus learning something about the kinds of dimensions intrinsic to the descriptions also seemed reasonable. We followed the latter course on the ground that the more important discriminations were those made by people in the organizational settings in which we are trying to assess change. This was consistent with the prior decision to make the form of the question open-ended in order to permit respondents to describe behavior changes using constructs that are both personally meaningful and organizationally relevant.

Inductively Derived Categories for Content Analysis[1]

A. Overt Operational Changes—Descriptive

1. Communication
   S. Sending. Shares information, expresses feelings, puts ideas across.
   R. Receiving. More effort to understand, attentive listening, understands.
2. Relational facility. Cooperative, tactful, less irritating, easier to deal with, able to negotiate.
3. Risk-taking. Willing to take stand, less inhibited, experiments more.
4. Increased interdependence. Encourages participation, involves others, greater leeway to subordinates, less dominating, lets others think.
5. Functional flexibility. More flexible, takes group roles more easily, goes out of way, contributions more helpful, less rigid.
6. Self-control. More self-discipline, less quick with judgment, checks temper.

B. Inferred Changes in Insight and Attitudes

1. Awareness of human behavior (intellectual comprehension). More conscious of why people act, more analytic of others' actions, clear perceptions of people.
2. Sensitivity to group behavior. More conscious of group process, aware of subcurrents in groups.
3. Sensitivity to others' feelings. More capacity for understanding feelings, more sensitive to needs of others.
4. Acceptance of other people. Able to tolerate shortcomings, considerate of individual differences, patient.
5. Tolerance of new information. Willing to accept suggestions, considers new points of view, less dogmatic, less arbitrary.
6. Self-confidence.
7. Comfort. Relaxed, at ease (must be specific as to setting or activity).

---

[1] Scoring depends upon an explicit statement of qualitative or quantitative difference. Changes may be positive or negative reflecting increases or decreases in quantity and greater or lesser utility. Precise category fit according to scoring conventions required for sets of categories A and B.

8. Insight into self and role. Understands job demands, more aware of own behavior, better adjusted to job.

C. Global Judgments—Gross characterological inferences, noncomparable references to special applications of learning, and references to consequences of change.

Following a long period of inductive derivation and testing, category specifications were determined and a team of coders were trained.[2] The scoring task involved assigning each mention of a specific change to one of 21 content categories. For each protocol a maximum score of one was assigned for each category in which there was one or more mentions. The categories were sufficiently fine that this did not waste any data, and the ease with which the scorers could make the present-absent discrimination had a salutary effect upon the interscorer reliability. Following training, the percentage of agreements between scorers in assignment of mentions to categories was consistently above 90 per cent.

Protocols were stripped of group identification prior to scoring so as to ensure a blind process. Also, at the end of the 18-month data collection period a mixed sample of 1960 and 1961 responses were independently recoded by two persons to check drift in the use of the categories. Score stabilities over this period of time again exceeded 90 per cent agreement in individual coding decisions.

Questionnaire Response

Since the rate of return for mailed questionnaires tends to be very low and the resultant problem of subject self-selection is so destructive of otherwise well-conceived research designs, special efforts were made to avoid this difficulty. The simplicity of the questionnaire, accompanying explanatory letters, numerous reminders, and commitments to provide a summary of research findings likely, combined to give quite astounding response statistics. Only a third of the control subjects and less than one-quarter of the experimental subjects did not reply or refused to cooperate. After others were eliminated because of job changes and intervening or preceding training experiences, 346 or 56 per cent of both the original experimental and control groups were included in the study. The describer response ratios were even more satisfactory. Eighty-four per cent of nearly 2,400 describers who

---

[2] The author was assisted by Eric Knowles, Ethel Hutchings, and Fred I. Steele in the development and application of the scoring system.

received questionnaires returned usable responses. On the basis of these figures, subject-selection can be eliminated as an important source of error variance in this study.

Change Scores

By combining cell values (zero or one) in the matrix of categories and describers for each subject, a variety of scores were obtained. The most comprehensive indices are a total-change score based upon the matrix sum, and a verified-change score developed by counting the number of observations of a particular subject in which two or more describers concur. Separate scores for category sets A, B, and C, and for self-ratings as differentiated from others' descriptions were also used.

Results and Discussion

Group Comparisons Using Summary Scores

The first analytic slice into the data is a comparison of total-change scores for those who had participated in laboratory training with those who had not. Examination of Table 13-1, which presents this analysis with the distribution divided into thirds, permits us to say that a significantly greater proportion of experimental subjects than controls were in the middle and top thirds of the distribution of change scores. The probability of a value of Chi-square as large as that obtained is less than .001 if the groups are not different. Further, when the same type of comparison is made independently for 1960 and 1961 data, subject and describer scores, and category-sets A and B, the pattern of results in Table 13-1 is reproduced.

Only when the experimental-control comparison is applied to set C data do we find no differences. A straightforward although somewhat after-the-fact interpretation of this negative result provides a reason to believe that the positive results obtained with total-change scores are not mere methodological artifacts. Category set C is the global and miscellaneous pit into which relatively nonspecific and other marginally scorable descriptions of change are cast. When respondents are asked to accommodate a researcher by providing a change description and they want to oblige, but do not have a concrete and specific behavioral referent, they tend to put down vague and global descriptions. This happens for both experimental and control

Table 13-1 Distribution of Experimental and Control Subjects, According to Total-Change Scores

	Experimental Subjects	Control Subjects	Total
Upper 9–23	99 (43.2%)	16 (14.3%)	115
Middle 5 to 8	81 (35.4%)	34 (30.3%)	115
Lower −3 to 4	49 (21.4%)	62 (55.4%)	111
N	229	112	341

$x^2 = 45.88$
(d.f. = 2)
$p\,(x^2 = 45.88) < .001$

describers with about equal frequency and is likely an important component of the base rate of change. These set C results are instructive in their contrast with other findings and in the emphasis they give to the discriminating power of scores based upon specific descriptions.

Further contrast between experimental and control groups can be seen in Table 13-2, in which the groups are compared with respect to the frequency of agreement among describers. The significance of the difference between the proportions of subjects with one or more confirmed change permits further credence in the interpretation that laboratory training tends to facilitate changes in behavior in the

Table 13-2 The Number of Subjects with One or More Verified Changes (Percentages in Parentheses)

	Experimental Group	Control Group	Totals
One or more changes verified by Describer concurrence	152 (66.7)	37 (33.3)	189
No Verifications	76 (33.3)	74 (66.7)	150
Totals	228	111	339

$x^2 = 33.75$, $p(x^2 \equiv 33.75) < .001$
d.f. = 1

job setting. The agreements in detailed descriptions of behavior changes make it difficult to attribute these differences to mere describer bias induced by awareness of the subject's participation or nonparticipation in training. It is more parsimonious to accept these independent but concurring change reports as largely objective.

The ways in which our subjects changed over the assessment period are revealed in the category descriptions for these categories were constructed so as to minimize the distortion of the original descriptions. We also need to know, however, what kinds of changes were reported most frequently and which categories discriminated most clearly between laboratory participants and controls. Data to answer these questions are provided in Table 13-3.

Eleven of the fifteen categories discriminate between experimental and control subjects beyond the .05 level of significance. The large number of sensitive categories and the fact that the most popular category includes only half of the experimental subjects indicate the

Table 13–3   An Analysis by Scoring Category of the Differences between Experimental and Control Groups in Proportions of Subjects Reported as Changed

		Proportions Perceived as Changed		
Scoring Category	Label	Experi-mentals	Controls	Differences
A-1S	Sending	.3275	.2328	.0947
A-1R	Receiving communication	.3406	.1638	.1768†
A-2	Relational facility	.3581	.2069	.1512†
A-3	Risk taking	.3188	.2241	.0947
A-4	Increased interdependence	.3843	.2741	.1102*
A-5	Functional flexibility	.2271	.1293	.0978
A-6	Self-control	.2620	.1552	.1068*
B-1	Awareness of behavior	.3362	.1638	.1725†
B-2	Sensitivity to group process	.2402	.0862	.1540†
B-3	Sensitivity to others	.3450	.1034	.2416†
B-4	Acceptance of others	.4934	.2931	.2003†
B-5	Tolerance of new information	.4192	.2328	.1864†
B-6	Confidence	.2882	.1897	.0985
B-7	Comfort	.3624	.2328	.1296*
B-8	Insight into self and role	.3581	.2414	.1167*

* $p < .05$
† $p < .01$

degree to which laboratory training outcomes tend to be individual and varied. A close look at some of the original data indicates that some subjects are perceived by their describers as having changed adaptively in the direction of an increase in assertive behavior and more willingness to take a stand, while other subjects are approvingly described as having decreased their aggressive behavior and become more sensitive to others' feelings. These findings indicate that in the training programs studied, there is no standard learning outcome and no stereotyped ideal toward which conformity is induced. In this respect these results are very similar to those reported by Boyd and Elliss:

> There were also wide differences in kind of response. The comparison of the cafeteria, which someone has applied to this form of development, comes to mind. Far from absorbing some standard lessons, each evidently chooses for himself. There were the quiet ones who came out of their shell to speak with greater confidence and definiteness. There were some who learned to consider more carefully before rendering a decision, while at the same time others received a spur to make up their minds. There were some with a chip on their shoulder who relaxed their defensive stance. There were those in the habit of expressing strong opinions or of holding decisions close to themselves who found that others had more to offer than they had supposed, and learned to listen, to consult, or to delegate. (Boyd and Elliss, 1962, p. 7)

Although changes are more frequent for experimental subjects in all categories, there are differences among categories in the proportion of subjects for whom change was reported. The cluster of categories with both the highest proportions of participants seen as changed and the largest experimental-control differences has increased openness, receptivity, tolerance of differences as its common content (B-4, B-5, A-1R). A second cluster (A-4, A-2, A-6) has a theme of increased operational skill in interpersonal relations with overtones of increased capacity for collaboration. A third major cluster has to do with improved understanding and diagnostic awareness of self, others, and interactive processes in groups (B-1, B-2, B-3, B-8). There are empathic as well as purely intellectual threads binding this third cluster. These three dimensions constitute the principal types of adaptive, self-directed changes accelerated by participation in laboratory education conferences.

A fourth cluster consisting of three of the categories which do not significantly discriminate between experimentals and controls arises from these data (A-1S, A-3, B-6). The common content of this set seems to be increased and more effective initiation and assertiveness.

While at least one-third of the participants made changes in this direction, when compared with the other categories and to the proportions of control subjects observed as changing in these ways, it appears that the training programs did not have their major impact in this area. The fact that within the wide individual differences in learning outcomes some subjects are rated as making their major move in this direction, may indicate that it is not the nature of the training activity that limits change in this direction. The composition of the trainee population may be the critical determinant. If the participants were selected heavily from among those whose reticence and reactive tendencies were inappropriately passive for the demands of their work environments, we might expect this fourth cluster to be more important as an ultimate outcome. Since the majority of laboratory participants are persons with leadership responsibilities and at least moderate influence in their home organizations, the three principal classes of change discussed above may reflect the participants diagnosis of particular organizational requirements. Although further research is needed to clarify these issues, the best answer on the basis of these findings is that the long-term outcomes of laboratory education tend to be increased capacity for adaptive orientation to the participants' particular situation rather than the stereotyped enactment of an ideology. The roots of such behavior changes lie in improved methods of collecting and processing information about the organizational environment and increased personal freedom to act on the basis of that information.

Training Processes and Long-Term Change

One recurrent finding relates to the question of the connection between behavior in the training situation and behavior changes following return to the home environment. A central proposition underlying laboratory education is that, in the laboratory, conditions are provided (contrast of social setting with the familiar, emotional support, access to knowledge of results of behavior) under which participants may more freely experiment with behavior and find alternative ways of dealing with their interpersonal environment. Responsible experimentation toward the development of more effective ways of attaining individual and group goals is the most direct laboratory learning process. But, there are individual differences in readiness to experiment and receptiveness to feedback about the consequences of one's action.

Some members of training groups take more risks, receive more feedback, and make more adaptive behavioral adjustments than others. If this conception of the learning process is approximately correct, these more involved and exposed participants should be those who are more often seen as having changed their behavior in their home organizations as well. We should expect then that observational measures of learning and change in the training group will be directly correlated with change scores obtained in the work environment 6 to 12 months later. Miles (1960) reported a product-moment correlation coefficient of .55 ($p < .01$) between his laboratory change ratings and organizational change scores about a year later.

A second test of this relationship was made by pooling data from a study by Harrison (1962) on training processes and immediate learning outcomes with the Bunker data on long range changes for the same subjects. The Harrison measure was based upon ratings by peers in the learning group of the amount of behavior change in response to feedback evidenced over the two-week training period. This measure and the Bunker verified-change score described above were found to correlate .32 ($p < .01$, $N = 57$). The laboratory rating was also positively correlated with the total change score ($r = .23$, $p < .05$) and with a composite score for category set A ($r = .24$, $p < .05$). Inspection of these data in Table 13–4 indicates that the principal contributions to co-variance are in the upper thirds of the long-range change score distributions. Seventy-four (73.7) percent of those in the upper third of the distribu-

Table 13–4 The Relation between an Immediate Measure of Laboratory Learning and Long-Range Change Scores

A.		Verified Changes			Proportion of
		L	M	H*	each row sum in H column
Laboratory	H	8	5	11	.458
Learning	M	9	3	5	.294
Score	L	9	6	1	.063

B.		Total Change Score			
		L	M	H	
Laboratory	H	6	4	14	.583
Learning	M	8	5	4	.235
Score	L	6	9	1	.063

* The distributions were divided as equally as their truncated nature would permit into Lower, Middle, and Upper Thirds for visual presentation. Statistical relationships are reported in the text.

tion of total change scores were in the upper third of the distribution of laboratory learning scores (proximal change). Back-home application of learnings appears to be much less probable for those who did not become actively involved in the training processes.

This pattern of results in which those who are most active tend to display long-term results supports a model of behavior change which approximates that described above. A parallel finding from these data is confirmation of the indication that some, but certainly not all, laboratory participants acquire transferable skills and attitudes that facilitate their interpersonal performance at work.

A very recent finding by Harrison and Oshry (1964) bears upon the issues just discussed. In a study of an organizational laboratory training program, they found that those who learned most in a T-group and applied their learnings most effectively tended to be those who were described by supervisors and peers before the training as being open to new ideas and to the expression of feelings. In the diagnosis of organizational problems they were seen as avoiding the assignment of blame to others and to the system. Those who were low in measures of learning and learning applications were described before the laboratory as inconsiderate of others and closed to new ideas. Their perceptions of organizational problems placed the causes outside themselves, in others and in the organization. If this pattern can be confirmed by other findings, it will appear that trainability has similar dimensions to training outcomes. Those who are open to new information can learn to become more so. The same characteristics and behaviors which block effective performance in working with others prior to laboratory participation seem to impair the ability to learn about self and social processes by laboratory methods.

The past five years have seen a good many new starts on research efforts to explicate the dimensions of laboratory training processes. Studies recently completed or under way examine individual personality factors, trainer characteristics and trainer behavior, group composition, group process variables, and features of training designs as determinants of laboratory education outcomes. In most cases, however, the outcome criteria have not included objective measures of long-range behavioral changes. Now that improved criterion measures are available, the next step is the systematic investigation of the relationship between each of these classes of determinants and application outcomes. There is strong evidence that groups, individuals and entire training programs have differential learning outcomes, but as yet there is no systematic evidence concerning the links between particular design components and observed applications.

Part IV

A THEORY OF LEARNING
THROUGH
LABORATORY TRAINING

This part of the book is our attempt to explain on a theoretical basis why laboratory training works as a learning method. In Chapter 14, we present an abstract overview of our theory of learning. In Chapter 15, we examine one aspect of the theory, that having to do with attitude change, in the context of the back-home setting. Here we are attempting to show why most organizations do not stimulate the kind of learning which laboratory training makes possible. We give a more detailed analysis of the forces which stimulate learning in the typical laboratory setting in Chapter 16. Finally, in Chapter 17, we state some hypotheses about the relative impact of different aspects of laboratories such as length and heterogeneity on the kinds and amount of learning.

This part of the book is written more abstractly because of our desire to develop the beginnings of some testable learning theory. It is of greatest relevance for our academic colleagues and for the laboratory trainer and designer. The lay reader wishing simply to acquaint himself with the uses of laboratory training could well skip this part and go on to Chapter 18.

14

A General Overview of Our Learning Theory

Introduction

Some of the commonest questions people ask about laboratory training are "why does it work, how do people learn in a laboratory, or in a T-group, how come they learn different things or more things in a laboratory than they do in more traditional educative experiences?" Curiously enough, we have as yet no satisfactory answers to these questions. In spite of the fact that one can witness dramatic learning in laboratory settings, we are desperately shy of good explanations of why and how it happens.

There is no lack of general models of the laboratory learning process, such as those presented in Chapter 3, but these models only identify broad phases of or minimum conditions for learning. They somehow miss the flavor or the essence of what goes on in a laboratory; they do not come to terms with the emotional flow, the tensions, the excitement, the trauma, and the discovery which are so much a part of life in the laboratory and in the T-group. They tend to be cognitive models, while the important learning is going on at the level of feelings and attitudes.

The dearth of good laboratory theory is reminiscent of the situation in psychotherapy where practice has also outrun credible theory. Outcomes can be systematically related to certain kinds of inputs on the part of the patient and the therapist, but the essential mechanisms of personal change remain somehow obscure.

Another way of focusing the dilemma of theory is to point particularly to the lack of *learning or change* theory, not of all theory. There are available excellent theories of group development, for example, just as there are excellent theories of neurosis. But such theories often leave one without any understanding of how to induce change or to create a learning situation, except by experience and/or intuition. The fact that a T-group reliably goes through certain phases of development concerning problems of authority and problems of intimacy tells us little about how delegates come to have greater awareness, different attitudes, or greater competence. Somehow, we need to focus on the why of it, the *learning* theory. This is what we will attempt to do in the next several chapters.

The Basic Learning Cycle

One of the major reasons why learning theory has been so difficult to develop in reference to laboratory training is that the learning outcomes involve at one and the same time a *cognitive* element (increased awareness), an *emotional* element (changed attitudes), and a *behavioral* element (changed interpersonal competence). How do we juggle these three levels of change simultaneously? Or, do we need three separate theories, one for each element?

We believe that the answer to this dilemma lies in the concept of a *cycle*, of a sequence of learning steps which are interdependent. Specifically, the learning cycle or sequence is a series of overlapping steps starting with dilemmas or with disconfirming information which produces attitude change. Attitude change in turn produces new behavior which serves as data for others, and thus produces new awareness in others; this new awareness produces more attitude change and more new behavior, and so on. Ultimately, the learning process in a laboratory is a constant flow of this sort of overlapping steps or stages. The flow is initiated by certain kinds of information input (dilemmas or disconfirmations) and is similarly terminated by certain kinds of information input (reconfirmations). The cycle could be diagrammed as follows:

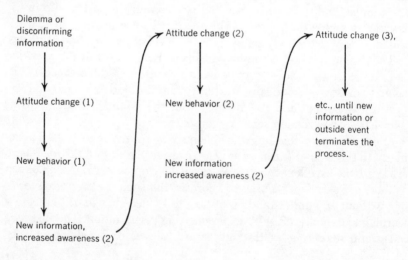

Having stated this highly abstract concept of the learning process, let us pin it down more concretely. The learning process starts with some dilemmas or some disconfirming information about the person's self; he obtains cues that not all is right in his relationships with others. Such information may come to him before or early in the laboratory. However, in order to be able to learn from the laboratory, the person must then change his attitudes about the learning process itself. In effect, he must come to accept some of the meta-goals of laboratory training, particularly those which pertain to a spirit of inquiry and a willingness to be more authentic in relationships. The person will not be able to obtain new awareness of himself and others unless he learns to pay attention to and to value the here-and-now data which he and others generate in the laboratory. *Learning to pay attention to and value such data involves a fundamental attitude change toward the learning process itself. This first attitude change step is, therefore, the single most important component in the total learning cycle.*

Let us emphasize this point by saying it another way. A person cannot learn about himself and others in a group unless he gets certain categories of information which are not readily available. And, he cannot get these categories of information unless his attitudes change about which kinds of data are relevant, which data he is willing to reveal about himself and which data he is willing to pay attention to in others. To put it even more concretely, the learning process at the outset, hinges upon a person's becoming willing and able to reveal his own feelings and reactions, and upon his becoming willing and able to listen and pay attention to the feelings and reactions of others.[1]

If this initial attitude change step is successfully accomplished by at least a reasonable percentage of the members of the laboratory, if they can accept some of the meta-goals of training, new behavior is generated. This new behavior is, at the same time, the kind of information which others need to increase their awareness of self, others, and the group. In other words, if attitudes toward the learning process change, group members will begin to reveal their reactions and feelings about each other and what the group is doing and will thereby generate the data which others need in order to increase their awareness of what is going on.

The new data (reactions and feelings) now serve as an information input which may well disconfirm certain other attitudes. Not attitudes about learning, but rather attitudes which the person has toward him-

---

[1] In Chapter 16, we will devote the bulk of the discussion to this very issue of how the laboratory culture and setting contributes to willingness to reveal and willingness to listen.

self, toward others, and toward groups. Such disconfirmations then require a new cycle of attitude change to begin. Let us underline that this time, the attitudes are not about the learning process; instead, they are about self, others, and the group. If some of these attitudes change in one or more members, this change will lead once again to new behavior which will serve as new data and information input to others, increasing their awareness and/or disconfirming still other attitudes which they may hold. So the process continues until either external forces bring it to a close, e.g., termination of the laboratory, or until an equilibrium is reached in which new behavior on the part of one member no longer proves to be disconfirmatory information for another member.

It should be noted that the basic elements of this cycle are (1) that information serves both as the source of attitude change and increased awareness, depending upon the degree to which it unfreezes the person, (2) that attitude change is the fundamental prerequisite to behavior change, and (3) that only behavior change makes new information available to others. In this sense, the three levels of learning are highly interdependent and must be treated as parts of a single learning process. By way of summary, we can now diagram this process as follows:

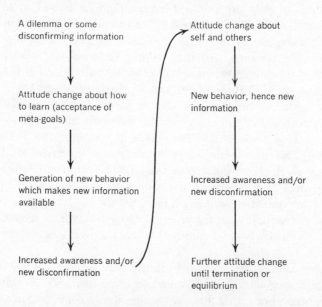

We do not expect that this relatively complex model of the learning process really communicates how delegates learn. In the next chapters, we will try to be more concrete and specific, to bring the model to life.

In the present chapter, we are attempting to present the theory *in general,* to provide an overview before we get into the specific illustrations of how the laboratory operates.

A Model of Attitude Change

In the basic learning cycle presented above, we have not said anything about the mechanisms or processes which characterize the step called "attitude change." Yet, this step is a crucial part of the theory because if we cannot understand how attitudes change we cannot really understand the learning process. Attitude change is a central component of the learning process and must, therefore, itself be understood.

We are talking about the changing of a certain category of attitudes —those attitudes which pertain to the learning process and those which pertain to self, others, and groups. One key characteristic of such attitudes is that they are generally quite central to the person and are likely to be integrated with his self-concept and his personality. Dilemmas and disconfirmations arise from and in turn produce powerful emotional responses and arouse what might well be called "social anxiety" or anxiety about basic sense of identity. Consequently, attitudes in this area are likely to be strongly held and to resist change. The kind of model of attitude change we will present is specifically designed to deal with the changing of such strongly held central attitudes.

In the present chapter, we will present the model in summary form, going into greater detail in the following chapter. Essentially, the model specifies that attitude change consists of three stages or phases which correspond closely to what Lewin identified as the stages of change—(1) unfreezing, (2) changing, and (3) refreezing. The first two of these stages are necessary conditions of change, the third is concerned with the stability of whatever change occurs. Under each of these stages, we can identify certain key mechanisms, as follows:

Stage 1. Unfreezing
    1. Lack of confirmation or disconfirmation.
    2. Induction of guilt-anxiety.
    3. Creation of psychological safety by reduction of threat or removal of barriers to change.
Stage 2. Changing
    1. Scanning the interpersonal environment.
    2. Identifying with a model.
Stage 3. Refreezing
    1. Personal—integrating new responses into the rest of the personality and attitude system.

2. Relational—integrating new responses into ongoing significant relationships.

Basically, we are saying that attitude change begins with a disequilibrium, with some information about a person that leaves him uncomfortable because it is unexpected or violates his image of himself. Often such disconfirming information leaves him feeling anxious or guilty. In order for change to occur, however, some psychological safety must be present in the situation or else the person will simply become defensive and more rigid. Though this process sounds somewhat cognitive, we wish to emphasize the basically *emotional* features of becoming unfrozen.

If the person comes to feel safe, he will begin to seek some new information about himself which will allow him cognitively to redefine some beliefs about himself or his relationships to others. Such new information will be obtained by one of two basic mechanisms:

1. *Scanning the available interpersonal environment for relevant cues.*
2. *Identifying with some particular other person whose beliefs seem to be more viable.*

The changee, in other words, may begin to try to view himself from the perspective of another person or from the perspective of an array of others. As his perspective, his frame of reference shifts, he develops new beliefs about himself which, in turn, lead to new feelings and behavioral responses.

If these new feelings and responses fit well with the rest of the person's personality and attitudes and/or if they are confirmed or reinforced by others, a new cycle of unfreezing and changing is initiated until the person finds attitudes (feelings, beliefs, and responses) which do fit and which are reinforced. This, in summary form, is our model of attitude change. As we have said above, we do not expect this model or theory to make sense until we provide concrete examples of how the process works on a day-to-day basis. This will be the task of the next two chapters.

15

Organizational Forces
That Aid and Hinder Attitude Change

Introduction

The present chapter will attempt to broaden our conception of the learning process by focusing on those forces which aid and hinder learning *prior to and after a laboratory training experience*. In particular, using our model of attitude change, we will examine (1) whether the typical organization unfreezes the potential participant, (2) what kinds of opportunities for scanning and identification exist in the typical organizational setting, and (3) whether or not organizational forces tend to refreeze attitudes learned in the laboratory.

The learning process for most people begins prior to the laboratory and continues long afterward. It therefore becomes important to understand clearly what the learning forces are in the back-home setting and what occurs in the boundary zone between the back-home system and the laboratory. It is no accident that delegates use the metaphor of space travel when talking about laboratory training experiences. Once they have made the transition to the laboratory, they use the imagery of "having been off the ground," and of "being in orbit." As the experience draws to a close, delegates talk of problems of "re-entry" and making a "safe return."

Another way to confront this issue is in terms of values. We have previously highlighted the difference between the value system of most organizations and those of laboratory training (see Chapter 10 in particular). If the acceptance of laboratory values is a prerequisite to learning, it becomes all the more crucial to understand how any readiness to learn or unfreezing occurs in the typical organization, or whether it occurs at all.

Unfreezing

Most delegates who come to laboratory training programs are involved in organizations of one kind or another, and whatever motivation they have is related to their organizational affiliation. However, the kind of motivation they bring and the degree to which they are unfrozen in the sense of actual readiness to learn from the laboratory process are highly variable. Several patterns are evident. Some delegates have had organizational experiences which provide a personal motivation to learn; some delegates are motivated to help solve problems generated by the organization, but they see their role as bringing back solutions to the organization, not personal change; some delegates come with nothing more than a vague curiosity or the desire to evaluate the experience in order to judge its relevance for someone else; some delegates are confused or unsure just why they are at the laboratory, whether they have been sent by the organization for appraisal, counseling, or man-to-man talks.

However, whether or not the existence of such cues actually leads to the unfreezing of the receiver, depends on a number of additional circumstances. There is a great deal more to successful unfreezing than merely having someone point something out over a period of time or disconfirm an attitude. For one thing, the recipient of disconfirmatory cues does not necessarily pay attention to them, nor does he necessarily attribute the problem to himself, if he does pay attention. Because our personal constructs and attitudes are highly valued, we put up powerful defenses against disconfirmation (Harrison, 1963). If the cues are the least bit ambiguous, we can easily dismiss them; if the cues are too blunt, we can attempt to dismiss the person who provided them; if we cannot evade the message at all, we can still rationalize the behavior which triggered the disconfirmatory cue as not being, after all, characteristic of our own *typical* behavior, and so on. In other words, successful unfreezing implies something more than mere disconfirmation or lack of confirmation.

Paradoxically, the additional thing required is both a heightening of anxiety and a reduction of threat. The heightening or *induction of guilt-anxiety* implies that the disconfirmatory cues have made contact with some of the person's major motivations and constructs, and have aroused in him the feeling that important goals or ideals are not being met now or may not be met in the future. To be told that he cannot run a group effectively is meaningful only if the person *wants* to run groups effectively or if he always *believed* that he did run them effectively.

The *reduction* of threat or the creation of a climate of psychological safety concerns the person's anxiety about being *basically* acceptable and worthwhile. Even though he may experience guilt-anxiety in relation to some of his attitudes and behavior and may also realize that some of his constructs are no longer working effectively, he will probably not drop his defenses until he feels that others value him enough to help him to change and to protect him during the painful process of change.

We would hypothesize that, in these terms, *effective unfreezing is not possible in most organizations.* The elements that are likely to be lacking are *clear* disconfirmatory cues (clear in the sense of unambiguous reactions or feelings of others with whom the person deals) and a climate of security which can offer protection during a process of change. The lack of clear cues is the result of the many cultural norms which discourage us from revealing our feelings directly to each other (see the list on pp. 291–292); the lack of a climate of security is the result, in most organizations, of the reality that there is a job to be done and that mistakes, whatever their reason, are too costly to be tolerated. In other words, the person knows he is playing for keeps, thus making it difficult for him to assume an attitude of experimentation if a safe traditional way exists.

Consequently, when delegates reveal to their fellow T-group members some of the problems which they say have brought them to the laboratory, we would assume that this revelation is the result of the great unfreezing forces present in the laboratory itself (see the next chapter) and the relatively greater climate of psychological safety and support in the laboratory that makes it possible to face up to and admit problems to self and to others. Somehow the *combination* of (1) the ambiguous disconfirmatory cues from the back-home situation, (2) the more specific unfreezing forces in the laboratory itself, and (3) the climate of security which the laboratory generates, produces a readiness for attitude change which none of these forces by themselves could have produced.

Some delegates initially arrive at the laboratory with the motivation to locate solutions or new ideas to help their organization solve specific problems. Thus, there may exist the desire to develop more collaborative superior-subordinate relationships or to make more effective use of committees or to improve interdepartmental communications. Delegates are sent to laboratories or volunteer themselves in order to obtain experiences that will help to make the organizational changes, *but they usually do not perceive themselves to be in need of personal learning.* They perceive the problem to be in the organization and do not, at the outset, see the connection between an organizational problem and their own pattern of organizational behavior.

For this group, and the others to be discussed, the laboratory carries a relatively greater burden if unfreezing is to occur at all. Part of the unfreezing must be to help the delegate realize the connection between his own personal learning and his goal of organizational improvement. Often, he arrives at the laboratory hoping to be told how to do things back home differently and is jarred to find in place of such proposed solutions an emphasis on *himself* as the first change target. In the case of these individuals, the organizational forces essentially hinder rather than aid the learning process in having failed to prepare them adequately for what laboratory training goals and values are.

Some delegates attend laboratories out of sheer curiosity or with the explicit intention of evaluating laboratory training in order to determine how relevant it really is for *others*. In a way, they are saying: "*I* don't really need to learn anything, but I will evaluate this allegedly potent experience in order to determine whether I should recommend it to others who do need to learn something." Sometimes this feeling masks a real motivation to learn which the delegate is not ready to reveal. In this case, he has already been partially unfrozen by the organization as in the first pattern described. In other cases this type of delegate finds himself in much the same situation as the second type—wishing to remain personally aloof, but finding the laboratory forces closing in on him personally. If the laboratory forces are powerful enough, this type of delegate will learn in spite of his initial aloofness.

A fourth category of delegates is the group who are unsure of why they are at the laboratory, either because they have been sent without knowing why or because they cannot clearly define their own learning needs. Those who are sent may arrive with the clear knowledge that they are expected to improve their interpersonal competence in some way, but they are usually completely unclear about the nature of their failings in the eyes of their boss or peers. Often these delegates initially perceive attendance at the laboratory to be a form of punishment for failure. This belief leads to feelings of resentment and defensiveness. In all these cases, the burden of unfreezing falls entirely on the laboratory itself. One of the remarkable things about many laboratories is precisely that they are capable of generating unfreezing forces powerful enough to overcome initial apathy, resistance, and hostility.[2]

---

[2] One might argue that this group of delegates should be excluded from laboratory participation because it slows down the learning of others who are already partially unfrozen. Perhaps, ideally, one would work only with delegates who are ready and

In summary, we have argued that attitude change must begin with the unfreezing of present attitudes and that such unfreezing rarely can occur in organizational settings. The process can *begin* there, however, with the vague and ambiguous disconfirmatory cues which reflect people's attempts to be both polite and critical at the same time. The laboratory, on the other hand, generates powerful unfreezing forces. The combination of back-home disconfirmation and laboratory forces is, therefore, more than adequate to set into motion a process of attitude change.

Changing

Unfreezing readies the person to pay attention to new categories of information about himself as a prelude to redefining his assumptions, beliefs, and constructs about himself and his relationships to others. Such new information can come to him in one of two ways: He can *scan* the interpersonal environment for cues, drawing different items of information from different people, or he can emotionally *identify* himself with one other person and acquire new information by attempting to see himself from the perspective of this particular other person.

An important difference between the two processes is that when the person changes through scanning, he selects only information relevant to his own change and growth needs, whereas when he identifies himself with a model, once he has chosen the model, he limits the new information he acquires to what that particular model makes available to him. In other words, scanning is more likely to lead to new attitudes which fit well into the rest of the personality; identification is more likely to lead to new attitudes which will be reinforced by the model but which may *not* fit as well into the rest of the personality.[3]

Change of either variety can occur in organizational settings as well as in laboratory settings, *provided the person is adequately unfrozen.* However, there are some forces operating in the organizational setting

---

eager to learn. Yet, if one made this decision, one might be depriving the very population that needs the training most of all. If it is true that organizations themselves do not effectively unfreeze people, the laboratory setting may be one of the few places where the more rigid, defensive person may learn something significant about himself.

[3] We have not treated the case of multiple identification or the use of both scanning and identification. Both processes probably occur but it is not within the scope of this discussion to explore fully the conditions under which they occur. For a fuller analysis of these processes, the reader is referred to Part III of *Interpersonal Dynamics* (Bennis, et al., 1964).

that make change somewhat more difficult even if adequate unfreezing has taken place. Probably the major obstacle is that change in one person generally involves change in a whole network of relationships. Organizations are patterns of shared and interlocking expectations. Often, it is easier for a group to continue to use ineffective but stable patterns of relationships than to go through the painful process of building new patterns while trying to get a job done.

Not only is it difficult to change *in* the organization, but organizational forces tend to undermine changes in the laboratory. The person who is about to go to a training program "gets the message" from his boss and co-workers to "learn a lot, but don't rock the boat when you get back," or "learn a lot, but only in terms of my expectations of what you should learn." If the person changes in directions other than those which are expected or sanctioned by his co-workers, subordinates, and boss, he is likely to be punished or seen as not having learned anything at all.

Another set of *organizational* forces that restrains change and growth is the resultant of certain patterns of organization. For example, giving the immediate superior practically complete authority over the career development of subordinates (which is a fairly common procedure) is likely to have the effect of preoccupying subordinates with "how to please their boss" rather than "how to develop themselves." Similarly, certain control systems which supply superiors with detailed information about a given person's performance in the organization tend to lead to dependence and/or insecurity, neither of which stimulates change or growth. Specialization and intergroup competition, while sound economically, can also stand in the way of personal growth in that the group member becomes more concerned about upholding group norms and being loyal than about his own inadequacies and/or needs for growth (Schein, 1963).

Organizational forces thus tend to be basically conservative. They discourage scanning for new solutions to interpersonal problems, while encouraging identification with those organizational models that reflect the organization's value system. To the extent that this value system is itself opposed to or different from the value system of the laboratory training, it will tend to lead to the learning of organizational attitudes. Consequently, even if the organization or the laboratory succeeds in adequately unfreezing the person, the chances are that genuine growth or the learning of *new* attitudes which may differ from organizational ones will not occur.

A major part of the impact of the laboratory is that it exposes the delegate to others with a *different variety of attitudes* about people, as reflected in the different delegate points of view. New attitudes can therefore be learned in a laboratory, *either* by scanning the environment and selecting in terms of need, or by identifying with another person and learning a new perspective through his eyes. The ultimate dilemma for the learner then is how to re-enter his organization without having to give up the new attitudes and behavioral patterns which he has learned.

Refreezing

Once the person begins to acquire new beliefs, perspectives, and points of view, his attitudes and behavioral responses begin to change. Whether or not these changes remain stable depends, however, upon the degree to which they fit into the rest of the personality (personal refreezing) or are reinforced and confirmed by important others with whom the person has a relationship (relational refreezing).

With respect to attitudes toward the learning process, the relevant refreezing occurs within the context of the laboratory itself. Once the person begins to pay attention to here-and-now data and comes to value a spirit of inquiry, he will likely get reinforcement, confirmation, and support from the staff members and some group members. If he values these relationships, his new attitude toward learning will stabilize. The person may also find that operating in terms of the meta-goals of training suits him well, fits his personality, and gives him greater satisfaction. If these responses are elicited, the new attitude toward learning will be refrozen on that basis.

Essentially the same argument would apply to attitudes about self, others, and groups. As these change, they may or may not become stable as a function of whether or not they fit with other attitudes and personality dimensions, and as a function of whether or not they are confirmed and reinforced by others whose opinions the learner values.

Inasmuch as the laboratory is itself a *temporary* system (Miles, 1964), one must consider *long-run* stability to be different from stability for the duration of the laboratory. We have pointed out above the kinds of organizational forces that make it difficult to change or learn in the first place. These same forces operate to undermine the new learning which the delegate brings back from the laboratory. It has long been known that training effects often tend to be temporary or, worse, that the person ends up being more committed to his original attitudes after training than he was before exposure to training. This phenomenon reflects the tremendous power of the organization to mold people to its own value system, either by failing to refreeze changes which have occurred during training, or by actually disconfirming these changes, setting a new cycle of attitude learning into motion.

The process involved in relational refreezing is similar to that involved in unfreezing. The person obtains cues from others about the impact of his attitudes and behavior pattern on them. To the extent that these attitudes and behaviors violate their expectations, and to the extent that the learner values the reactions of these others, he will either abandon what he has learned or relearn the organizational patterns all over again. But, as was pointed out above, the degree to which this will occur depends upon the degree of personal refreezing, i.e., the degree to which the new attitudes and behavior fit the rest of the person's attitudes and personality traits.

Summary

In Chapter 14, we argued that the basic learning cycle consists of a series of steps—acquiring new information which creates dilemmas or disconfirms, changing attitudes, and changing behavior which releases new information and sets a new cycle into motion. We argued that the first set of attitudes which have to change in order for learning to occur are concerned with the learning method itself. Only if the delegate can come to value and pay attention to here-and-now data about himself and others can the learning cycle be initiated.

In the present chapter, we attempted to present, in somewhat more detail, what is involved in the particular step which we have labeled "attitude change." We have attempted to discuss the difficulties in all the phases of this process by highlighting the *organizational* forces in our day-to-day life which militate against learning something new. Fortunately, the laboratory itself generates powerful unfreezing forces, making it possible for the person to begin to re-evaluate his attitude and learn new ones based upon scanning or identification. If the new attitudes fit and are reinforced, they will stabilize until new disconfirming information is perceived.

We would now like to move to a more detailed and concrete description of the forces which are unleashed in a typical residential laboratory setting. In particular, we must attempt to understand how, given the organizational forces against learning, the laboratory comes to be able to change the delegate's views of the learning process and to teach him new values of how and what to learn.

16

The Laboratory as a Force toward Learning

Introduction

In a sense, all of the previous theoretical material about the learning process has been a prelude to the present chapter. We would now like to explain how learning really takes place. To do this, we will focus on those forces in the laboratory setting, culture, staff value system, and training design that initiate the first and most important attitude change —that of learning how to learn, of coming to value the meta-goals of laboratory training. Once this step has been accomplished, the learning process almost takes care of itself. The data are there, ready to be looked at and learned from. All that is really needed is the willingness to look at them and the ability to pay attention to them.

The residential laboratory has, from the outset, a social structure and a culture (normative system) that have been created largely by the staff and are imposed on the delegate.[1] This social structure in combination with the training design creates the essential forces that make learning possible. These forces can be grouped into three major categories as follows:

Forces That Motivate Learning by Unfreezing the Delegate. We have pointed out that unfreezing may begin with dilemmas and disconfirmations which occur in the organizational settings prior to entry into the laboratory. But the laboratory creates a whole new set of dilemmas and

---

[1] This imposed culture should not be confused with the particular norms and structures built by the groups as the laboratory proceeds, although the interaction of the initial and emergent cultures is of obvious relevance to the full understanding of how and why people learn in a laboratory.

exposes the delegate to a new set of disconfirming cues which serve as powerful motivators for learning.

Forces That Enhance Willingness To Be Open and Authentic by Reducing Threat from Others. All of the activities of a laboratory are built around the collection of observations and reactions of the delegates to the here-and-now events of the laboratory. Learning can occur only if delegates come to be willing to be open and honest about their observations, reactions, and feelings. What ordinarily militates against such openness and authenticity is fear of the reactions of others. To be open and honest is to expose oneself to *danger from others.* They may take advantage of the person, retaliate if they feel he has been hostile, or demean him by not taking him seriously. Consequently, to understand how the laboratory enhances learning requires us to examine those forces in it that reduce threat from others and promote openness and authenticity.

Forces That Enhance Willingness and Ability To Listen to and Pay Attention to the Reactions and Feelings of Others by Reducing Threat from Within. The basic learning in a laboratory results from a delegate discovering what impact he has on others, what impact others have on him, and what the consequences of the various reactions which members have are for group functioning. This learning requires that the delegate listen to the reactions of others and pay attention to them. What ordinarily militates against listening and paying attention is his own defensiveness or fear of his own reactions. To listen and to pay attention is to expose oneself to *danger from within oneself.* The delegate may learn things he does not wish to hear, he may become anxious or be overwhelmed by guilt, or he may lose self-esteem. Consequently, understanding how the laboratory enhances learning requires us to examine those forces in the laboratory which reduce threat from within and promote the willingness and ability to listen and pay attention to the reactions of others.

Forces That Motivate Learning by Unfreezing the Delegate

Isolation and Loss of Support for Accustomed Routines.

The laboratory setting, particularly in a total residential laboratory, requires the delegate to become involved in a social system and to suspend for one or two weeks his membership in the back-home social system. The laboratory isolates him from co-workers, family, and daily work routines. Such isolation is a powerful unfreezing force because to a large extent our beliefs, attitudes, and values derive their stability from the daily confirmation which others provide us with. If we are removed from our usual pattern of relationships, we lose the support which others provide us with. Beliefs, attitudes, and values become less stable as the person is isolated from his normal routine and pattern of relationships.

This process of loss of support through isolation is particularly acute in the area of self-concept or identity. Our beliefs about ourselves and our feelings of self-esteem are learned from and supported by the reactions of others. We learn to define ourselves partly in terms of the reactions we elicit in those others whose reactions we particularly value. Hence the loss of the daily feedback from bosses, co-workers, family, and friends, exposes the delegate to uncertainty about himself: who he really is and how much worth he should attach to himself. Whatever anxiety is generated by isolation is, of course, reinforced by the knowledge the delegate has that the laboratory may be a place where he will learn something about himself which he did not know before, where people will "tell him the truth about himself" or expose his weaknesses. Thus, the very transition to the laboratory social system is likely to be inherently a potent experience.

The isolation of the delegate from his back-home setting is usually reinforced by the immediate removal of what might be called "self-defining equipment"(Goffman, 1959). The delegate is told and shown by the example of the staff's informal attire that the laboratory is a highly informal place. Uniforms, business suits, and other external symbols of status are discouraged. Even clerics who attend a laboratory find themselves attending sessions without their collars or habits. Nothing is more surprising than to see, on the last day of the laboratory, the informal gathering of people who have learned to know each other in the T-group, donning their back-home clothes for the plane and train trips home.

In addition to the loss of identifying clothing, the delegate usually suffers the loss of his title and full name. In the pre-laboratory information folders, there is usually a card asking him to give his preferred nickname so that it can be put on his name tag. The name tag he is given when he arrives bears this nickname and his last name, but no title, company affiliation, or other identifying information is shown. The delegate soon learns, through staff example, that regardless of relative age, status, formal rank, or personality attributes all members of the laboratory community address each other by first name. It is often quite traumatic for the person used to being called Mr., Dr., or Sir to find himself nothing more than Jim, John, or Teddy in a group of strangers.[2] The laboratory imposes a surface intimacy which can be very upsetting to those not used to it.

Reinforcing the loss of distinguishing clothing, formal titles, and organizational affiliations is the loss of privacy which results from sharing a room with one or more people, eating meals family style, and using public toilet and shower facilities. The delegate finds himself in a life situation where his daily needs are routinely taken care of, but where there are no established routines or status props behind which to hide. The person is suddenly on his own with respect to others, and there are not clearcut cues as to what sort of behavior is appropriate. His consciousness of himself is thus greatly heightened, as is the likelihood of his discovering in himself feelings and reactions which he did not know he had. In Goffman's terms, in the laboratory setting the front and back stages of life become merged to a great extent, exposing the person more fully and increasing the probability of social anxiety or identity crises.[3]

Thus far, we have pointed out how various aspects of the laboratory setting create for the delegate a situation in which his accustomed roles are not supported by any of the props and routines which are typical in the back-home situation. Instead, he encounters a number of forces which actually disconfirm certain of these roles and push him toward something which might be called the "learner role."

New Learning Norms

The process of learning new norms, particularly norms which pertain to the learning process itself, is most visible in the unstructured setting of the T-group. Basically what happens to the delegate is that he discovers that methods of handling other people and groups that have worked well in the back-home setting fail to work in the T-group. As most of the group members experience such failure,

---

[2] The full import of this informal norm was only recently brought home to us through a program for M.I.T. graduate students and their wives (a group who had accepted two-year internship appointments in African nations). One of the wives found herself in a T-group in which the staff member was also an M.I.T. faculty member. This young woman admitted near the end of the laboratory, with obvious discomfort, that one of the most difficult aspects for her had been to call the trainer and other older members of the T-group by their first name. She was 20 years old and totally unused to such "disrespectful" behavior on her own part.

[3] Another recent analysis has pointed out the similarity between laboratory culture and adolescent culture. The forces active in the laboratory are seen as stimulating varying degrees of regression which take the person back to a time of life when values were being formed, thus making possible their reassessment (Mill, 1962).

they are forced to re-examine and redefine their goals and their method of operation. Out of this process arise the norms which make learning possible.

For example, the person who has been successful as an aggressive leader in the back-home setting finds few followers in the T-group; the skillful manipulator finds that others can see through him and resent his manipulation; the silent observer finds others demanding to know what he thinks; and so on. The delegate finds that he does not have the protection of a formal power position; he cannot just adjourn the meeting at an appropriate moment, walk out rather than answer a question, or employ other strategies which he may have employed with success in his past interpersonal and group relationships. Often this leaves the delegate with a genuine sense of helplessness and forces him to seek other solutions.

As back-home norms fail to be confirmed, new norms are confronted and worked on: "we are here to learn, i.e., to change or be influenced"; "the correct ways to behave is to help the learning process along"; "we are all equal and all enjoy high worth in the eyes of the staff"; "success in the laboratory is defined by how much we learn, i.e., how much we change"; "we are here to test and re-evaluate our basic approach to ourselves, other people, and groups"; "learning is an important and valuable activity; if you are not willing to learn, there is something wrong with you and you should not be in the laboratory"; "we are on our own and have to manage our own learning; the staff will not be of much help."

In addition, the key norm, that anything which occurs in the group can be legitimately scrutinized and analyzed, is communicated in lectures and through trainer example. Thus, the decision which a minority railroaded through the group can be re-examined and undone; various roles and strategies which members exhibited can be focused on, discussed, and reacted to.

There is a definite moral overtone to all of these norms: being a successful learner is good; being unwilling or unable to learn is bad. No single activity communicates these messages to the delegate. Rather, they come out of the brochures, introductions, trainer remarks and behavior in the T-groups, and the pressure from other delegates who are already highly motivated to learn. There is little doubt that the laboratory exerts powerful conformity pressures on the individual who does not accept to some degree the norms about the learning process.

Somewhat related norms tend to develop in the T-group, are imposed in exercises, and are mentioned explicitly in theory sessions: "in order to learn you must be an *active* participant, you must *expose* to some degree your typical behavior"; "you must be interested in and *help* in trying to understand why you, others, and the group are behaving the way you or they are"; "you must be *willing to tolerate a certain amount of tension,* because learning usually provokes some tension"; and "you must initially *trust the basic method* of the laboratory and the staff."

Supporting these norms, particularly the one about equality and group responsibility, is the manner in which the staff present themselves to delegates. *First,* even though there is a formal staff structure with a laboratory dean and informally defined senior and junior staff, trainers tend to present themselves as professional equals unconcerned about hierarchical formal authority. The emphasis is on individual responsibility, getting the man most qualified for any particular situation, and on a "collaborative concept of authority."

Second, the staff attempts to communicate that "we are all in this together"; "we must collaborate and help each other to learn"; "no one of us has all the resources necessary"; "each of us has some of the resources we will need." In saying this to delegates, the staff is not being devious or dishonest. Rather, we must distinguish between norm• that concern *how to learn,* and norms that concern *what will be learned.* The staff creates a setting which, in effect, *imposes norms of how to learn,* but such norms do not prejudge what will actually happen in the groups, what observations will be made, what feelings will be revealed, and therefore, *what will be learned.* Genuine collaboration is needed in maximizing *what will be learned.*

To reinforce the norms about learning and the image of staff-delegate equality, staff members attempt to exemplify the laboratory philosophy in their own interactions with each other. One extreme has been to invite delegates to observe staff meetings to see for themselves how the staff operates. A more common situation arises in theory sessions if staff members supplement each other's lecture material, raise questions, or disagree with each other. Extra efforts tend to be made in these situations to listen to and to deal constructively with the issues posed. When staff members violate their own learning norms, it often has severe repercussions among the delegates.

In summary, the main thrust of the forces described thus far is toward (1) the destruction of norms associated with a formal hierarchical social structure, (2) the establishment of a more informal peer culture in which status is achieved based on acceptance of new norms, and (3) the acceptance of a learner role and learning norms which reflect the underlying values of laboratory training.

Summary. The unfreezing forces which are generated in a laboratory setting can be roughly classified into the following categories: (1) isolation from accustomed sources of support—colleagues, family, and regular routines; (2) removal of self-defining equipment, status, title, etc.; (3) loss of certain areas of privacy; (4) lack of confirmation or actual disconfirmation of roles which are appropriate in the back-home setting; (5) breakdown of hierarchical authority and status structures in favor of a kind of peer culture and informal status based on laboratory norms; (6) a set of laboratory norms about the value of the learning process and the method of learning; and (7) deliberately created lack of structure to heighten consciousness of self and to create unavoidable dilemmas.

It is these forces which motivate and initiate the learning process by unfreezing the delegate, by arousing social anxiety through disconfirmation, and by focusing the delegate on himself in his relationship to others.

Forces That Enhance Willingness to be Open and Authentic by Reducing Threat from Others

If learning is to occur in the laboratory setting, delegates must be willing and able to be open and authentic with each other. The primary barrier to openness and authenticity is the danger of being hurt by others. A person may be hurt in retaliation for something he has said or be punished because he has broken one of a number of cultural rules about not stating feelings openly.

Blake, Mouton, and Blansfield (1961) have given an excellent summary of some of these norms which are deeply ingrained in Anglo-Saxon culture:

1. *Norms designed to protect the feelings of another person:* "don't say anything if you can't say something nice"; "don't criticize if you can't provide a constructive alternative"; "never talk about someone behind his back."

2. *Norms designed to increase self-protection*: "people who live in glass houses should not throw stones."
3. *Norms suggesting that feelings only cause trouble*: "let sleeping dogs lie"; "don't stir up a hornet's nest"; "don't rock the boat"; "when ignorance is bliss, it's folly to be wise."
4. *Norms suggesting that emotions are immature and should be masked*: "only sissies cry"; "keep a stiff upper lip"; "learn to take it on the chin."

In addition to such norms, there are a variety of informal "rules of the game" such as not criticizing people in front of others, never carrying tales out of school, and keeping feelings out of work relationships. Cultural norms in favor of openness like "call a spade a spade," "shoot straight from the shoulder," and "call them as you see them," refer mostly to the area of work performance rather than to interpersonal feelings.

We are all overtrained culturally to accept others for what they are, not to tell them anything which conceivably might hurt them, and to give compliments whenever possible, even if they are not sincere. In order to maintain our self-esteem at the highest possible level, we present ourselves in the most favorable light possible. Others collude with us in whatever self-deception is involved by granting us whatever they feel they can. Only rarely do we get direct forthright reactions to our behavior.

The laboratory setting provides the delegates with an opportunity to obtain information about themselves and others which is ordinarily unavailable. Such information, the feelings and reactions of others, is essential for us to have if we are to understand why others behave toward us as they do. For example, one of the biggest discoveries which members of T-groups make is that the seemingly random events which occur in the group become highly understandable once the feelings of the members are brought out into the open.

For the laboratory setting to enhance learning at this level, it must help delegates suspend the norms *against* openness, reduce threat from others, and provide opportunities for building new norms *in favor* of openness. The laboratory must create a psychologically safe environment to minimize the risks of openness. A number of factors work in this direction: the temporariness and "game" quality of the laboratory, the learning method itself, psychological theory, and the presence of the staff. Let us examine each of these in detail.

The Laboratory as a Temporary Game[4]

A number of conditions make the laboratory and its setting different from the usual back-home settings. *First,* it is clearly understood by all participants that the laboratory is a temporary and short experience. However traumatic it may be, it will not last forever. *Second,* it is highly informal and egalitarian. Those dangers which arise from direct formal authority and power are minimized. Staff members use only veiled sanctions, minimizing the use of any direct authority. *Third,* the laboratory is isolated and self-contained. The only witnesses to whatever goes on are fellow participants and staff. A clear norm is established early: Whatever happens at the laboratory is confidential. It will be learned by others only if delegates themselves tell about it. There is no outside audience; those inside the cultural island share the same fate. *Fourth,* there is no product to be manufactured or service to be performed for anyone else. All participants are there only for their own and each other's benefit. *Fifth,* none of the relationships formed during the laboratory are permanent or carry necessary implications for the back-home situation (except in the special case of team training). Delegates who come from the same organization or know each other well are generally put into different T-groups. *Sixth,* most of the basic needs for food and lodging are automatically taken care of by dormitory living, thus freeing the delegate from distracting choices and helping him focus attention on learning. *Seventh,* there is a clearcut routine of activities for each day that further minimizes choices. In short, the temporariness provides a culture which minimizes responsibilities while focusing on learning and change.

The atmosphere which these conditions create in the residential laboratory is not unlike that of an ocean cruise or retreat. The demands of real life are temporarily suspended, permitting people to concentrate on themselves and each other. Threats from others are reduced because the stakes for which people are playing are temporary. The person may get emotionally hurt in the laboratory but he does not lose his job or take a cut in salary. He can engage others in the context of a game and experiment with open communications in

---

[4] In a recent paper, Miles (1964a) has analyzed in detail the socio-psychological characteristics of "temporary systems" such as laboratories, workshops, trips, meetings, and the like. Many of the points made here are similar to the ones he has identified.

trivial ways before raising the stakes. Such experimentation permits him to feel out the others to see what kind of danger, if any, they represent. The fact that most delegates come to the laboratory with the constructive intent of learning and helping each other reduces the likelihood that such experimentation will have disastrous outcomes.

The Learning Method as Protective

The learning method serves to reduce threat from others by promoting an emphasis on (1) here-and-now *specific* events and acts rather than people, (2) objective reaction and analysis rather than evaluation, and (3) the legitimacy of experimentation.

1. One of the major assumptions which the staff makes about effective learning is that it is safer and more productive to collect observations, reactions, and feelings about some *specific* group incident or *specific* member behavior than about a group member in general. For example, the trainer may respond or ask others to respond to "Harry's attempt to get his point across," not to a question such as "how do the group members feel about Harry in this group." Whereever possible, the trainer by example or direct suggestion focuses the group on the specific behavior of a member rather than on his total character or personality.

The major assumption which underlies this strategy is that it is easier both to give and to receive feedback on specific behavior because this feedback does not represent an evaluation of the person as a whole. If the feedback is too threatening, the person is offered the defense that the behavior was not really typical of him.

A second assumption which underlies this strategy is that by focusing on specific behavior the group members learn to be better observers of their own and others' behavior. From being forced to make more *precise* observations, they learn how easy it is to stereotype another member and to miss the important fact that his behavior may be highly variable.

A third assumption which underlies this strategy is that only by reference to specific behavioral data is it possible to compare, contrast, and accumulate reactions. If one person sees Harry as hostile whereas another sees him as supportive, it cannot be determined how to reconcile these observations without knowing which behavior of Harry's produced each of the reactions. The two persons may be reacting to the same behavior differently, or they may simply be focusing on different behavior which Harry has exhibited at different times.

2. By focusing on specific behavior rather than on the total person, it is also easier to establish a norm of *objectivity*. The trainer encourages by example and suggestion that observations and reactions be an accurate *description* of how the person felt or what he saw, not an *evaluation* of the other person's behavior. Of course, true objectivity is never possible where human interactions are involved. What we mean by objectivity in this context is the attempt to be as explicit as possible about what our feelings and reactions are and to distinguish these from judgmental evaluations of either our own or the other person's behavior and feelings. Being descriptive is an important aid in the achievement of this kind of objectivity. In general, it is easier to be descriptive in reference to some event than about the totality of impressions one has gained of another person, although eventually group members become skillful in giving objective feedback on general impressions as well.

As members achieve skill in objective reporting, the climate becomes safer for all concerned. For example, hostile reactions can be controlled and neutralized by being objectively analyzed—what triggered these reactions, what earlier feelings were present between the combatants? We do not mean to imply here that successful learning requires the elimination of direct outbursts of feelings. Rather, we wish to underline that the norm of objectivity and the sanction to analyze any behavior that occurs, serves in the member's fantasy life as a safety valve. If feelings run too high, the group can use as a coping device an objective analysis of why feelings were high, how they were being handled, and how they might be handled in the future.

3. The norm of *experimentation* is also critical in promoting openness and authenticity. As group members, possibly under the goading of the trainer, try small experiments in being open, they usually discover that this leads to more mutual acceptance and support, not to rejection and hostility. The discovery that openness leads more often to acceptance than to rejection is one of the most powerful forces toward a re-examination of cultural norms about interpersonal relationships and communication. If group members experience success in trying to be open, they become more strongly committed to the laboratory norms about learning.

Psychological Theory as a Source of Protection

Theory sessions, staff behavior, and trainer comments all attempt to underline several basic points about emotions that, if understood, serve to protect the delegate psychologically from the threat of others: (1) emotions exist within all of us, whether we are aware of them or not; (2) all people have both tender, loving emotions and tough, aggressive emotions, although they may be more comfortable expressing one set or the other (Wallen, 1963); (3) emotions generally have specific causes, though the causes may be multiple; (4) once the cause is identified, the emotions often are not as threatening to the person himself or others as they initially seemed; (5) emotions, even if quite violent, are normal, can be understood, and must be analyzed objectively if interpersonal and group relationships are to be understood. In short, every attempt is made to legitimize the existence and expression of feelings, to help delegates accept their own and others' feelings, not as something to be frightened of and retaliated against, but as something to be understood and learned from.

For example, a common incident in T-groups or exercises is some hostile remark by person A to person B that results in an open or veiled fight and raises the general level of tension in the group. If the group can stop the fight and analyze the prior events or feelings, it often turns out that person A was tense, not hostile, and that some behavior of B triggered A into showing his tension through hostility. The group can then explore further what the sources of tension were, an exploration that often reveals that A was not alone in being tense and that the group can do something constructive about its sources of tension.

The eventual outcome is that A's hostility is revealed to be something other than rejection of B. It may well have reflected a total group problem rather than some specific problem of A's. The group may also learn that hostility is generally a *symptom of tension*, even closeness (not necessarily of *malice*), and that hostility, therefore, need not be fearful or mysterious. As different kinds of feelings are brought under control and scrutiny, the environment becomes safer for the expression of new feelings, helping to make communication more open and authentic.

The Staff as a Source of Protection

It is difficult to assess the exact impact of the staff. On the one hand, staff members vary greatly in how they present themselves to the delegate population, and, on the other hand, delegate *fantasies* about the staff are as important as actual staff behavior. Such fantasies usually involve the attribution of omniscience and omnipotence to staff members. The staff does have some real power and authority. For example, their power to manage whatever dangers arise in the laboratory is communicated in a number of ways.

First, the staff clearly has a plan and a theory. Whether staff members say "we are all in this together as equals" or "we are here to help you learn," it is clear that they know what they are doing. They exhibit relatively little tension themselves, particularly in the presence of strong feelings. If they are tense they often are able to communicate that it is all right to feel tense and to demonstrate actual resources in dealing with situations when danger gets too high (e.g., the trainer will protect a group member who is getting-attacked too strongly or will intervene in tense situations and help the group to analyze the source of the tension).

Second, the staff is professionally trained and is granted the authority of knowledge and experience. Whether this makes the individual staff member more competent to create a learning situation or not is less important than the *faith* that his experience and training elicit in the delegates. Their belief that the trainer has "been here before" and "will rescue us when the going gets too rough" is important in stimulating the taking of psychological risks by exposing feelings. The trainer may, in fact, not have experienced the kind of situation the group is in, and may feel completely inadequate on occasions. Nevertheless faith in his abilities is crucial for delegates to feel early in the laboratory. This faith is often evidenced by their reluctance to believe any statements on the trainer's part that he is in the dark or feels powerless. The fact that he exhibits some power and knowledge often leads to the fantasy that he has total power and omniscience.

Third, the staff member attempts by personal example to establish a norm of openness and authenticity. While there are many variations in trainer behavior, most trainers attempt by one means or another to demonstrate to group members that it is possible and profitable to reveal feelings and reactions, and that this can be done in a manner that minimizes threat.

Some trainers attempt to establish this norm by being completely open about their own feelings, not only in the T-group but in all contacts with delegates. At the other extreme, there are trainers who will withhold their *feelings* but be quite open about their *observations* of what is happening in the group. They may suggest the sharing of feelings but not necessarily set a personal example. In between lies a gamut of trainer styles—some trainers are more comfortable expressing tender emotions; some will express their feelings after other delegates have done so, others will initiate the process; some will blurt out their feelings almost as soon as they become aware of them, others will report their feelings at a later time. Whether the personal example turns out to be helpful to the group in achieving a safer psychological climate probably depends more on the trainer's authenticity than on his actual style. If he is unaware of his own feelings or distorts them in the process of communicating them, he probably does more damage than if he withheld them altogether. If he has strong feelings which are valid reflections of group process (in contrast to being primarily a reflection of his own needs) and fails to share them explicitly, he may be working against the norm of openness.

Fourth, the staff member attempts to demonstrate by example and by presentation of theory that feelings are always present and can be harnessed to aid the group in getting work accomplished when properly modulated and integrated. In other words, the sharing of feelings not only produces personal learning for the group members, but also enables the group to consider the question of how feelings can be integrated into work activities. The staff member often plays a crucial role here in showing the role of *timing* in the expression of feelings, in showing how the *modulation* of strong feelings can make their expression less threatening and more constructive, and in showing how the group can alternate its activity from high *task* orientation to a high group building and *maintenance* orientation. He shows this by his personal example in how he times and modulates his own feeling expression and by pointing out examples of good timing and modulation when they occur in the group.

The problem for the group is to find a principle of appropriateness that supersedes the simple norm that authentic open communication is always a good thing. If learning is the only goal, the simple norm is probably valid for all times and all situations. Whether open authentic communication is useful when a group is trying to accomplish a task depends on some principles of appropriateness (when and how and about what to be open and authentic).[5]

---

[5] In actual fact such principles have to be consciously or unconsciously applied even in the pure learning situation. We can never be open about all feelings at all times, partly because there are too many of them, partly because we always select and filter our communication in terms of the goals we are trying to accomplish and the norms operating in the situation.

One such principle of appropriateness would be that the expression of feeling must be relevant to the group or interpersonal situation. The staff member will encourage a group whenever it is ready to develop principles of appropriateness in terms of its own needs, anxieties, and concepts of relevance. Some groups will be conservative, others daring in the kinds of feelings they declare to be appropriate. The role of the trainer is not to set the limits personally but to help the group work out its own limits.

Fifth, every laboratory of any size designates one of its staff members as counselor for those delegates who feel the need of individual counseling. He is usually a psychiatrist or clinical psychologist hired explicitly for this purpose. His presence, alone, communicates a sense of security that all contingencies which may arise can be taken care of. His presence also heightens anxiety in some by communicating the possibility that someone may be sufficiently upset to need counseling.

A final point which must be made is that the very presence of the staff arouses feelings about authority figures that are imported from the larger culture. In some delegates, staff members arouse feelings of dependency, in others, feelings of counter-dependency, and in still others they arouse neither. For the delegate to learn fully from his experience, he must also come to recognize and analyze his feelings toward the staff authorities, particularly the T-group trainer. But the analysis of the role of the staff member and the feelings aroused by him and in him also make him less available as the omnipotent protector. Consequently, it is unlikely that the group will be able to face up to and discuss these feelings until enough of a climate of trust and safety has been built up to make the staff member less omnipotent.

Summary.

We have argued that learning depends on some degree of openness and authenticity of communication. Openness and authenticity in turn depend upon the willingness of the participant to violate cultural norms that discourage such communication. The primary danger in openness and authenticity is that others will be hurt and will retaliate or that others will punish the person for violating cultural norms. In assessing how a laboratory setting stimulates openness and authenticity, it is necessary to examine forces that reduce threats from others and encourage new norms in favor of authentic communication.

Several sets of such forces or conditions are identified. *First,* the laboratory is temporary and isolated from the permanent back-home situation. It is a situation similar to a game in which the stakes are real but not as high as the stakes back home. The relationships formed are temporary and have no direct relation to back home. The laboratory is an artificial situation and not automatically governed by traditional norms.

Second, the learning method itself offers some protection and forces re-evaluation of traditional norms. The focus on specific incidents or pieces of behavior rather than on the person as a whole minimizes total rejection. The norm of objectivity permits even highly evaluative communications to be examined and reassessed. The norm that any incident or behavior is fair game for analysis and reconstruction permits better understanding of the feelings that have arisen and, if necessary, the clarification or the undoing of damage done by their expression. The analytical approach also provides a safety valve in giving the group a safe detour when feelings run too high to be handled directly. Finally, the norm of experimentation leads to the discovery that authentic communication leads to less hostility and rejection than nonauthentic communication—the more of it members do, the safer the climate becomes (partly because protective mechanisms also develop alongside the climate of openness).

Third, psychological theory offers protection in declaring that feelings are ubiquitous and normal, that everyone has both tender and tough emotions, that feelings have causes which can be understood, and once understood are not as threatening, and that the specific and seemingly isolated feelings of a given member are often merely symptoms of tensions which are more widely shared in the group.

Fourth, the staff is a source of protection both in reality and in fantasy. The existence of a planned set of learning experiences and a theory of learning reassures the delegate that the staff knows what it is doing and will not let anyone get really hurt. The staff tends not to be tense in the presence of strong feelings and to have ways of coping with such feelings. It is professionally trained and has the authority of knowledge and experience. It sets a personal example of openness and authenticity and thereby demonstrates its value for the learning process. It attempts to show by example and theory presentation that not only does feeling expression and authentic communication lead to more learning, but also that feelings can be integrated into work activities to the mutual enhancement of both. Finally, the staff helps the group define principles of appropriateness to integrate feelings into ongoing work situations.

Fifth, many laboratories designate a psychiatrist or clinical psychologist as counselor to help any delegate who develops personal problems during the laboratory.

Forces That Enhance Willingness and Ability to Listen to and Pay Attention to the Reactions and Feelings of Others by Reducing Threat from Within

The major forces that stand in the way of listening and utilizing feedback are the personal tensions which most delegates experience prior to and during the early parts of the laboratory. These tensions preoccupy the delegate and force him to cope; his attention is focused on reducing tension rather than on learning about himself.

The tensions have several different sources: (1) dilemmas created by the unfreezing forces—how to establish a viable identity in the group, how to control others, how to insure that the group goals will include his own needs, and how to keep the group discussion at an *appropriate* level of intimacy; (2) the heightened consciousness of self that brings with it the possibility of discovering something within himself that will prove to be unacceptable; (3) the actual possibility of getting honest reactions to himself from others, which have always been relatively unavailable and may prove to reveal unacceptable parts of himself or, worse, may prove himself to be entirely unacceptable; (4) defensive reactions to feedback already obtained, either because it was hostile and retaliatory, or because it was too threatening; (5) the belief or assumption that he may not be able to change behavior which is unacceptable to others (therefore it may be better not to learn about it in the first place); (6) the belief or assumption that feedback is always evaluative and always deals with inadequacies or with things that are wrong.[6]

Given this kind of initial constellation of forces, how can the delegate relax enough to be able to listen and utilize feedback? Let us look at the same set of factors we discussed in reducing external dangers: the laboratory as a temporary game, the learning method, psychological theory, and the role of the staff.

---

[6] Miles (personal communication) has suggested that this particular belief or assumption grows out of our childhood experiences where we received direct reactions to our own behavior only when we exceeded bounds or did something wrong. Even if feedback was positive, it was still evaluative. Most people, in other words, have no experience with objective feedback (nonevaluative reactions of others to one's behavior).

The Laboratory as a Temporary Game

The temporary nature of the laboratory experience, the fact that it is not for keeps, that the stakes are not as high as they would be back home, that many people share the same fate, and that there are no witnesses to whatever interpersonal disasters might occur, serves to reassure the person somewhat and to give him hope. In his own mind, he can liken the tension he experiences to the tension which he has experienced in other novel situations or in strange social situations to which he has been exposed. He can dismiss the tension as being irrelevant to his real self and can retreat to the safer assumption that the laboratory is some kind of human relations game dreamed up by academics. He might say to himself, "who wouldn't be tense in a situation where you sit around all day talking."

At the same time, the recognition that the situation is strange and is more like a game makes it easier to take an experimental attitude or a devil-may-care kind of philosophy toward the learning possibilities. The person can say to himself that because it is not for keeps and does not involve his real self anyway, he might as well get his money's worth and find out what others think about him. He generally knows that the situation is very much for keeps, but he can rely on the game culture as a defense if what he hears is too threatening. It may help therefore for the staff to support the fiction of the game in the early parts of the laboratory.

The fact that the laboratory is temporary and has unreal "as-if" qualities makes it easier for norms of mutual acceptance to be established. Not only do delegates have fewer cues about each other and confront each other in a more genuine sense, but also the temporary game quality makes it possible for delegates to extend themselves to other people in ways they would not ordinarily. In effect, they say, "I might not accept this guy back home or on the job, but I guess I can accept him and try to get to know him here since we are going to be together only for one or two weeks anyway." Here again the analogy to the isolated vacation spot or the ocean cruise is meaningful. To the extent that people engage each other only in terms of certain limited parts of themselves, and in a temporary context, they can suspend some of the evaluative reactions they might have if they knew the total person in his own setting.

The presence of a large heterogeneous population, combined with adequate recreation facilities and free time for informal get-togethers, also stimulates acceptance and a climate of mutual support. Even if the person loses some self-esteem in his T-group, or is too tense to play a role well in an exercise, or feels the trainer has rejected his ideas, he can always find at least one or two others in the total laboratory community who are having similar experiences and who will accept him unconditionally. Thus, in the community room, over drinks, or under a tree, pairs or trios are seen sharing their anxieties with each other, trying to make sense of the experiences of the day, working through some of their feelings about the feedback that they received during a T-group session, or just asking each other whether they are basically acceptable or not. In a real sense, delegates get together to test a wide set of assumptions and realities. They ask themselves questions like: "Do they really dare to listen," "Is there an island of escape for them if what they hear is too traumatic," "Is there someone who will help them work through the real meaning and import of what they have heard?" To the extent that each delegate can find at least one other person in the laboratory with whom to establish such a mutually accepting relationship, he can begin to listen and utilize feedback.[7]

The Learning Method as Reassurance

Most of the points previously made about the learning method apply as much to reducing threat from within as they do to reducing threat from others. Once the delegate learns that feedback from others can be limited to certain of his behaviors, that it can be objective and nonevaluative, and that the reactions of others to his behavior will vary, he becomes somewhat reassured that he will not be traumatized by his laboratory experience. Once some of his tensions about what he may learn about himself are reduced, he becomes more ready to expose himself and to listen for reactions.

It is probably safe to say that, for most delegates, their fantasies of being rejected and criticized far outrun reality. Even if a delegate arouses a thoroughly negative reaction in others, it is likely that the group would have enough wisdom and sensitivity not to give direct threatening feedback in this area, until it felt that the person was prepared to hear such feedback. Therefore, the realities of the T-group and the laboratory are likely to be reassuring rather than threatening, once the initial tension of getting started has been mastered. Even if initial feedback is unequivocally negative, its *unambiguous* quality

---

[7] In a sense, these informal contacts create *new* temporary systems within the laboratory system. As T-groups and laboratory culture stabilize, the base for learning perhaps shifts to ever newly created temporary systems.

may result in some relief from tension. Often what has bothered the person is a history of receiving ambiguous feedback.

The learning method helps reduce threat from within in another way. Laboratories, as we have said, develop clear norms about the legitimacy of inquiry. We have already pointed out how these norms can help the group neutralize violent emotional issues. The norms also have a direct impact on the delegate's fantasies and fears about loss of self-esteem which result from revealing feelings that may be unacceptable to others. We believe that the primary impact of the climate of inquiry and analysis is the reassurance of the person. Analysis of feelings inevitably leads to their modulation and to mechanisms for shunting aside feelings that are too difficult to cope with. As each delegate witnesses how the group successfully manages the emotional expressions of others, he becomes more reassured about his own emotions. He learns that the environment is safe and that the group is strong enough to cope with his feelings.

We have examined how the learning method helps the delegate indirectly. It helps him to cope with those inner tensions which operate as preoccupiers and prevent him from listening to feedback. But the learning method also deals *directly* with the problem of listening, either by having structured exercises and theory sessions on the topic, or through interventions by the trainer when he observes conspicuous failure to listen.

Exercises, theory sessions, and interventions tend to be very helpful to the group primarily because most people assume they know all about listening and are convinced that they do it reasonably well. Once they understand and have demonstrated to them in their own behavior the distortions and failures in the listening process, they become more interested in listening to all aspects of the group process. They learn that listening is a much more active process than they had ever assumed, and that it involves getting into a helping relationship with others (helping others to communicate more clearly as well as to understand better). As they become more active in their listening, they find that this too reduces some of their tensions, particularly those revolving around the fear of loss of control.

We may cite one very simple but highly effective exercise. The trainer suggests that the group introduce into its discussion the simple ground rule that, before a speaker makes his own point, he should repeat what the previous speaker said, *to the previous speaker's satisfaction*. As the group attempts to do this, individuals discover not only how little of a previous speaker's comments they have actually heard, but also that different people have heard different things. The listeners suddenly discover how preoccupied they are with their own next point, various tensions, irrelevant observations, and so on.

Psychological Theory about Problems of Listening

One of the most common topics covered in theory sessions is communication. No matter how long or short the laboratory, one or more sessions dealing with the problems of accurate sending and receiving of information and feelings are almost always found. The topic of communication is covered in many different sessions, but a common thread in most of them is the difficulties of listening. The major points which, if understood, would reduce threat from within could be stated as follows: (1) it is difficult to listen effectively because of various preoccupations of the listener and various filters he uses to sift out the incoming messages; (2) such preoccupations are primarily symptomatic of overconcern with oneself and one's own points, rather than a reflection of concern for the other person who is trying to communicate; (3) the filters used are primarily defensive in nature, designed to protect the person from disconfirming information; (4) the filters operate as implicit assumptions and may deprive the person of important information about himself; (5) the only way communication can be improved is for the person involved to become more consciously aware of the filters used both by sender and receiver, which in turn can be accomplished only by a more active collaboration between the parties to the communication, thus, (6) both talking and listening are active complex processes requiring making an effort and checking out whether the message has gotten across or not.

Theory sessions dealing with this type of content serve to focus delegates on the communication process and thereby help them recognize and deal with some of their own defenses against feedback.

Most laboratories will also introduce specific theory on the problems of giving and receiving *feedback*. The difficulties of being objective and nonevaluative in *giving* feedback are contrasted with the difficulties of *hearing* it without immediately rejecting it or worse, retaliating if the feedback is seen as hostile. The problems of creating a climate conducive to feedback are talked about and brought into the open. The problem of timing and assessing the readiness of a potential receiver of feedback is analyzed. The tremendous difficulty of listening to and utilizing feedback is acknowledged as normal, not as insurmountable. By intellectual discussion of defense mechanisms, the groundwork is laid for helping people make explicit what they have been doing implicitly. Once the delegate can acknowledge his own defenses and accept them as normal, he can also begin to question their overall utility for him. Once he has asked himself how useful his defenses are, he has laid the groundwork for surmounting them.

The Staff as a Source of Protection

Just as the presence of the trainer protects members from each other (at least in the members' fantasies), so it also makes possible the fantasy that the trainer will protect each person from himself. Particularly in the early stages of the laboratory, it is important for delegates to believe in the omniscience and omnipotence of the staff because, for many of the delegates, identification with the staff serves as an important mechanism of borrowing strength for coping with the tensions generated within the delegates themselves. We are suggesting here a re-creation of earlier processes of identification with parents as a way of coping with uncontrollable impulses arising from within the person. The delegate can see that the trainer is not upset by his own feelings and can believe that the trainer can control any feelings that might arise in the group. Hence he can use the trainer as an absorber of and protector against his own feelings.

The importance of this mechanism can be seen if the trainer actually shows weakness, loss of control, or feelings which are incongruent with this powerful image. Those group members who have relied on him will become very tense, show great disappointment, and will tend to withdraw from further self-exposure in the group. Their ability to listen to feedback will drop proportionately because of new preoccupations. Other members will rejoice and attempt to step into the leader role themselves. If they have the requisite personal qualities, they may successfully reassure the more dependent members just as the trainer did.

The example which the staff member sets in how to deal with the person's own feelings and how to receive and utilize feedback as an important reality factor. By reality factor, we mean something which depends on the trainer's actual behavior rather than on delegate fantasies about him. Usually the trainer has little opportunity early in the group life to set an example of how to receive feedback because he gets very little. He can, however, set an example of how to give objective nonevaluative feedback when he shares his own reactions with the group, and can point up examples of such feedback when they occur among other group members. If the group has had incidents both of evaluative and non-evaluative feedback, he can invite them to compare their reactions to the two types, and thereby help them build norms of appropriateness for giving as well as receiving feedback.

Norms about receiving feedback can also be built around incidents involving different reactions which members have had to how others were hearing and utilizing feedback. For example, some members deny the feedback and exhibit overt defensiveness; others look and act so hurt that they arouse guilt in the group; still others ask questions and attempt to explore the implications of what was said to them; still others listen silently but then attempt to experiment with other modes of behavior. Some reactions will leave the group much more comfortable and ready to proceed; others will block further communication. The trainer can help, by inviting an analysis of different incidents, to establish norms for future member behavior.

The presence of a staff member designated as counselor is a final source of support. If any delegate finds himself unable to cope with feelings welling up within him, he knows that he can seek professional help as well as informal support from his friends. Delegates do utilize the laboratory counselor as well as their T-group trainers in this manner and derive obvious benefit from it, as judged by their own reports and observations of their behavior.

Summary.

We have argued that a major barrier to listening is the variety of personal tensions that preoccupy the person, particularly early in the laboratory. A second barrier is the pattern of defenses and filters the person sets up to screen out certain kinds of communications directed to him. A third barrier is the erroneous assumption which most people make that they are able to listen reasonably effectively, and therefore do not need additional knowledge or skills in this area. A fourth, and perhaps most important barrier of all, is the tendency to maximize *self*-esteem and to devalue, from the outset, what others attempt to tell us. This is an attitude that the group experience must change before effective listening can commence. These various barriers reflect primarily threats from within the person himself.

Many of the forces which were identified as reducing external threat also reduce threat from within by providing reassurance, support, and an atmosphere of unqualified acceptance. The temporary nature of the experience and the egalitarian atmosphere work toward such reassurance. The possibility of finding one or two close friends with whom to share problems is another force which the heterogeneous population and free time makes possible. The unreality or game quality of the laboratory makes it possible to rationalize a feeling as unreal and therefore not ultimately threatening.

The learning method with its emphasis on objectivity, nonevaluation, and focusing on incidents and behavior rather than total people, also operates to reassure the delegate and help him cope with inner feelings. For one thing, he learns that his fantasies about how horrible feedback would be are not borne out by the reality of what goes on in the group. The learning method also helps the delegate achieve greater knowledge about the problems of listening and, through exercises, increases his actual listening skills. Defenses can be made explicit and analyzed in the context of the exercise in which they are less threatened.

Psychological theory about the problems of listening, giving feedback, and receiving feedback supports exercises and trainer interventions. The assumption is made that the more the person can intellectually understand the process of threat and defense, the better his chances are of coping with his own feelings as they really operate.

Staff members help delegates cope with their inner threats partly by being available as powerful figures whose strength can be borrowed through identification and partly by setting an overt example of how to give and receive feedback. By their interventions, they can focus on incidents and help the group build norms appropriate to its members and their needs. The opportunity for individual delegates to obtain counseling help is a final source of support.

Conclusion

Let us conclude this detailed analysis by recapitulating what we have been trying to do in the past few chapters. In Chapter 14, we outlined a learning model consisting of successive cycles of disconfirming information—attitude change—new behavior, which in turn provided new information. We noted that the most important attitude change concerned the attitudes about the learning process itself, because if people did not learn to value the meta-goals of training, i.e., the here-and-now emphasis, and the value of open and authentic communication, they could not elicit any of the data they would need to learn about themselves and groups.

In Chapter 15, we examined in some detail what is involved in the attitude change process. In particular, we examined the kinds of forces which play on the delegate prior to his attendance at the laboratory that make it difficult for him to change any of his attitudes. We talked about attitude change in general and discussed its broad phases of unfreezing, changing, and refreezing.

In the present chapter, we focused on the conditions and forces operating in the laboratory which make it possible and, indeed, likely that attitudes about how to learn will change during the course of the laboratory. We noted that the major barriers to open communication and better listening were threats from others and threats from within oneself, and we attempted to show how the actual laboratory setting and activities reduced these threats. Most of our emphasis was on the unfreezing of the delegate through the creation of dilemmas, disconfirmations, and, concomitantly, through the creation of psychological safety. As delegates get unfrozen and learn new attitudes about revealing reactions and feelings, they make possible the achievement of the ultimate learning goals—to learn about self, others, and group.

Actually, we need to say very little about subsequent learning steps. Once attitudes about how to learn have changed, the rest of the process flows naturally in terms of the impact of the actual data revealed. As we indicated before, the new behavior in the form of reactions, observations, and feelings that the delegate has learned to reveal now provides information for other delegates. For some, this information will be disconfirming and will set in motion further attitude change; for others, it will be a confirmation thus refreezing where they already are; for still others, it will be irrelevant in terms of the kinds of attitude areas they are working on, although the information will greatly heighten their awareness of how others feel and how groups work.

Finally, a word must be said about increased interpersonal competence. We have put our emphasis on attitude change because this underlies so much of the learning process, but we cannot assume that interpersonal competence increases automatically with attitude change. What we can say is that attitude change is a prerequisite for increased competence in the sense that any new behavior which does not reflect new attitudes will not be internalized or stable. Behavior may change as an adaptation to group pressures, but such change will neither last, once the group pressures are off, nor be integrated with other parts of the self. Learning new competence means to us stable, internalized, integrated, new behaviors.

Attitude change about the learning process sets the stage for such learning by encouraging experimentation and the collection of data about oneself. Once the person realizes that he has alternatives, that he can make a choice about how he relates to others, and can choose responses partly on the basis of how others react to him, he has won more than half the battle. The laboratory setting and particularly the T-group provide him with an ideal opportunity to re-examine his previous behavior, to try new behaviors toward others, and to study their reactions to determine the impact of his new behavior.

Competence then will increase as a function of the degree to which the person systematically seeks out attitudes and behaviors that, on the one hand, fit into his own personality and, on the other hand, are more effective in helping him achieve his goals without thwarting the goals of others. This is often a slow and difficult process of trial and error which only starts in the laboratory, continuing, maybe for years, in the back-home setting. But what sets the process into motion is the fundamental attitude change about the learning process itself—the recognition of choice and the use of data about oneself as the basis for choice.

17

Some Hypotheses about
the Relative Learning Impact
of Different Kinds of Laboratories

Introduction

As a conclusion to our theoretical section, we would like to state some hypotheses about the relative impact of different kinds of laboratories. We have repeatedly stated that attitude change lies at the heart of the learning process and have specified that the likelihood of attitude change is a function of the effectiveness of the laboratory in unfreezing, changing, and refreezing attitudes. In the present chapter, we would like to discuss several of the major variables which have particular relevance for these stages of the attitude change process. The variables derive their particular importance from the fact that they involve the earliest kinds of decision which laboratory planners make about laboratories. Once decisions at this level are reached, certain learning possibilities are already opened or closed.

The variables which we will consider are the following: (1) the length of the laboratory; (2) the degree of isolation of the laboratory; (3) the nature of the delegate population and (4) the kind of staff to be utilized. We will not consider such matters as laboratory design because, to a considerable extent, the design is predetermined once decisions about the above four characteristics have been made. The design can generally accentuate forces which have already been built in; only under unusual circumstances would it reverse or obviate such forces.[1]

---

[1] We have deliberately ignored certain other variables, such as the personality of the delegate, not because they are irrelevant to learning, but because of our focus on those aspects which are easier to control by the planner of laboratory training.

1. *Length of laboratory.* For purpose of distinguishing different kinds of laboratories, we will consider short (3 days), medium (1 week), and long (2 weeks) laboratories, and examine the implication of length for unfreezing, changing, and refreezing.

2. *Degree of isolation.* Four degrees of isolation will be examined. *None*—this condition is obtained in the nonresidential part-time laboratory characteristic of some college courses in group dynamics. *Some*—some isolation is achieved in the nonresidential but full-time laboratory. *Considerable*—this condition would be reflected in the part-time residential laboratory such as a typical Bethel laboratory where the delegate is away from work but brings his family and lives outside the immediate laboratory community. *Total*—total isolation is achieved in those laboratories where the delegate is removed completely from work and family and lives full-time in the laboratory community, e.g., Arden House.

3. *Nature of delegate population.* We will examine three kinds of populations. *Team or family groups*—delegates who come from the same organization and have direct working relationships with each other. *Homogeneous but not teams*—delegates who come from the same occupational group and maybe even the same organization, but who do not have any direct working relationships with each other. *Heterogeneous*—delegates drawn from different occupations and different organizations.

4. *Staff characteristics.* As indicated earlier (Chapter 4), we can identify many different bases for differentiating among staff members, such as personality, experience, preference for certain types of laboratories. In the present context, we wish to focus on a characteristic that reflects both personality and training style, that characteristic having to do with how the staff member presents himself to delegates, how he interacts with them, and the kind of learning model he holds implicitly. We feel that staff members should be differentiated in terms of their particular orientation to the teaching-learning transaction: whether they encourage learning through *identification* or learning through *scanning.*

The trainer who is committed to a theory of learning through scanning would tend to reduce his salience and visibility in the group and would actively encourage delegates to seek information from many sources in the group. By contrast, the identification-oriented trainer consciously and deliberately allows himself to become a model, an ideal member, or good member and encourages delegates to learn to become like him or like anyone else in the group who is exhibiting appropriate behavior. The scanning-oriented trainer puts more emphasis on group process, on the value of different styles of behavior, and on the learning *process*, letting what is learned take care of itself. The identification-oriented trainer has a conception of "good group member behavior," attempts to behave in terms of it, and highlights instances of it in other members. There are, of course, many styles which combine elements of the two extremes; most trainers would fall somewhere in between. For purposes of stating some hypotheses, however, it is useful to consider the extreme types.

Our hypotheses about these laboratory characteristics are attempts to state how likely it is that a given characteristic affects the learning process by aiding or hindering unfreezing, changing, or refreezing. We are not attempting to assert that one kind of laboratory produces more learning than another. Because of the complexity of the learning process itself, such global hypotheses are not, in our opinion, fruitful at this point. Rather, we are asserting our belief that certain laboratory characteristics have a direct impact on certain phases of the learning process, and it is at this more specific level of analysis that we can state some hypotheses about laboratories.

We have attempted to summarize our hypotheses in the form of a chart, shown in Table 17–1. Along the vertical axis, we have indicated the laboratory variables that have just been discussed. Along the horizontal axis, we have shown the phases of the learning process as these have been described in the previous three chapters. If we felt that a particular characteristic had a particular impact on a phase of the learning process, we indicated this by marking pluses, minuses, or zeros in that part of the chart depending on whether it was our hypothesis that the variable had a positive enhancing effect (plus), no effect (zero), or a negative undermining effect (minus). In some cases, we felt that the *amount* of positive and negative effect could be assessed, hence we indicated one, two, or three pluses or minuses to indicate the strength of the enhancing or hindering forces. In a number of cases, we could not decide whether a particular variable did or did not affect a particular learning phase or process. In those instances, we placed a question mark in the chart. Let us examine the chart and try to spell out some of the major hypotheses which we feel are warranted.

I. Hypotheses about Laboratory Length

As our chart indicates, we have a number of hypotheses which pertain directly to the length of laboratory experience. These can be stated as follows:

Ia. *The longer the laboratory, the greater the likelihood of delegates being successfully unfrozen.*

Table 17–1 Hypotheses about the Effect of Selected Laboratory Variables on the Stages of Attitude Change*

	Unfreezing	Changing		Refreezing	
		Scanning	Identi-fication	Personal	Relational
Length of Laboratory					
Short (3 days)	+	0	++	+	0
Medium (1 week)	++	+	++	++	−
Long (2 weeks)	+++	++	+++	+++	−−
Degree of Isolation					
None (nonresidential, part-time)	−−	−−	?	+	+
Some (nonresidential, full-time)	0	−	?	+	0
Considerable (partial residential)	++	++	++	++	−
Complete (total residential)	+++	+++	+++	+++	−−
Delegate Population					
Teams or family group	−−	−	+++	0 or −	+++
Homogeneous but not teams	+	+	++	0 or −	++
Heterogeneou	++	+++	0 or +	++	0 or −
Staff Characteristics					
Identification, modeling oriented	?	0 or −	+++	−−	−,0, or +
Scanning oriented	?	+++	0 or −	+++	−−

* Pluses denote positive effects, the number of pluses referring to the degree of effect; zeros denote no effect (irrelevance); minuses denote a negative effect, hindering of that phase of the change process; question marks indicate that we do not have a hypothesis.

Ib. *The longer the laboratory, the greater the likelihood of successful learning either through scanning or through identification.*

Ic. *The shorter laboratory, the more possible it is to learn through identification (one can find a model quickly), and the less possible it is to learn through scanning (it takes longer to locate useful sources of personally relevant information).*

Id. *The longer the laboratory, the greater the likelihood that what is learned will be personally refrozen, i.e., will become integrated with other parts of the self.*

Ie. *The longer the laboratory, the greater the likelihood that what is learned will be out of line with back-home norms and values, hence the less the likelihood of it being relationally refrozen.* The degree to which this hypothesis holds depends upon the degree to which the delegate population is homogeneous. The more homogeneous the population, the greater the likelihood of things learned being acceptable back-home, i.e., relationally refrozen.

II. Hypotheses about Degree of Isolation

IIa. *The greater the degree of isolation of the laboratory, the greater the likelihood of delegates being sucessfully unfrozen.* If there is minimum isolation, there is a likelihood that unfreezing will actually be hampered (because of the continued involvement of the delegate in his day-to-day routine and relationships).

IIb. *Given a considerable amount of isolation, the greater the isolation, the greater the likelihood of learning either through scanning or identification.* Very low isolation actually is likely to undermine scanning, but we do not have a hypothesis about its effects on identification possibilities.

IIc. *The greater the degree of isolation of the laboratory, the greater the likelihood of personal refreezing.*

IId. *The greater the degree of isolation of the laboratory, the less the likelihood that what is learned will be relationally refrozen back home.*

III. Hypotheses about the Nature of the Delegate Population

IIIa. *The more homogeneous the delegate population, the less likely delegates are to become unfrozen.* At the extreme of team training or family group training, unfreezing is actually hindered because delegates may not wish to take the risks of opening up to others with whom they have long relationships. The more that delegates are strangers to each other, the easier it is for them to become unfrozen.

IIb. *The more heterogeneous the population, the greater the likelihood of learning through scanning* (largely because heterogeneity makes available a wider range of solutions for the delegate to whatever problems he is working on).

IIIc. *The more homogeneous the population, the greater the likelihood of learning through identification.* This is true because the potential models are already salient, are clear by virtue of their similarity to the delegate, and are more trustworthy because he is likely to know them already.

IIId. *The more heterogeneous the population, the more likely it is that the person will find personally meaningful solutions, hence the greater the likelihood of personal refreezing.* This is the case because the heterogeneous laboratory exposes each delegate to more different patterns of how to deal with interpersonal problems.

IIIe. *The more homogeneous the population, the more likely it is that the person will find organizationally acceptable solutions, hence the greater the likelihood of relational refreezing.* In the heterogeneous laboratory, the delegate may well find solutions which are personally acceptable but not acceptable back home. In the homogeneous laboratory solutions are by definition acceptable because the back-home norms are represented in the laboratory.

IV. Staff Characteristics

IVa. *The greater the degree of scanning orientation of the staff member, the greater the likelihood that the delegate will learn through scanning, and the less likely he is to learn through identification.* This is true because a scanning emphasis lowers the salience of others as potential identification models.

IVb. *The greater the degree of identification orientation of the staff member, the greater the likelihood that the delegate will learn through identification, particularly through identification with the staff member, and the less likely he is to learn through scanning.* This is true because identification focuses the delegate on the model and lowers his attention to other potential sources of information.

IVc. *The greater the degree of scanning orientation of the staff member, the greater the likelihood that things learned will be personally relevant and therefore personally refrozen, and the less likely that things learned will be organizationally relevant and therefore relationally refrozen (unless the population is homogeneous).*

IVd. *The greater the degree of identification orientation of the trainer, the less the likelihood that things learned will be personally relevant and therefore personally refrozen; whether or not they are organizationally relevant and will be relationally refrozen depends upon the nature of the delegate population and the congruence between trainer values and organizational values.*

V. Hypotheses Based on Combinations of Characteristics

In a number of instances, we have had to qualify our hypotheses because of the interdependence of some of the variables we have mentioned. In the present section, we would like to state more global hypotheses which take account of these interactions.

Va. *Unfreezing will be facilitated most in the long, isolated, heterogeneous laboratory.*

Vb. *Change through scanning will be facilitated most in long, isolated, heterogeneous laboratory with a scanning-oriented staff.*

Vc. *Change through identification will be facilitated most in the long, isolated, homogeneous laboratory with an identification-oriented staff.*

Vd. *Personal refreezing will be facilitated most in the long, isolated, heterogeneous laboratory with a scanning-oriented staff.*

Ve. *Relational refreezing will be facilitated most in the homogeneous laboratory with an identification-oriented staff.*

Vf. *Maximum personal learning is likely to occur in the long, isolated, heterogeneous, scanning-oriented laboratory, but at the possible expense of learning organizationally unacceptable things.*

Vg. *Maximum organizationally relevant learning is likely to occur in the long, isolated, homogeneous, identification-oriented laboratory, but at the possible expense of learning things which are personally less acceptable.*

A Dilemma for Designers of Laboratory Training. The last several hypotheses point up the fact that the conditions for maximum personal learning and maximum organizationally relevant learning are not necessarily the same. The dilemma posed brings us back to the issue of laboratory goals, the implied contract with the delegate, and the concept of "who is the ultimate client?"

If it is true, as our observation bears out, that laboratories oriented toward deep personal learning may stimulate organizationally dysfunctional attitudes and behavior changes, it is crucial that they advertise openly what they are capable of providing and what risks the delegate may run by attendance. This is essentially what most laboratories do when they point out the importance of sending teams to the training program. The integration of personal learning into a team during the laboratory is the first and most crucial step in integrating it into wider organizational relationships. On the other hand, those laboratories which are primarily concerned with refreezing, i.e., changing permanent organizational relationships in a more than temporary sense, should point out that the learning opportunities for the delegate are focused on his role and organizational behavior rather than on deeper personal issues.

Each staff, when planning the laboratory, faces the dilemma of how to balance personal learning goals with the goals of helping delegates integrate what they have learned into the back-home setting. It has been known from the inception of laboratory training, that it is very difficult for the individual delegate to hold on to the insights and changes which occur in the laboratory setting if there is no social support present in the back-home organization. Various back-home exercises which have been tried have had only limited success in consolidating and strengthening the learning.

The resolution appears to lie *first*, in a clearer recognition of the dilemma—the complex interaction between the organizational context in the process of personal change, and the complex interaction between types of laboratory settings, delegate composition, staffing patterns, and the possible outcomes of the experience.

Second, it would appear to be mandatory for the original planners of the laboratory experience to be very clear about their goals, the kind of contract they are entering into with the delegate, and who their ultimate client is. One of the important reasons for using only professionally trained help in planning and designing laboratory experiences is that professionally competent decisions must be made from the very beginning of the planning process. Organizations which first decide to have a laboratory and then go about hiring a staff to run it, have already confused the issue. They should allow the staff to reconsider the whole question of whether a laboratory is appropriate or not, and, if so, what kind of laboratory it should be.

Third, it appears crucial that we invent better approaches to training the back-home environment. If we care about stable, functional attitude change which is both personally and organizationally useful, we must go outside the laboratory setting in order to prepare the back-home environment for the changes which the laboratory can produce.

Summary and Conclusions: Training Design Vulnerabilities

In this chapter, we have attempted to show how the processes of attitude change—unfreezing, changing, and refreezing—are affected by some of the major aspects of laboratory settings, i.e., length, degree of isolation, homogeneity of delegate populations, and kind of staff employed.

We have also attempted to highlight a dilemma of laboratory planning by focusing attention on the complex interaction between personal learning and organizational refreezing, and the demands that this dilemma places upon laboratory planners to be clear about their implied contract with the delegates.

In conclusion, we would like to provide another frame of reference for considering the laboratory variables we have discussed. This frame of reference may be most useful to the designers of laboratory training experiences. If the hypotheses stated prove to be correct, we can use Table 17-1 to identify the major *vulnerabilities* of different kinds of laboratories. By vulnerabilities, we mean *potential* weak spots which must get special attention in order to prevent actual training design flaws. The patterns of minuses identify these vulnerabilities. By taking them into account, we can obtain a clearer idea of what must be built into the training design in the way of compensating forces, or what limitations of laboratory goals have to be accepted.

For example, the nonresidential laboratory is most vulnerable at the level of unfreezing. If the delegates arrive unfrozen, a great deal can be done. If not, the training will probably amount to little more than appreciation training, giving delegates a feeling for the kinds of learning which are possible in a laboratory.

The long, residential laboratory is most vulnerable at the level of relational refreezing. There is little question that they can unfreeze and induce personally meaningful change, but the new responses may not fit into organizational expectations. If relational refreezing does not occur, the person must (1) give up the new responses, producing the well known fade out effect, or (2) seek new significant others, which may mean leaving the organization, or (3) attempt to change the organization.

Team or family training is vulnerable in that it may not facilitate unfreezing and may fail to build a climate for learning through scanning because of the ease of learning through identification. Its strength lies in the fact that whatever learning occurs is relationally refrozen, at least within the team.

The vulnerable point in maximally heterogeneous laboratories, as in the long residential laboratories, is that the learning produced may be personally meaningful but difficult to integrate back home.

Laboratories which are staffed by modeling-oriented trainers are vulnerable to producing learning which may not be easily integratable personally. Scanning-oriented staffs have the opposite problems of producing learning which may not be integratable organizationally.

To avoid these pitfalls, a careful diagnosis of the client system is required before a laboratory is even under consideration, followed by a careful working out of the elements of the setting in terms of the training goals, the characteristics of the client population, staff availability, and training design. Preplanning is essential so as to avoid being limited by a laboratory that has vulnerabilities for which one cannot compensate with the training design.

18

Our Questions about Laboratory Training

Heywood Broun is said to have become a Communist during his student days at Harvard. During his junior year, the story goes, he was taking a survey course on Political Institutions. The format of the course was apparently crucial in Broun's conversion. Each *Monday*, the Professor in charge of the course would have a lecturer in to talk to the students about a particular political movement with which the lecturer was identified as a proponent and practitioner. The same week, on *Wednesday*, the Professor would summarize and demolish, point-by-point, the main arguments of the Monday speaker. The visiting lecturers were known to have an amazing impact. Like medical students who "caught" the diseases they were studying, these students became converts of this or that political cause—if only for two days. When Norman Thomas spoke to the class, for example, everyone converted to Socialism until the following Wednesday when each of Thomas' points was disputed by the Professor and the students' conversions carefully righted.

When Earl Browder came to speak, he was so effective that the entire class, *en bloc*, converted to Communism. Heywood Broun was one of those who became a Monday Communist, but it so happened that on that particular Wednesday, when the Professor was to refute Communism, the Boston Red Sox were opening the season at Fenway Park against the New York Yankees. Heywood Broun was a fervent baseball fan. . . .

This anecdote conveys the power of criticism and the importance of presenting two sides of every issue. We do not intend now to "demolish, point-by-point" the arguments and ideas we have presented thus far, but we do want to express some of our own criticisms, doubts, and

321

ambivalences. We have wondered about the appropriate way to express these concerns. In the course of writing this book, this dilemma was never very far from our minds: How do you present an idea objectively—and at the same time indicate your own doubts—without sacrificing clarity and directness? How do you expose weaknesses without sounding apologetic or cynical to dubious friends and without paying false homage to critics? How do you reveal ambivalence without blunting your point? And how do you qualify, give vent to, skepticism and doubts without distracting the reader and without diverting the rhythm and progress of the exposition?

The strategy for dealing with our ambivalences in this book is indirect. We tried to be as cautious and conservative as we dared, and we tried to avoid the cant and dogma of the True Believer. Now, however, we would like to present those criticisms and concerns about laboratory training which, thus far, we have tended to suppress. We hope to go beyond mere criticisms; like Broun's Professor we hope to provide a dialectic which will include some of our own concerns, some of laboratory training critics' concerns (occasionally they are difficult to distinguish from our own), and some responses to our own and to others' questions. This chapter gives us an opportunity to wonder aloud with the reader, to engage in an internal dispute with ourselves, and to expose some of our deepest concerns, not as apology or defense, but by way of producing a balance and perspective that our text may not have reflected.

We can organize our concerns about laboratory training around four questions we will take up in order: (1) Is laboratory training professional; (2) is laboratory training ideology rather than inquiry; (3) is laboratory training therapy in social science disguise, and (4) is laboratory training a "Quest for Omnipotence?"

Is Laboratory Training Professional?

Laboratory training purportedly is a professional activity, and it must be professional if it is to continue the delicate and important work it has set out to do. It affects people's lives and attempts to change social systems. Any social mechanism with these aims *must* satisfy the requirements of a profession. A profession must fulfill certain criteria if it is to achieve professional status and among the most crucial of these are three. Professional practice must be founded on basic research and on reliable knowledge, i.e., a profession must be scientifically based. A profession must enforce a codified system of ethics. A profession must be staffed by adequately trained and certified practitioners.

On all three counts, questions must be raised about the professional status of laboratory training.

Scientific Basis of Laboratory Training

Laboratory Training presumes to be rooted in the behavioral sciences and most of its practitioners combine practice with a research-academic life. While there is promise in the research potential generated by the Intern Program (see Chapter 4) and other activities, at the present time practice still outstrips research. This is serious, for there is so much to be done. As Stock (1964, p. 437) says in her peroration of a chapter on laboratory training research: "Each reader is invited to provide his own ending to the incomplete sentence, 'Why doesn't someone study————?' "

Discouragingly, but not unexpectedly, the research effort seems weakest in those situation where the risks are highest and the tasks are most complex. We are referring to the uses of laboratory training in inducing change in organizations. *In some organizational change programs, a great deal of attention is being paid to research, but not enough research is yet being done.*

Of course, there are tremendous pressures against conducting research in organizations. For one thing, the research designs have to be intricate and are difficult to implement. These are not college laboratories where subjects can be carefully controlled. For another thing, the practical demands on the staff member's time appear to sap the energy necessary for good research. Just as it takes an extraordinary effort for a clinician to conduct research, so it takes a laboratory training practitioner that extraordinary effort.

As we hinted earlier, the future holds genuine promise for renewed research emphasis. National Training Laboratories itself now has a full-time behavioral scientist who is coordinating all NTL research activity. The effects of this investment in time, energy, and dollars is already noticeable.[1] The Intern Program has attracted competent researchers to tackle laboratory training related research projects and has been instrumental in linking laboratory training to other behavioral science research centers. Laboratory training pioneers, such as R.

---

[1] A research committee was recently formed by NTL's Research Director, Charles Seashore. Members are Warren Bennis, Douglas Bunker, Roger Harrison, Harold Leavitt, Ronald Lippitt, Henry Riecken, Herbert Shepard, and Goodwin Watson. A journal for research, *Applied Behavioral Sciences,* is now being launched under the editorship of Goodwin Watson.

Lippitt, M. Miles, and R. Blake, are developing interesting methods to study its processes and outcomes. So the future looks brighter than it has for some time.

In any case, the basis of Laboratory Training must always rest on the foundation of the behavioral sciences. Without this footing, we cannot safeguard adequately against obscurantism, cultism, malpractice, and downright foolishness. Research must lead the way and fuel the practice of laboratory training, rather than the reverse.

A Codified System of Ethics

With the exception of clinical psychology, which borrows its ethical system from medicine, the behavioral sciences have not worked out or codified as careful a system of ethical practices—vis-à-vis a lay public —as have other professions such as medicine and law. This is so for a simple reason: It is only relatively recently that behavioral scientists have *had* clients. However, the formation of a codified system of ethics is one of the pressing current needs of laboratory training.

As we see it, the main deficiency in this area is the ambiguity of the contract between laboratory training staff and the client (whether individual or organization). Frequently, the nature of the contract is unstated, unclear, or ambiguous. There seems to be a kind of reluctance or unwillingness to subject the contract to careful examination so that purpose can be defined in reasonably similar and realistic terms by both parties to the relationship. Although this articulation may be difficult—and often it is, given the inevitable communication gap between professionals and their lay clientele—it is essential.

It is essential because laboratory training advocates and promotes certain kinds of changes, and, if a contract is to be established, the proposed changes must be clarified and communicated, however arduous this task is, so that the anticipated consequences are dealt with and agreed upon. Laboratory training is not like medicine or law where clients seek out help to correct deficiencies or to be repaired, cured, or remedied. In those cases, the client has a fairly clear idea of his problem, an intimation of its cure, and comes to the relationship voluntarily and often without an alternative. And the law protects both parties to the contract. Laboratory training, on the other hand, actively seeks out clients in order to influence them.[2] And clients may not have a realistic picture of the intended changes. So the nature of the relationship, the contract, must be carefully elucidated.

---

[2] Clients, too, in increasing numbers seek out laboratory training. In any case these remarks hold.

If we sound stern on this issue, there is a good reason for it. We fear, on occasion, that training relationships are agreed to in a nonchalant manner without a thorough understanding on both sides. (Chapter 10 provides some examples of this.) One of the reasons why we have placed so much emphasis on voluntarism for clients is to safeguard against false pretense. But more than this, a professional must take responsibility for spelling out implications of the relationship and from time-to-time must *examine its validity*.

There is still another important reason for considering the ethical elements of laboratory training. It has to do with what society allows or "legitimizes" education to do to its clients. In our society, training or education is undertaken almost exclusively in order to acquire some knowledge or ability. We do not ordinarily attend school in order to acquire or change *motivation* or *attitudes*. Only people defined as "sick" are supposed to seek help in this respect in terms of our social values.

So-called normals and society often regard induced changes in motives or attitudes as "brainwashing," or as an "invasion of privacy." Quite frequently these charges have been leveled at laboratory training, and they must be considered seriously rather than dismissed as reckless or as evidence of resistance.

Recently Rosow (1964) has discussed this issue in relationship to socialization practices in a way that we find helpful for clarifying some of the ethical issues. Rosow asserts that a person must acquire three things before he is able to perform satisfactorily in a social role: knowledge, ability, and motivation, and that the person's life cycle dictates priorities for each of these. In other words, Rosow argues that socialization processes vary with phases of the life cycle, that what might be appropriate for infancy and childhood may not be appropriate for adulthood. For example, we consider the learning of motivation and values to be legitimate and appropriate primarily in childhood. By the time a person is an adult he should only need knowledge or training in abilities. Adult retraining in motives and values is ordinarily only legitimate for the sick and delinquent. Yet laboratory training purports to change attitudes and values. How this dilemma is resolved so that laboratory training can oblige society and yet satisfy its goals and clients is difficult to say. We believe that only through recognizing these societal norms and exploring thoroughly some of their consequences with potential clients can some of the ethical pitfalls be avoided.

Value and attitude change—even a change toward a spirit of inquiry, which we have been advocating—is a serious business and must rely on a carefully considered ethical system. The foundation of this ethical system must be based, most of all, on a thoroughly understood contract. That is to say that both parties to the contract should be aware of and voluntarily accept the obligations involved.

Adequately Trained and Certified Practitioners

Until 1959 the training of laboratory staff was undertaken casually without much self-consciousness about the process of selection, induction, and training of new staff. There were occasional planned courses, but by and large the training that was conducted evolved informally. The usual pattern was for a promising social scientist to be invited to a laboratory training activity by a senior staff member who then tried to place the newcomer in a position in which he would learn. Usually, the new staff man would act as an observer, junior trainer, or research assistant. Until very recently, the demand for new staff was small, and the informal training methods reflected this.

In 1959, foreseeing increased demands for staff, NTL formed a committee on "Trainer Development" to examine future needs and a "variety of problems relating to the recruitment and training of trainers" (Bennis and Miles, 1960). This committee recommended an Intern Program which would select, train, and induct new staff. The first eight-week program began at Bethel in 1960; since 1961 the program has been supported by the National Institutes of Health. (See Chapter 4 for a more complete description of the Intern Program.)

Undoubtedly the Intern Program has helped in strengthening the quality of laboratory training staff. The Interns typically are drawn from academic centers and are PhD's with careers that already show genuine promise. Since the start of the program in 1960, more and more Interns are playing key roles in laboratory training affairs. Nevertheless, we still desire more formal supervision of new staff members and more training opportunities for senior staff. Too often, there is a sense of finality about the training programs. We would like to see the idea of continuing education that we advocate to our clients extended to laboratory training staff, as well.

But even more bothersome to us is that there is no accreditation for laboratory training staff. Too many individuals, we fear, with too little training experience, with insufficient grounding in the behavioral sciences, and with dubious motivation become trainers. Presently, there is no way of controlling this. One stopgap possibility, which appeals to us, is to use only the Fellows and Associates of NTL as an accredited list. We would encourage this so that official members of the NTL roster may become, in time, the certified group.[3]

The early years of professional development are those when a profession can least afford malpractice. Yet evaluation data of training effects are difficult to obtain and interpret, which makes for difficulty in discerning the actual value of one trainer style over another or one type of trainer personality over another. While the present training *methods* of new staff are vastly superior to what they were ten years ago, more progress has still to be made and better methods of certification enforced before we will be more relaxed and confident about the training and selection of trainers.

Is Laboratory Training Ideology, Rather than Inquiry?

Critics of laboratory training have often pointed to the zeal and enthusiasm its supporters manifest, an enthusiasm that reaches at times a shrill evangelical tone that is annoying to the neutral observer and embarassing to us. Perhaps, we occasionally rationalize, it is only the newcomers who hold those attitudes. But the strident and innocent enthusiasm seems more widespread, and it besets us with a vexing problem: Is laboratory training more of an ideology, a faith, than a method for inquiry? Talleyrand's epigram also comes to mind: "I can take care of my enemies; it's my friends I have to worry about."

Laboratory training must operate on the basis of a system of values which emphasizes inquiry, not ideology. The entire normative and ethical structure rests on this distinction, so it might be useful to elaborate on it.[4] The primary task of laboratory training is to create an orientation toward learning that leads to the development, within the learner, of the motivation for and capacity to make his own decisions. So primarily, laboratory training is about *how to learn*, about *choice*, and about developing competencies to learn efficiently those values we grouped under a spirit of inquiry (See Chapter 3). We believe that the business of laboratory training is to transmit these values and to create conditions where individuals can have experiences which can be evaluated. However, even inquiry is an ideology of a kind. So let us be specific about what we are objecting to.

---

[3] In Appendix I, we have listed the Associates and Fellows of NTL and the performance criteria for their selection.
[4] We have set forth our own *normative* view of social systems elsewhere. See Bennis, Schein, Berlew, and Steele (1964).

We are objecting primarily to inappropriate employment of laboratory training. On occasion we have observed a total lack of discrimination in prescribing laboratory training, whether the client is an individual or an organization. Distinctions have always to be realized between *real life* and the highly controlled life of laboratories. In Chapter 10 we discussed some cases where laboratory training was almost literally smuggled into a client system without formal, or even informal, legitimization, and, certainly, with little understanding of its appropriateness. We cannot stress this point enough. No client is going to live or die because of laboratory training. Thus, its utilization can always be assessed cautiously and carefully.

We have other worries along these lines and it is always difficult for us to know where critics' distortions end and our own begin. Laboratory training is regarded in many quarters as promoting a kind of togetherness, other-directedness, and group dynamic smorgasbord that denies the reality and importance of *power* relationships. For some, laboratory training has been associated with socialism and anarchy; to others, it has been guilty of failing to recognize the importance of formal lines of authority. Still other complaints have to do with its preaching of a certain set of values that may or may not be functional and that can most *certainly not* be justified by hard data. For example, laboratory training is seen as purchasing affiliation at the price of achievement and cohesiveness at the price of individualism. It is also seen as promoting a naive wish to implant democratic principles anywhere and everywhere.[5]

To what extent these perceptions are valid does not concern us here. Laboratory training is *not* in the business of suggesting this or that model of organization or *any* action alternative except insofar as these models and alternatives aid the development of learning, diagnosis, and inquiry. Thus, we view T-groups as *learning* groups and wish they were called L-groups instead of T-groups. We view laboratories as controlled learning environments where people learn, *not* that democracy or autocracy is a good thing or that cohesive and/or leaderless groups are good or bad (they may be, but that is not the point), but that they can study and inquire about the *consequences* of autocracy, democracy, leadership types, and cohesiveness. They can then choose with greater knowledge what form or practice might be most appropri-

---

[5] Only recently we got word from a former government official of an NTL alumnus stationed in the Far East on government duty. The latter tried to impose laboratory training on a Buddhist monastery he had had some contact with. The monks tolerated this for awhile, but finally rebelled and evicted the well-intentioned but seriously misled "change-agent."

ate. Clearly, it is possible that autocracy might be more appropriate under certain conditions.

Laboratory training aims to enhance the range and validity of alternatives and to improve the processes of choice. It does this by promoting conditions where an individual can learn the importance of data collection in the sphere of human affairs and those interpersonal competencies which can aid in the collection, evaluation, and feedback of these data. *All of these competencies are slanted toward the development of better mechanisms of choice.*

Thus laboratory training can be defined as an experientially-based learning technique that attempts to create an attitude of inquiry and openness toward human phenomena. As Thomas Mann expressed it: "I wear my eyebrows, so to speak, continually raised." This attitude of skepticism and scrutiny is what we hope delegates and clients internalize and what laboratory training should emphasize.

Where and how laboratory training fails to carry out its primary task of imparting this spirit is not altogether clear to us. And it is difficult to know how justified our fears are. But so often delegates seem to come away from a laboratory with the belief that we have been advocating that work groups be run like T-groups, that organizations should abandon formal authority and traditional principles of organization, that democratization will work better always. We worry whether the real goals of inquiry have been eclipsed by more grandiose, ideological aims. We wonder if, somehow or other, laboratory training is not firmly established in the public's mind as representing a political platform rather than an open forum, as a prescription rather than a diagnosis. We worry about whether or not we have exercised sufficient vigilance in recognizing the limits of our competence, techniques, and ambition. We cannot afford to forget that the main product is the devolopment of inquiry.

One final word is in order. The action-oriented person sometimes asks, quite rightfully: "How do I know when to stop inquiring and take action?" "When do I know enough?" "When does further diagnosis reach the point of diminishing returns?" We wish we had a clear answer to these legitimate questions. But at the present we can only say that our emphasis on inquiry results from our feelings that most people could do more of it, not from our feelings that it should replace action.

Is Laboratory Training Therapy in Social Science Disguise?

An issue, never far from the surface and all too easily agitated, has to do with the relationship between group psychotherapy and T-groups, specifically whether or not T-groups and therapy groups can really be distinguished from each other. The fact that the issue lingers despite endless debates, tirades, and symposia probably betrays its seductiveness and lack of resolution.[6]

The issue usually takes on a classic simplicity. It goes like this: Psychiatrists, clinical psychologists, or other individually-centered therapists accuse laboratory training staff of "irresponsibility," of "doing therapy without knowing it," of being "Sorcerer's Apprentices," of adding needless pathological elements by setting off explosive and dangerous anxieties without the knowledge or competence to deal with them. Staff are accused of being "therapists in disguise" and possibly doing untold damage to their clients, most of all, by causing or activating acting-out neuroses of various kinds.

Laboratory training staff, for their part, respond defensively by going into explanations of how laboratory training differs from therapy, by indicating that their antagonists really do not understand it, by implying that groups threaten the therapists' highly controlled doctor-patient sanctuary, and by asserting that they (the unwashed) really do not understand the group's supportive and restorative functions, and so forth.

These discussions are often engaging but rarely productive. Typically they end in fruitless complexity and increased mutual disdain. Undoubtedly there is room for disagreement and valid reason for conflict between the various helping professions: doctrinal, theoretical, jurisdictional, political, and even personal. And yet the intensity and the persistence of the perennial charges and counter charges make us think that the real issues go beyond the actual arguments.

It is surprising, too, for certainly the fundamental aims of therapy and laboratory training are similar. They are both interested in bringing about a greater degree of consciousness; they are both interested in bringing about a greater degree of self-determination and responsibility in human affairs; they are both dedicated to the pursuit and love of truth. Of course, there are profound differences which should not be ignored. The domain of psychotherapy, the area it probes and explores, is the unconscious and its mysteries. The unit of analysis for laboratory training is the interpersonal encounter. Therapy throws its analytic searchlight into the past and into the genetic and develop-

---

[*] For a recent examination of the differences and similarities between laboratory training and group psychotherapy, see J. Frank's excellent essay (1964) and Section B of Chapter 7.

mental roots of conflict. Laboratory training focuses almost exclusively on the present. For the therapist, a dream is laden with symbolic meaning and unconscious intent. For the trainer, a dream is a specimen of social interaction; he looks at its impact on the group, and so forth.

There are other differences and Frank's essay (1964) summarizes these. The trouble with all of these comparisons is that the differences *within* the domain of group therapy and laboratory training may be as great or greater than the differences *between* the two domains. Rosenbaum and Berger (1963) in a recent survey of group therapy list at least a dozen different approaches. In the recent book on T-group theory (Bradford et al., 1964), nine explicit theoretical statements are presented, all vastly different in scope, in variables examined, in trainer interventions, in developmental processes, and so forth. So what good does it do to compare therapy groups with T-groups when neither of these is a clearly defined, homogeneous unit, and when both contain so many variants that their status as a particular "thing" is unreliable?

Recognizing that there are extreme variations among training and group therapy groups may help us get to what may be the core issue. We can view T-groups along a continuum. One extreme of this continuum contains trainer styles that resemble group therapy; at the other extreme, we can find trainers and training styles that have only a remote resemblance to group therapy. It may be useful to summarize some of these training theories[7] in a crude way and then return to the implications of this framework for the therapy-training issue.

Theory A: Problem Solving. This theory states that learning takes place through identifying group problems, finding the relevant behavioral science theory for the problem which will suggest the direction of the resolution, and then practicing the skills needed to resolve the problem. This approach is similar to Blake's "dilemma–invention–experimentation–feedback" model discussed in Chapter 3. This theory focuses primarily on group membership, and only secondarily on personal learning. It is an approach that is highly cognitive and skill-oriented.

Theory B: Personality Development. This theory states that learning takes place through becoming sensitive to one's own and others' feelings. The trainer and training activities attempt to produce a psychologically safe climate which focuses on emotional processes.

---

[7] We are using the word "theory" in the vernacular, really as a notion or model which provides a framework for action and which guides the trainer's style.

Self-actualization, inducing creativity, treasuring and evoking personal responses are encouraged and rewarded. Theory is based on emotional dynamics, existentialist and humanistic psychology.

Theory C: Valid Communication and Authentic Relationships. Overlapping with Theory B, this one states that learning in the laboratory takes place through the development of more authentic interpersonal relationships, learned primarily with and through the trainer who presents a role model of how to be authentic or congruent. The focus of inquiry for the group is the entire range of communicative acts, their distortions and reliabilities. A great deal of attention is paid to developing consensual validation. Theory is based on the interpersonal theories of Harry Stack Sullivan and Carl Rogers.[8]

Theory D: A Model of Inquiry. This theory states that learning takes place through the development of a new attitude toward the learning process itself and the discovery that intrapersonal, interpersonal, and group phenomena can be studied systematically by gathering data, analyzing them, and drawing conclusions from them. Part of the learning is a *sensitization* process whereby formerly unnoticed behavior now becomes salient, and a *recognition* process whereby data about one's own and others' feelings can be observed. This theory focuses primarily on the learning process itself.

Theory E: Unconscious Motivation. This theory states that learning takes place through making conscious certain feelings and reactions in group members toward key issues that are unconscious or unnoticed. The assumption is made that bringing unconscious feelings to the level of awareness in itself leads to personal growth.

The preceding five categories represent a very rough approximation of reality. We have to stress this because certainly there are some trainers who range over all five theories and others who would deny membership in any one. Nevertheless, we believe that most trainers can be included in one or two categories. We feel fairly certain that these emphases exist (i.e., we venture to say that trainer acts could be coded along these lines) and that trainers do vary along the very crude dimensions we have suggested.

Now we can return to the original issue confronting us: the relationship between laboratory training and group therapy. If our framework is valid, the terms of the relationship between laboratory train-

---

[8] See Bennis, Schein, Berlew, and Steele. (1964, Parts I and II) for a more detailed discussion.

ing and group therapy have to be stated differently. First of all, we can assert that *if* laboratory training practitioners operate with Theories A and/or D, their similarity to group therapy is doubtful. *If*, on the other hand, practitioners operate within the frameworks of B and C, then there may be some overlapping with group therapy. And if they operate as in Theory E, then there may be little to distinguish laboratory training from group therapy.[9]

But there is another, more important conclusion to be drawn from our framework. We can say that some trainers some of the time are, indeed, acting like group therapists. That is to say that some trainers *perform acts* which can be identified as therapeutic. Similarly, we can say that some therapists, some of the time, are acting like T-group trainers. The point of all this is that therapy and training have to be defined empirically in terms of the enacted roles of the trainers and the therapists. To a great extent therapists and trainers probably reverse roles at times, that is they *act* in ways that are associated with the other. It is senseless to brand anyone with any label, therefore, unless we can look more closely at the whole range of their behavior in groups.

We are not proposing to pigeonhole laboratory training staff by saying that every trainer *must* have a clearly visible style. Nor do we think it is important to rank-order certain styles as better or more appropriate than others. What *is* important to us is that trainers (1) know what they are doing and have a rationale for doing it, (2) know when they are doing therapy and when they are steering clear of it, (3) are clear about their motivation, (4) realize what their primary tasks in the group are, and (5) are adequately professionally trained for the roles that they take.

Until the day comes when these conditions can be met (and progress is being made through the Intern Program) laboratory training will continue to be involved in wrangles with group therapists and other representatives of the helping professions. More important, until then, laboratory training cannot guarantee uniform results from its training efforts. Consequently, it is particularly important for practitioners of laboratory training to be explicit and open about their goals, and to insure that potential clients know what they are getting into when they participate in a program.

---

[9] We mean here that the groups *processes* may be extremely similar. Important differences still remain: healthy vs. sick participants, psychiatrists vs. social scientists conducting groups, two week laboratory vs. once or twice a week meetings, differences in underlying theory, etc.

Is Laboratory Training a Quest for Omnipotence?[10]

In part II of this book we indicated the range and volume of laboratory training's impact on social organizations of all types: government bureaucracies, hospitals, factories, universities, and so on. There is no question in our minds but that this trend will continue and that laboratory training's effects on individuals and social systems will become even more marked. There seems to be a large, growing demand for its product.

This is quite natural and possibly desirable over the long run. Social systems do need help in understanding and controlling their human environments, and laboratory training seems to be in a remarkably strategic position to give help on these matters. Probably, over the next decade or so, given the increasing complexity of organizational life, more and more laboratory training staff will be called on as change-agents.

This trend of which we speak will also expose and exacerbate an important problem which is currently latent, one which will have to be dealt with more directly over the next several years. A change-agent can exploit his role to gratify certain basic (often unconscious) wishes, most particularly, the need for power and control. We are referring to this as the quest for omnipotence. The possibilities for unconscious gratification in the change-agent's role are enormous and because of their potential consequences (for the health of the client as well as the change-agent) they must be examined.

Most people's callings are partially determined by psychological (often unconscious) factors and academic man (including the psychologist) is not immune to these. Generally speaking, his role contains elements of research, teaching, consultation, and reflection. Vis-à-vis the outside world and within the community, it is a role without a great deal of *direct* power and control. And when academic man is called on to consult, as he is being asked to do more and more, his main role is to *advise*. Only indirectly and passively does academic man exercise power, yet he is often in direct contact with leaders who do wield vast amounts of power.

Given this recent contact with men-in-power and the ability of the change-agent to influence them, we occasionally wonder about the change-agent's detachment and scientific attitude regarding his clients. Is there an intoxication, a fascination with influencing the big shots, that goes beyond the ordinary demands of the contract?

---

[10] We are indebted to Daniel Levinson for this phrase.

If so, can we really *count* on the change-agent's objectivity and skepticism? Might change-agents not be tempted simply to exploit the relationship? We doubt it, but we worry because it seems that change-agents can wield power vis-à-vis client organizations without conscious recognition and without the full realization of the client. In the change-agent's case, he is "having it both ways." On the one hand, he is the consultant, the passive one, and, on the other hand, he is the leader, the power behind the throne. He achieves that infantile dream of *power without responsibility*.

No profession is immune to these dreams of omnipotence and glory. All we can ask is that the practitioners are aware of them and able to distinguish reality from fantasy. Particularly today, when academic man is being wooed and courted in the highest councils, when his services have never been more in demand, he has to watch his own need to develop better worlds, which may be the acting out of omnipotent fantasies.

Laboratory training staff members are in a particularly vulnerable state with respect to these matters. They possess a powerful learning method which may lead to some quite radical revisions of the way life is conducted. With this power, there does come a responsibility: that of guarding very closely their own power motives and of facing up to their own motivation. Without this confrontation, we are afraid that change-agents and their clients may get trapped in false dreams with perhaps dangerous consequences for all.

This quest for omnipotence is visible also during the conventional residential laboratories. There, the staff plays a role which, by most standards is extremely (though covertly) powerful. Who else in society has the right to set up temporary systems where a total community is developed from scratch according to detailed staff specifications? Only in total institutions such as hospitals, prisons, and military compounds is there anything like the control laboratory training staff possesses. Meal times, roommates, and housing accommodations, recreational activities, and contact with the outside world as well as training activities are all regulated to some extent by the laboratory ground rules. Not that these rules are transmitted in an arbitrary way or dictatorial manner; they are not. And in some cases, delegates are asked to participate in planning with the staff some of the laboratories activities, including, on occasion, training activities. Nevertheless, laboratories are worlds where the staff is supreme. It "knows the ropes" and has gained an intimate familiarity with the vicissitudes of a laboratory. Usually staff members are the only individuals who are relatively free from the initial anxieties which unfreezing typically releases. They become central and are usually perceived as having tremendous insight and possessing extraordinary interpersonal gifts. And some staff admittedly participates in laboratories because it gives the staff members an opportunity to set up "instant utopias," a cultural island, free from cultural barriers and amenable to shaping according to internal wishes. The exhilaration and intoxication which it feels during the laboratories, and the often noticed depression immediately following it results from the "Godlike" role staff plays. Practitioners in the helping professions often take on a "Godlike" aura to their clients,[11] laboratory training staff simply has to recognize and deal with this, to refuse to collude in these matters (tempting as it is), and to understand its own quest for omnipotence.

Away from the laboratory setting, it may be difficult to distinguish the quest for omnipotence from an imaginative recommendation which a change-agent offers to a client. Recently, staff has been warned against being overly optimistic, utopian, and even romantic concerning its ideas for changing human organizations. It has been felt in some quarters that it is no use trying to alter existing bureaucratic structures, for example, "they exist," the argument goes, "so all you can possibly do is change some key individuals in the structure. Bureaucracy is endemic." Perhaps these criticisms of laboratory training are justified; we know so little about the possibilities, alternatives, and potentialities of human organizations and their capacity to change and adapt. Yet we think that either an overly optimistic or overly pessimistic orientation, at this stage, is unsuitable. Aristotle thought slavery was endemic to all men since it existed in all societies in his day. Suggesting anything else in ancient Greece would have been utopian too, we guess. In any case, attempts to develop more adaptive organizations with more potential for releasing the productive and creative forces of the human resources should not be labeled utopian until the results of the change-agents can be carefully evaluated.[12]

❖   ❖   ❖

---

[11] Psychiatrists, for example, have even more of a problem along these lines. Transference fantasies may reach monumental proportions. A psychiatrist has been defined as "a man who pretends he doesn't know everything." However, psychiatrists are traditionally aware of omnipotent fantasies unlike laboratory trainers.

[12] If we have betrayed biases here, we would like to acknowledge that we certainly have them. But hopefully, a commitment to laboratory training values leaves us open to negative evidence if our hypothesis about better organizations fails to be confirmed.

Now, where are we? What have we been trying to do in this chapter? Essentially, we attempted to air our consciences, to come to terms with our ambivalences. At times, it is unclear to us whether or not we are tilting at imaginary windmills, jousting with real criticisms, fighting some distortion, or shadow boxing with ourselves.

These dilemmas and conflicts will probably always surround laboratory training. For that matter, they will always infiltrate any profession which helps other human beings. What we ask for is conscious and honest confrontation of the dilemmas raised. This means that no relationship should materialize with a client unless it is based on a realistic and thoroughly explored contract. One should be aware of one's conscious motives in conducting laboratory training and sensitive to the possibility of unconscious motives. And some method should be developed for discerning that point at which the client's needs end and the change-agent's begin. This means, in effect, that a spirit of inquiry must govern in all contacts with clients and colleagues.

Appendix I

If You Want to Run a Laboratory

In Chapter 4, we indicated that there are basically two different patterns of laboratory sponsorship. Laboratories are either sponsored by NTL or university related human relations training centers, or are brought into being at the request of some group or organization, such as a professional group or business concern. This appendix is written for those representatives of groups or organizations who may already have faced or will in the future be facing the decision of whether or not to engage in laboratory training. This appendix is for you if you are the director of training or management development, the president of the organization, or the key change agent in your group, if you have to help in making the decision about the appropriateness of laboratory training for your group. We believe that most of the mistakes in the use of laboratory training are made in the earliest decisions concerning it. This appendix is written as a simple set of guidelines in the hope that such mistakes can be avoided.

In chapter 10 are found the general considerations in deciding whether or not to think about laboratory training. Assuming that those considerations have been taken into account and assuming that a rational decision to run a laboratory has been made, what are your next steps in organizing a program? This is the question of this chapter. As the initiator of a laboratory program, you face a basic choice between two alternatives:

1. Locating an experienced trainer and turning the responsibility for actually planning and staffing over to him;

2. Hiring your own training staff and making the administrative arrangement yourself.[1]

The following information is provided to help you do the best job, in the case of either alternative.

Alternative 1: Hiring a Trainer as Laboratory Coordinator

If you, the laboratory planner, wish to hire a coordinator for the training program, you should consider the following points:

1. Locate a highly reliable, well-recommended individual who has had experience in organizational situations similar to the one you face. At the end of this section, we present some guides for locating such individuals.

2. Be prepared to enter into a period of close consultation with such an individual, lasting anywhere from one day to several weeks depending upon the particular circumstances. During this time, the coordinator you hire needs to become familiar with the background of the decision to have a laboratory, with the organizational characteristics of the sponsor, with the training goals specified, and with other administrative matters pertaining to staffing, location of the laboratory, etc.

3. Be prepared to change some of the training goals or laboratory characteristics which may have been initially decided upon. Often the consultation with the coordinator reveals issues not previously faced. Any good trainer would be unwilling to take on the job unless he could himself become convinced that the training goals and the laboratory idea had validity, given the organization and its situation.

4. Be prepared to drop the idea of a laboratory if the potential coordinator is convinced that for some reason a laboratory training experience would be a mistake. Resist the impulse to keep shopping around for a trainer until one is finally found who is willing to take the assignment as presented.

5. If, following the consultation, the trainer agrees to be the coordinator of the laboratory, give him as much freedom and support as he desires in organizing it. If there are limitations of money, time, facilities, etc., *present these at the outset*, so that they can be evaluated during the period of consultation. Do not start hedging in the coordinator once you have hired him. In particular, it is important to give the coordinator a

---

[1] A third alternative is to hire an organization such as NTL to create a total training design suited for the particular needs of your organization. If this alternative is followed, most of the questions we raise in this chapter are automatically dealt with. Hence, we will not give special attention to this alternative.

free hand in hiring other members of the training staff. In order for the laboratory to be an integrated experience, it is important that the training staff member feel comfortable with each other and have high confidence in each other. Such integration is best achieved by leaving the further staffing to the coordinator. Do not put him into the position of being obligated to take on members of the organization as junior or senior staff members, unless this genuinely makes sense and has been explored during the consultation period.

6. Continue to work with the coordinator as a consultant-helper to him. He will need information, guidance, administrative support, and an opportunity to test out training ideas with you or other representatives of the organization who launched the idea. It would be a mistake to hire a coordinator and then dump the whole job into his lap. Rather, what is required is continuous collaboration and an open channel of communication between you and him. It is particularly important that you be available during the early stages of laboratory training when many administrative questions may come up unexpectedly.

7. Once a training staff has been hired and has begun to plan, refrain from trying to introduce into the laboratory design any extraneous activities such as social affairs, visitors from the organization, and the like. If some of these activities seem unavoidable, share your dilemma with the staff but accept its final decision concerning whether to go ahead or cancel the visit. Some excellent laboratories have been ruined by the inopportune arrival of a high organization official or an ill-planned social affair, as the cases in Chapter 10 illustrated.

8. Attempt to generate in yourself an open-minded experimental attitude about the laboratory until it is over. Do not attempt to evaluate the activity during the time it is going. Above all, do not panic if something seems to be going wrong. If you have hired a responsible training staff, it will know how to cope with whatever happens; it will keep you informed if there are risks or dangers, and it will help you make an accurate evaluation of the experience.

Resistance to laboratory training is usually high early in the laboratory. If you expose yourself to some of the negative reactions you may hear and are tempted to try to influence the training staff because of what you have heard, resist the temptation. By all means, report what you have heard, but let the training staff decide whether to let things ride or whether to change anything. In other words, don't start raising *fundamental* questions halfway through. Save them for the final evaluation.

9. Unless you have the background and experience yourself to make valid training decisions about laboratory training, do not try to second-

guess the training staff or to influence the design in terms of your own theories. The training staff needs whatever *information* you can give it about the organization, the training needs, and the goals. But let the training staff decide how best to use the information and to accomplish the goals. If the planning time is short, do not interrupt the planning with questions which require the staff to justify in detail whatever it is planning. It will have some shorthand ways of talking about things, and it can be a genuine interference to force the staff to spell them all out. Seek staff members out during off hours and inquire then why certain decisions were made and how the training design meets the goals. The time to influence the staff is in the initial consultation period; do not try to influence once the implementation phase has begun unless there is plenty of time to work things through.

10. After the laboratory is over, allow plenty of time (at least half a day) for evaluation of the laboratory with the training staff. Write this time into the initial contract so that you will be sure to have the benefit of a complete post-mortem and recommendations for future training activities. During this time, be completely frank and open about your questions and concerns. The staff, or at least the coordinator, owes you an explanation of whatever was done. Do not be afraid to ask for it. If the situation is amenable to research on laboratory effects, encourage the training staff from the outset to build in a research design and provide financial and other support to complete it.

How to Locate a Coordinator

The best source for competent trainers is the NTL network. We have listed on pp. 350–356 the names of all NTL Fellows and Associates as of the 1963 elections. A person must pass a rigorous screening procedure to be nominated, and must be elected by two-thirds of the present Fellows. The criteria for Fellowship are as follows:

Members of the NTL Fellows are persons trained in one of the social or behavioral sciences or in one of the professions of social practice. They must have achieved a high degree of competence in the training and research methodologies for which NTL stands and/or competence in consultation with groups or organizations on training or training-relevant problems. In addition, they must have published contributions to the advancement of knowledge, have served satisfactorily on at least six assignments in positions requiring the assumption of autonomous professional responsibility, and have expressed interest in a continuing relationship with NTL. NTL Fellows are available for recruitment and assignment to the staffs of various NTL projects and activities, and for referral to other organizations.

Admission of a person to the NTL Fellows requires the following actions:

1. Nomination by a member of the NTL Fellows, to be accompanied by biographical data from the nominee, and a listening of the nominee's publications beyond his dissertation. A written statement by the nominee that he desires to be considered for the NTL Fellows will also accompany the nomination. For consideration as a Fellow, the candidate will ordinarily possess a doctor's degree. However, in exceptional circumstances, a candidate will be considered upon nomination and presentation by a nominating Fellow of extensive evidence of equivalent experience and/or qualification.

2. References from other Fellows or Associates.

3. Screening by the Committee on Staff Resources and Utilization of the NTL Board, which will apply in a systematic way the following criteria:

a. Ability to diagnose situations
b. Ability to develop training designs
c. Ability to conduct T-groups
d. Ability to lecture on social science topics
e. Ability to organize and direct training projects
f. Past service on staffs of training laboratories and election as an NTL Associate
g. Concern for application of social science knowledge or human relations training as a major part of his professional life
h. Ability to plan and conduct structural exercises
i. Ability to work in team situations
j. Past contributions to theory and research
k. Background in basic and applied behavioral science
l. Experience in working with a variety of occupational groups
m. Experience with follow-up training (other than a residential laboratory)
n. Likelihood of continuing to utilize his energies to advance knowledge and practice in the general area of training
o. Experience in working in the field of organizational or community change
p. Experience on multi-levels in organizational or community change
q. Adequate consulting experiences with a variety of organizations
r. Perception of Fellows as a qualified peer

4. Approval by the NTL National Board

5. Election by a two-third vote of those NTL Fellows who cast their vote (the total number of votes to be at least one-half of the current Fellows)

6. Acceptance in writing by the person invited, agreement to help maintain NTL training and other activities and to participate in NTL committees from time to time, and payment of such annual fee as the Board may set.

Removal of a person from the NTL Fellows may be accomplished by any of the following procedures:

1. Resignation, death, nonpayment of fee.

2. Authenticated violation of such codes of ethics as the NTL Board may establish for its trainers and consultants, such action to require a two-thirds vote by a meeting of the NTL Board.[2]

In order to become an Associate, a person must also be screened and elected by the Board. Criteria for Associate status are:

Members of the NTL Associates are persons trained in one of the social or behavioral sciences or in one of the professions of social practice. They must have demonstrated themselves to be competent in the training and research methodologies for which NTL stands and/or competent in consultation with groups or organizations on training or training-relevant problems. NTL Associates are available for recruitment and assignment to the staffs of various NTL projects and activities, and for referral to other organizations.

Admission of a person to the NTL Associates requires the following actions:

1. Nomination by a member of the NTL Fellows or Associates, to be accompanied by biographical data from the nominee, and a listing of the nominee's publications beyond his dissertation. A written statement by the nominee that he desires to be considered for the NTL Associates will also accompany the nomination.

2. References from other Fellows or Associates.

3. Screening by the Committee on Staff Resources and Utilization of the NTL Board, which will apply in a systematic way the following criteria, of which at least ten must be met satisfactorily:

a. Ability to diagnose situations
b. Ability to develop training designs
c. Ability to conduct T-groups
d. Ability to lecture on social science topics
e. Ability to organize and direct training projects
f. Past service on staffs of training laboratories
g. Concern for application of social science knowledge or human relations training as a major part of his professional life
h. Ability to conduct structural exercises
i. Ability to work in team situations
j. Past contributions to theory and research
k. Background in basic and applied behavioral sciences
l. Experience in working with a variety of occupational groups
m. Experience with follow-up training (other than a residential laboratory)

4. Election by a two-thirds vote of the members attending an NTL Board meeting.

---

[2] This and the next section are quoted from the NTL Internal Organizational Rules.

5. Acceptance in writing by the person invited and payment of such annual fee as the Board may set.

The Associate serves for a term of three years. At the end of this term, he is reviewed by the Committee on Staff Resources and Utilization and by the Board, and if he continues to meet the qualifications he is entered as a permanent Associate.

Removal of a permanent member of the NTL Associates may be accomplished by any of the following procedures:
1. Admission to the NTL Fellows.
2. Resignation, death, or nonpayment of fee.
3. Authenticated violation of such codes of ethics as the NTL Board may establish for its trainers and consultants, such action to require a two-thirds vote by a meeting of the NTL Board.

In terms of locating a coordinator for a laboratory, the likelihood is greater of finding someone from the Fellow's list. The Fellows represent the group with the most experience and most commitment to the advancement of laboratory training. If you are already acquainted with one or more Fellows, you can start your search for a coordinator by consulting them. It is perfectly acceptable procedure to ask any of them to recommend someone else. You are not committing yourself to any given person by asking him to help you locate a coordinator.

If you do not know any of the Fellows, there are two options: (1) Locate the name of someone in your geographical area and either call or write him. Most members of the network are used to dealing with this kind of request even if it comes from a stranger. (2) Write directly to NTL central office in Washington and ask them to recommend someone. You can check qualifications by consulting professional directories such as those put out by the American Psychological or Sociological Associations.

A recommendation from the NTL central office may be a more informed one in that they generally are better acquainted with the background, specific interests, and particular qualifications of the network members. However, most of the Fellows know each other, which means that consulting any of them also can lead to a relatively informed opinion.

Not all competent trainers are included in the NTL network. For a variety of reasons, some people who have the requisite experience, background, and training have decided not to affiliate with NTL. If you know of such a person and know that he is competent, there is no reason not to use him. If you have a name of a person who is not affiliated with NTL and wish to get an evaluation of him, you are most likely to get an accurate assessment by consulting NTL Fellows or writing to the central office. Anyone who is active in the training field is likely to be known to NTL, and you are likely to obtain an accurate and fair assessment of him from NTL, whether he is part of the network or not.

Alternative 2: Acting as Your Own Coordinator

In many instances, the person who wishes to organize some laboratory training decides that he knows clearly enough what he wants and needs to obtain. In that instance, he may decide to serve as coordinator himself, hire his own staff, and make all administrative arrangements. If you find yourself wishing to organize the laboratory in this manner, we have listed below some of the points you should consider as you proceed.

Staffing the Laboratory

Staffing the laboratory involves three separate questions: (1) how many staff members to hire in terms of getting an adequate staff-delegate ratio; (2) what rank or experience differentials there should or could be between staff members and (3) whom actually to call with an offer.

1. *Number of staff.* If the laboratory involves T-groups, the administrator should generally aim toward a ratio of one trainer to twelve delegates. If only two groups are involved, two staff members may be enough. As the size of the laboratory increases, however, it becomes desirable to add some extra staff members to help with lectures and exercises. The larger the staff, the more difficult it becomes to coordinate and the greater the likelihoood of a less integrated design. For this reason alone, an optimum size laboratory may well be one involving only two groups with two or three staff members.

2. *Differential status among staff members.* Differences in experience, age, background, etc., can be important as sources of strain within a staff group. If there are T-groups, there should be at least one experienced senior trainer for each group. If there are less experienced staff members present, they could concentrate on exercises or other activities and serve as junior trainers in the T-groups. One of the best ways of avoiding possible staff conflicts resulting from status differences or differences in training philosophy is to hire a coordinator and let him pick his own staff. If you pick your own staff, you have the problem of having to guess who will be compatible with whom.

3. *How to locate staff and how to decide whom to invite.* The considerations involved in staff selection are basically the same as those involved in finding a coordinator. A good place to start is the NTL network. If you do not know the people on the Fellows and Associates

list, it would be advisable to obtain information from NTL concerning who is active, who has what areas of interest, relative age and experience of different potential staff members and so on. Often such information can be obtained locally from one or two NTL Fellows.

Locating an Adequate Physical Setting for the Laboratory

It is essential for good laboratory training that the proper physical facilities be available. Two basic considerations must be taken into account: (1) the laboratory location should be away from normal day-to-day job or family pressures, preferably in some nonurban setting, and (2) the laboratory should be in a facility that is physically comfortable, provides adequate meeting rooms, living arrangements, and serves good food. Nothing can undermine a laboratory more quickly than dissatisfaction with the daily living arrangements in a setting in which the person is asked to remain for several days. It is well worth the extra money to find good quarters which enhance rather than detract from the laboratory.

The training area should include an adequate size room for each T-group and make possible an informal seating arrangement. In addition, a general meeting room is required of a size adequate to handle the entire delegate group. A small administrative office in which a typing and reproducing facility can be established is crucial since many important training materials are generated after the laboratory begins.

It is also important that the training area be reserved solely for the use of the laboratory, since it is often desirable to put charts on the wall, create special seating arrangements, and the like. The laboratory is usually a full-time activity and should therefore have facilities available at all times.

Noise is often a problem. T-group rooms should not be adjacent to each other to prevent noise from one disturbing the activities of the other. The general meeting room should be protected from noise to give maximum opportunity for lecture material to be heard.

Motels, small hotels, lodges, unused schools or campuses during the summer can make excellent training facilities provided they meet the criteria mentioned above. If a resort area is chosen, there is the additional advantage of recreational facilities which are an important adjunct to good laboratory training. It is important for delegates to have free time and to have facilities which encourage recreation during this time. If no regular recreational facilities exist, provisions should be made for ping-pong, volleyball, or whatever other sport can be conveniently set up.

Administrative Support for the Training Staff

Every laboratory should have a full-time secretary or administrator attached to it. The training staff is usually tied up with training activities that prevent it from working on duties such as typing and reproducing training materials, answering phones during training sessions, helping delegates with daily living problems such as mail and laundry, keeping laboratory records, analyzing data gathered in exercises, and so on. The secretary may be idle much of the time but should, nevertheless, be on hand at all times.

In those instances in which an organization runs a series of laboratories, it is desirable to have an administrator who handles the whole series and who provides administrative continuity from one laboratory to the next. An experienced administrator can be of immense help to the training staff, particularly during the early stages when many decisions have to be made on the spur of the moment.

Training Materials and Equipment

For most laboratories, there is a standard list of items which you should provide the training staff or at least consult with it about. These are as follows:

1. Chartpads, easels, and felt marking pencils in sufficient numbers to permit one to be placed in each T-group room and one or two in the general meeting room.

2. One tape recorder for each T-group and sufficient tape to cover the entire number of T-group meetings. (Check this item with the training staff because they may decide not to use tape recorders.)

3. At least one typewriter and a ditto machine or something equivalent to produce training materials on short notice.

4. Notebooks or folders, one for each delegate, in which to clip all training materials received.

5. Name tags for each delegate and name cards (manilla or other cardboard pieces folded in half to stand up in front of a person at the table) for delegates to write their names on.

6. Pads and pencils for each person in each T-group.

7. Equipment for projecting slides and films. (Check with the training staff on likelihood of use, but be prepared to rent one on short notice if a film is suddenly decided upon.)

8. Books, reprints, and handouts of material to be covered should be obtained in advance wherever possible to avoid delivery delays.

Fees for Delegates and Salaries for Staff

What you charge the delegate or the organization for the training experience depends upon its length of time, the cost of living facilities, whether you are running it nonprofit for your own organization or are inviting members of other organizations in, and your assessment of the delegate's ability to pay. Some NTL labs run chronically in the red because tuitions are deliberately kept down in order to enable members of that particular profession to attend.

What you pay the training staff has to be more or less in line with emerging standards of a fair daily rate, given the unique blend of skills and background which good trainers bring with them. This fair rate varies considerably from organization to organization. If you are uncertain about these rates, informal inquiries of NTL or any of the Fellows will provide you with them. Trainers with little experience are often paid less although the responsibility they bear in the laboratory is as great as that borne by senior staff.

The demand for good trainers is outrunning the supply. This fact necessitates that organizations become aware, as quickly as they can, of the difficulties of getting good trainers and plan to pay at a scale which will permit the attraction of such trainers.

Orienting the Delegate to the Laboratory[3]

Laboratory training has received sufficient publicity in the last several years so that most potential participants have some kind of stereotype of what it is all about. These stereotypes are difficult to correct until the laboratory has begun, and efforts to do so run the risk of raising, rather than lowering, anxieties about the laboratory. Therefore, a useful guideline would be either to give a complete and detailed orientation, during which participants can ask questions about the laboratory, or simply to announce it with a minimum of fanfare and publicity. Sending reams of literature about laboratory training is probably not as effective as having a meeting with the group who will go, during which an exchange of questions and answers can take place. If such a meeting or series of meetings is impractical, it would be enough to send an announcement or a one paragraph description based on some standard laboratory literature. The delegate should not be given the feeling that it is going to be something special, way out, super-potent, or the like. It should be presented as an intensive training experience with goals somewhat different from other training.

In the literature sent to the delegate, it *is* important to tell him about the physical facility, the general schedule, the kinds of clothing to bring, and so on. Delegates who come with too much formal clothing or expecting to be able to play 18 holes of golf every day will have their expectations upset causing needless strain. Therefore, the more than can be said about living arrangements and schedule, the better.

Summary

We have outlined the basic considerations which should be taken into account in planning a laboratory. After deciding between the two basic alternatives of whether to hire a coordinator or perform that function yourself, questions arise of how to staff the laboratory, where to hold it, what facilities and equipment to have ready, how to orient delegates, how to pay staff and charge delegates, and so on. If the issues we have covered do not exhaust the kinds of questions you may have, you should feel free to raise them with NTL.

List of NTL Fellows as of May, 1964

Chris Argyris, Department of Industrial Administration, Yale University, New Haven, Connecticut

Richard Beckhard, Richard Beckhard Associates, New York City

Kenneth D. Benne, Human Relations Center, Boston University, Boston, Massachusetts

Thomas R. Bennett, II, Graduate Studies, George Williams College, Chicago, Illinois

Warren G. Bennis, Sloan School of Management, Massachusetts Institute of Technology, Cambridge, Massachusetts

Max Birnbaum, Institute of Human Relations, The American Jewish Committee, New York City

Willard W. Blaesser, The City College of New York, New York City

Robert R. Blake, Scientific Methods, Inc., Austin, Texas

Michael G. Blansfield, Blansfield, Smith & Co., Inc., Pasadena, California

Leland P. Bradford, National Training Laboratories, National Education Association, Washington, D.C.

Paul C. Buchanan, Yeshiva University, New York City

Douglas R. Bunker, Graduate School of Business Administration, Harvard University, Boston, Massachusetts

Hubert S. Coffey, Department of Psychology, University of California, Berkeley, California

---

[*] See Chapter 10 for the strategic considerations involved in participant orientation.

Campbell Crockett, The Graduate School, University of Cincinnati, Cincinnati, Ohio

William G. Dyer, Department of Sociology and Anthropology, Brigham Young University, Provo, Utah

Charles K. Ferguson, Department of Conferences and Program Consultation, University of California Extension, Los Angeles, California

Jack R. Gibb, Western Behavioral Sciences Institute, La Jolla, California

John C. Glidewell, Social Science Institute, Washington University, St. Louis, Missouri

Max R. Goodson, High School Division, Ginn and Company, Boston, Massachusetts

Roger L. Harrison, Department of Industrial Administration, Yale University, New Haven, Connecticut

Gordon Hearn, School of Social Work, Portland State College, Portland, Oregon

Murray Horwitz, Research Center for Human Relations, New York University, New York City

David H. Jenkins, Group Dynamics Center, Temple University, Philadelphia, Pennsylvania

Robert L. Kahn, Institute for Social Research, The University of Michigan, Ann Arbor, Michigan

Donald C. Klein, Human Relations Center, Boston University, Boston, Massachusetts

Paul R. Lawrence, Graduate School of Business Administration, Harvard University, Boston, Massachusetts

Harold J. Leavitt, Graduate School of Industrial Administration, Carnegie Institute of Technology, Pittsburgh, Pennsylvania

Gordon L. Lippitt, Center for the Behavioral Sciences, The George Washington University, Washington, D.C.

Ronald Lippitt, Institute for Social Research, The University of Michigan, Ann Arbor, Michigan

Bernard Lubin, Indiana State Department of Mental Health, Indianapolis, Indiana

Joseph Luft, Department of Psychology, San Francisco State College, San Francisco, California

H. Curtis Mial, National Training Laboratories, National Education Association, Washington, D.C.

Matthew B. Miles, Teachers College, Columbia University, New York City

Edward O. Moe, Institute of Urban Research and Service, University of Utah, Salt Lake City, Utah

J. Weldon Moffitt, Extension Division, University of Utah, Salt Lake City, Utah

Donald Nylen, Consultant to The Ford Foundation in Africa, Hadlock, Washington

Don A. Orton, Lesley College, Cambridge, Massachusetts

Barry I. Oshry, College of Business Administration, Boston University, Boston, Massachusetts

Henry W. Riecken, Social Science Department, National Science Foundation, Washington, D.C.

Edgar H. Schein, Sloan School of Management, Massachusetts Institute of Technology, Cambridge, Massachusetts

Warren H. Schmidt, Graduate School of Business Administration, University of California, Los Angeles, California

Charles N. Seashore, National Training Laboratories, National Education Association, Washington, D.C.

Edith Whitfield Seashore, Training consultant, Washington, D.C.

Herbert A. Shepard, Department of Management, Case Institute of Technology, Cleveland, Ohio

Frank F. Tallman, University of California Medical Center, Los Angeles, California

Robert Tannenbaum, Graduate School of Business Administration, University of California, Los Angeles, California

Richard W. Wallen, Personnel Research and Development Corporation, Cleveland, Ohio

Goodwin Watson, Newark State College, Newark, New Jersey

John R. Weir, Division of the Humanities, California Institute of Technology, Pasadena, California

Dorothy Stock Whitaker, Private consultant, Leeds, England

Henry H. Work, University of California Medical Center, Los Angeles, California

Abraham Zaleznik, Graduate School of Business Administration, Harvard University, Boston, Massachusetts

Dale E. Zand, Graduate School of Business Administration, New York University, New York City

Alvin F. Zander, Research Center for Group Dynamics, The University of Michigan, Ann Arbor, Michigan

List of NTL Associates as of May, 1964

Robert F. Allen, Department of Psychology, Newark State College, Newark, New Jersey

Edmund J. Amidon, Group Dynamics Center, Temple University, Philadelphia, Pennsylvania

Louis B. Barnes, Graduate School of Business Administration, Harvard University, Boston, Massachusetts

Richard P. Barthol, Department of Psychology, University of California, Los Angeles, California

Bernard M. Bass, Graduate School of Business, University of Pittsburgh, Pittsburg, Pennsylvania

Howard Baumgartel, Department of Human Relations, University of Kansas, Lawrence, Kansas

Walcott H. Beatty, Department of Psychology, San Francisco State College, San Francisco, California

David E. Berlew, Sloan School of Management, Massachusetts Institute of Technology, Cambridge, Massachusetts

F. Kenneth Berrien, Department of Psychology, Rutgers University, New Brunswick, New Jersey

Arthur Blumberg, Group Dynamics Center, Temple University, Philadelphia, Pennsylvania

Edward S. Bordin, Department of Psychology, The University of Michigan, Ann Arbor, Michigan

David S. Brown, Department of Business and Public Administration, The George Washington University, Washington, D.C.

Racine D. Brown, South Carolina Mental Health Commission, Columbia, South Carolina

James F. T. Bugental, Psychological Service Associates, Los Angeles, California

J. Alfred Cannon, Division of Social and Community Psychiatry, University of California Medical Center, Los Angeles, California

André Carrière, Centre de Recherches en Relations Humaines, Montreal, Canada

Robert Chin, Human Relations Center, Boston University, Boston, Massachusetts

James V. Clark, Graduate School of Business Administration, University of California, Los Angeles, California

Jan E. Clee, Department of Management, Case Institute of Technology, Cleveland, Ohio

Arthur M. Cohen, Department of Sociology and Anthropology, Emory University, Atlanta, Georgia

Robert M. Cox, Wainwright House, Rye, New York

Burns Crookston, Colorado State University, Fort Collins, Colorado

Gilbert David, Leadership Development, Inc. New York City

Jamie Dennis, Employee Relations Department, Standard Oil Company of New Jersey, New York City

Vladimir A. Dupre, Department of Psychology, Grinnell College, Grinnell, Iowa

Delwyn A. Dyer, Cooperative Extension Service, Michigan State University East Lansing, Michigan

Richard M. Emerson, Department of Sociology and Anthropology, University of Cincinnati, Cincinnati, Ohio

F. Martin Erickson, Student Activities, University of Utah, Salt Lake City, Utah

Ralph V. Exline, Center for Research on Social Behavior, University of Delaware, Newark, Delaware

Robert S. Fox, University School, The University of Michigan, Ann Arbor, Michigan

Richard C. Franklin, Community Development Institute, Southern Illinois University, Carbondale, Illinois

Boris Gertz, Graduate Programs, Lesley College, Cambridge, Massachusetts

Thomas Q. Gilson, Department of Management, University College, Rutgers University, New Brunswick, New Jersey

William P. Golden, Jr., Downtown Center, San Francisco State College, San Francisco, California

Franklyn S. Haiman, The School of Speech, Northwestern University, Evanston, Illinois

Tilden Harrison, Personnel Services, National Council of YMCA's, New York City

Jerry B. Harvey, National Training Laboratories, National Education Association, Washington, D.C.

Kenneth F. Herrold, Teachers College, Columbia University, New York City

William G. Hollister, Utilization Branch, National Institute of Mental Health, Bethesda, Maryland

Leonard Horwitz, The Menninger Clinic, Topeka, Kansas

Marie M. Hughes, College of Education, University of Arizona, Tucson, Arizona

Harrington V. Ingham, Student Health Service, University of California, Los Angeles, California

Shepard A. Insel, Department of Psychology, San Francisco State College, San Francisco, California

Gale E. Jensen, School of Education, The University of Michigan, Ann Arbor, Michigan

Allan Katcher, Employee Relations, Missile and Space Systems Division, Douglas Aircraft Company, Inc., Santa Monica, California

Sherman Kingsbury, Arthur D. Little, Inc., Cambridge, Massachusetts

Marvin A. Klemes, Industrial consultant, Beverly Hills, California

Malcolm S. Knowles, School of Education, Boston University, Boston, Massachusetts

Theodore C. Kroeber, Department of Psychology, San Francisco State College, San Francisco, California

Dolores G. LaCaro, Lesley College, Cambridge, Massachusetts

Martin Lakin, Departments of Psychology and Psychiatry, Duke University Medical Center, Durham, North Carolina

Alvin A. Lasko, Psychological Service Associates, Los Angeles, California

George F. J. Lehner, Department of Psychology, University of California, Los Angeles, California

Morton A. Lieberman, Department of Psychiatry. The University of Chicago, Chicago, Illinois

Rensis Likert, Institute for Social Research, The University of Michigan, Ann Arbor, Michigan

Traugott Lindner, Consultant, Vienna, Austria

Thomas M. Lodahl, Graduate School of Business and Public Administration, Cornell University, Ithaca, New York

Thomas J. Mallinson, Department of Psychiatry, University of Toronto, Toronto, Canada

Floyd C. Mann, Institute for Social Research, The University of Michigan, Ann Arbor, Michigan

Richard D. Mann, Department of Social Relations, Harvard University, Cambridge, Massachusetts

Fred Massarik, Graduate School of Business Administration, University of California, Los Angeles, California

Paul B. Maves, Religious Education, Drew University, Madison, New Jersey

W. J. McKeachie, Department of Psychology, The University of Michigan, Ann Arbor, Michigan

Laurence K. McLaughlin, Consultant, San Bernardino, California

J. H. McPherson, Psychology Department, The Dow Chemical Company, Midland, Michigan

Dorothy J. Mial, National Training Laboratories, National Education Association, Washington, D.C.

Cyril R. Mill, Rohrer, Hibler, and Replogle, Minneapolis, Minnesota

Daniel R. Miller, Doctoral Program in Social Psychology, The University of Michigan, Ann Arbor, Michigan

Richard C. Mills, Communication Workshops, North Hollywood, California

J. Robert Mitchell, Training Programs, The Ford Foundation, Lagos, Nigeria

David Moment, Graduate School of Business Administration, Harvard University, Boston, Massachusetts

Jane S. Mouton, Scientific Methods, Inc., Austin, Texas

Alvin J. North, Department of Psychology, Southern Methodist University, Dallas, Texas

Charles D. Orth, 3rd, Graduate School of Business Administration, Harvard University, Boston, Massachusetts

Udai Pareek, Small Industry Extension Training Institute, Yousufguda, Hyderabad, India

George L. Peabody, Division of Christian Education, The National Council, Protestant Episcopal Church, New York City

Robert F. Pearse, Leadership Development, Inc., New York City

Hilda D. Perlitsch, Department of Psychology, Boston University, Boston, Massachusetts

A. Terrence Polin, Graduate School of Business Administration, University of Southern California, Los Angeles, California

Charlton R. Price, Department of Sociology and Anthropology, University of Kansas, Lawrence, Kansas

Jessie Rhulman, Department of Psychology, University of California, Los Angeles, California

Miriam Ritvo, Human Relations Center, Boston University, Boston, Massachusetts

V. M. Robertson, Peninsula YMCA, San Mateo, California

Alexander C. Rosen, The Neuropsychiatric Institute, University of California Medical Center, Los Angeles, California

Juan A. Rossello, School of Medicine, University of Puerto Rico, Río Piedras, Puerto Rico

Fernand Roussel, Institut de Psychologie, University of Montreal, Montreal, Canada

George Saslow, Department of Psychiatry, University of Oregon Medical School, Eugene, Oregon

William C. Schutz, Division of Social and Community Psychiatry, Albert Einstein College of Medicine, New York City

Stanley Seashore, Survey Research Center, The University of Michigan, Ann Arbor, Michigan

Mary Settle, The American National Red Cross, Washington, D.C.

Robert Sevigny, Department of Sociology, University of Montreal, Montreal, Canada

Paul H. Sheats, University Extension, University of California, Los Angeles, California

Arthur J. Shedlin, School of Business Administration, University of California, Los Angeles, California

Clovis J. Shephard, Department of Sociology-Anthropology, University of California, Santa Barbara, California

Robert S. Soar, School of Education, University of South Carolina, Columbia, South Carolina

John Anthony Stout, Human Relations Training, Uganda Electricity Board, Kampala, Uganda

Leslie This, Personnel Division, Agricultural Research Service, U.S. Department of Agriculture, Washington, D.C.

Elmer E. Van Egmond, Research and Laboratory Schools, Lesley College, Cambridge, Massachusetts

Thomas J. Van Loon, General Board of Education, The Methodist Church, Nashville, Tennessee

Richard E. Walton, School of Industrial Management, Purdue University, Lafayette, Indiana

Cynthia Wedel, National Council of the Churches of Christ, New York City

Thomas A. Wickes, Consulting psychologist, Missoula, Montana

Alexander Winn, Staff Training and Research Division, Aluminum Company of Canada, Ltd., Montreal, Canada

Eli F. Wismer, National Council of the Churches of Christ, New York City

Donald M. Wolfe, Department of Management, Case Institute of Technology, Cleveland, Ohio

Appendix II

If You Want to Read Further:

A Selected Bibliography

Our intention in this appendix is to provide the reader with suggestions for further reading. This bibliography is by no means complete. It does offer a fairly adequate coverage of most of the relevant materials. And the items we have cited will undoubtedly fill in the omissions and blind spots in our listing.

We have organized the bibliography into the following categories:

I. *General books and articles.* Here we have listed a number of overviews of laboratory training.

II. *Popular articles.* This section includes articles which were written originally for a lay audience and which communicate the essence of laboratory training with a minimum of fuss and jargon.

III. *The uses of laboratory training.* This section includes readings which describe and analyze how laboratory training is employed in a variety of organizational settings.

IV. *Evaluation studies.* This section includes research papers and summaries of research on Laboratory Training processes and outcomes.

V. *Related group theory.* In this section we have attempted to list readings which encompass the theoretical structure of laboratory training as well as some related theory from group psychotherapy. We have also cited some papers which utilize group process for teaching purposes but which employ a somewhat different, but related, orientation.

VI. *Criticisms of laboratory training.* We have attempted to list in this section the most articulate opinions and evidence for making a case against laboratory training.

I. GENERAL BOOKS AND ARTICLES

Blake, R. R., and Mouton, Jane S. (1961), *Group Dynamics—Key to Decision Making*, Houston, Texas, Gulf Publishing.

Bradford, L. P. (Ed.) (1961), *Group Development*, NTL Selected Readings Series No. I Washington, D. C., National Education Association.

Bradford, L. P., Gibb, J. R., and Benne, K. D. (Eds.) (1964), *T-Group Theory and Laboratory Method*, New York, Wiley.

Goetz, B. E., and Bennis, W. G. (1962), "What We Know about Learning and Training," *Personnel Administration*, Vol. 25, pp. 20–30.

Miles, M. B. (1962), "Human Relations Training: Current Status," in I. R. Weschler, and E. H. Schein (Eds.), *Issues in Human Relations Training*, NTL Selected Reading Series No. 5, Washington, D. C., National Education Association.

Miles, M. B. (1960), "Human Relations Training: Processes and Outcomes," *Journal of Couseling Psychology*, Vol. 7, pp. 301–306.

Miles, M. B. (1959), *Learning to Work in Groups*, New York, Bureau of Publications, Teachers College, Columbia University.

Schutz, W. C., and Allen, V. L. (1961), *On T-Groups*, Berkeley, Calif., School of Education, University of California, unpublished manuscript.

Tannenbaum, R., Weschler, I. R., and Massarik, F. (1961), *Leadership and Organization: A Behavioral Science Approach*, New York, McGraw-Hill.

Trist, E. L. and Sofer, C. (1959), *Explorations in Group Relations*, Leicester, England, Leicester University Press.

Weschler, I. R., and Reisel, J. (1959), *Inside a Sensitivity Training Group*, Industrial Relations Monograph, No. 4, Los Angeles, Institute of Industrial Relations, University of California.

Weschler, I. R., and Schein, E. H. (Eds.) (1962), *Issues in Human Relations Training*. NTL Selected Readings Series No. 5, Washington, D. C., National Education Association.

II. POPULAR ARTICLES AND BOOKS

Argyris, C. (1964), "T-Groups for Organizational Effectiveness," *Harvard Business Review*, March-April, pp. 60–74.

Bennis, W. G. (1963), *The Marked Deck: A Non-Objective Playlet for Four Characters*, Washington, D. C., National Training Laboratories, Subscription Service, No. 2.

Bradford, L. P. (1953), *Explorations in Human Relations Training: An Assessment of Experience, 1947–1953*, Washington, D. C., National Training Laboratories, National Education Association.

Ferguson, C. K. (1959), "Management Development in 'Unstructured' Groups," *California Management Review*, Vol. 1, pp. 66–72.

Hoy, G. A. (1959), "A Brand-New Breakthrough in Management Development," *Factory*, July, pp. 74–79.

Klaw, S. (1961), "Two Weeks in a T-Group," *Fortune*, August.

Marrow, A. J. (1964), *Behind the Executive Mask*, New York, American Management Association.

III. THE USES OF LABORATORY TRAINING

An *Action Research Program for Organizational Improvement* (in *Esso Standard Oil Co.*) (1960), Ann Arbor, Mich., Foundation for Research on Human Behavior.

Argyris, C. (1962), *Interpersonal Competence and Organizational Effectiveness,* Homewood, Ill., Dorsey Press.

Argyris, C. (1964), "T-Groups for Organizational Effectiveness," *Harvard Business Review,* March-April, pp. 60–74.

Bennis, W. G. (1963), "A New Role for the Behavioral Sciences: Effecting Organizational Change," *Administrative Science Quarterly,* Vol. 8, pp. 125–165.

Bennis, W. G., Benne, K. D., and Chin, R. (Eds.) (1961), *The Planning of Change,* New York, Holt, Rinehart and Winston, see particularly Part IV.

Blake, R. R., Blansfield, M. G., and Mouton, Jane S. (1962), "How Executive Team Training Can Help You," *Journal of American Society of Training Directors,* Vol. 16, pp. 3–11.

Blake, R. R., and Mouton, Jane S. (1962), "Headquarters—Field Team Training for Organizational Improvement," *Journal of American Society of Training Directors,* Vol. 16, pp. 3–11.

Blake, R. R., and Mouton, Jane S. (1963), "Improving Organizational Problem Solving through Increasing the Flow and Utilization of New Ideas," *Training Directors Journal,* Vol. 17, 48–57.

Blake, R. R., and Mouton, Jane S. (1962), "The Developing Revolution in Management Practices," *Journal of American Society of Training Directors,* Vol. 16, pp. 29–50.

Blake, R. R., and Mouton, Jane S. (1964), *The Managerial Grid,* Houston, Texas, Gulf Publishing.

Blake, R. R., and Mouton, Jane S. (1964), "The Managerial Grid as a Framework for Inducing Change in Industrial Organizations," in P. Worchel and D. Byrne (Eds.), *Personality Change,* New York, (1964), Wiley.

Blake, R. R., and Mouton, Jane S. (1961), "Reactions to Intergroup Competition under Win-Lose Conditions," *Management Science,* p. 7.

Blake, R. R., Shepard, H. A., and Mouton, Jane S. (1964), *Intergroup Conflict,* Ann Arbor, Mich., Foundation for Research in Human Behavior.

Blansfield, M. G. (1962), "Depth Analysis of Organizational Life," *California Management,* Vol. 5 pp. 29–42.

Blansfield, M. G., Blake, R. R., and Mouton, Jane S. (1964), "The Merger Laboratory: A New Strategy for Bringing One Corporation into Another," *Journal of American Society of Training Directors,* Vol. 18, pp. 2–10.

Buchanan, P. C. (1964), *Innovative Organizations—A Study in Organization Development,* Washington, D. C., (1959), National Training Laboratories Subscription Service, No. 1.

Ferguson, C. K. (1959), "Management Development in 'Unstructured' Groups," *California Management Review,* Vol. 1, pp. 66–72.

Gertz, B. (1963), *Human Relations Training with Mental Hospital Personnel,* Columbia, S. C., unpublished manuscript, Department of Psychology, South Carolina State Hospital.

Lippitt, R. (1949), *Training in Community Relations*, New York, Harper.

Lynton, R. P. (1960), *The Tide of Learning: The Aloka Experience*, London, Routledge and Kegan, Paul.

Mial, C., and Mial, Dorothy (1962), "Leadership Training," *National Civic Review*, May.

Miles, M. B. (Ed.) (1964), *Innovation in Education*, New York, Bureau of Publications, Teachers College, Columbia University, particularly Chapters: 1, 3, 11, 19, 25.

Reddin, W. J., and Beckett, E. N. (1962), "Sensitivity Training in Canadian Industry," *The Canadian Personnel and Industrial Relation Journal*, Vol. 9, pp. 1–4.

Schein, E. H. (1961), "Management Development as a Process of Influence," *Industrial Management Review*, Vol. 2, pp. 59–77.

Shepard, H. (1965), "Changing Interpersonal and Intergroup Relationships in Organizations," in *Handbook of Organization*, J. March (Ed.), New York, Rand-McNally.

Shepard, H., and Blake, R. R. (1962), "Changing Behavior through Cognitive Change," *Human Organization*, Vol. 21, pp. 88–96.

Tannenbaum, R., Weschler, I. R., and Massarik, F. (1961), *Leadership and Organization: A Behavioral Science Approach*, New York, McGraw-Hill.

Thelen, H. A. (1954), *The Dynamics of Groups at Work*, Chicago, University of Chicago Press.

This, L., and Lippitt, G. (1963), "Managerial Guidelines to Sensitivity Training," *Journal of American Society of Training Directors*, Vol. 17, pp. 3–13.

IV. EVALUATION STUDIES*

Durham, L. E., and Gibb, J. R. (1960), *An Annotated Bibliography of Research*, National Training Laboratory, Washington, D. C., National Training Laboratories.

House, Robert J. (1963), *T-Group Training: A Review of the Scientific Evidence and an Appraisal*, Ann Arbor, Mich., unpublished manuscript, University of Michigan.

Meigneiz, R. (Ed.) (1962), *Evaluation of Supervisory and Management Training Methods*, Paris, DECD, Part IIIA.

Miles, M. B., Michael, S. C., Whitman, F. L., and Harris, T. M. (forthcoming), *To Bethel and Back: The Processes and Results of a Human Relations Training Laboratory for Educators*, New York, Bureau of Publications, Teachers College, Columbia University.

Smith, P. B. (1963), "Attitude Changes Associated with Training in Human Relations," *British Journal of Social and Clinical Psychology*, Vol. 2, pp. 105–113.

Stock, Dorothy (1964), "A Survey of Research on T-Groups," in L. P. Bradford, J. R. Gibb, and D. K. Benne, (Eds.), *T-Group Theory and Laboratory Method*, New York, Wiley, Chapter 15.

---

* In this section we list two review articles (Durham and Gibb, 1960; Stock, 1964) which thoroughly cover what research has been conducted. The only other references are to works which have come out since the publication of the review articles. The reader is also referred to Chapters 12 and 13 for two other recent studies by Miles and Bunker.

V. RELATED THEORY

Bennis, W. G., Benne, K. D., and Chin, R. (Eds.) (1961), *The Planning of Change,* New York, Holt, Rinehart and Winston, Chapters: 6, 11, 12.

Bennis, W. G., Schein, E. H., Berlew, D. E., and Steele, F. I. (1964), *Interpersonal Dynamics,* Homewood, Ill., Dorsey Press.

Bion, W. R. (1959), *Experiences in Groups,* New York, Basic Books.

Bradford, L. P. (1958), "The Teaching-Learning Transaction," *Adult Leadership,* Spring.

Bradford, L. P., Gibb, J. R., and Benne, K. D. (Eds.) (1964), *T-Group Theory and Laboratory Method,* New York, Wiley, Chapters 6–14.

Foulkes, S. H., and Anthony, E. S. (1957), *Group Psychotherapy: The Psychoanalytic Approach,* Baltimore, Penguin Books.

Freud, S. (1949), *Group Psychology and the Analysis of the Ego,* New York, Liverwright.

Friedman, L. J., and Zinberg, N. E. (1964), "Application of Group Methods in College Teaching," *The International Journal of Group Psychotherapy,* Vol. 14, No. 3, pp. 344–359.

Gibb, J. R. (1964), "The Present Status of T-Group Theory," in L. P. Bradford, J. R. Gibb, and K. D. Benne, (Eds.), *T-Group Theory and Laboratory Method,* New York, Wiley, Chapter 6.

Harrison, R. (1962–1963), "Defenses and the Need to Know," *Human Relations Training News,* Vol. 6, pp. 1–4.

Harvey, O. J., Hunt, D. E., and Schroder, H. M. (1961), *Conceptual Systems and Personality Organization,* New York, Wiley.

Horwitz, L. (1963), *Transference in Training Groups and Therapy Groups,* Topeka, Kansas, unpublished manuscript, Menninger Clinic.

Jones, R. M. (1960), *An Application of Psychoanalysis to Education,* Springfield, Ill., Charles Thomas.

Luft, J. (1963), *Group Processes,* Palo Alto, Calif., National Press.

Mill, C. (1962), "A Theory for the Group Dynamics Laboratory Milieu," *Adult Leadership,* November.

Psathas, G., and Hardert, R. (1964), *Normative Patterns in the T-Group,* St. Louis, unpublished manuscript, Washington University.

Rosenbaum, M. and Berger, M. (1963), *Group Psychotherapy and Group Function,* New York, Basic Books.

Scheidlinger, S. (1952), *Psychoanalysis and Group Behavior,* New York, W. W. Norton.

Schutz, W. C. (1958), *FIRO: A Three Dimensional Theory of Interpersonal Behavior,* New York, Holt, Rinehart and Winston.

Semrad, E. V., and Arsenian, J. (1961), "The Use of Group Processes in Teaching Group Dynamics," in W. G. Bennis, K. D. Benne, and R. Chin (Eds.), *The Planning of Change,* New York, Holt, Rinehart and Winston, pp. 737–743.

Shepard, H. A., and Bennis, W. G. (1956), "A Theory of Training by Group Methods," *Human Relations,* Vol. 9, pp. 403–414.

Slater, P. E. (1962), "Displacement in Groups," in W. G. Bennis, K. D. Benne., and R. Chin (Eds.), *The Planning of Change,* New York, Holt, Rinehart and Winston, pp. 725–736.

Stock, D., and Thelen, H. A. (1958), *Emotional Dynamics and Group Culture*, New York, New York University Press.

"A Symposium on the Relationship of Group Psychotherapy to Group Dynamics" (1963), *The International Journal of Group Psychotherapy*, Vol. 13, No. 4.

Whitaker, D. S, and Liberman, M. A. (1964), *Psychotherapy through the Group Process*, New York, Atherton Press.

VI. CRITICISMS OF LABORATORY TRAINING

Dubin, R. (1961), "Psyche, Sensitivity, and Social Structure," in R. Tannenbaum, I. R. Weschler, and F. Massarik, *Leadership and Organization: A Behavioral Science Approach*, New York, McGraw-Hill, Part IV.

Gunderson, R. G. (1961), "Group Dynamics—Hope or Hoax?" in W. G. Bennis, K. D. Benne, and R. Chin (Eds.), *The Planning of Change*, New York, Holt, Rinehart and Winston, pp. 255–259.

House, R. J. (1963), *T-Group Training: A Review of the Scientific Evidence and an Appraisal*, Ann Arbor, Mich., unpublished manuscript, University of Michigan.

McNair, M. P. (1957), "Thinking Ahead: What Price Human Relations?" *Harvard Business Review*, March-April, pp. 15–39.

Odiorne, G. (1963), "The Trouble with Sensitivity Training," *Journal of American Society of Training Directors*, Vol. 17, pp. 9–20.

Whyte, Jr., W. F. (1953), *Leadership and Group Participation*, Bulletin No. 24, Ithaca, N. Y., New York State School of Industrial and Labor Relations.

References

An Action Research Program for Organization Improvement (in Esso Standard Oil Co.) (1960), Ann Arbor, Mich., Foundation for Research on Human Behavior.

Allport, G. (1945), "The Psychology of Participation," in G. Allport (1960), *Personality and Social Encounter*, Boston, Beacon.

Argyris, C. (1962), *Interpersonal Competence and Organizational Effectiveness*, Homewood, Ill., Dorsey Press.

Argyris, C. (1964), "T-Groups for Organizational Effectiveness," *Harvard Business Review*, March-April, pp. 60–74.

Baritz, L. (1960), *Servants of Power*, Middletown, Conn., Wesleyan University Press.

Bavelas, A., and Strauss, G. (1955), "Group Dynamics and Intergroup Relations," in W. F. Whyte (Ed.), *Money and Motivation*, New York, Harper, pp. 90–96.

Bennis, W. G. (1963), "A New Role for the Behavioral Sciences: Effecting Organizational Change," *Administrative Science Quarterly*, Vol. 8, pp. 125–165.

Bennis, W. G., Benne, K. D., and Chin, R. (1961), *The Planning of Change*, New York, Holt, Rinehart and Winston.

Bennis, W. G., and Miles, M. B. (1960), *Memo on Trainer Development*, mimeographed, Washington, D.C., National Training Laboratories.

Bennis, W. G., Schein, E. H., Berlew, D. E., and Steele, F. I. (1964), *Interpersonal Dynamics: Essays and Readings on Human Interaction*, Homewood, Ill., Dorsey Press.

Bennis, W. G., and Shepard, H. A. (1956), "A Theory of Group Development," *Human Relations*, Vol. 4, pp. 415–437.

Blake, R. R. (1960a), *Action Research Training Lab*, West Point, N. Y., Tenth Proceedings.

Blake, R. R. (1960b), "Typical Laboratory Procedures and Experiments," *An Action Research Program for Organization Improvement (in Esso Standard Oil Co.)*, Ann Arbor, Mich., Foundation for Research on Human Behavior.

Blake, R. R., and Mouton, Jane S. (1961a), "Competition, Communication, and Conformity," in I. A. Berg and B. M. Bass (Eds.), *Conformity and Deviation*, New York, Harper.

Blake, R. R., and Mouton, Jane S. (1961b), *Group Dynamics—Key to Decision Making*, Houston, Texas, Gulf Publishing.

Blake, R. R., and Mouton, Jane S. (1961c), "Union Management Relations: From Conflict to Collaboration," *Personnel*, Vol. 38, pp. 38–51.

Blake, R. R., and Mouton, Jane S. (1961d), "Reactions to Intergroup Competition Under Win-Lose Conditions," *Management Science*, Vol. 7, pp. 420–435.

Blake, R. R., and Mouton, Jane S. (1962a), "The Developing Revolution in Management Practices," *Journal of the American Society of Training Directors*, Vol. 16, pp. 29–52.

Blake, R. R., and Mouton, Jane S. (1962b), "Intergroup Therapy," *Journal of Social Psychiatry*, Vol. 8, pp. 196–198.

Blake, R. R., and Mouton, Jane S. (1962c), "The Instrumented Training Laboratory," in I. R. Weschler and E. H. Schein (Eds.), *Issues in Human Relations Training*, Washington, D.C., National Training Laboratories, NTL Selected Reading Series No. 5.

Blake, R. R., and Mouton, Jane S. (1963), "Improving Organizational Problem Solving through Increasing the Flow and Utilization of New Ideas," *Training Directors Journal*, Vol. 17, pp. 48–57.

Blake, R. R., and Mouton, Jane S. (1964a), "The Managerial Grid as a Framework for Inducing Change in Industrial Organizations," in P. Worchel and D. Byrne (Eds.), *Personality Change*, New York, Wiley.

Blake, R. R., and Mouton, Jane S. (1964b), "Organization Development and Performance," in R. R. Blake and Jane S. Mouton, *The Managerial Grid*, Houston, Texas, Gulf Publishing, pp. 290–311.

Blake, R. R., Mouton, Jane S., Barnes, L. B., and Greiner, L. E. (1964), "Breakthrough in Organizational Development," *Harvard Business Review*, November-December, pp. 133–135.

Blake, R. R., Mouton, Jane S., and Bidwell, A. C. (1962), "The Managerial Grid," *Advanced Management—Office Executive*, Vol. 1, pp. 15–18, 36.

Blake, R. R., Mouton, Jane S., and Blansfield, M. C. (1961), *Team Action Laboratory*, Internal Revenue Service, Dallas Region, pp. 34–39.

Blake, R. R., Mouton, Jane S., and Blansfield, M. G. (1962), "How Executive Team Training Can Help You and Your Organization," *Journal of the American Society of Training Directors*, Vol. 16, pp. 3–11.

Blake, R. R., Shepard, H. A., and Mouton, Jane S. (1964), *Intergroup Conflict in Organizations*, Ann Arbor, Mich., Foundation for Research on Human Behavior.

Blansfield, M. G. (1962), "Depth Analysis of Organizational Life," *California Management Review*, Winter, pp. 29–42.

Blau, P. (1961), "The Dynamics of Bureaucracy," in A. Etzioni (Ed.), *Complex Organizations*, New York, Holt, Rinehart and Winston, pp. 343–355.

Bloom, S. W., Boyd, Ina, and Kaplan, H. B. (1962), "Emotional Illness and Interaction Process: A Study of Patient Groups," *Social Forces*, Vol. 41, pp. 135–141.

Boyd, J. B., and Elliss, J. (1962), *Findings of Research into Senior Management Seminars*, Toronto, Personnel Research Department, The Hydro-Electric Power Commission of Ontario.

Bradford, L. P., Gibb, J. R., and Benne, K. D. (Eds.) (1964), *T-Group Theory and Laboratory Method*, New York, Wiley.

Bradford, L. P., Lippitt, R., and Gibb, J. R. (1956), "Human Relations Training in Three Days," *Adult Leadership*, Vol. 4, pp. 11–26.

Buchanan, P. (1964), *Evaluating the Effectiveness of Laboratory Training in Industry*, paper read at American Management Association seminar, New York, February 24–26.

Bunker, D. R. (1963), "The Effect of Laboratory Education upon Individual Behavior," *Proceedings of the 16th Annual Meeting, Industrial Relations Research Association*, December.

Burke, R. L., and Bennis, W. G. (1961), "Changes in Perception of Self and Others during Human Relations Training," *Human Relations*, Vol. 14, pp. 165–182.

Campbell, D. T., and Fiske, D. W. (1959), "Convergent and Discriminant Validation by the Multitrait-Multimethod Matrix," *Psychological Bulletin*, Vol. 56, pp. 81–105.

Chin, R. (1960), "Problems and Prospects of Research: Research Approaches to the Problem of Civic Training," in F. Patterson et al., *The Adolescent Citizen*, New York, The Free Press of Glencoe.

Clark, J. V. (1963), "Authentic Interaction and Personal Growth in Sensitivity Training Groups," *Journal of Humanistic Psychology*, Vol. 2, pp. 1–13.

Cleveland, S. E. (1961), "Changes in Projective Data in Relation to Patient Training Laboratory," in R. B. Morton (Ed.), *Proceedings No. 2 Patient Training Laboratory*, Houston, Texas, Veterans Administration Hospital.

Durham, L. E., and Gibb, J. R. (1960), *An Annotated Bibliography of Research, National Training Laboratories, 1947–1960*, Washington, D.C., National Training Laboratories.

Fairweather, G. W. (1961), "The Social Psychology of Mental Illness: An Experimental Approach," *Newsletter for Research In Psychology*, Washington, D.C., Veterans Administration, Vol. 3, pp. 3–9.

Frank, J. D. (1964), "Training and Therapy," in L. P. Bradford, J. R. Gibb, and K. D. Benne (Eds.), *T-Group Theory and Laboratory Method*, New York, Wiley.

Goffman, E. (1959), *The Presentation of Self in Everyday Life*, Garden City, N. J., Doubleday Anchor.

Hanson, P. G., Rothaus, P., Cleveland, S. E., Johnson, D. L., and McCall, D. (1964), "Employment after Psychiatric Hospitalization," *Mental Hygiene*, Vol. 48, pp. 142–151.

Harrison, R. (1962), *The Effects of Training on Interpersonal Perception, Bethel, 1961*, unpublished mimeographed paper, Yale University. (Also additional personal communications.)

Harrison, R. (1963), "Defenses and the Need to Know," *Human Relations Training News*, Vol. 4, pp. 1–4.

Harrison, R., and Oshry, B. I. (1965), personal communication based on data contained in forthcoming manuscript.

Hjelholt, G., and Miles, M. B. (1963), "Extending the Conventional Laboratory Training Design," *NTL Subscription Service*, No. 1.

Holtzman, W. H., Thorpe, J. S., Swartz, J. D., and Herron, E. W. (1961), *Inkblot Perception and Personality*, Austin, Texas, University of Texas Press.

Hyman, H. H., Wright, C. R., and Hopkins, T. (1962), *Applications of Methods of Evaluation*, University of California Publications in Culture and Society, Vol. 7, Berkeley, University of California Press.

Johnson, D. W. (1964), "Title III and the Dynamics of Educational Change in

California Schools," in M. B. Miles (Ed.), *Innovation in Education*, New York, Bureau of Publications, Teachers College, Columbia University.

Lewin, K. (1947), "Group Decision and Social Change," in T. Newcomb, and E. Hartley (Eds.), *Readings in Social Psychology*, New York, Holt, Rinehart and Winston.

Likert, R. (1961), *New Patterns of Management*, New York, McGraw-Hill.

Lippitt, R., Watson, J., and Westley, B. (1958), *Dynamics of Planned Change*, New York, Harcourt, Brace and World.

Lorr, M., Klett, C. J., McNair, D. M., and Lasky, J. J., (1962), *Manual: Inpatient Multidimensional Psychiatric Scale (IMPS)*, Washington, D.C., Veterans Administration.

McGregor, D. (1960), *The Human Side of Enterprise*, New York, McGraw-Hill.

Maslow, A. H. (1962), "Deficiency Motivation and Growth Motivation," in A. H. Maslow, *Toward a Psychology of Being*, Princeton, N. J., Van Nostrand.

Miles, M. B. (1957), *Personal Change Through Human Relations Training: A Working Paper*, (unpublished working paper).

Miles, M. B. (1959), *Learning to Work in Groups: A Program Guide for Educational Leaders*, New York, Teachers College, Bureau of Publications, Columbia University.

Miles, M. B. (1960a), "Human Relations Training: Processes and Outcomes," *Journal of Counseling Psychology*, Vol. 7, pp. 301–306.

Miles, M. B. (1960b), "Training Designs for Human Relations Laboratories 1959," in B. Dyer (Ed.), *Workbook and Reader Series, NTL*, Washington, D.C., National Education Association.

Miles, M. B. (1961), "The Training Group," in W. G. Bennis, K. D. Benne, and R. Chin (Eds.), *The Planning of Change*, New York, Holt, Rinehart and Winston, pp. 716–725.

Miles, M. B. (1964a), "On Temporary Systems," in M. B. Miles (Ed.), *Innovation in Education*, New York, Bureau of Publications, Teachers College, Columbia University.

Miles, M. B. (1964b), *Learning Processes and Outcomes in Human Relations Training: A Clinical-Experimental Study*, paper read at the meetings of the Eastern Psychological Association, April.

Miles, M. B., Michael, S. C., Whitman, F. L., and Harris, T. M. (forthcoming), *To Bethel and Back: The Processes and Results of a Human Relations Training Laboratory for Educators*, New York, Bureau of Publications, Teachers College, Columbia University.

Mill, C. (1962), "A Theory for the Group Dynamics Laboratory Milieu," *Adult Leadership*, Vol. 11, pp. 133 ff.

Morton, R. B. (Ed.) (1961a), *Proceedings, Patient Training Laboratory I–V*, Veterans Administration Hospital, Houston, Texas.

Morton, R. B., Rothaus, P., and Hanson, P. G. (1961a), "An Experiment in Performance Appraisal and Review," *Journal of the American Society of Training Directors*, Vol. 15, pp. 19–28.

Morton, R. B., Rothaus, P., and Hanson, P. G. (1961b), "Adaptation of the Human Relations Training Laboratory to a Psychiatric Population," *Newsletter for Research in Psychology*, Washington, D. C., Veterans Administration, Vol. 3, pp. 23–29.

Mouton, Jane S. (1961), "Leveling: Key to Relationships Reviews," in R. R. Blake, Jane S. Mouton, and M. G. Blansfield, *Team Action Laboratory*, Internal Revenue Service, Dallas Region, pp. 34–39.

Mower, H., Hunt, J., and Kogan, L. (1953), "Further Studies Utilizing the Discomfort-Relief Quotient," in H. Mower (Ed.), *Psychiatric Theory and Research*, New York, Ronald Press, Chapter 11.

Odiorne, G. (1963), "The Trouble with Sensitivity Training," *Journal of the American Society of Training Directors*, Vol. 17, pp. 9–20.

Pepinsky, H. B., Siegel, L., and Van Alta, E. L. (1952), "The Criterion in Counseling: A Group Participation Scale," *Journal of Abnormal and Social Psychology*, Vol. 17, pp. 415–419.

Rosenbaum, M., and Berger, M. (1963), *Group Psychotherapy and Group Function*, New York, Basic Books.

Rosow, I. (1964), material on Rosow's work was summarized by Brim, Jr., O. G., "Socialization through the Life Cycle," *Items*, Vol. 18, pp. 1–5.

Rothaus, P., Hanson, P. G., Cleveland, S. E., and Johnson, D. L. (1963), "Describing Psychiatric Hospitalization: A Dilemma," *American Psychologist*, Vol. 18, pp. 85–89.

Rothaus, P., and Morton, R. B. (1961), *Proceedings No. 2 Patient Laboratory*, Houston, Texas, Veterans Administration Hospital.

Rothaus, P., and Morton, R. B. (1962), "Problem Centered Versus Mental Illness Self-Description," *Journal of Health and Human Behavior*, Vol. 3, pp. 198–203.

Rothaus, P., Morton, R. B., and Hanson, P. G. (1963), "The Fate of Role Stereotypes in Two Performance Appraisal Situations," *Journal of Personal Psychology*, Vol. 16, pp. 269–281.

Rothaus, P., Morton, R. B., Johnson, D. L., Cleveland, S. E., and Lyle, F. A. (1963), "Human Relations Training for Psychiatric Patients," *Archives of General Psychiatry*, Vol. 8, pp. 572–581.

Sanford, F. (1962), "Revolutionary Trends in Mental Health," *Research Bulletin of the Division of Mental Health*, State of Washington, Mental Health Research Institute, pp. 5–6.

Schein, E. H. (1963), "Forces Which Undermine Management Development," *California Management Review*, Vol. 4, pp. 23–24.

Seashore, C., and Van Egmond, E. (1959), "The Consultant-Trainer Role in Working Directly with a Total Staff," *Journal of Social Issues*, Vol. 15, pp. 36–42.

Sharaf, M. R., and Levinson, D. J. (1964), "The Quest for Omnipotence in Professional Training," *Psychiatry*, Vol. 27, pp. 135–149.

Shaw, G. B. (1924), *Saint Joan*, Baltimore, Penguin Books, 1962, p. 153.

Shepard, J. A., and Bennis, W. G. (1956), "A Theory of Training by Group Methods," *Human Relations*, Vol. 9, pp. 403–414.

Sherif, M., Harvey, O. J., White, B. J., Hood, W. R., and Sherif, C. W. (1961), *Intergroup Conflict and Cooperation*, Norman, Okla., The University of Oklahoma Book Exchange.

Slater, P., and Bennis, W. G. (1964), "Democracy Is Inevitable," *Harvard Business Review*, March-April, pp. 51–59.

Stock, D. (1964), "A Summary of Research On Training Groups," in L. P. Bradford, J. R. Gibb, and K. D. Benne (Eds.), *T-Group Theory and Laboratory Method*, New York, Wiley.

Stone, A. E., Frank, J. D., Nash, E. H., and Imber, S. D. (1961), "An Intensive Five Year Follow-up Study of Treated Psychiatric Patients," *Journal of Nervous and Mental Disorders*, Vol. 133, pp. 410–421.

Tannenbaum, R., and Bugental, J. F. T. (1963), "Dyads, Clans, and Tribe: A New Design for Sensitivity Training," *NTL Human Relations Training News*, Vol. 7, pp. 1–3.

Tannenbaum, R., Weschler, I. R., and Massarik, F. (1961), *Leadership and Organization: A Behavioral Science Approach*, New York, McGraw-Hill.

Wallen, R. W. (1963), "The 3 Types of Executive Personality," *Dun's Review*, and *Modern Industry*, February.

Weschler, I. R., Massarik, F., and Tannenbaum, R. (1962), "The Self in Process: A Sensitivity Training Emphasis," in I. R. Weschler, and E. H. Schein, (Eds.), *Issues in Human Relations Training*, Washington, D.C., National Training Laboratories, NTL Selected Reading Series No. 5.

Weschler, I. R., and Reisel, J. (1959), *Inside a Sensitivity Training Group*, Industrial Relations Monograph, No. 4, Los Angeles, Institute of Industrial Relations, University of California.

INDEX

BF
637
C653

23,744

CAMROSE LUTHERAN COLLEGE
LIBRARY

D

← Everett Thykeson →

447 KARP CT
COQUITLAM BC